Field Collecting
Gemstones and Minerals

Field Collecting Gemstones and Minerals

(Formerly titled *Gemstones and Minerals: How and Where to Find Them*)

JOHN SINKANKAS

E P B M

ECHO POINT BOOKS & MEDIA, LLC
BRATTLEBORO, VERMONT.

Published by Echo Point Books & Media
Brattleboro, Vermont
www.EchoPointBooks.com

Field Collecting Gemstones and Minerals
ISBN: 978-1-63561-064-2 (paperback)

Cover design by Justine McFarland

Front cover images: *Center*—Chrysocolla mineral stone,
with reflection on black surface background by Madlen,
courtesy of Shutterstock; *Bottom right*—rock climber's
hands by Galyna Andrushko, courtesy of Shutterstock;
Bottom center—Close-up of gold-painted shovel head by
Peter Vandenbelt, courtesy of Shutterstock; *Bottom left*—
Untitled by Jon Flobrant, courtesy of Unsplash.com

Back cover image: Untitled by Mathew MacQuarrie

Dedicated to my wife **MARJORIE**

Preface to the First Edition

Sooner or later every collector of minerals and gemstones realizes the need for information on *how* and *why* mineral deposits form. If he is to find deposits for himself, or become more skilled in exploiting those already known to him, he must be able to recognize those few places in vast expanses of rock most likely to yield valuable minerals and specimens. There are few experiences more frustrating than to take considerable time and trouble to find a locality only to face a blank wall which gives little hint as to where to dig.

Although much information on mineral deposits is available, it has been written largely for the advanced student who expects to make geology or one of its related sciences a lifelong profession. Very little has been written for the amateur. In this respect, the plight of the beginner is even worse than that of his more experienced fellow collectors because popular books on collecting designed to help persons like himself, speak mostly of the assembly and care of collections without giving much practical information on just how to go about finding worthwhile material in the field.

For these reasons, the subject matter in this book has been carefully selected to help the amateur obtain knowledge which he otherwise could not get without taking special courses at college level or digging out the information for himself from a number of technical books. Naturally it is impossible to include everything on rocks and the mineral deposits found in them in a book of this size, but there is no need to because after all the problems of the amateur collector and prospector are different from those of the professional geologist or mineralogist. The aim of this book is mainly to help and not to instruct, although some instruction cannot be avoided if reasons for the how and why of mineral deposits are to be made clear.

Accordingly, after several chapters on field trips and the use of equipment and tools, three chapters are given on rocks, mineral deposits, and field features of deposits, with all of them emphasizing the vital relationships between minerals and the rocks in which they are found. Only those deposits of greatest interest to the amateur collector of mineral specimens and gemstones, and also to the prospector, are discussed. The outward signs of deposits, particularly outcrops and float are described in word and picture, and instructions are given as to how to follow up these signs. Chapters then follow on the techniques of collecting, placing greatest emphasis on skillful removal of crystals from cavities, and what to do with specimens after they are collected. This last part discusses trimming and cleaning specimens, including the use of chemical agents, and the care and display of specimens; it concludes with a chapter on marketing specimens which contains useful advice to fortunate persons who have found more than they need for their own collections.

Paterson, New Jersey

Preface to the Second Edition

In 1961, the First Edition of this work appeared under the title *Gemstones and Minerals—How and Where to Find Them*. Since that time it has been thought advisable to make a number of corrections to the text, dispense with outdated material, and expand slightly some sections in the light of new information. The new title was adopted to reflect more accurately the content of this work.

The changes in this edition are new information on the use of portable gasoline motor drills and the rearrangement of material in Chapter 2, to present it in a more consistent fashion. Numerous corrections have been made in the titles and addresses of government agencies offering publications and services to prospectors. The bibliographies in Appendix V. have also been revised to incorporate newer publications of interest to readers and to eliminate those which have been superseded. A substantial number of better photographs have been substituted to show more clearly the features which they illustrate, and one new drawing, Figure 21, appears in Chapter II. For the latter I am indebted to Miss Bonnie Swope of San Diego.

San Diego, California   JOHN SINKANKAS

Acknowledgments

An author, whose name, I am ashamed to say, I cannot at this moment recall, said in prefatory remarks to one of his works that it is impossible to write a book completely by one's self. He of course alluded to the many authors who had written before him, and whose ideas he had borrowed for his own book. After writing several of my own, I can only say that I agree most heartily—it is impossible to write strictly solo. But perhaps equally true, it is almost impossible to acknowledge the assistance of the many unselfish persons who cheerfully took the time and trouble to help in preparing this book, not to mention those who were instrumental in the preparation of others used by me as references. Speaking of reference books, I found Alan M. Bateman's *Economic Mineral Deposits* and *Formation of Mineral Deposits* most valuable. The clearly stated concepts concerning the genesis of minerals in L. G. Berry and Brian Mason's *Mineralogy* were also most helpful, while that model of uncomplicated and wonderfully descriptive writing set forth in the *Rock Book* by Carroll and Mildred Fenton served as inspiration. Other references and texts were used, but space does not permit detailing their authors and titles; however, the best I found are included in the bibliography in Appendix V.

Individuals who helped are also numerous. My special thanks are due to Paul E. Desautels, Associate Curator in the Division of Mineralogy and Petrology of the Smithsonian Institution, who critically examined the appendix on chemical treatment of minerals and made many helpful suggestions for its improvement. His help and that of Dr. George Switzer of the Institution were also instrumental in obtaining a large number of the many fine photographs which appear in the text. Helpful suggestions for the chapter on the preparation of specimens were supplied by Neal Yedlin. Field trip procedures, the use of tools, and many other phases of practical field work too numerous to mention were learned under the guidance of Elbert H. McMacken. Much useful data on maps was supplied by the Map Information Office of the U. S. Geological Survey, while Elizabeth Wellshear of the Denver Branch

Library was especially helpful in selection of appropriate photographs from the Survey's voluminous files. Other photographs supplied by individuals and concerns are separately credited wherever appearing and their use gratefully acknowledged. Lastly, I wish to express gratitude for the help given to me during every stage of manuscript and drawing preparation by my wife Marjorie.

Contents

List of Illustrations

1

Prospecting and Collecting Trips

Time is wasted and opportunities are lost by failure to plan prospecting and collecting trips carefully. One-day trips to local quarries and mines may be successful with the minimum of planning, but longer excursions taking several days, or involving hiking cross-country, can be utterly ruined by forgetting some essential item of equipment or not having facts straight as to where to go. Planning includes travel arrangements to the area, location of exact positions of mines or quarries on maps or charts, check-offs of equipment for camping and digging, to be sure nothing is left behind, and any other arrangements which must be made to insure success. Finding minerals and gemstones is uncertain at best and there is no point to complicating matters by failure to plan properly.

GENERAL PLANNING

There are several distinct types of trips. The most informal excursion is the day's outing to some easily accessible place. Such trips require the fewest preparations of all, although much better results can be had if there is careful planning. The second type is the scouting or reconnaissance trip, whose object is to cover considerable ground in order to spot places deserving of careful attention at a later time. The third type of trip involves actual prospecting and collecting, in which the sole purpose is to recover ores and specimens from a deposit previously located. It is sometimes possible to combine scouting and prospecting in a single trip, depending on the local situation.

Before any kind of trip is taken, the very first preparation must be to learn as much as possible about the area or deposit to be visited: where to go, what to look for, and, perhaps most important, what difficulties or obstacles must be overcome. For example, an uninformed collector may decide to visit Mount Antero in Colorado, having heard that the area furnishes handsome specimens of beryl and other minerals. Unless he is aware that the collecting grounds are located on the summit, at an altitude of about 14,000 feet above sea level, and cannot be reached except by arduous climbing near the summit, he may be in for a rude awakening when he arrives in the area and begins to inquire for details on how to reach the mountain. Another preliminary item of information which must be learned is the mineralogical history of any mineral deposit to which a trip is planned. As so often happens, the dumps of a mine or quarry famous for its ore or mineral production may be absolutely worthless to the collector because of the nature of the deposit and perhaps the nature of the material discarded. Examples of mines with uninteresting dumps may be any of a number of gold mines in the Sierra Nevada of California. Certainly their operators will not throw out quartz specimens shot with wire gold, and indeed may not discard any material whatsoever except finely crushed tailings from the stamp mills. On the other hand, mines can be found with extensive and interesting dumps; if information on which dumps to collect can be obtained from someone familiar with the area, so much the better.

WHERE TO FIND INFORMATION

Among the most valuable sources of information on collecting localities are the several popular mineral science magazines, which appear monthly or bi-monthly, and which frequently include in their issues stories of actual collecting experiences, along with detailed directions on how to reach localities. Such articles sometimes provide the only useful information available anywhere upon localities which may be commercially unimportant but still of great interest to the amateur. These fine magazines also contain many advertisements for field guides covering general as well as specific collecting sites. All kinds of equipment, mineral and rock specimens, books on mineralogy and geology, and many other items useful to the collector and prospector are also advertised.

One of the magazines, *Lapidary Journal*, publishes an annual *Rockhound Buyer's Guide*, in which dealers in equipment as well as all mineral and gem cutting clubs in North America are listed. Each issue contains several reports on selected collecting localities. *Gems And Minerals* magazine specializes in field trips in the western United States, while *Rocks And Minerals* similarly specializes in field trips that can be taken in the eastern United States. A relatively new magazine, *The Canadian Rockhound*, provides field trip articles for residents of Canada and visitors from across the border. Many libraries stock one or more of these magazines and provide access to back numbers, as well as to current issues. Persons seriously interested in collecting and prospecting should subscribe to at least one. Magazines, guides, books, and other publications of interest are listed in Appendix V.

In order to acquaint oneself with the appearance of rocks and minerals expected to be found in collecting areas, visits should be made to museum, school, and privately-owned collections. Excellent public exhibits are on view in many places, particularly in larger cities, but tend to stress showy minerals and to subordinate drab species or equally drab rocks. Although it may be necessary to make special arrangements with curators to view locality specimens, kept in drawers as "study" collections, the effort is easily worth the trouble. Besides, if one expresses a sincere interest in some locality or area, the curator often responds by giving valuable advice in respect to where to go, how to get there, and what to look for. Ardent private collectors are often glad to help beginners and, when faced with visiting collectors, sometimes offer to lead field trips to places which would be extremely difficult to find otherwise.

Since this book emphasizes the importance of rocks in respect to mineral deposits to be found in them, it is strongly urged that special study be given to rocks, even to the extent of acquiring samples of the kinds described in the third chapter. Too many collectors have become skilled in the study of minerals but not in the study of rocks, and have unnecessarily handicapped themselves in prospecting by their inability to read rock formations and thus guide themselves to places likely to contain deposits. Sample rock and mineral collections such as shown in Figure 7 may be purchased at modest cost from a number of dealers and provide excellent ways of becoming familiar with the most common materials of the earth's crust.

SOURCES OF GEOLOGICAL PUBLICATIONS

Professional information on geology, mineralogy, mining, and prospecting in North America is truly enormous, with thousands of pages of fine print devoted solely to compilations of what is available. Most of this material is designed to provide scientific and technical information, rather than popular information, and is therefore valuable chiefly to persons who are already professionally qualified in some branch of the mineral sciences. Although professional geological literature is seldom fully understood by the average collector or prospector, its many reports and papers often contain the only authoritative information on certain areas and deposits, and they are therefore worth the time and trouble required to read and understand them. A good glossary of geological terms often helps in making meanings clear; several are recommended in the bibliography in Appendix V.

Geological literature is available from many sources, but for citizens of the United States the publications of the U. S. Geological Survey and of state geological surveys provide the wealth of material. Since its formation, the Geological Survey has published about 2,000 professional papers, bulletins, monographs, and circulars dealing with a wide variety of subjects, from strictly theoretical problems to practical explanations of geology and mineralogy. Complete lists of published works are furnished in *Publications of the Geological Survey* (latest edition 1961), a paper-bound catalog which is kept revised by means of annual *Supplements*. The latest *Supplement* as well as the basic publication may be obtained free of charge from:

U. S. Geological Survey
Washington, D.C. 20242

For states west of the Mississippi River, including Louisiana and Minnesota, and for Alaska, requests for this book should be addressed to:

U. S. Geological Survey   U. S. Geological Survey
Distribution Section   310 First Ave.
Federal Center   Fairbanks, Alaska 99701
Denver, Colorado 80225

The Distribution Sections named above also supply circulars which describe Geological Survey literature relating to individual states. Each circular lists publications, maps, and special publications, and indicates libraries within the state where reference can be made to Geological Survey publications, many of which are out of print and unobtainable from any government source. Libraries regularly receiving publications of the Geological Survey and the Bureau of Mines are listed in Appendix IV, but not all receive every publication, the requirements of each being tailored to suit conditions within the state concerned. However, where a collector or prospector does not wish to incur the considerable cost of purchasing a large number of publications or must refer to a publication out of print, he may be reasonably certain that one or more of the libraries near him will have fairly complete files of publications concerning the geology of his state. IMPORTANT: Publications of the U. S. Geological Survey, except maps and the catalog and lists noted above, must be ordered from:

Superintendent of Documents
Government Printing Office
Washington, D.C. 20402

Price lists of government publications in stock at the Government Printing Office may be obtained free of charge by writing to the above address. The following lists are of interest to the collector and prospector: PL-10, *Laws, Rules and Regulations;* PL-15, *Geology;* PL-58, *Mines;* PL-84, *Atomic Energy and Civil Defense.* Certain Bureau of Mines publications of interest to prospectors and miners are also listed in the bibliography in Appendix V.

Geological investigations in Canada and its Provinces are conducted mainly by the Geological Survey of Canada and by provincial geological agencies. Publications are in "series," that is, Paper Series, Memoir Series, Economic Geology Series, and Bulletin Series. *Papers*, giving preliminary reports and maps of specific areas, are commonly issued before a field project is completed. Geological maps accompanying papers are patterned but not printed in color. *Memoirs* are full reports with colored maps, while *Economic Geology* publications deal with specific minerals, generally on a nation-wide scale, or are used to publish reports which do not fit other categories. *Bulletins* are used for miscellaneous special investigation reports. Indexes and catalogs of the above publications are contained in *Geological Survey of Canada Paper 54-1;* it may be obtained from:

The Director, Geological Survey of Canada
Department of Mines and Technical Surveys
601 Booth Street
Ottawa, Ontario, Canada.

Or from branch offices at:

739 West Hastings Street, Vancouver 1, British Columbia
406 Customs Building, Calgary, Alberta
Whitehorse, Yukon Territory
Yellowknife, Northwest Territories.

Provincial departments of mines also publish geological reports and some publish catalogs. Addresses are given in Appendix III.

Geological literature upon Mexico and Central America is meager and difficult to obtain; however, a few publications are available and may be obtained by addressing inquiries to:

Instituto de Geología
Universidad Nacional Autónoma de Mexico
Ciudad Universitaria, Mexico 20, D.F.

A good bibliography of publications, reports, and articles dealing with the geology of Central American republics is contained in U. S. Geological Survey Bulletin No. 1034—*Mineral Deposits of Central America*, by R. J. Roberts and E. M. Irving.

THE USE OF MAPS

Although the majority of collectors would not dream of launching upon an extensive automobile tour without a supply of road maps covering every inch of the way, many will blithely set off through forest or desert in search of some mineral deposit with nothing more than vague directions and abundant optimism. If optimism were enough, we would all have far better collections, but optimism, unfortunately, never makes up for the lack of specific directions, and there are no better directions than those which are placed upon accurate maps.

Many guide books designed to meet the needs of the collector, as well as good articles in mineral science magazines, often furnish excellent sketch maps, complete with mileage and conspicuous landmarks. Most such maps require cautious use because they fail to give a complete picture of terrain. The best field trip maps are laid out upon topographic maps which show terrain features of the entire surrounding area. With such a map it is possible to look ahead and recognize some prominent landmark long before it is reached and not depend entirely upon carefully recording mileage to guide one to the proper place. Topographic maps are specially important for those last few miles which may be closed to cars and which require taking to the trail. In such cases, mileage becomes meaningless and dependence must be placed on recognizing landmarks previously selected from the map.

Topographic Maps

Topographic maps attempt to show on a flat paper surface the actual form of the land by means of curved lines called *contour lines*. A common example of a contour line is the shoreline of a lake. Since the water of the lake is perfectly level, all points of the shoreline will be at the same level too. If the surface happens to be exactly 1,000 feet above sea level, then we can say that the shoreline of the lake is the 1,000 foot contour line. If we were to fly over the lake, we would see that the shoreline twists and turns to delineate the shape of the land at the places where the lake level, or the 1,000 foot level intersects the land. The same kind of delineation is attempted by the map-maker except that he must use imaginary lines derived from careful measurements to show how the land changes its form at each level of altitude. Figure 1, reproduced from a small explanatory map supplied by the U. S. Geological Survey, shows very clearly the relationship between contour lines and the actual forms of the land.

Several features of this map are worthy of study, the first being the bunching of lines along the face of the cliff on the left, indicating a steep drop-off. All steep hillsides, cliffs, and promontories on topographic maps will show this same bunching of lines, some exceedingly steep places being represented by so many contour lines squeezed together into a narrow band that they appear blurred. In contrast, note how the gently-sloping hill on the right is depicted by uniformly spaced lines and how the flat places in the valley have very few lines at all because elevations change so slightly from one place to another. By understanding contours on a topographic map it is easy to form a mental picture of the landscape even if one has never seen it before. This is a very important consideration when planning a cross-country trip on foot, working an area on horseback, or attempting to penetrate roadless areas by jeep. By consulting a topographic map it is possible to select routes which offer easiest and safest access and least chance of becoming lost.

Elevations on maps are shown in two ways, first, by placing figures on contour lines corresponding to elevations, and second, by indicating elevations of identifiable points such as mountain summits, passes, surfaces of lakes, and road intersections. To prevent confusion, every fifth line only is given elevation figures and the line further identified by heavier ink. Elevations are shown on the sample map of Figure 1. The vertical distance between contours, or *contour interval*, is selected

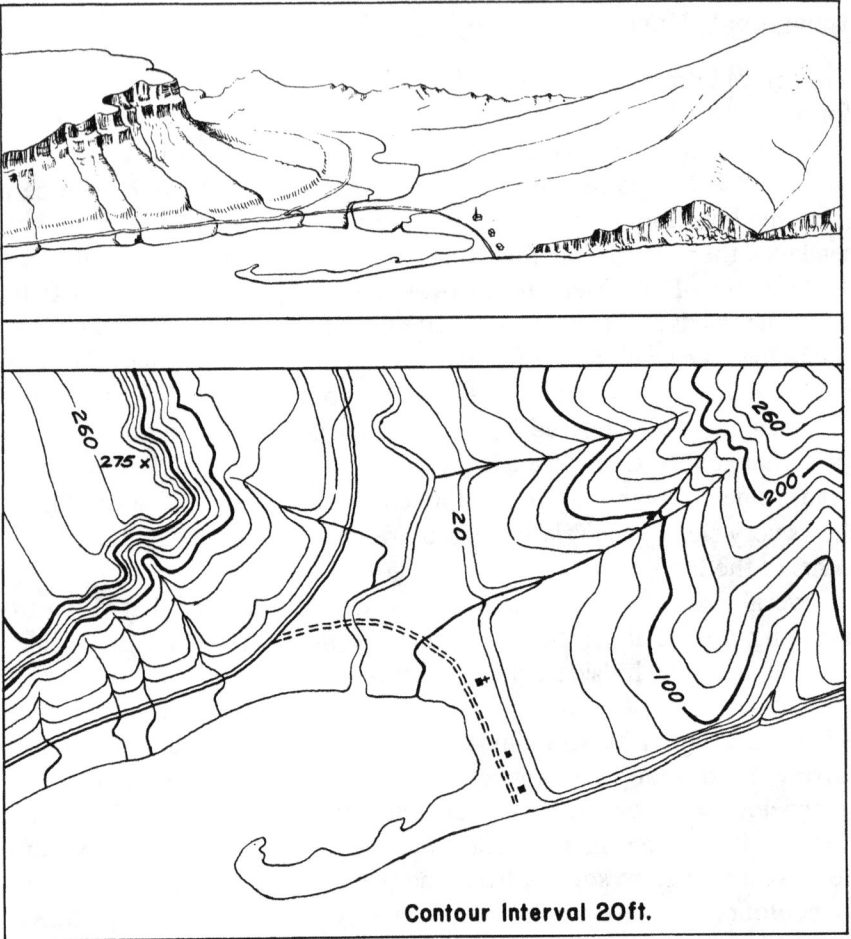

Contour Interval 20ft.

FIGURE 1. The upper illustration is a view of a river valley and surrounding hills. The river flows into a bay partly enclosed by a hooked sandbar. On both sides of the valley are terraces cut through by small streams. The hill on the right slopes gradually whereas the one on the left forms cliffs. These features, as well as others, are shown by lines and symbols on the topographic map below. This same system of representation is used on all topographical maps and is actually very easy to understand once the meanings of contour lines are made plain. *Courtesy U. S. Geological Survey.*

according to steepness of terrain. Obviously an interval of only 5 feet in the Rocky Mountains would result in a hopelessly confused map but one of 100 feet would supply both adequate information and a map easier to read. Standard intervals are 5, 10, 20, 40, and 80 feet; intervals of 25, 50, and 100 feet are used for certain areas of the Western States. The interval used on any U. S. Geological Survey map is shown upon the bottom center margin.

In addition to natural features, such as land forms, rivers, creeks, and lakes, cultural features or works created by man, are also shown. These include roads, trails, mines, prospects, railroads, dams, buildings, boundary lines, etc. Land features are printed in light brown, water features in light blue, and cultural features in black. Recent maps use red for principal highways and township and other land subdivision boundaries; woodlands are shown on some maps in light green overprint.

Maps can be any size of course, but few persons wish to be bothered with large sheets of paper which require tricky folding to put back together. Most topographic maps therefore stick to modest sizes which can be laid flat on the average desk or can be folded easily for carrying in the field. The most frequently used maps of the U. S. Geological Survey are standardized on paper sizes of from 17″ x 21″ to 23″ x 27″ so that storage and handling are greatly simplified.

Scales used on topographic maps vary with the need for detail. Near population centers where many engineering projects require accurate position information and considerable detail appears, maps use the largest scales, that is, they cover least ground on the same size paper; this in effect magnifies detail. On the other hand, in wilderness areas small scales will be used, or, to put it another way, a great deal of area appears on a map of equal paper size. The U. S. Geological Survey accordingly employs the following scales for many of the topographic maps likely to be used by the prospector or collector:

Scale	One inch upon the map equals:
1: 20,000	approximately 1,667 feet
1: 24,000	exactly 2,000 feet
1: 30,000	exactly 2,500 feet
1: 31,680	exactly one-half mile
1: 62,500	approximately one mile
1: 63,360	exactly one mile
1: 125,000	approximately 2 miles
1: 250,000	approximately 4 miles

The Federal Topographic maps issued by the Department of Mines and Technical Surveys, Ottawa, Canada, for areas within that country use the following scales:

Scale	One inch upon the map equals:
1:50,000	4,166 feet
1:125,000	approximately 2 miles
1:250,000	approximately 4 miles

Map scales appear at bottom center margins of map sheets and include three scales which can be used for measuring distances upon the map with dividers or strips of paper. One scale gives miles and tenths, another provides a scale of feet, and a third gives kilometers.

Standard topographic maps, or *quadrangles* as they are commonly called, show land areas included between north-south lines of longitude and east-west lines of latitude. Since lines of longitude in North America converge upon the North Pole, each quadrangle shows a corresponding convergence of its side boundaries; however, the amount is very slight and as one proceeds farther south in the Continent, it becomes even less noticeable. The least area covered in standard quadrangles of the U. S. Geological Survey measures 7½ minutes of latitude along the top and bottom, and 7½ minutes of longitude along the sides. Latitude and longitude are given at each corner along with tick marks upon the margins from which measurements can be made to locate geographical positions according to latitude and longitude. Next in area are quadrangles measuring 15 minutes by 15 minutes, which of course require a smaller scale to depict on standard size paper, followed by 30 minute by 30 minute quadrangles which call for an even smaller scale. Maps covering larger areas are also available.

Miscellaneous Maps

The following maps are issued by the U.S. Geological Survey in addition to the standard quadrangles previously described.

City Area Maps—Approximately 50 major cities in the United States, including Alaska and Hawaii, are depicted on special maps made by combining portions of standard quadrangles. Topography is shown.

Alaska Maps. Certain areas of economic importance are covered by maps to a scale of 1:63,360.

Alaska Base Maps. Show railroads, highways, settlements, streams, lakes, mountain ranges, etc. Topography not shown.

Hawaii Maps. Major islands are covered by single maps to a scale of 1:62,500. Standard quadrangles to a scale of 1:24,000 are available for Oahu, Molokai and Maui. Topography is shown.

Puerto Rico Base Maps. Several types are available, including those showing contours and others in Spanish editions.

State Maps. All states are covered but not by all types of maps. Base maps show counties, cities, towns, railroads, streams, and public land boundaries. Some show highways also; others show topography plus highways upon base maps.

National Park Maps. Approximately 43 parks, monuments and historical sites have been mapped topographically.

Geological Maps

The kinds of rocks, their distribution and their structure are shown upon geological maps as overprinted information on topographic maps. Areas underlain by various rocks or sediments are indicated in several ways, the most commonly used being by color overprint, with or without special patterns such as dots, bars, stripes, etc. Sometimes only pattern overprints are used to save the expense of color printing, and at other times, areas underlain by similar rocks are merely outlined and identifying symbols placed within each space.

Geological maps have been prepared for areas as small as a few thousand feet across, as for individual mines or ore deposits, and as large as entire states and provinces. It is obvious that as larger areas are encompassed, maps become only approximate indicators of geology, since it would be impossible for teams of geologists and mappers to cover every square foot of ground even within areas of only several square miles, no less hundreds of square miles. Detailed coverage is really not necessary except in places where mineral deposits or special geological features occur. Despite their limitations, geological maps are of great value to prospectors and collectors, and have led to the discovery of many mineral deposits.

Geological maps are frequently prepared to accompany reports of surveys, and many publications in book or pamphlet form carry maps in small pockets pasted to back covers. Smaller maps are printed in the text or pasted in as separates in appropriate places. Unlike topographic quadrangles, which cover most areas of interest to the prospector and collector, relatively few standard geological maps are available covering the same areas. However, the U. S. Geological Survey publishes a series of geologic quadrangle maps of 25″ x 30″ paper size in various scales from 1:24,000 to 1:125,000; also a series of miscellaneous geologic investigation maps and a series of 7½ minute quadrangles on a scale of 1:24,000. The first two groups cover sections of 24 states, but the last group is confined to Utah, Arizona, and Colorado.

In recent years the Geological Survey of Canada has published a series of colored geological maps on scales of 1 inch to 1 mile, and 1 inch to 4 miles. Preliminary maps are sometimes published on scales of 1 inch to ½ mile and 1 inch to 2 miles, while special detailed maps may take scales of 1 inch to 400 feet and 1 inch to 1,000 feet.

How to Obtain Maps

U. S. Geological Survey topographic maps may be obtained by mail or at sales counters in certain Survey offices, and at a number of private agencies. However, unless the exact map can be identified, it is necessary to send to the U. S. Geological Survey for a free copy of the Index Circular for the state concerned. Index Circulars show a map of the state overprinted with rectangles corresponding to maps published. Maps are given names for prominent cities or distinctive geographical places. Circulars additionally give information on map scales, whether maps are in print, full details for ordering, lists of special maps, map agents, Federal distribution centers, and map reference libraries located within the states covered by the Index. Request state Index Circulars from:

U. S. Geological Survey
Distribution Section
1200 S. Eads Street
Arlington, Va. 22202

For states west of the Mississippi River, including Louisiana and Minnesota, request Index Circulars from:

U. S. Geological Survey   or: U. S. Geological Survey
Distribution Section   310 First Ave.
Federal Center   Fairbanks, Alaska 99701
Denver, Colorado 80225

Geological maps for sale by the U. S. Geological Survey are also listed in *Publications of the Geological Survey*, previously described. Additional Federal agency maps available to the public are listed in Price List 53 of the Government Printing Office; the price list can be obtained free of charge by writing to:

Superintendent of Documents
Government Printing Office
Washington, D.C. 20402

Information sheets on special maps, or inquiries concerning maps issued by Federal agencies, as well as information upon the activities and publications of all Federal mapping agencies and some State and private organizations, is supplied to the public, free of charge, by the Map Information Office at the U. S. Geological Survey in Washington.

Topographic and geological maps of Canada are also shown upon Index Maps. These may be obtained by writing to:

Map Distribution Office
Department of Mines and Technical Surveys
601 Booth Street
Ottawa, Ontario, Canada.

Maps of Mexico are very few in number and difficult to obtain. However, inquiries may be addressed to:

Commision Cartografica Militar   or: Instituto de Geologí
Lomas de Sotolo, Tacubaya   Universidad Nac. Autonoma
Mexico, D.F.   de Mexico
                                        Ciudad Universitaría
                                        Mexico 20, D.F.

Aeronautical charts covering Mexico and Central America are published by the U. S. Coast and Geodetic Survey and, although designed primarily for aerial navigation, do show terrain, approximate elevations, and many cultural features in color. They may be purchased from:

U. S. Coast and Geodetic Survey
Department of Commerce
Washington, D. C. 20355

LAYING OUT TRIPS

Short, one-day trips call for careful planning only in respect to knowing exactly where to go, since a great deal of time can be wasted by depending upon local inquiries. It is best to ask someone who has already been there all about those important details which are necessary to cover the last mile or so. In wooded or rolling terrain, so typical of the Eastern United States and Canada, one cannot depend upon seeing a quarry or mine but must know exactly the trail or woods road to follow. A great many localities are listed as ". . . about 1 mile northeast of Smithville crossroads . . ." which seems a fairly precise location, all things considered, but if the countryside is heavily wooded and several roads lead in the general direction, one begins to experience the frustrations which all collectors have suffered at one time or another in looking for nebulous localities. A map, almost any kind of map, would help in such a situation. This is but one reason why mines and quarries located off highways should be pin-pointed ahead of time upon topographic maps, if it is at all possible to do so. In many instances, mine or quarry locations are already marked upon maps, especially upon more recent editions, by the usual crossed-picks symbol. Some especially well drawn maps even go so far as to indicate trails leading into the deposits by single-dashed lines, or woods roads by double-dashed lines. These visual directions are often worth more than the best verbal instructions. In this connection, it will be found that woods roads leading into mines or quarries are often paved with crushed rock from the deposit.

For laying out long trips into remote localities, whether they be made on foot, on horseback or by jeep, topographic maps should be used. Terrain features are examined closely to determine easiest routes, and extremely steep climbs which may be dangerous or tiring are ruled out. If a compass is to be used, conspicuous landmarks are picked out and bearings laid down upon the map for reference in the field. Positions can be fixed also by visual *cross-bearings*, established first on the map, then applied in the field—that is, by lining up a set of mountain peaks or hill tops by eye and merely turning to line up another set at about right angles to the first. Another good cross-bearing is provided by a double set of peaks for one line of sight and some point along a river bed where this line crosses. When the two peaks swing into line, as one walks up the stream bed, position is unmistakably fixed. If many peaks surround the area and present a confusing picture, only the highest, steepest, or those which for some reason are the most distinctive, should be selected as landmarks. Other useful check points are watercourses, especially junctions of branches, waterfalls, steep rapids, and similar unmistakable features. Falls and rapids are distinguished on maps by bunching of several contours as they cross stream beds. Incidentally, watercourses provide excellent guide paths in and out of unknown areas. Since water selects direct routes to lower elevations, usually along paths of least steepness, experienced woodsmen stick to them in preference to striking off into terrain which may be far more rugged. Furthermore, topographers are usually careful to show even the smallest brooks upon their maps since they recognize the value of watercourses for getting about and for providing position information. Several methods for keeping track of position are illustrated in Figure 2.

Plotting Locality Positions

Assuming the appropriate topographic map is at hand, it is necessary to plot localities accurately in order to lay out the best way to approach a mine or quarry. Localities given in books, field guides, and magazine articles are described in one of the following ways: by *bearing and distance*, by *latitude and longitude*, or by *township subdivision*. There are other ways, but these are the most accurate and most commonly used.

Bearings and distances are given in reference to easily found, conspicuous points on maps, as for example: prominent peaks or hilltops, stream branches, crossroads, or centers of small villages. Bearings are given in cardinal compass points, in degrees and cardinal points, or in degrees alone. Distances may be in feet, yards, or miles. Cardinal points are familiar to everyone, e.g., N—north, NNE—north by northeast, etc., however, some older locality descriptions using cardinal points in combination with degrees may be confusing and deserve a word or two of explanation. Typical descriptions may read "... bearing 10° west of south ..." or "... bearing north 30° east. ..." In the first example, if the observer stood facing south, the bearing would be 10 degrees to his right, or toward the west. In the second example, an observer facing north would find the bearing 15 degrees to his right, or toward the east. Referring to the drawing of a compass rose in Figure 3, 10 degrees west of south is equivalent to 190 degrees, or a bearing

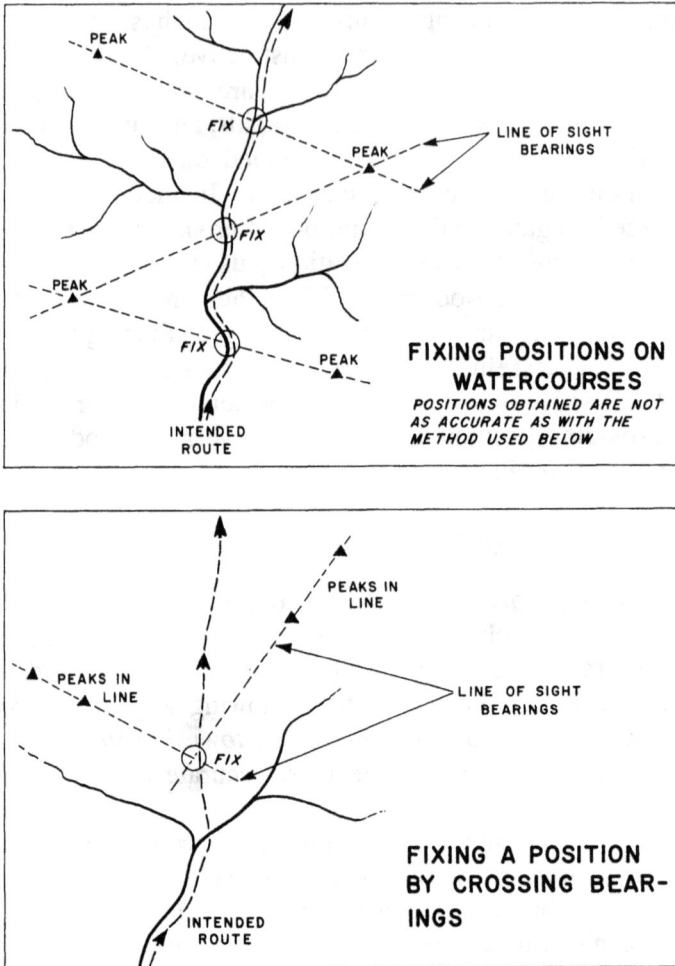

PEAK
FIX
PEAK
LINE OF SIGHT
BEARINGS
FIX
PEAK
FIX
PEAK
INTENDED
ROUTE

**FIXING POSITIONS ON
WATERCOURSES**
*POSITIONS OBTAINED ARE NOT
AS ACCURATE AS WITH THE
METHOD USED BELOW*

PEAKS IN
LINE
PEAKS IN
LINE
LINE OF SIGHT
BEARINGS
FIX
INTENDED
ROUTE

**FIXING A POSITION
BY CROSSING BEAR-
INGS**

FIGURE 2. Several methods of keeping track of position. In each method, the intended paths and reference fixes are laid out beforehand and followed in the field. Position keeping by these methods is a very good idea since few persons are good judges of distances traveled on foot, especially over rough terrain.

between S and SSW, while north 30 degrees east is equivalent to 30 degrees, a bearing between NNE and NE.

Most modern references to localities give accurate bearings in degrees alone, for example: "The prospect on the southern slope of Thomas Mountain bears 253 degrees, 5,300 yards from Colfax Crossroads." This locality is plotted by first finding Colfax Crossroads upon the topographic

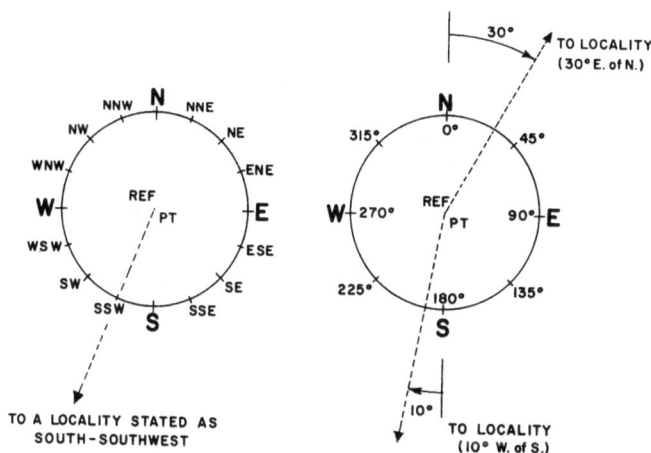

FIGURE 3. Methods of stating bearings and distances.

quadrangle, laying a protractor so that its center hole is exactly over the crossroads, and then swinging the protractor around until its cross-leg is parallel to either the top or bottom margin of the map. Since 253 degrees is 17 degrees away from west (270 degrees), a like number of degrees are counted off on the curved edge of the protractor and a pencil mark made at that point. Now by connecting this point with a straight line drawn with a ruler from Colfax Crossroads, the bearing to the locality is established. With a pair of dividers or a strip of paper, a distance of 5,300 yards is measured on the scale at the bottom of the map and transferred to the bearing line to fix the exact point of the deposit sought. Every topographic map has tick points along the edges which can be connected with pencil lines to opposite points in order to provide the horizontal lines necessary for use of a protractor. Half-circle protractors can be bought very inexpensively from stores selling school supplies. This plotting exercise is illustrated in Figure 4.

Positions given in latitude and longitude may be plotted on topographic maps by measuring up the sides to the proper latitude and across the bottom or top for the longitude. Lines drawn across the map will then intersect at the proper position. Because so few latitude and longitude tick marks are furnished along the margins of maps, it is necessary to measure distances between marks and divide by the number of minutes in order to obtain the distance covered by each minute, or to simply estimate distances along the margins, accepting the possibility of

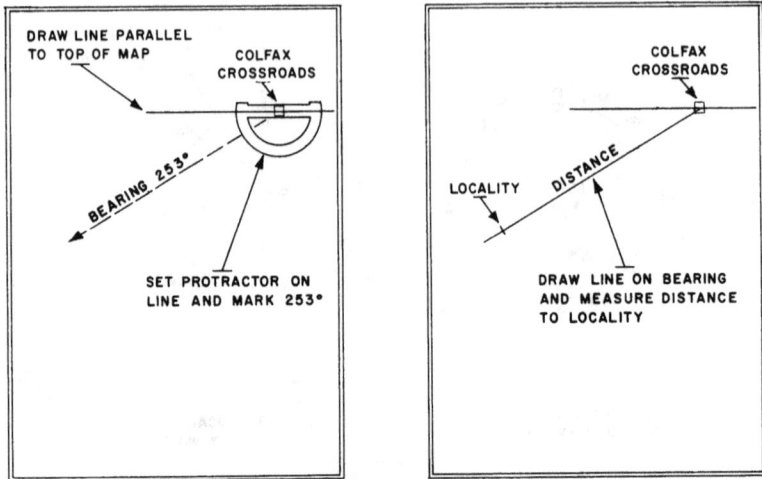

FIGURE 4. Plotting a position on a topographic map.

error. The following information will be useful in plotting positions in latitude and longitude:

(a) All latitudes in North America are North and increase toward the top of maps.

(b) All longitudes in North America are West and increase toward the left on maps.

(c) One degree = 60 minutes; one minute = 60 seconds. Fractions of minutes may be given in seconds or as decimals.

(d) The symbol of a degree is a small zero (°) to the upper right of the figure. The symbol of a minute is a small vertical dash ('). The symbol for a second is two small vertical dashes (").

(e) The length of a degree of latitude (always measured along the north-south direction) is 60 nautical miles, but since each nautical mile is 6,080.2 feet in length, the equivalent in statute miles is a little over 69 miles.

(f) The length of a degree of longitude is 60 nautical miles *only at the equator*, and decreases as the poles are approached. This is the reason why standard topographic quadrangles, although measuring 7½ minutes of latitude by 7½ minutes of longitude, are rectangular in shape instead of square.

The final common method of describing localities is based upon the system used to subdivide public lands into *townships*, or plots of land measuring 6 miles square and hence containing 36 square miles, or 36

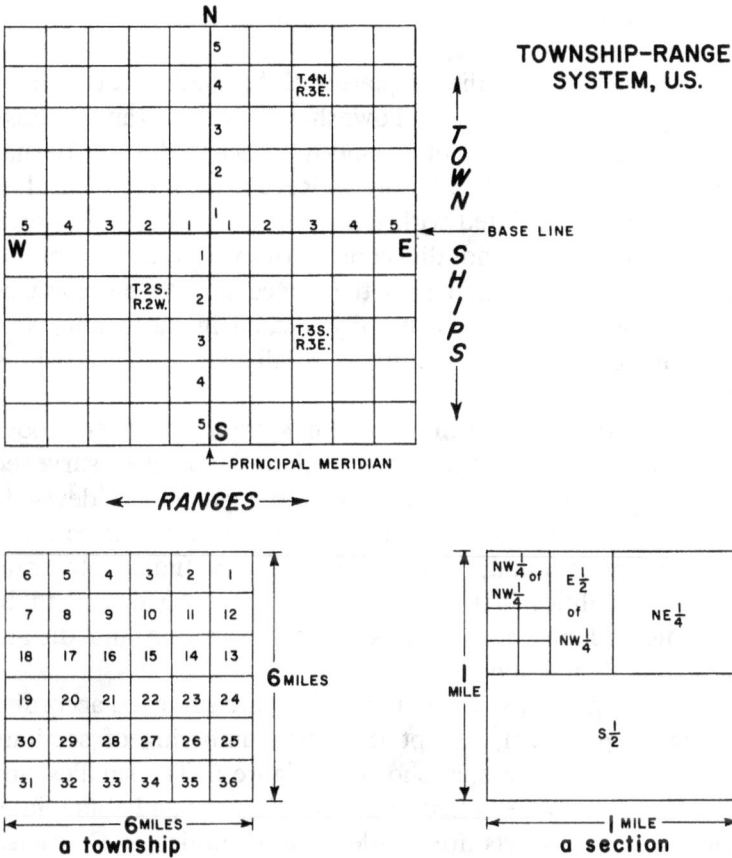

FIGURE 5. Subdivision of land according to the township-range system in the United States.

sections. Figure 5 shows how townships are surveyed. Points are selected from which two lines are run, a north-south line called a *principal meridian*' and an east-west line called a *base line*. There are 30 principal meridians spaced across the United States, and a number of base lines which divide the whole into enormous blocks. A north-south strip of townships is called a *range*, and may be either east or west, depending on which side of the principal meridian it is located. Each range is divided into east-west strips, resulting in *townships*. In Figure 5 several examples are shown of townships identified according to their position.

The bottom diagrams in Figure 5 show how a township block is divided into *sections* and how each section is further divided into *quarters* or *halves*, and fractions of quarters. Thus the meaning of a position given as SE¼ of SW¼ of NW¼ Sec. 27, T. 29N., R.7E.S.B. M. translates into: the southeast quarter of the southwest quarter of the northwest quarter of Section 27, Township 29 North, Range 7 East, San Bernardino Meridian. The plot of land is 10 acres; the San Bernardino Meridian, incidentally, is in California. Recent U. S. Geological Survey quadrangles are overprinted with red dashed lines indicating township boundaries and other land divisions. However, older maps do not contain this information and it is then necessary to purchase county maps from County Surveyors, usually located in the county seats, in order to find out how the county is subdivided into townships and sections.

Exceptions to the township division system described above are common in the Eastern United States, where lands were surveyed and claimed many years before the township system was devised. Old Spanish land grants in California are other exceptions, also certain tracts of National Forest Land, National Parks, and Indian Reservations. Accordingly, localities in these areas will never be described by the township method but may be described by bearing and distance or latitude-longitude methods.

In Canada, large tracts of land in the West are surveyed according to a similar township system, except that the numbering of sections and section subdivisions differs, as shown in Figure 6. The smallest subdivisions within a section are called Legal Subdivisions and abbreviated LS. In Eastern Canada, tracts are divided into Counties or Districts, with some townships being 10 miles square but others being irregular in form. Townships may be named or numbered and are laid out in 1 mile wide strips running east to west. In Ontario, townships are called "concessions," and in Quebec "ranges"; both are numbered with Roman numerals north to south. Each strip is divided into "lots," numbered in Arabic numerals from east to west. A typical description of an Ontario lot may be: "Lot 22, Concession X, Hale Township, Hardy County." Some recently surveyed portions of Ontario use the 6-mile square township system. In Quebec, the term "parish" is used instead of township.

PUBLIC AND PRIVATE PROPERTY RIGHTS

Considerable land in the public domain still remains available for homesteading, prospecting, and mining in the United States, particularly in Alaska, and also in Canada. As populations grow, more and more

31	32	33	34	35	36
30	29	28	27	26	25
19	20	21	22	23	24
18	17	16	15	14	13
7	8	9	10	11	12
6	5	4	3	2	1

6 MILES

← 6 MILES →

a township

13	14	15	16
12	11	10	9
5	6	7	8
4	3	2	1

1 MILE

← 1 MILE →

a section—DIVIDED INTO QUARTER SECTIONS AND LEGAL SUBDIVISIONS.

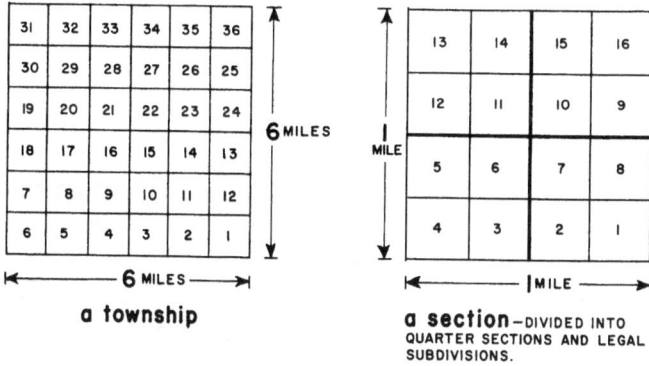

FIGURE 6. Township-Section system of West Canada.

land is being claimed through the procedures provided by the laws of each country and its political subdivisions, but much remains which is forbiddingly cold, dry, or barren. Regulations for claiming land are issued by national, state, and provincial governments and should be consulted if prospecting aimed at establishing mining claims is being considered. A brief but excellent summary of United States Federal laws governing mining claims on public lands is contained in Bureau of Mines Information Circular 7535, Part II, *Locating Mining Claims on the Public Domain*, by Marion Clawson, February 1950. This circular may be obtained free of charge from:

Bureau of Mines
U. S. Department of the Interior
Washington, D. C. 20242

Many areas which were once unbroken stretches of public land are now cut up into complicated patchworks of public and private lands. It is dangerous to assume that barren or wild lands are open to collecting and prospecting merely because there are no houses, roads, or other signs of civilization. State, provincial, and county land or surveyor's offices should be visited to determine the boundaries of lands still open, and this information should be plotted upon maps covering the area in order to avoid trespassing. Copies of local regulations issued by National Forest Headquarters should also be obtained, since they govern access to and activities within National Forest lands. Entry to National Forests— for any reason whatsoever—may be suddenly barred during dry spells when critical fire conditions exist.

Where private lands appear worthy of prospecting or contain known mineral deposits from which specimens or ores are wanted, it is necessary to make collecting arrangements beforehand with owners. Prospecting privileges ordinarily are granted on the basis of outright lease of mineral rights if deposits are found, or may be a combination of lease, plus royalties, on the wholesale value of ore and minerals recovered. The last ten years have seen many collecting localities on private lands barred to the general public because of abuse of privileges. Common complaints range from failure to close cattle gates to failure to clean up rubbish and litter, the regrettable practice of persons whose camping manners are not the best. Cases are on record where fences have been torn down, gate locks broken or sawed through, machinery and tools damaged or stolen, windows smashed, and many other acts committed which can only be called vandalism in its worst sense. In addition, most mines and quarries carry insurance compensation and are reluctant to allow persons not in their employ to enter their grounds, for fear that serious injuries or even fatalities may be incurred. Most insurance policies require that positive steps be taken to prevent illegal entry, otherwise settlement of suits and claims are refused, leaving the mining or quarrying companies liable to civil suits by damaged parties or their heirs and relatives. However, many owners are sympathetic to the desires of serious collectors and frequently arrange visits in charge of a company employee or some other responsible person.

In recent years, the increasing number of mineral and gemstone collectors has led property owners, or owners of mineral rights, to permit collecting after payment of modest fees. This scheme provides some recompense to owners for the inconvenience or damage inflicted upon property, and at the same time, removes any shadow of doubt as to collecting rights. In many instances, such localities are advertised in the magazines devoted to the mineral sciences and reference to past issues may assist in planning pleasant and successful trips.

CAMPING TIPS

In general, the same camping procedures used by hunters and fishermen are employed on collecting and prospecting trips. Only tips found by experience to apply specially to collecting and prospecting trips will be described here. However, excellent books on woodcraft and camping are usually available from any library or bookstore, and one of the best is listed in the bibliography in Appendix V. Persons without previous outdoor experience should study at least one camping textbook in order to avoid mistakes which may ruin an otherwise pleasant excursion.

One of the important things soon learned by collectors and prospectors is that time spent in camp is time wasted in the field. A camp is a place to cook and sleep but nothing can be collected there except rubbish. For this reason, it is necessary to so order the affairs of the camp that everyone in the party shares in the chores and does everything at the proper time. For example, the time to make up beds, lay firewood, and otherwise ready the camp for eating and sleeping is not at night, when everybody is dead tired, but in the morning before the day's work begins. A great many frictions and annoyances can be avoided by previous assignment of tasks and agreement upon camping routines. Careful planning is needed in stocking food, and one individual should be assigned the job of making up a list of items beforehand and getting them together. Most campers manage to buy major items such as meats, vegetables, and bread but forget salt and pepper, butter or cooking grease, sugar for coffee and other small but important accessories. Also commonly forgotten are utensils and other kitchen hardware, particularly a can opener, and anyone who has attempted to open a can without one knows how annoying the experience can be. If much camping is done, it pays to assemble a special cook-out kit, containing cheap but durable items such as plates, cups, knives, forks and spoons, etc., cooking utensils, serving spoons, and many others, all kept in a special box and ready to go at a moment's notice. Standard "check-off" lists should be at hand for food items and supplied to the person responsible for the commissary.

In respect to camp drinking water, it is best to depend on home rather than upon field sources. However, tablets for purifying water of doubtful character are available and work well in destroying possibly harmful organisms. Water containers must never be made of glass since normal rough handling about a camp is sure to break them. Even worse is to take along glass containers to quarries or mines, especially if the water must be used to replenish carbide lamps when working underground. When estimating how much water to take along, it is best to err on the high side, but as a general rule, two persons need about 5 gallons for two days for all purposes. If some lack of cleanliness can be tolerated, the same quantity will do for drinking and cooking purposes for two men for three days. How much drinking water is used depends also upon the climate and how hard members of the party work. If excessive perspiration takes place, heat stroke may be avoided by taking salt tablets; one or two a day are usually enough. Porous water bags are popular in dry regions because water evaporating from the outside cools the contents, however, considerable water is lost in the process and if one does not mind drinking warm water, it is less wasteful to store water in sealed cans, canteens, or five-gallon metal containers of the kind used on jeeps.

Personal Injuries

The greatest hazard on all collecting and prospecting trips is personal injury. Climbing over piles of rock, venturing into quarries and mines, and using unfamiliar hand tools are not the safest occupations by any means, although the vast majority of persons seldom receive harmful injuries if they use care and common sense. Nevertheless, dangers are present everywhere and what may not be a serious injury at home may be a risk to life itself in the field, far away from help. For this reason alone, no trip should be taken to remote areas without at least one companion. Even a short trip to a local quarry should not begin without telling someone where you are going, if you must go alone. A companion provides an added safety factor because it isn't likely that both members of a party will be subjected to the same hazard at the same time. However, there are many other reasons for taking along a companion, not the least of which are sharing work which may be too much for one person, and the enjoyment of each other's company during the long evening hours when nothing can be done in the field. Perhaps it is true that "he travels fastest who travels alone" but it is wise to consider the drawbacks before doing so.

Another place where a companion can spell the difference between serious illness or uncomfortable but not disabling injury, is in the case of snake bites. Poisonous snakes are present over much of Mexico, United States, and some southern portions of Canada; no poisonous snakes are found in northern Canada nor in all of Alaska or Hawaii. Because snake venom exercises much greater toxic effect if it spreads through the blood system, it is extremely important that the victim be prevented from moving about unnecessarily and that as much venom as possible be extracted immediately after the bite has been suffered. A companion is vital in preventing serious consequences because he can administer to the wound, withdraw venom, make the victim comfortable, and finally go off to summon help necessary to move out the injured party by stretcher. Needless to say, one of the several kinds of small and compact snake bite kits available upon the market should always be carried on the person or in the packsack. Additional first aid items which are also extremely handy on most mineralogical trips are a stock of small bandages and cloth or plastic adhesive tape for covering over small cuts. A more complete first aid kit should be kept in camp and regularly included in the cook-out kit.

Clothing

Another hazard not fully appreciated by the inexperienced is severe chilling brought on by failure to wear proper clothing. Except in desert regions, it is almost impossible to depend on dry weather at all times, and it is foolish not to take along at least one change of clothing, in the event of becoming wet from rain or from working in wet mines or quarries. Water is incredibly efficient in removing heat from the body, and if one is not young and bursting with energy, it is best to keep dry, or, if this is impossible, to have a change of clothing ready at camp. When working in continually wet places such as in mines, or prospecting in the open in rainy climates, waterproof, southwester-type hats, jackets, and trousers are essential items of outer clothing. Even on one-day trips it is a good idea to have rain clothing and extra inner clothing available in the car; it takes up little extra room and may be extremely useful before the day is out. On longer trips, extra clothing is even more necessary, since the chances are better that clothes will be soaked by rain or by perspiration brought on by heavy work. In many of our North American deserts, it isn't at all unusual to experience temperatures in the 80's during the day and below freezing at night. Lack of warm dry clothing after a hard day's work can ruin comfort, if not health. Extra socks and a pair of moccasins to slip upon the feet after camp is reached also add blessed comfort and, at the same time, give socks and shoes worn during the day a chance to air and dry.

In selecting clothing, remember that it is best to be sheathed in several thin layers than in a single thick layer. For example, it is better to wear a shirt, sweater, and light jacket, than a single very heavy shirt or jacket. Several layers of clothing trap air in pockets and prevent escape of heat from the body better than single heavy items. Furthermore, excess layers can be peeled off during the hottest part of the day, or after hard work has caused perspiring, and put on again when needed later. Clothing should also be selected for protection against sunburn and physical injury. To avoid undue loss of perspiration and to prevent sunburning in hot sunshine, it is important to wear a hat, and a shirt with sleeves. If work is being done in close quarters, sleeved shirts are far better than sport shirts for protecting the elbows and forearms from scratches and bruises. If there is a possibility of being struck by falling rocks or bumping into low overhangs in tunnels, a metal or pressed fiber miner's helmet should be worn. In any event, wearing some kind of headgear is always a good idea; if it is in the way, it can always be taken off. In cold weather, or during desert nights, a wool pullover cap is worth its weight in gold. It can be worn as a cap, stretched over the ears or pulled down even farther to cover part of the neck and sides of the face. In mosquito-infested regions, it covers most of the head and provides a thick enough layer to discourage drilling operations by these pests.

Good tough mittens or gloves are absolutely essential, because the hands and wrists are the parts of the body most likely to be injured. Although cuts and bruises on hands and fingers may be small, they prove most irritating and, unless covered over, prevent further use of the hands. Dangers from deep cuts are greatest when digging in crystal-lined pockets filled with clay or dirt which obscure view of the contents. In such openings, quartz is very likely to be present as thin sharp slivers which cut like razor blades. Persons who do not regularly use their hands for manual labor are sure to develop blisters very shortly after commencing work, merely from gripping shovels, picks, and other tools. The best protective gloves for collecting work are made of horsehide and are sold in various models in practically every hardware or general store. Country stores are especially likely to stock large selections, in all sizes. Although most expensive, the best kinds are full leather with plenty of room for the fingers. They should not fit too tightly, in order to allow perspiration from the hands to escape easily. Less satisfactory kinds are those which are palmed and fingered with leather but are cloth upon the backs. Gloves of this sort tend to fall apart quickly at the seams because sharp stone fragments quickly cut the stitching. Cloth gloves are cheapest of all but last a fraction of the time. In this connection, very cheap or very expensive clothing should be avoided. The best clothes of all are those meant for workmen, in which stout fabrics are employed, sewn with good strong stitching.

For work in muddy or wet situations, the best trouser and shirt fabrics are smooth, hard-surfaced cotton twills and denims. Dirt and mud cling to them least, while, conversely, napped fabrics such as wools, should be avoided because they are sure to become deeply caked with mud and are almost impossible to keep clean. Because cottons are cold fabrics, however, inner shirts and inner trousers should be of warmer material if outside temperatures require warmer clothing. Miners regularly use outer trousers and jackets made from canvas, for protection both against moisture and against injuries. Still the best inner clothes are the part wool, part cotton "long handle" underwear, or "union suits." Single-piece versions are satisfactory and least bulky but double-piece models afford greater flexibility, since one part or the other can be worn if not both. Wool is unbeatable for maintaining warmth even when soaked with water or perspiration, however, 100% wool underwear is seldom made because wool directly against skin is too irritating to most persons. If woolen underwear is found to be too warm, a good trick is to wear flannel pajamas instead underneath outer clothing; the weight and bulk are negligible yet good insulation is provided.

Many prospectors and collectors like to wear sweaters because they can be slipped on and off easily and, when not in use, can be stowed or tucked under the straps of backsacks. They can be used also for wrapping fragile specimens in an emergency, or rested upon the shoulders to ease the bite of knapsack straps.

The greatest discomfort experienced by beginners usually arises from improper footwear, of the wrong type or incorrectly fitted. Ordinary street oxfords offer no protection against ankle bruises or cuts, nor against ankle twisting. The kind of footwear selected depends on the kind of trip to be taken. If it is a scouting trip involving considerable hiking, then the shoes should be light in the tops with strong but resilient soles and should provide some protection for the ankles. The author's favorite model for this kind of work is the Maine hunting shoe, which consists of a rubber shoe topped by a soft leather upper extending well above the ankle to about four inches below the knee. The leather uppers extend high enough to permit tucking in trousers so that they cannot pull out while hiking or working. With socks worn beneath the leather, the area of the lower leg most vulnerable to injuries or to snake bites is well protected. Because Maine hunting shoes are soft-rubber soled, it is customary to buy them large enough to take inner soles made from felt or horsehair. The latter not only furnish additional cushioning but also absorb perspiration. Whenever shoes are not in use, the inner soles are removed and hung up to dry. Similar all-leather hunting shoes are less desirable because foot parts are not waterproof and seam stitching in the so-called "moccasin" models is quickly cut by sharp stones. Because plain rubber slips on wet rocks, some collectors prefer to use footwear shod with neoprene or with leather studded with hobnails. Hobnailed boots are almost a necessity when climbing over smooth rock and also have the advantage of wearing out less rapidly than plain leather.

The ordinary military field shoe is very popular, being light yet strong enough to take abuse and to protect the ankles. Thousands of pairs have been sold as surplus, but watch for those which are so old that the leather is brittle and weak, and the stitching rotten. For work which involves removal of heavy rock masses, or for digging upon dumps where rolling rocks are real hazards, steel-capped shoes are invaluable. Shoes of this type are sold in stores catering to workingmen, especially in industrial cities where factories and foundaries process heavy objects which could drop and crush toes of workmen.

Regardless how fine a pair of shoes may be, if they do not fit properly they are worse than the sleaziest pair of cheap shoes which do fit. Everyone who has done much walking in ordinary street shoes on hard pavements knows how hot and tired the feet become; in outdoor work, the problem is far greater, and it is therefore absolutely essential that shoes be fitted properly before they are bought. However, due allowance must be made for socks, one pair of cotton for wear next to the skin, and two pairs of light wool socks, or one pair of heavy woolen socks for wear over the cotton. This is the absolute minimum protection for feet, and in fact some persons wear still another pair of socks despite added bulk and warmth. If feet are encased in thinner layers, severe blistering is almost certain to result and from that point on, each step will be a painful one. The necessary socks should therefore be taken along to the store, and actually worn when trying on shoes. The fit should be snug but not cramped and should be tested by putting on both shoes and walking about a bit. Avoid all shoes which narrow toward the toes; shoe toes must be generously wide to accommodate natural spreading of the forepart of the foot when weight is placed upon it, plus the slight swelling which always takes place after considerable walking.

Bedding

For overnight trips, good bedding is essential for comfortable sound sleep. Comfort is stressed because adequate rest is vital to success in collecting or prospecting. When one is well rested, the senses are keener and better work is possible, and it is a well-known fact that fatigue promotes accidents. Never plan to sleep on car seats; they are simply not long enough and one is apt to be more exhausted at the end of the night than before going to bed. The most generally used bedding arrangement is a sleeping bag plus inflatable air mattress, with or without a military style collapsible canvas cot. A sleeping bag alone is not thick enough for comfort when placed directly upon the ground. However, if this must be done, comfort can be increased by preparing a bed of leaves or boughs to spread the bag upon. It is much better to use an air mattress, either a very light plastic model which can be folded into a very small package when deflated, or a larger kind made of rubberized fabric, which, although more comfortable, is far bulkier. A cot is desirable not only for increased comfort but also to raise the body above the ground in places where dampness prevails or snakes abound. Light sleeping bags are generally more useful than heavy ones because their warmth can be increased by spare blankets in colder weather while their light weight in warm weather prevents them from becoming too hot. Buy only those bags which can be unzipped along one full side and the bottom, permitting them to be opened out flat. This feature permits easy airing and cleaning, and also makes it a simple task to fold in extra blankets when needed. Sleeping bags may be treated with water repellant but are far from waterproof. For this reason it is a good idea in regions where sudden showers fall at night, to take along a tarpaulin to spread over the bedding. One last hint in respect to sleeping comfort: to avoid that feeling of cliff-hanging during the night, take special pains to level cots by cutting away earth beneath the legs until the top of the cot is absolutely horizontal.

Insect Pests

The problem of protection against insects, especially mosquitoes, gnats, and wood ticks, is a serious one in many regions of North America. In the South, the red-bug, or chigger, is particularly annoying and, by virtue of his nasty habit of burrowing beneath the skin, provides discomfort for days if not weeks afterwards. In the West, the tick carries Rocky Mountain spotted fever. In the North, the frozen muskegs and tundras are paradises for mosquitoes, which appear in appalling abundance during warmer seasons. The best general protection against insects is snug clothing seals at wrists, neck, and next to boot tops. Tucked-in trousers are effective in preventing any kind of insect from reaching leg areas, while a woolen cap worn over the top of the head prevents attacks upon the scalp. However, these measures cut down exposed areas but do not protect the face, hands, and wrists; for these areas it is necessary to use one of several currently available insect repellants. Modern preparations are a far cry from the tar and citronella mixtures used some years ago, most being quite odorless and far less messy. Liquid preparations are easy to spread upon skin but are a nuisance because they must be replaced frequently. Some campers like repellants put up in stick form because evaporation is much slower and replacement less frequent. All repellants sting when touched to mucous membranes of the mouth and especially so when accidentally introduced into the eyes. For this reason, only small quantities should be used upon the forehead, lest perspiration dissolve part and carry it down into the eyes. If no head covering is used, an ordinary handkerchief can be used; knot the corners to form a cap, sprinkle or rub with repellant, and place over the scalp. If knots are tight enough, the handkerchief will not fall off while moving about.

Where insects are numerous, mosquito netting to cover sleeping bags during the night is very desirable indeed. Two sticks jammed into the ground can be used to raise the netting well away from the face since mosquitoes probe easily through netting lying directly in contact with the skin. Repellants can be used of course but tend to evaporate or rub off on bed clothing during the night.

The favorite haunts for red-bugs and for wood ticks are the very tips of twigs and branches of trail-side brush. Ticks station themselves on the extremities, clinging with several legs to the branch and reaching outward with several others, ready to let go and attach themselves to animal passers-by as soon as they are disturbed. To avoid them avoid brush; always hike in clear spaces, if possible. In tick-infested country, it is a good idea to stop frequently and inspect clothing for ticks, especially trouser legs, where the greatest numbers will usually be found. Although all contacts with brush cannot be avoided, take special pains to stay out of brush which is head high or which is liable to put ticks on the scalp or neck.

Firearms

A few words on the use of firearms is appropriate in this chapter because the author has noted far too many instances of careless discharge of lethal weapons by persons who should not be permitted to own such weapons, no less use them. Too many persons feel that a field trip is an excursion to a wide open shooting gallery, in which any feature of the landscape is a legitimate target. Although there are many places where one can fire a high-powered rifle at maximum trajectory without the least danger of striking any living thing, this fact still does not excuse taking along the weapon, since it is only an unnecessary and possibly hazardous piece of equipment. Farmers and ranchers are intensely hostile to any collector or prospector who brings in firearms or, even worse, fires at nothing in particular. Many wild areas are grazed by cattle, and when it is recalled that a steer is worth several hundred dollars on the hoof, it is easy to see why an armed field tripper is not greeted with warmth. As far as shooting rattlesnakes is concerned, the marksmanship required is probably best left to the unerring gunmen of television.

Desert Travel

A great source of danger in desert regions is automobile breakdown in remote places, necessitating either repairs on the spot, waiting for help, or walking out, possibly at great personal risk. It is surprising how many accidents to automobile parties are reported each year in California, Arizona, Nevada and other states which include expanses of desert. However, such accidents happen mostly to the unprepared, and not to the wise collectors and prospectors who take great pains to be sure their cars are in top notch working order before embarking on desert jaunts. Whenever taking desert trips by car, be sure to take along extra tires and tubes, tire and tube repair kit, chains and shovels, extra water, fuel, and food. Be prepared to repair damage or to stay a week if necessary until help comes. Partly clogged radiators which manage to stay cool in ordinary climates are almost certain to boil over in high desert temperatures. Boiling over is even more certain where elevations are considerably above sea level. At least five gallons of water in a jeep can should be taken along for radiator replenishment in addition to full canteens and thermos jugs of drinking water. If emergency water must be used for the radiator, it is best to wait until darkness to travel, for then the air is much cooler and evaporation losses will be held to the minimum. Extra fuel is also very desirable for a number of reasons, not the least of which is the possibility of losing one's way and having to do considerable backtracking.

PLANNING THE DAY'S WORK

Organization is just as necessary in actual collecting and prospecting as it is in camping, and again efficiency demands that each member of the party know what he is to do. A check should be made of all equipment and tools which will be needed for work, including lights, water, collecting bags, and other items in addition to hand tools. One never feels quite so foolish as when one realizes, after taking a long hike or climb to a collecting site, that some vital tool or accessory is still at camp.

In reconnaissance work, it is a good idea to furnish each member of the party with copies of the map covering the areas which will be prospected, assigning each person a reasonably small area which he is to inspect. It is better to cover carefully a small area at a time, remaining fresh and untired, than to attempt covering too much. A time of return to camp is specified as a safety feature, in case someone becomes lost or injured. Failure of a member to return on schedule will be the signal to search for him within his assigned area. When everyone has returned, notes are compared and additional areas laid out for the afternoon or next day. In this way it is possible to obtain far better prospecting than by permitting all persons of the party to wander about at will.

Where actual work is to be done upon a prospect or deposit, it is generally best for one person to work, another to assist, and if the party contains a third member, for him to fetch tools, furnish water, hold a light or take care of incidental chores. Duties are rotated so that no member becomes unduly tired. A well-knit team shortly finds that certain members are best able to do certain jobs and almost automatically a routine procedure is set up which is followed from that time on. A smoothly-functioning team can remove a surprising amount of rock, a fact well known to professional miners everywhere, who regularly employ organized work teams. Within the team each member knows his job and also knows the jobs of others, thus permitting each to anticipate the other's needs without a great many questions, answers, and explanations.

Especially good teamwork is needed where old mines are being explored, for many boobytraps await the unwary. Members of the party should not separate unless each knows the workings; even in this case, no one should wander off without telling another member of the party exactly where he is going and what he intends to do. It is very easy to receive injuries in underground workings, and extraordinary care must always be taken, regardless of how quiet and peaceful things seem.

FIELD NOTES AND SAMPLES

Systematic prospecting calls for taking notes as areas are covered, if for no other reason than to be able to return to points of interest. It is amazing how memory fails and old landmarks change after a lapse of several years. A well trodden trail quickly becomes overgrown with grass and brush, an abandoned quarry fills with trees until its presence is wholly camouflaged, and many other features of the landscape change. A small notebook, with pencil attached by a cord, is very handy to take along. In it should be jotted down directions for reaching places of interest. These would be expressed as bearings and distances from prominent landmarks, such as mountain peaks, plus bearings and distances from closer features which would serve to narrow down the area of search during a later trip. If a topographical map is taken along, it is better yet to locate the point upon the map and mark it accordingly.

When scouting in unknown terrain, prospectors should take rock and mineral samples for later identification, if their identity cannot be established in the field. Rock types are important in determining what kind of mineral deposits may be found in them. To avoid confusing many samples taken over a period of days from within the area scouted, it is necessary to note, in the field, where each one was collected, numbering accordingly by affixing some kind of label. Some professional geologists use adhesive tape labels, writing the data upon the tape and then affixing it to specimens at the time they are collected; at the same time, appropriate remarks are made in the notebook. It may turn out that some area given a quick inspection may really deserve a careful examination, and to be able to return exactly to the places previously visited is obviously important.

In the event a mineral deposit of unknown character is found, it is extremely important to collect as many different kinds of minerals as possible, in order to be sure an important mineral or ore is not missed. Sometimes the most valuable minerals look the least impressive, while valueless species may be flashy and colorful. A classic story is told of the early days of the Comstock Lode in Nevada. Miners seeking gold were continually annoyed by a heavy grayish mineral which cluttered their gold washing equipment and had to be removed by hand. This grayish mineral later turned out to be an extremely rich ore of silver, which, when identified, set off the famous rush to Virginia City. Even in deposits previously exploited, new and interesting minerals overlooked by previous amateur and professional mineralogists are being found. The author recalls the day he found the rare mineral hambergite upon the dumps of the Little Three Mine at Ramona, California, and was the first to identify this species at this locality, although its bladed crystals must have been exposed to everyone's view since the mine was opened about 1903, a period of almost 55 years. In taking samples it is, therefore, necessary to take a little of anything and everything which in any way looks peculiar or differs from those minerals which can be positively identified. Even those which are recognized should be taken back because they may prove to contain valuable metals, as for example, masses of pyrite found in quartz veins which may contain finely-disseminated gold.

FIELD IDENTIFICATION

Unless one camps out for a lengthy period or works from a field headquarters, such as a cabin or tent, it is generally inadvisable to attempt chemical field testing of minerals to determine what they are. The necessary equipment is rather cumbersome and it is best to avoid the very considerable trouble which testing procedures demand. However, some practical tests are easy to do and should be done since one of them may be enough to identify the species.

Before the tests described below are performed, it is assumed that specimens have been carefully examined first, noting color, luster, crystal forms, habits, transparency, cleavage planes, nature of fracture surfaces, and any other marks which distinguish the minerals concerned. If identity is still uncertain, one or more of the following tests may be performed: hardness, streak, toughness, magnetic properties, and "hefting" to obtain some idea of specific gravity. When one or more properties are determined, a mineralogy book with determinative tables should be consulted and a tentative determination made.

Hardness is judged according to the Mohs Scale which assigns the following values of hardness from low to high:

HARDNESS VALUES—MOHS SCALE

Hardness	Mineral	Remarks
1	Talc	The softest mineral and therefore scratched by every other; very easily scratched by the fingernail.
2	Gypsum	Easily scratched by the fingernail.
3	Calcite	Can be cut by a steel knife blade.
4	Fluorite	Scratched easily by a steel point.
5	Apatite	Difficultly scratched by a steel point.
6	Feldspar	Barely scratched by steel point but readily scratched by a file.
7	Quartz	Scratches glass readily.
8	Topaz	Scratches quartz.
9	Corundum	Readily scratches quartz and topaz.
10	Diamond	Deeply and easily scratches quartz; readily scratches corundum.

Of the above minerals, quartz, feldspar, and calcite are very common in the field and provide readily available standard hardness specimens. Steel and glass which are sure to be present in almost every camp, provide other standards of hardness. With the use of these five materials, it is possible to obtain fair ideas of hardness of unidentified minerals.

Streak is the colored mark left upon an unglazed white porcelain plate when a mineral is drawn across its surface. The backs of ordinary bathroom floor tiles make excellent streak plates and it is a simple matter to include one in the field kit. If no streak plate is available, the same test can be made in the following manner. Select a hard, smooth-surfaced rock and place upon it a small fragment of the mineral to be tested. Pound gently with a hammer until the mineral is reduced to powder, trying not to grind the rock itself. Pour some of the powder upon a white surface such as paper or cloth. Note the color; it will be the same as noted on a streak plate.

Toughness is measured in terms of how easily a mineral breaks, that is, is it brittle or does it require strong blows of a hammer to break apart. Some idea can be gained by attempting to break samples, beginning with small slivers between the fingers to light tapping upon other samples with a hammer. At the same time, freshly-fractured surfaces can be examined for the character of fracture, i.e., conchoidal, irregular, etc., and the presence and character of cleavage planes.

Magnetism is easily determined by crushing a sample of mineral to sand size and noting whether grains adhere to a small alnico magnet. Very few minerals respond to this test; the principal ones are magnetite, ilmenite, and pyrrhotite. Very finely crushed samples of minerals containing iron may also be attracted and then indicate the presence of this metal in the specimen.

The last practical test, "hefting," is almost idiotic in its simplicity and is one which everyone has used, without necessarily knowing the principle involved. This test merely compares the relative weights of various minerals to familiar substances such as metals. Some persons skilled in estimating specific gravities of minerals by hefting specimens in the hand, can judge quite accurately both the value of specific gravity and the weight of the sample. Others can do well if a sample of a known substance is held in one hand and the unknown mineral is held in the other; better judgment is obtained if samples of about the same size are used. The following minerals and metals commonly available in the field or present among camp tools can be used to compare against unknown minerals:

SPECIFIC GRAVITY OF COMMONLY AVAILABLE
MINERALS AND METALS

Mineral or Metal	Approximate Specific Gravity
Quartz, feldspar, calcite	2½
Garnet	4
Magnetite, pyrite	5
Iron or steel	7
Copper, brass, bronze	8½
Lead	11
Gold	17

Identification Tables

Mineral identification tables in handy form are found in my *Mineralogy for Amateurs*, also in *Getting Acquainted with Minerals* by English & Jensen, and Berry and Mason's *Mineralogy*. Especially complete testing procedures appear in Smith's *Identification and Qualitative Chemical Analysis of Minerals*. In the event the beginner is not at all familiar with rocks and minerals, it is extremely helpful to get a small study collection like the one shown in Figure 7. Small collections can also be assembled from bits and pieces donated by interested friends who are collectors. The materials need not be of fine quality but should be typical.

FIGURE 7. Small rock and mineral collections designed to familiarize students with the more important constituents of the earth's crust. The upper illustration shows a streak test being applied to a piece of hematite using an unglazed porcelain tile for a streak plate. *Courtesy Ward's Natural Science Establishment.*

2

Tools and How To Use Them

The removal of rock and soil in search of mineral specimens and ores involves many kinds of tools, from heavy sledges to slender picks suitable for dislodging the most delicate crystals. Techniques vary according to the tools used and how much care is needed in removing specimens without damage. Taking out crude or massive ores can be done with very little attention paid to preservation because crystals are not involved. However, if the primary object is to collect crystallized specimens, methods must be far more refined and work must be pushed cautiously. The drop in value of specimens showing broken or chipped crystals or tool marks is astonishing to the novice collector, who is all too often inclined to judge value solely by size.

Because of the above considerations, the collector is well-advised to curb his natural enthusiasm and not rush headlong into digging out a pocket likely to contain valuable specimen material. This advice also applies to the prospector developing an ore deposit, because many ore samples covered with crystals are often worth far more as specimens than as ores. A good example is gold-quartz, which is dull and unattractive in ordinary forms because so little gold is visible to the naked eye. However, if small vugs are found in which the gold is handsomely crystallized or forms bright shining wires or plates, the value of the specimen jumps well above that of its gold content alone. English, in an article on the valuation of mineral specimens published in an early issue of the *American Mineralogist*, tells of a famous collector of means, who unhesitatingly gave a sum much over the bullion value of gold for a small but fine octahedral crystal of this native metal. He cheerfully paid the price because of the rarity of gold crystals in general, and the exceptional scarcity of crystals of the form and size purchased. No matter how or where specimens are gathered, the fact remains that the best, and hence the most valuable, are obtained by hand, using the proper tools in proper fashion.

DIGGING TOOLS

A shovel is almost indispensable on any collecting trip if for nothing else than removing debris generated with other kinds of tools. Because of the weight of rock fragments, very large and wide shovels such as coal scoops are to be avoided because they take up too much at a time to make easy throwing loads. Garden spades must also be avoided since the square nose does not easily penetrate a mass of rock pieces. Shovels with small pointed blades are best, either in the short models with hand grips or in the very popular long-handled models with straight round wooden shafts. A smaller shovel is useful in cramped quarters and is less tiring to use because less leverage is needed to throw the load; however, the long-handled shovel is much better for sinking pits or digging deep trenches because a longer reach is possible. Several useful shovels are shown in Figure 8.

The small collapsible trenching shovel used by the U. S. Army during World War II and still available in surplus goods and camping equipment stores, is extremely popular because of its light weight, rugged construction, and its ability to fold up for carrying in knapsacks. It has the further advantage that it can be used as a scoop by locking the blade in a position at right angles to the handle. For very close quarters, or for digging in narrow vertical cavities, it has few equals.

Another excellent Army surplus tool is the small combination mattock and pick forged from a single piece of steel and fitted with a removable wooden handle. This tool also fits in knapsacks and is very light yet strong. Its chief drawback is the tendency for the handle to loosen during use; to avoid this, insert a screw in the handle just below the head to prevent the latter from backing off. This mattock, plus other useful pick tools, is shown in Figure 9. Heavy mattocks employed in construction or on farms for digging or chopping roots are seldom useful unless similar work is necessary in collecting or prospecting. Ordinary picks are also of limited usefulness, but some miners find use for the kind in which one end is flattened like a chisel. When the chisel end is inserted into a crevice and the handle twisted, enormous leverage can be exerted. However, the pick most preferred for mining is a special lightweight model (see Figure 9) with flattened narrow head and wooden handle

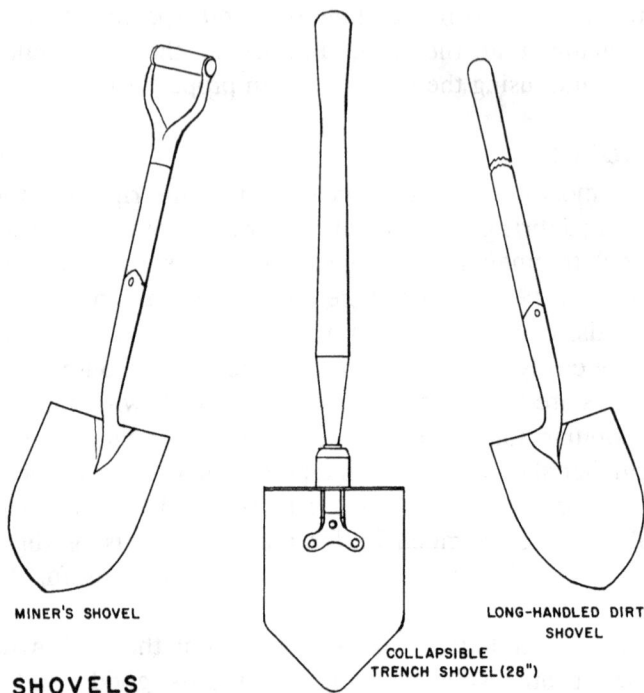

MINER'S SHOVEL

LONG-HANDLED DIRT
SHOVEL

SHOVELS

COLLAPSIBLE
TRENCH SHOVEL(28")

FIGURE 8. Several shovels useful for the collector and prospector. The center shovel is actually much smaller than either of the shovels on the sides but has been enlarged to show details. It is operated by unscrewing the collar just above the blade; this permits the shovel blade to be folded to a right angle position or folded back on the handle to reduce the total size for stowing in a knapsack.

shaped to match. It is far superior to ordinary picks, being less tiring to use, slimmer, and less likely to snag along the sides when used in cramped quarters.

The combination hammer-pick also illustrated in Figure 9 is popular with some miners underground because it serves to shatter rock or break up ore blocks into more manageable pieces without having to change off tools and waste time when both picking and hammering must be done alternately.

All picks should be kept sharp since they then penetrate much deeper with far less effort. Picks should never be used as hammers or bludgeons. They cannot strike as strong or as direct blows as hammers and they will lose their sharp, penetrating points. Mica miners of North Carolina use the slender miner's picks referred to above with great delicacy and

MINER'S PICK (21"-26")

EYE NO. 10

POLL OR ORE HAMMER (16")

EYE NO. 7

PICK-MATTOCK (14")

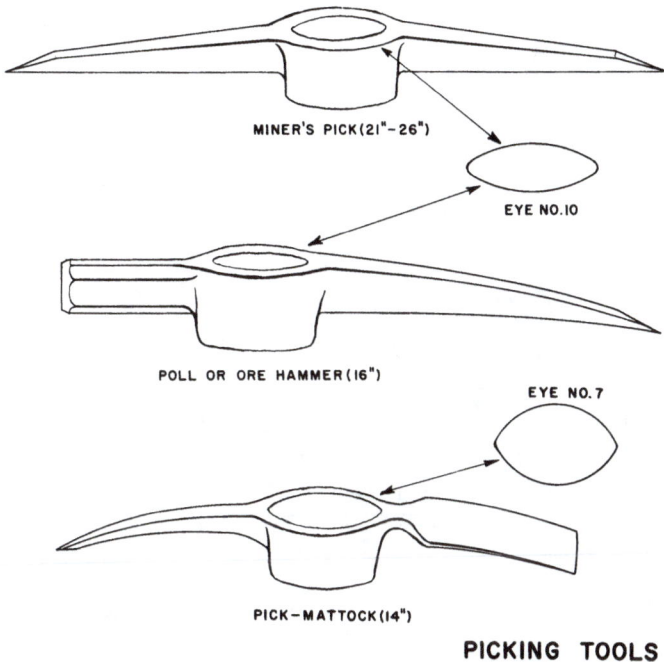

PICKING TOOLS

FIGURE 9. Several useful tools designed for picking, hammering and digging. Approximate lengths of heads are indicated, as well as the shapes of the wooden handles.

accuracy, dislodging books of mica which would be ruined by heavier picks wielded in clumsy fashion. When working in pegmatite, collectors strike only feldspar with their picks, as a rule. It is far less likely to dull points than quartz and has the further advantage of possessing several cleavage planes which cause it to break up readily.

HAMMERS

For light collecting work, the standard mineralogist's pick-hammer is by far the best all-around tool to use. It can be bought in several weights and in steel head, wooden handle combinations, or all-steel, leather or plastic-handled models. All-steel models are very strong and generally heavier than wooden-handled hammers of the same dimensions; however, weight may be a disadvantage if much swinging is to be done. Wooden-handled models last a much shorter time; misdirected blows often shatter the wood just below the head, or the handle loosens in time and must be replaced. On the favorable side, however, it may be

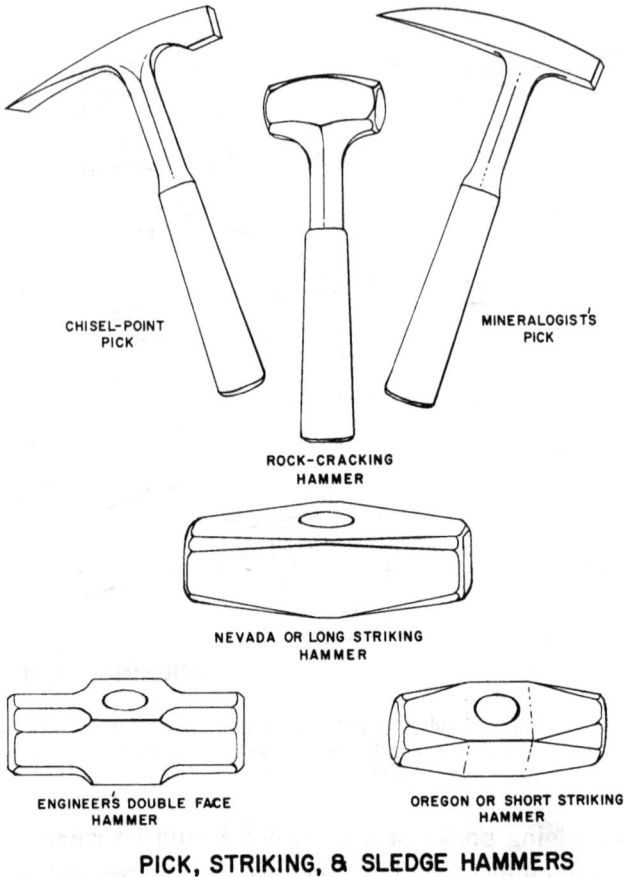

CHISEL-POINT
PICK

MINERALOGIST'S
PICK

ROCK-CRACKING
HAMMER

NEVADA OR LONG STRIKING
HAMMER

ENGINEER'S DOUBLE FACE
HAMMER

OREGON OR SHORT STRIKING
HAMMER

PICK, STRIKING, & SLEDGE HAMMERS

FIGURE 10. The best all-around hammer is the mineralogist's pick, shown in the upper right-hand corner, although the small rock-cracking hammer is also extremely useful in situations where considerable rock must be broken to free specimens or a hammer of medium weight is required to drive chisels and gads. The Nevada sledge hammer is better for cracking rocks than either of the other sledges illustrated but the broader faces of the engineer and Oregon hammers make them less likely to miss in striking drills or gads.

mentioned that wooden-handled hammers have better balance, transmit less shock and vibration to the hand, and are less fatiguing to use. Makers of all-steel hammers now market hammers with shock-absorbing handles and in lighter weights to meet the objections noted above. All-steel hammers may be used successfully as gads because any slip of the striking hammer will not shatter the handles as would be the case if wooden handles were fitted. A number of hammers and heavy striking hammers are illustrated in Figure 10.

Another light hammer popular with collectors of rock and fossil specimens, and also useful for trimming specimens in general, is the mason's hammer. The business end is chisel-shaped while the other end may be an ordinary square hammer-head or another chisel point. It is heavier for a given length of head than ordinary rock hammers but for trimming sedimentary rocks it is exceptionally efficient.

Whenever considerable rock must be removed or shattered, heavy hammers, known as striking hammers, prove extremely useful. The head shape of a striking hammer is like that of a small sledge; its two ends are of squarish shape, have slightly curved faces, and are of the same size, so that both ends can be used interchangeably. Weights range from two to four pounds, but perhaps the most useful size weighs three pounds. All are fitted with short wooden or steel handles of about a foot or less in length. Striking hammers are most useful for shattering rock around cavities and pockets, especially if brittle quartz is present, and are also used for striking chisels, gads, and hand drills. For collecting in tough rocks where heavy trimming or cracking is required to free specimens from matrix, the striking hammer is almost a necessity.

One or more sledges should also be in the possession of the collector who finds it necessary to break up rock. A light sledge of six or eight pounds is probably most useful, particularly for persons of slight to medium physique, but heavier models up to fourteen pounds may be used by stronger individuals and are of course more effective. Most sledge heads are squarish in shape, with ends brought to octagonal cross-sections next to striking faces. Some models are octagonal at one end and chisel-pointed at the other, chisel points often being preferred for splitting rocks along desired directions. To be fully effective, sledges must be fitted with long hickory handles, which must be gripped close to the ends to permit circular swinging blows.

GADS AND CHISELS

A gad differs from a chisel only in coming to a point instead of terminating in a thin wedge, but its uses vary considerably because of this. It cannot cut or split along a desired direction as a chisel is capable of doing, but merely pries apart rock when the point is started and driven home by repeated blows of a hammer. Gads can be forged to long thin tapers or short stubby tapers, depending upon the use to which they will be put, but as a general rule, most gads used in mining or quarrying are relatively slender, since the idea is to use them as wedges in places where ordinary chisels will not fit. On the other hand, if the points are too slender, the tips will break off when a glancing blow is struck or when the gad is knocked along the shank to loosen it. Compared to gads, chisels are far less useful to the collector, since they fail to penetrate rock as easily and lose point sharpness quickly. If a choice must be made between gads and chisels, it is best to select gads. The collector or prospector can make up his own gads from carbon steel bar stock of various diameters, or can ask a local blacksmith to make up a set. For most purposes, gads ranging from 6″ in length, of ½″ diameter stock, up to 10″ or 12″ in length, of 1″ to 1¼″ stock, are most useful.

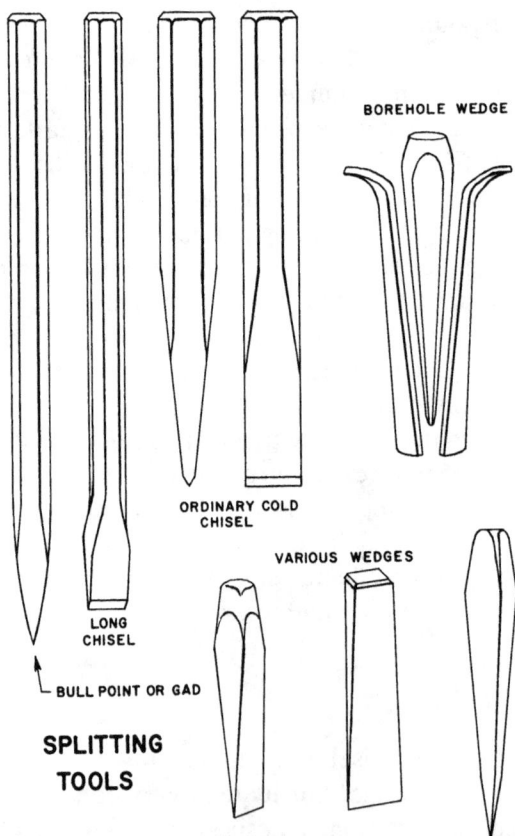

BOREHOLE WEDGE

ORDINARY COLD
CHISEL

VARIOUS WEDGES

LONG
CHISEL

BULL POINT OR GAD

SPLITTING
TOOLS

FIGURE 11. A variety of useful tools for splitting rock. The borehole wedge is meant to be used in drilled holes to split rock. The side pieces or "feathers" are inserted in the holes, followed by the tapered pin or "plug." Repeated blows on the pin cause exertion of enormous pressure on the rock. Although this is a professional piece of equipment, similar sets can be made up from wedges and plates of sheet steel. See also Figure 12.

Several small gads of identical size should be made up, because it is handy to insert them in cracks, several at a time, and then strike them alternately to pry apart rock. A typical gad or bull point, as it is sometimes known, is illustrated in Figure 11, along with other splitting tools.

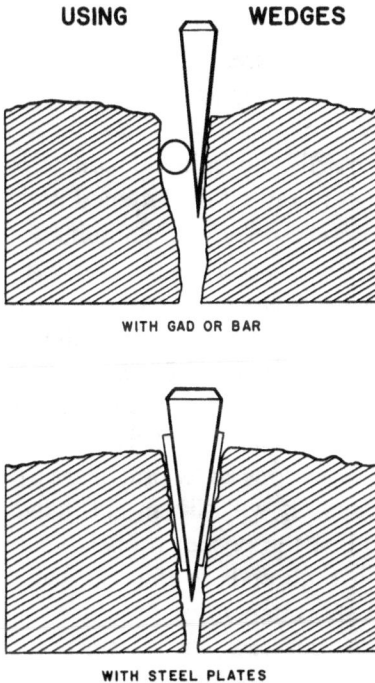

USING　　　WEDGES

WITH GAD OR BAR

WITH STEEL PLATES

FIGURE 12. Single wedges or a series of wedges used by the methods shown above can be very effective in splitting relatively large masses of rock. The better of the two methods is illustrated in the lower drawing. Wedges should be driven home by a three or four pound rock cracking hammer or a light sledge. Note that the impact surfaces of the wedges, as well as similar surfaces on other tools meant to be hammered, are beveled to prevent "mushrooming." Frequent regrinding may be necessary to keep the tops of such tools in proper shape.

WEDGES

Steel wedges of long taper are often very effective for splitting rock along cracks but cannot be used unless the sides of cracks are relatively straight. Very thin cracks can be opened by using one or more gads and, when the cracks are enlarged enough, inserting wedges to complete parting. When used alone, wedges tend to score heavily along the sides and mushroom on the tops because of repeated heavy hammer blows. To avoid these difficulties, it is good practice to insert two flat pieces of steel plate in the crack first, and start the wedge between them. Smooth bearing surfaces are thus provided and the wedge is hammered down most easily. Another trick is to place a short gad along one side of the crack in the rock to act as a roller for the descending wedge, as shown in Figure 12.

CHIPPING AND PRYING BARS

Where considerable rock must be removed around cavities and pockets too narrow or too deep to reach into, scarcely any tool is as useful as a properly designed prybar. The unique value of a prybar is its ability to exert leverage, greater of course as the bar increases in length. Bars are also extremely useful for chipping slabs of rock away from walls of cavities in order to obtain more elbow room or to provide direct access to contents deep within a pocket. For such purposes, prybars are used with jabbing motions to sink the points, followed by leverage to pry off slabs of rock.

Although many kinds of bars are pressed into mineral collecting service, from simple straight steel shafts with pointed or flattened ends, to bars for prying up nails, very few can compare to the combination chipping-prying bar developed to perfection by the collectors and miners of San Diego County in California, who use them extensively in working the gem pegmatites of that region. This bar, locally called a "pocket robber," is made from carbon steel bar stock, of hexagonal or octagonal cross-section of from 5/8" to 7/8" in diameter. Thin stock is used for bars of about 18" in length, while thicker stock is used for those up to 45" in length, which are about as long as is practicable to use. Round stock must not be used because it will slip in the hands while being twisted and turned. The secret of the pocket robber lies in its unusual shaping of points, the same on both ends so that the bar is doubly useful. The points are forged to short tapers of square cross-section and then bent off approximately 30 degrees. The length of the bent sections ranges from about 1 1/4" to 1 3/4"; anything shorter is not capable of penetrating when the bar is used for chipping, while anything longer results in tips breaking off when the bar is used as a lever. The tip offset angle is very important: if too shallow, the bar is not effective as a lever, but if too steep, it fails to "sink" when used with a jabbing motion because of rebound. A series of bar points is illustrated in Figure 13 while Figure 114 shows a prybar in use.

Enormous leverage can be exerted with pocket robbers because of the offset points, which automatically provide fulcrums only short distances past the tips. Thus in a bar 24" in length with an offset one inch in length, leverage is 24 : 1, or put another way, only 10 pounds of force applied to one end will result in a prying force of 240 pounds at the other. A 45" bar with 1 3/4" offset gives an advantage of about 26: 1, but since it is thicker and stiffer, a much greater force can be applied

SQUARE
CROSS-SECTIONS

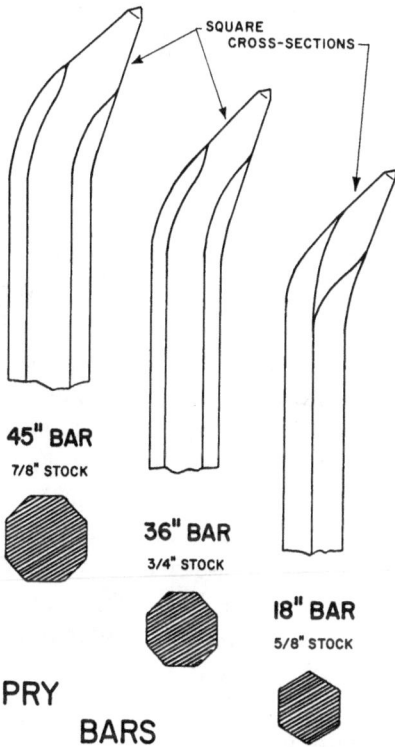

FIGURE 13. Extremely useful prybars. The patterns shown here must be followed closely to insure best results in their use. Although the prybars are not shown full length, the opposite ends of the bars are exactly the same except that the points turn in opposite directions.

45" BAR
7/8" STOCK

36" BAR
3/4" STOCK

18" BAR
5/8" STOCK

PRY

BARS

without bending the bar. It is possible, for example, to apply 100 pounds on the outer end merely by leaning on the bar, and realize well over one ton of force at the point. With such leverage it is not difficult to "walk" slabs of rock several feet wide and over a foot thick out of the way.

The use of the pocket robber calls for some discretion and common sense. Like other pointed tools, it is best to avoid striking quartz, which, by virtue of its hardness, rapidly chips or dulls points. Obviously solid rock should not be struck hard but may be probed to detect cracks. The bar works best in small cracks in rock tough enough to withstand the enormous leverage developed without chipping away. If a section of rock is to be detached, it is examined for cracks and a place is selected which looks large enough for the bar point. The bar is then jabbed firmly into the crevice and gradual leverage applied until the rock yields. If it does not, more leverage is applied until yielding is obtained or the rock chips off. It is important not to use the very tip of the bar because this is liable to break off; it is better to insert the point until the rounded portion, or fulcrum, is seated. If the rock begins to move but falls back as soon as pressure is relaxed, a gad or hammer point is inserted in the crack to hold it open until another "bite" can be taken. The procedure is repeated as necessary until the rock is dislodged.

The use of the pocket robber for chipping follows the same pattern except that each short jab directed at material adhering to walls of pockets or cavities is immediately followed by a twist of the bar to lever off fragments. If a cavity is extremely narrow, the bar point is turned toward the wall and jabbed into the crevice between slab and wall rock; when seated, the bar is held firmly in place and then rotated so that the fulcrum is next to the wall. Pressing down the end of the bar results in prying loose wall material. This process is shown in Figure 114. It is impossible to describe every trick of using this bar and it is enough to say that each collector should make up at least one model, preferably about 24″ in length to start, and try it out for himself. One word of caution: do not be tempted to make one end of the bar a chisel end; this may appear logical but experience has shown chisel ends to be useful perhaps one time out of a hundred while pointed ends are useful every time.

Ordinary construction work prybars with chisel-ends are used by some for moving rock, especially where great leverage must be applied. However, excessively long bars are awkward to handle and are apt to bend if made from stock too small in diameter. If made stiff enough, they weigh a great deal and are a nuisance to carry. Lumber and flooring prybars sold in hardware stores can be converted into useful tools for rock work by taking them to a blacksmith for forging into pocket robbers. A handy shovel-bar combination used by Swiss collectors may appeal to some readers because it dispenses with carrying an ordinary shovel. This tool consists of a long octagonal steel bar forged to a square point on one end. A shovel blade made from stout sheet steel fits over the point and is held in place by two steel straps riveted to the shovel; one of the straps fits over the taper of the point and permits jamming the blade securely in place. The square cross-section prevents the shovel from rotating.

HYDRAULIC AND SCREW JACKS

Large blocks of stone which interfere with further work can often be eased out of the way or toppled from their positions by using automobile jacks. Perhaps the best are hydraulic models which are simple and smooth in their operation, and tremendously powerful. With blocks of wood to place against walls of large cracks or openings, they may be positioned quickly and safely to exert pressure without slipping. It is dangerous to use them directly against rock because of the possibility they may slip, or to use them to lift rocks rather than to push rocks aside. Attempts to raise rock slabs usually result in sudden, unpredictable lateral movements, which tip them over, trapping tools underneath, or possibly injuring the person operating the jack.

POCKET CLEAN-OUT TOOLS

A wide variety of small tools can be profitably employed in the delicate work of detaching crystallized specimens from the walls of cavities, several of which are illustrated in Figure 14. Among the most useful

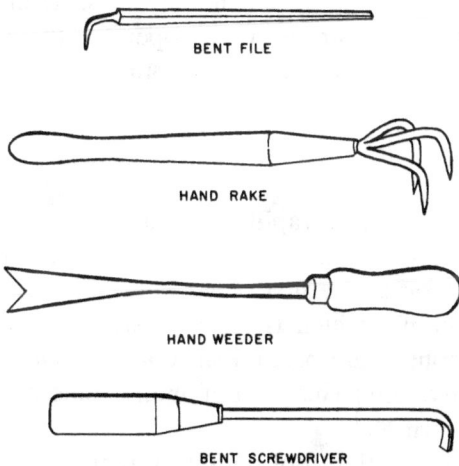

BENT FILE

HAND RAKE

HAND WEEDER

BENT SCREWDRIVER

FIGURE 14. Several small tools useful for cleaning out cavities and pockets. The hand rake is popular with many collectors for digging in dumps, while the hand weeder often serves as both a chipping and prying tool in close quarters when working out specimens from pockets. By inserting the point in a crack and twisting the handle, it is possible to dislodge specimens very gently.

MISCELLANEOUS TOOLS

are small pocket robbers, used to pry off slabs of rock which interfere with further work. Loose floor deposits within openings are best probed with very small tools such as three-cornered files with tangs bent over 90 degrees, or screwdrivers with bent blades. Hand weeders and other small garden tools are sometimes useful. Small chisels and gads are especially serviceable for prying off matrix specimens. Because of the delicacy of crystals and the need to protect them from damage, collecing bags with some newspaper or cloths should be at hand to receive specimens. Several gunny sacks are extremely useful for lying or sitting upon, or for stuffing into cavities to cushion crystals from shock or to prevent them from dropping to the floor when loosened.

GOGGLES

Plastic or safety glass goggles are inexpensive insurance against serious eye injuries due to flying chips of stone and slivers of steel knocked from tools. Although steel slivers can be detected easily because of their dark color, chips of transparent quartz or feldspar are almost impossible to see when bathed in the fluids of the body. Furthermore, steel can be extracted quickly by using a magnet, but mineral chips usually must be located by careful examination of the eyeball and socket with magnifying glasses and then extracted by tweezers or dislodged with needle points. Many miners, quarrymen, and collectors develop a quick reflex action, taught by painful experience, in which they close their eyes at the instant the point of a tool strikes rock, opening them immediately afterwards. However, the better, and safer practice is to protect eyes by wearing goggles.

TOOL TEMPERING

Excessively soft points on rock tools wear so rapidly that it becomes a nuisance to keep them sharp. On the other hand, excessively hard points are so brittle that they break off at the first blow. Between these two extremes lies a hardness or temper which is most satisfactory for general use. Tools used only occasionally are best taken to a blacksmith or iron worker for reshaping and retempering, but if many tools are used frequently it pays to do your own.

The process of forging consists of heating tool points to light cherry red and beating them with a heavy hammer upon an anvil, reheating as necessary to maintain malleability. About four to six inches of the point must be heated to be sure pounding does not develop cracks in metal too cold to be worked properly. It is best to remove wooden handles to prevent charring and later loosening.

Retempering may be combined with reforging or may be done separately if desired. In any case, a point needing retempering is heated to light cherry red as before, and then chilled rapidly by dipping into ordinary water for about five seconds. Approximately three-quarters inch of the point is immersed. A file, kept handy during the process, is immediately applied to the very tip, and a spot about three-quarters inch long is filed clean and bright. The heat remaining in the shank of the tool now creeps toward the point, announcing changes in temperature by colored bands which pass across the bright spot from shank to tip. The first color to appear is very pale yellow followed by straw yellow, brown, purple, and finally blue. When the pale straw yellow reaches to within the last half inch of the point, the entire tool is plunged into water to arrest the temper. If possible, tempering should be done in daylight where colors are easily observed in their true values. The color changes referred to are shown in Figure 15.

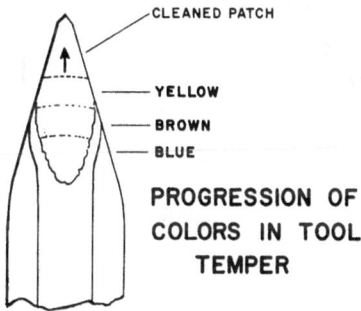

CLEANED PATCH

YELLOW
BROWN
BLUE

PROGRESSION OF COLORS IN TOOL TEMPER

FIGURE 15. Color changes used to temper carbon steel tool points. When the yellow color reaches about one half inch from the tip, the entire head of the tool is plunged into water to arrest the temper.

Emergency hammering and tempering can be done in the field by heating tools in a bed of glowing wood embers. Hammering can be done on any convenient mass of steel such as the head of a sledge hammer resting upon a large flat rock, or even upon a rock itself, providing it is smooth and hard. Points to be tempered can be rubbed against a piece of flat sandstone or other suitable rock to develop the bright spot necessary for observing color changes prior to quenching.

SCREENS AND SCREENING

Where desirable minerals occur as small fragments or crystals mixed with much soil, clay, sand, gravel, or other rubbish, screens are used to separate them quickly from unwanted material. Screens may be used with perfectly dry material which crumbles readily but moist or damp material is almost impossible to handle because it balls up or is so permeated by dirt that the identity of minerals cannot be told unless each piece is wiped between the fingers. If water is available, a much better job can be done because dirt and clay will be washed away and remaining material will be left clean and sparkling.

The size of the openings in screen wire is determined by the size of the fragments it is desired to save. For example, a collector faced with the problem of recovering sapphire crystals from gravel determines that the largest crystalls are not more than a half inch in diameter but the smallest are no more than one-eighth inch in diameter. He therefore decides to use screen wire with half-inch openings for his first screen, and wire with one-eighth inch openings for the second screen. By passing his material through the larger mesh screen first, all large rubbish will be discarded; the screened material is now passed through the second screen, and material smaller than one-eighth inch is also discarded. The remaining material is then put to one side and looked over carefully for sapphire crystals of the size range from ⅛″ to ½″. In case other desirable minerals, or even extraordinary sapphire crystals larger than one-half inch should be present, the material left in the first screen is examined carefully before it is thrown away. The value of water in making everything bright and clean is apparent.

In the screening arrangement just described, the usual method of making the screens is as follows: the upper screen is rectangular in shape and fitted by the corners to four upright posts; it can be lifted off if desired. The second screen rests on rails attached to the uprights underneath and is also removable. Mine run material is thrown upon the top screen, thoroughly flushed with water, and stirred by hand to be sure that all fines pass through. At the same time, it is examined for minerals of value which may be too large to fit through screen openings. When nothing of value remains, it is lifted off and the contents dumped. The lower screen is also lifted off and the material dumped upon a stock pile to await later examination. The process is repeated until mine run material is used up. Fines accumulating beneath the lower screen must be removed regularly to prevent clogging.

The simplest screens are hand screens meant to be used by a single operator. Experience has shown that rectangular screens of no more than 18″ x 24″ in size are large enough to take a good charge, yet are small enough so that they can be shaken easily from side to side to assist the screening action. Larger screens are extremely awkward to handle unless another person assists in the operation. Where dry material is being processed, it is sometimes possible to make up long narrow rectangular screens upon which material is thrown; sliding down by gravity along a tilted side, this material automatically screens itself. Circular screens are sometimes used, and no doubt are very good, but unless thin flexible wood or metal is available to make them from, they do not offer enough additional advantages to take the considerable trouble involved in their manufacture. Where a great deal of material must be processed, particularly without the benefit of water, cylindrical revolving drum screens are sometimes used. In operation, a charge of material is introduced in the upper end of the inclined drum, which is then revolved by hand with a crank arrangement. The material rolls over and over as it slowly works its way toward the lower end, knocking off dirt and clay in the process, until it finally pours out in relatively clean condition. However, in order to be effective, cylindrical screens must be rather long, strongly constructed, and yet easy to load and turn. Because of these reasons, most persons prefer not to go through the trouble involved in making them.

Small rectangular or square hand screens such as shown in Figure 16 are made of one inch hardwood stock cut no deeper than four inches. Pieces for the sides are cut off square and fastened by angle straps and screws; use of ordinary nails or screws without corner reinforcement is

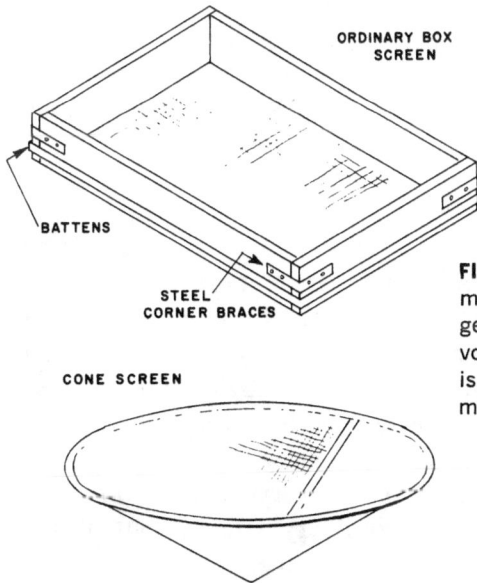

ORDINARY BOX SCREEN

BATTENS

STEEL CORNER BRACES

CONE SCREEN

FIGURE 16. Screens are indispensable for many recovery operations, especially if small gemstone fragments or crystals are involved. The cone screen is seldom used but is extremely useful for separating heavy minerals from lighter worthless material.

SCREENS

unsatisfactory and will result in the screen falling apart after a short period of use. All edges of wood boards are planed off to prevent splintering. One-half inch screen, or screen of other mesh size, is laid across the bottom of the wooden frame and fastened with thin hardwood or metal strip battens. Screen should overlap the sides by one inch when folded over. The raw ends of the screen are fastened down with additional battens so that no sharp wires project anywhere. The kind of screen wire used is very important. Chicken wire or mosquito gauze are absolutely useless. The best screen material is galvanized iron wire with square openings.

In use, a box screen is filled with a shovelful of material and shaken from side to side immediately if the material is absolutely dry. If the material is moist, the screen should be immersed and shaken in water, or the material left to dry until it does not stick or ball up. Shaking is done from side to side at first, and then forward and backward, repeating the process as necessary. Large and obviously useless stones should be thrown out as soon as recognized although some persons permit a few to stay in the screen to rub against smaller material and hasten breaking up of balls of dirt or lumps of clay. If much clay or dirt is present, it may be necessary to rub the charge by hand to be sure that valuable crystals are not caught up in balled clay or soil and hidden from view. Hand rubbing is particularly necessary when screening pegmatite pocket contents because pocket clays frequently enclose some of the finest crystals to be found. Pegmatite dump material must be similarly treated for the same reason.

CONE SCREENS

Ordinary screens are intended only to separate loose material into particles of uniform size but cone screens can be used to separate minerals according to their specific gravity by taking advantage of the fact that minerals of greater density sink faster through water. Precious metals and many gemstones are much heavier than common minerals of the same size which accompany them in gravel deposits, and therefore it is possible not only to screen out very small or very large waste material, such as is done with ordinary screens, but also to concentrate the heavy minerals in the cone screen apex, where they can be easily separated from useless minerals of similar size. A cone screen, as the name implies, is shaped like a flattened cone, about one third as deep as it is wide (see Figure 16). Thus, in a cone screen of 15″ diameter, the depth at the center will be about 5″. Cone screens made from wire or from woven reeds, split wood or bamboo, are used in many areas of the world, particularly for recovering gemstones such as diamonds, rubies, sapphires, and others of similar density.

The operation of a cone screen is very simple. When the screen is filled about half full with unsorted material, it is taken to a stream or to a tub of water, and moved up and down and occasionally from side to side to cause settling of heavier minerals. Each downward stroke momentarily suspends the gravel in the water, permitting heavy minerals to fall at a slightly faster rate than the lighter ones, in time resulting in them working their way downward toward the apex of the cone. Slight sideward motions are necessary to allow heavy minerals to pass by and displace lighter minerals. After this process has been carried on for a few minutes, or until the operator judges that heavy material has had time to settle, the cone is taken to a flat area and quickly flipped over to dump its contents. Heavy minerals settled into the apex of the cone now appear on top of the pile where they are easily picked out. In Brazil, where diamond miners use cone screens or "bateas," expert observers claim that very few diamonds are missed by the method just outlined. A cone screen works best when the particles in the charge are of about the same diameter.

Where large numbers of small stones must be saved in each cone screen charge, it helps to do preliminary screening to remove part of the waste, and save the concentrated charge to screen again for further concentration. This is how the process works. A cone screen is charged and then shaken up and down in water until most of the heavy minerals have settled. Instead of dumping at this time, waste material on top is carefully scooped off with a spoon or flat stick until "pay dirt" appears underneath. The screen is returned to the water and pumped up and down again until more waste appears on top; this is again scooped off, being careful not to include valuable minerals. By this time the charge has become very concentrated and of course much smaller in size. This material is now dumped and saved. The process is repeated with more unsorted material until a sizeable quantity of concentrates has been accumulated. Now by charging the screen with concentrates only, and then removing any remaining waste material that appears on top, a final concentrate is left which is virtually pure. The author tested this method upon a large lot of cleavelandite feldspar in which was mixed numerous fragments of spessartine garnet, the garnet being considerably higher in specific gravity than the feldspar. In about one hour of work, about 15 pounds of garnet were separated from over 100 pounds of unsorted material. It is estimated that less than 1% of the garnet was lost and that a fraction of 1% of the final concentrate consisted of feldspar grains. This work was done with a cone-shaped kitchen sieve, about 8" in diameter.

GOLD PANS

In principle, gold pans work in the same way as cone screens but are far less efficient because no openings can be tolerated in the bottom of the pan. For this reason, it is impossible to generate the up and down "pumping" action proved to be so effective in cone screens, and the concentration process therefore takes longer and much more handwork is needed later to separate gold from the final concentrates. Gold pans are made from sheet iron, stamped into shapes which closely resemble ordinary pie tins except sides are carried up farther. Pans may be purchased in several sizes from those about 12" in diameter to some about 20" across. A popular size is 16" in diameter and measures 2½" in depth. For easy backpacking, smaller sizes are better although for production panning, larger pans are more efficient.

In use, the gold pan is filled with unsorted gravel, then with water, and the mixture stirred by hand to wash away clay or dirt which obscures a clear view of contents. Large pebbles of no value are taken out and thrown away immediately; also smaller material as soon as it is evident that it is valueless. About half the water is now poured off and the pan shaken from side to side to cause settling of heavy materials. The pan is finally given a wobbling motion which causes the water to run around in a circular path, climbing higher upon the rim as its speed increases until it begins to spill over the edge. As it does so, light minerals are taken with it, resulting in concentration of the remainder of the charge. More water is dipped as necessary to continue concentration until practically all light minerals have been removed. A miner using a gold pan is shown in Figure 17. Gold, platinum, diamonds, magnetite, chromite, and other heavy minerals which may be present in the gravel, now remain resting upon the flat inner portion of the pan. All that is left, usually, is very fine sandy material which can be further concentrated by adding very little water and causing the sand to sweep from one side to the other. Gold will show up in a small "tail" on the high side of the pan bottom. Most miners pick out nuggets of gold as soon as they are spotted, saving them in a jar or can kept handy for that purpose. Very fine material is scraped off the bottom and placed in a separate container for later removal of impurities, or, if gold occurs in flakes, removal of the latter with tweezers. A magnet is useful for removing magnetite, a mineral very commonly associated with gold in panning concentrates.

FIGURE 17. A "sourdough" demonstrating the final stages of gold-panning on Boulder Creek, Alaska. Only a handful of small gravel and sand now remains in the pan, plus whatever flakes and nuggets of gold have been concentrated. *Courtesy U. S. Geological Survey.*

LIGHTS

Many kinds of lights have been used by miners and collectors but only a few are really efficient. It is extremely important that bright steady light be available when working out a pocket or cavity. Gloom is the enemy of deftness and accuracy, and it is safe to say that more fine specimens have been ruined by collectors because they could not see clearly what they were doing than for any other reason. In underground workings, lights are certainly essential but many collectors fail to realize lights should also be used on the surface any time that a pocket or cavity is not flooded directly with natural light. It is very little additional trouble to have a light of some kind handy, even a flashlight is of some use, although quite feeble in power as compared to other kinds.

The best general purpose light is the carbide lamp which burns acetylene gas generated within itself from the chemical reaction of water upon calcium carbide. Two sizes are commonly used, a small lamp for miner's helmets and a larger model meant to be hand-held or hooked to tunnel walls or timbers by a pointed bail. Both models are illustrated in Figure 18. The smaller model measures about four inches tall and two inches in diameter and can be obtained with polished reflectors of either 2½″, 4″ or 7″ diameter. The smallest reflector is meant to be used for lamps fitted to miner's helmets or caps, although the intermediate and large sizes can also be used but are more likely to be knocked off. Larger reflectors provide more spotlight effect and are therefore better suited to mineral collecting purposes where good light is generally wanted only upon some small area; the preferred size is 4″. The larger model measures 6½″ tall and 3″ in diameter across the base and may be obtained with reflectors of the sizes noted above. In all models the principles of operation are the same, and understanding them will help in keeping lamps efficient and in good working order, a

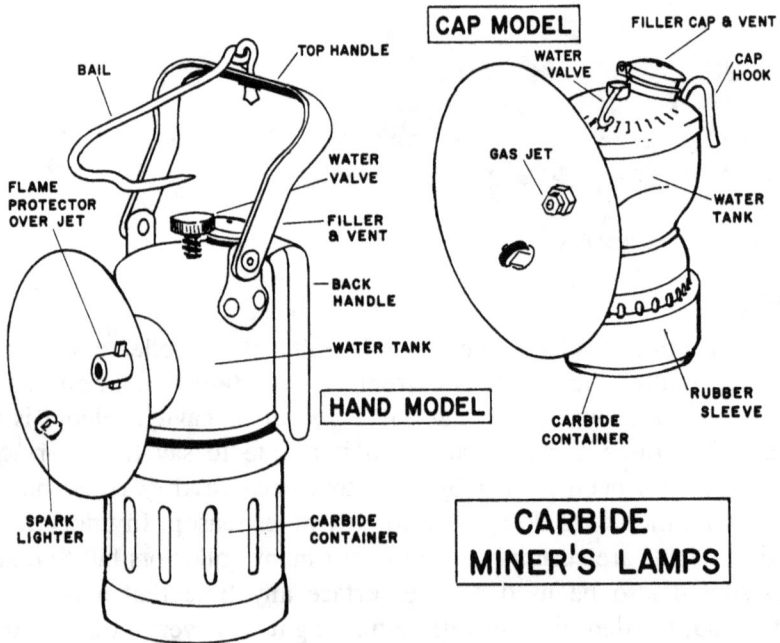

FIGURE 18. Carbide lamps are generally conceded to be the best sources of light in mines where explosive gases present no dangers. Although the small cap model is light in weight it lasts much less than the larger model and for this reason experienced collectors prefer the larger hand model.

vital point when it is considered that all work underground depends upon introduced lighting.

Carbide lamps are divided into two chambers, one above the other (see Figure 18). The upper chamber contains water and is fitted with a tight cap in which a small hole is bored in order to release gases which may force their way into the chamber from below. This hole must be kept clear. The lower chamber contains the carbide and is screwed into the base of the upper chamber when charged with carbide lumps and ready to operate. A rubber gasket provides the necessary seal between halves. Gas leakage is very common along the seal and may be enough to flow upward into the flame and ignite, much to the consternation of the user. To prevent leaks, it is a good idea to rub a little paraffin or other kind of wax upon the threads of the lower chamber, however, oil or grease must not be used since these rapidly rot the rubber. Lubricating the threads permits easier joining of top and bottom sections with much less likelihood of leaks.

When the lamp is used, the bottom chamber is filled about half-full with ½" carbide lumps. Carbide is available in cans at camping goods stores. The top is then screwed down firmly and filled with water. A small lever or key which protrudes above the water chamber is turned to open the valve, releasing water into the lower chamber, which, as soon as it drips into the carbide, reacts to form acetylene. The gas passes through a filter into a tube leading to the flame jet in the center of the reflector. After a few seconds to permit air in the system to clear out, a match or spark is placed in front of the jet to light the gas which issues forth in a narrow stream. Most reflectors are fitted with a sparking device, similar to those used in cigarette lighters, and this may be used to light the flame but some practice is necessary to do so. The technique is to hold the palm of the hand over the shallow depression formed by the reflector, with the side of the palm resting firmly upon the sparking wheel; after waiting a few moments for an explosive mixture of gas to fill the depression, the hand is stroked briskly to the side, actuating the sparking wheel and lighting the gas and the flame. Most persons, however, content themselves with lighting the jet with a match or a cigarette lighter.

The duration of a single charge of carbide depends upon the size of the charge and the size of the flame; the flame size, in turn, is determined by how fast water is permitted to drip into the lower chamber. Small lamps last from one to two hours while the larger and more effective lamps may last from four to eight hours. The jet size in all lamps is the same although each can be regulated to some extent by feeding less water to the carbide. It is a nuisance to clean the white muddy debris left in the lower chamber after carbide is consumed, especially in the dark, and for this reason when a lengthy period of work in darkness is contemplated, a larger lamp should be used. As a back-up to a large lamp, a small lamp can be taken along in the knapsack, or perhaps, a plastic-body, plastic-lens flashlight which can survive drops without being damaged. Another satisfactory and simple emergency light is an ordinary candle kept in a small plastic bag or plastic box. It is most important that alternate lighting be available when working in a mine; one cannot depend on only a single source of illumination regardless of how foolproof it seems to be, and one cannot be sure of finding one's way out of the mine without benefit of a light.

Accessories for carbide lamps are water, preferably in small canteens which can be poured handily; thin wires or special reamers for cleaning out jets which often become clogged by carbide powder, especially if the lamp is accidentally dropped; and finally, an airtight can or plastic container to hold a supply of fresh carbide, plus reamers, matches, etc. After each use, lamps should be emptied of water, washed out and dried, and reflectors burnished with soft cloth, first rinsing gently to remove rock dust and clay. Reflectors often become coated with soot from flames and then require cleaning with metal polish.

Electric flashlights or camplights are generally poor sources of light both in respect to intensity and duration. When it is considered how much new batteries cost, it will be quickly realized that hours of illumination with carbide cost but a fraction of the sum involved in replacing batteries. Gasoline camping lamps are often used for underground work because they provide brilliant powerful light which far outshines any produced by carbide or electric lamps of the same size. However, gasoline lamps depend for their dazzling light on the incandescence of a Wellsbach mantle, a very fragile bullet-shaped envelope of cerium oxides. Needless to say, jarring or dropping the lamp will result in an abrupt disintegration of the mantle and an eclipse of the light. Replacing a mantle in darkness or even in daylight is not exactly a simple task. Furthermore, the mantle chamber is enclosed by a glass bowl and this too is liable to be broken. For these reasons, the employment of a gasoline lamp during collecting work should be carefully considered despite the strong attraction of the brilliant light offered. The powerful light of a gasoline lamp is not generated without some penalty in respect to oxygen consumption, and if a carbide lamp is found to be feeble due to contamination of the air within a mine working, one may be sure that a gasoline lamp will not improve matters much. In camp, however, a gasoline lamp provides unsurpassed illumination.

Oil lamps and candles are old time favorites of miners but because of their feeble yellow flames, they are now seldom used. In this connection, it should be mentioned that carbide flames are also decidedly yellow in hue and some care must therefore be employed when trying to discriminate colors of minerals. The author remembers well an incident when a fine etched morganite beryl crystal of some value was almost thrown out upon a heap of rubbish from a gem pocket because it looked like an ordinary piece of flawed quartz. Only by cleaning off adhering clay was it possible to distinguish the characteristic crystal form of beryl, but in respect to color, it seemed exactly like quartz under the yellow flame of the lamp.

HAND DRILLS

Where it is absolutely essential that holes be drilled for dynamiting, and no power rig is available, the collector may use a series of hand drills forged from carbon steel stock. However, there are few tasks in the field which are so tedious and time-consuming as drilling rock by hand, and such a job should be avoided if at all possible. The work can be "single jack," in which one person holds the drill with one hand and strikes it with a 4-pound striking hammer held in the other, or it can be "double jack" in which one person holds the drill and the other strikes it with a sledge. The latter method is obviously not very appealing from the standpoint of possible injuries from a poorly directed blow, but the first method is not attractive either. Considerable skill is required in either case, and of course accuracy diminishes as fatigue increases.

For hand drills, the shape of the points is important; the common "star point" of compressed air jackhammer drills is almost completely unsuitable because the unavoidable lightness of hand-delivered blows does not allow much penetration. It has been found that the "fishtail" point, as shown in Figure 19, is best because good chipping takes place

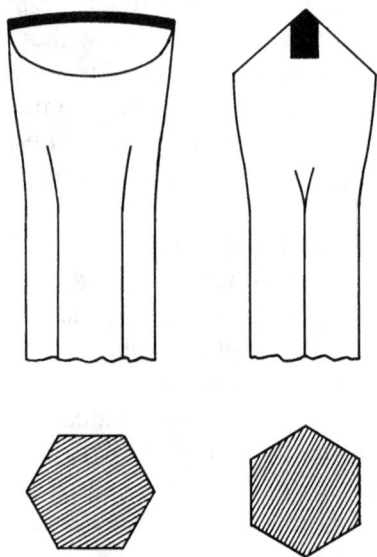

FIGURE 19. The shape of a hand drill for boring rock. Although the example shown is fitted with a carbide insert, the same shape is used in making up drills from carbon steel rod.

CARBIDE-TIPPED DRILL

with each blow. However, careful and consistent rotation of the drill is necessary to prevent formation of a groove at the bottom of the hole instead of a nicely rounded face. Therefore, after each blow, the hand drill must be rotated 45 degrees before it is struck again. Fishtail points are similar in shape to ordinary chisel points but the cutting edge is gently curved instead of being perfectly square. Points must be flared during forging in order to provide the necessary clearance for the shanks. Hand drills are made from ¾″ to ⅞″ diameter carbon steel octagonal bar stock and tempered and hardened, as described earlier in this chapter. Because ordinary steel drills lose their edges so rapidly, many prospectors now use drills provided with carbide cutting edge inserts (see Figure 19). Such drills are available from mining equipment suppliers. Carbide points cannot be forged but must be ground to shape with carborundum wheels, however, this is not a serious disadvantage because they last so much longer than ordinary steels.

Several hand drills are used in series. beginning with a short drill of 18″ in length and flared widely at the point, to drills up to 36″ in length with point diameters of one inch or wider to accommodate dynamite sticks. If a series of three or four drills of different lengths are being used, it is necessary to add 1/16″ to ⅛″ in diameter at the cutting point for each drill of shorter length in order to be sure that succeeding drills will not jam in the hole. A vital accessory piece of equipment is a "spoon" for cleaning out rock chips from the base of the hole. Spoons are usually made of slender steel rods fitted upon the ends with disks of steel, smaller in diameter than the narrowest drill in the set. If a forge is handy, they can be made in one piece by merely flattening the end of the rod and bending it over to a right angle.

SELECTION OF DRILL HOLE SITES

The selection of a place to drill is of greatest importance. Beginners are often tempted to drill along cracks or crushed zones in rock, reasoning that easier penetration should be possible. Easier going may occur for a few inches, but inevitably loose material below will jam the drill so tightly or will cause blows to so lose their effect that further work will have to be abandoned and drilling started all over again in firm rock. Even if a hole of considerable depth could be sunk along crushed or cracked places, the looseness of the formation would cause easy escape of gases generated by explosion of the dynamite and much of its force would be wasted. It is best therefore to select good firm rock, avoiding, however, schistose material full of mica, or zones where this mineral is abundant. In any case, selection of exactly the right place to drill is likely to be worth the extra few minutes of careful inspection. The next consideration in deciding where to drill is the availability of elbow room since swinging a hammer in cramped or restricted quarters is excessively tiring as well as annoying. Another important consideration is to place holes so as to take advantage of the natural splitting of rock, if this is a characteristic. Again, careful examination before settling upon a place to drill may enable one well-placed shot to remove a great deal of rock in a manner best calculated to expose the area of interest.

As a general rule, holes less than 12″ in depth are apt to result in "cratering," or dislodgment of only a cone-shaped mass of rock directly around the hole. If drilling is to be done at all, the hole should be taken down to at least 18″. On the other hand, if it is desired only to crack the rock, as when working close to a pocket, short holes may be used, but they should be charged with only half a stick or less of dynamite.

PORTABLE DRILLING MACHINES

In the last few years, portable drilling machines have been received with much favor by prospectors and miners. Perhaps the lightest in weight and therefore easiest to transport and handle is the Swedish-made Atlas Copco "Cobra" drill shown in Figure 20. Without a drill-steel inserted, its overall length is 24 inches and its weight is only 53 pounds. It accepts drill-steels of ¾ inch shank diameter and 1⅛ inch tip diameter which produce holes just large enough to take 1-inch diameter dynamite sticks without jamming. Other equally useful portable drills are made but most are considerably larger and heavier. The author has used the "Cobra" machine with much success.

FIGURE 20. Atlas-Copco portable gasoline motor drilling machine in operation. This unit is entirely self-contained. It weighs slightly over 50 pounds and is easily transported and operated in the field. Photograph taken at the Hercules Mine, near Ramona, California.

The principle of this and similar portable machines is that rapid blows are supplied to the drill-steel via a floating piston, which is forcibly slammed against a buffer piece during each explosion in the cumbustion chamber of the machine. At the same time, some of the explosive power pushes against another piston which spins the flywheel-magneto. During the cycle, the movement of the piston also compresses air which is forcibly ejected through the tip of the hollow drill-steel. The vital function of this compressed air is to continually blow out rock chips which form at the bottom of the bore hole. If these were not removed as fast as they formed the drilling would quickly come to a halt. Another feature of this machine is that it provides positive turning of the drill-steel thus preventing "wedging" at the bottom of the bore.

When the machine is working efficiently and is used with sharp drill-steels, it can bore through ordinary granite at rates of about 2 feet per 8 to 10 minutes. However, while drill-steels up to 10 to 12 feet in length can be handled, the rate of drilling slows down as the bore hole becomes longer and much slower drilling speeds must be expected for holes over several feet in length.

Because the motive power is a two-cycle gasoline-oil fueled engine, similar in principle to many outboard motorboat engines, sufficient fuel for a normal day's work can be carried in a one-gallon can. The fuel mixture is ordinary non-leaded gasoline to which is added outboard motor oil in the ratio of one part of oil to sixteen parts of gasoline. Because the engine is a two-cycle motor, it is subject to the same starting and operating difficulties experienced in motors of similar design used in other applications. However, once the proper adjustment of the fuel valve is learned, both for starting and running, no unusual difficulties will be encountered.

The air intake is provided with a very efficient, closely woven felt filter which is absolutely necessary to prevent rock dust from entering the engine and causing excessive wear. However, it becomes clogged with dust after several hours of drilling and unless cleaned by rinsing in gasoline, the air is prevented from passing through as readily as it should. This causes difficulties in starting, especially if the engine is cold. When this happens, the following procedure will cure the trouble. Before starting, unscrew the filter cartridge part way to allow unfiltered air easy entry. Place the machine on some surface where there is no chance of sucking in dirt or dust, start the motor, and allow it to warm up. After several minutes, screw down the cartridge and commence drilling. When this does not help, it means that the filter is too badly clogged and it should either be cleaned thoroughly or replaced.

Drill-Steels

The best drill-steels to use are similar to those shown in Figure 19 and similarly employ a single, wedge-shaped bar of tungsten carbide for the cutting tip. The angle made by the tip is of greatest importance to efficient drilling. If it is too shallow, or blunt, the drill operates very slowly. If it is too sharp, the tip is likely to chip badly and require frequent regrinding. The maker of the drill-steel furnishes a template and data on what angle is best for the tip. His recommendations should be followed whenever the tip is sharpened. It is perfectly feasible to sharpen the tips on a silicon carbide grinding wheel but water should be supplied to the grinding face to keep both wheel and tip cool, and the angle should be checked frequently to be sure that it is close to that recommended. Under no circumstances should the *sides* of the tip be ground away because this will decrease the diameter of the bore hole and result in longer drills sticking when they are inserted, or cause dynamite sticks to jam when the holes are being loaded.

For ordinary light drilling and blasting, two drill-steels are desirable, one of at least 1½ feet in length, and another of from 2 to 3 feet in length. Steels shorter than 1½ feet are too shallow to prevent "cratering" at the top of bore holes when the latter are loaded with dynamite and detonated. On the other hand, excessively long steels are very awkward to use because they necessarily raise the machine much above the ground level and cause difficulties in balancing it until a good hole is begun. It is always best to start with a short steel and switch to longer steels as the bore hole deepens.

Drilling in Confined Spaces

While the portable drill will be used mostly upon surface outcrops, it may be required in pits, shafts, and in tunnels. In confined, windless places the dust from drilling and the exhaust fumes are dangerous and must be avoided. A respirator mask to trap dust is strongly recommended at all times when the drill is not being operated in a good breeze which will blow away the dust particles before they can be inhaled. In the case of exhaust fumes, this problem is most easily solved by attaching a flexible steel hose to the exhaust with some stout wire and leading the other end away from the drill. For the "Cobra" machine, a 1¼-inch-diameter flexible hose, as much as 25 feet in length, will permit completely satisfactory operation.

EARTH AUGERS FOR DRILLING

A useful drilling tool in certain situations where clay, soil, or decomposed rock are involved is the earth auger, shown in Figure 21, a hand-cranked spiral drill much like a larger version of the ordinary carpenter's wood borer. Augers can be bought in various diameters and lengths and are used with a kind of brace-and-bit arrangement similar to those used for driving wood bits. The earth auger is primarily

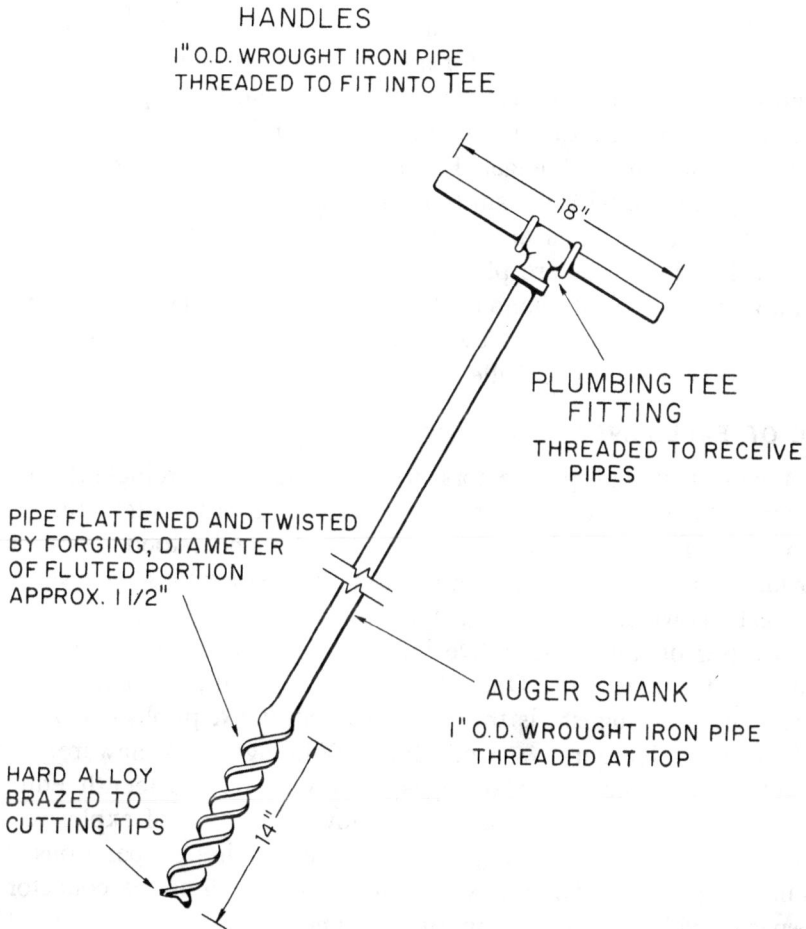

HANDLES
I" O.D. WROUGHT IRON PIPE
THREADED TO FIT INTO TEE

18"

PLUMBING TEE
FITTING
THREADED TO RECEIVE
PIPES

PIPE FLATTENED AND TWISTED
BY FORGING, DIAMETER
OF FLUTED PORTION
APPROX. I 1/2"

AUGER SHANK
I" O.D. WROUGHT IRON PIPE
THREADED AT TOP

HARD ALLOY
BRAZED TO
CUTTING TIPS

14"

EARTH AUGER
OVERALL LENGTH APPROX. 44"

FIGURE 21. The earth auger shown here is used for making boreholes in decomposed rock, clay, or earth. It can be made up on order by any blacksmith. In some
rural districts where farmers are clearing land, a similar type of auger is used for
boreholes beneath tree stumps which are later charged with dynamite to shatter
the stumps and facilitate removal. In such districts it is often possible to buy similar augers at reasonable prices from local hardware stores.

employed for drilling dynamite holes underneath stumps to blow them out of the ground, or for blowing up or loosening hard pan soils; however, it is also very useful for mining. In the Himalaya Mine in San Diego County, California, rock enclosing the gem-bearing pegmatite is often so decomposed that it can be drilled parallel to the edges of the pegmatite with an earth auger. Holes from 24″ to 36″ are run close to the seam, charged with dynamite in the usual fashion, and then set off with powder fuse. Shots are very effective despite the softness of the material in which they are placed, and the pegmatite is readily broken up into smaller, easy-to-handle blocks. Much of the decomposed granite found in Colorado and New Hampshire in which pegmatite bodies occur is soft enough to be drilled by augers.

USE OF EXPLOSIVES

Most collectors and prospectors are understandably reluctant to use dynamite or other explosives for reasons of safety, but when their properties, handling, and uses are clearly understood, explosives provide means of removing rock when nothing else will do. However, if practical knowledge is lacking, it is absolutely essential that the prospective user obtain authoritative information on how to use explosives from the manufacturer. One of the best manuals, written in clear, understandable English, is the *Blasters' Handbook*, published by E. I. DuPont de Nemours & Co., Inc., Wilmington, Delaware. This pocket-sized volume of 516 pages is now in its fourteenth edition. Although much of the text is directed toward the use of explosives on grand scales, such as in large quarrying and mining operations, full details are given on dynamites, caps and fuses, such as the collector or prospector will want to use from time to time.

Before contemplating use of explosives, it is necessary to determine local, state or province, or other laws or regulations governing the use of explosives in the area where work is to be done. Some states and lesser political subdivisions closely regulate transportation, storage, and use of explosives, and it is necessary to comply with such regulations not merely to remain within the law but because each regulation is aimed at eliminating a practice found to be extremely dangerous. The following sections deal with the kind of dynamiting most useful to the collector and prospector with practices and procedures carefully checked against the best information available; however, readers are expressly cautioned to observe the two steps recommended above, namely, obtain a copy of a handbook on blasting practice and learn laws and regulations governing use of explosives in the area where work is to be done before proceeding with the actual use of dynamite.

Explosives for farm and mining work are frequently sold by hardware stores in rural areas. Local inquiries will usually turn up a retailer who can supply explosive, caps, and fuse in small or large quantities. The most common explosive handled, and the one generally used by collectors and prospectors is *dynamite* which is manufactured in cylindrical paper-wrapped "sticks," eight inches long and one and one-eighth or one and one-fourth inch in diameter. However, where hand drilling is resorted to, sticks of only seven-eights inch in diameter should be used to fit the smaller diameter hand-driven bore holes. Dynamite is set off with blasting caps which are fired by burning fuse or by electricity, depending on which is more convenient to use or whether careful timing of several shots is needed. In the latter event, electrical blasting caps must be used. However, since electrical caps cannot be set off reliably with ordinary dry cell batteries, it is necessary to use a hand generator or blasting machine, both of which are expensive and add weight to material which must be back-packed into remote localities. For these reasons, most prospectors and collectors prefer to use caps set off by burning fuse.

Dynamite can be purchased in various "strengths," a term meaning how much total power the explosive develops. In "straight" dynamites, the strength refers to how much of the weight of the explosive mixture is pure nitroglycerine. Cartridges are therefore sold in 20%, 40%, 60% and other percentage strengths; the highest mentioned, or 60% dynamite, is about one and a half times as powerful as 20% for equal quantities of explosive, and also faster in its speed of explosion. Other kinds of dynamite to which are added less powerful or less sensitive explosives such as ammonium nitrate, are also designated by percentage strengths but may vary considerably in properties, although they develop the same total energies. Straight dynamites are so rapid in their action that they produce a shattering effect rather than a lifting effect, and are therefore excellent to use in situations where this is wanted. For example, if a small crevice is to be enlarged, or the rock around the crevice to be cracked so that it can be pried loose with hand tools, and a small charge, say half a stick, is used, then 60% straight dynamite or even more rapid explosives are called for. On the other hand, if a long hole has been drilled with the object of removing as much rock as possible, it may be better to use a larger charge of slower acting dynamite. When much dynamite is to be employed, less expensive types should be purchased; they will generally provide about the same total explosive energy at less cost.

Gelatin dynamites are also available and provide even greater shattering effects than straight dynamites due to their greater speed of detonation. They are soft and easily molded into crevices if need be, and waterproof. Quick detonation also makes them useful for cracking large boulders and rock masses in the process known as "mud capping," which is explained later in this section.

Blasting caps are purchased in boxes of one hundred for burning fuse types and in lots of fifty for electric types, but smaller quantities are often available from retailers. Unlike dynamite, which is practically explosion proof under normal use, blasting caps are far more sensitive and must be handled with due care. Caps cannot be hammered, squeezed, bitten into or otherwise tampered with if unwanted detonations are to be prevented; they will go off if thrown into a fire. It cannot be overemphasized that caps must be handled with great care since it is their very sensitivity which enables them to set off the far less susceptible dynamites. Caps measure about 1½" in length and are about ¼" in diameter. Those meant to be fired with burning fuse are open at one end with recesses about an inch long, into which fuse is inserted and crimped in place. Electric caps are sealed completely and only two waterproof wires emerge from one end. Cap wires are connected to lead wires which run to an electrical firing device located far enough away to protect personnel from blast and flying debris. The standard cap for ordinary stick dynamites is a No. 6 whether fired by fuse or electrically.

Burning or "safety" fuse is black powder enclosed in spirally-wrapped cloth tapes and yarns, waterproofed with asphalt, and resembles thick white cord. It is sold in rolls of 100 feet but retailers frequently sell smaller lengths when requested. Due to great care in manufacture, safety fuse is very reliable but must not be mistreated by bending too sharply or permitting it to be crushed or cut. Fuse burns at the rate of two minutes per yard or 40 seconds per foot. Most miners and prospectors test speed of burning by cutting off a sample of twelve inches and time the speed by wristwatch, thus determining the burning rate to be expected from the remainder. This is not an important point in respect to single charges since the fuse is always cut to a generous length to allow enough time to reach a safe point and enough over in case a stumble or some other mishap prevents gaining the proper distance at the proper time. It is a good idea never to use less than three feet for even the smallest charges while at least four feet of fuse should be used when two or more sticks are being detonated. This rule of thumb is not so much because of the danger of the blast effect as from flying rocks. In any event, before fuse is cut, all factors of retreat should be considered and the following questions asked: "Is the path to safety clear of obstructions which may cause stumbling?"; "Is there a place behind which one can hide to avoid flying rocks?"; in leaving a mine, "How long does it take at a leisurely deliberate pace to reach a point of safety?"; and finally: "Is there a possibility of a cave-in or roof collapse because of shock waves transmitted through the rock by the explosion?" Examination of the retreat problem will do much to decide upon the proper length of fuse. In any case, fuse is cheap, and if doubt exists, another foot will furnish a little extra safety at practically no cost and little wasted time.

Fuse is cut square upon a wooden board using a very sharp knife; one end is slit to one half-inch for easy lighting with a flame and the other end is left perfectly square for insertion into the cap. If fuse has not been used recently, at least an inch from each exposed end should be cut off and discarded in case it has deteriorated with standing. The square end of the cut fuse meant for the cap is now inserted gently without twisting into the open end of the cap until it can go no farther. The fuse is secured in place by a special crimping plier, applied well away from the end of the cap containing the explosive. The process of priming is shown in Figure 22. One must *never* attempt crimping with the teeth or by striking or tapping the cap; one slip or miscalculation can result in explosion and extremely serious injuries. The special preparations described here are not needed for electric caps which need only have their wires unfolded and connected to the lead wires laid over the ground to the blasting machine or battery. However, electric caps are just as sensitive as fuse caps and must be treated with the same respect. Electric caps are reasonably waterproof and may be used in holes where water is present, however, caps used with burning fuse require waterproofing to be applied at the junction between cap and fuse. Some miners use cup grease for this purpose, others use soap or soft paraffin rubbed into the minute opening along the edge of the cap where it joins the fuse. Rubber electrician's tape is also useful for sealing.

Safety fuse is most positively lighted by hot wire "sparklers," but several ordinary matches will do just as well when employed in the following manner (see Figure 22). Break off the head of a large striking

MAKING A CAP-FUSE PRIMER

AN EASY WAY TO LIGHT FUSE

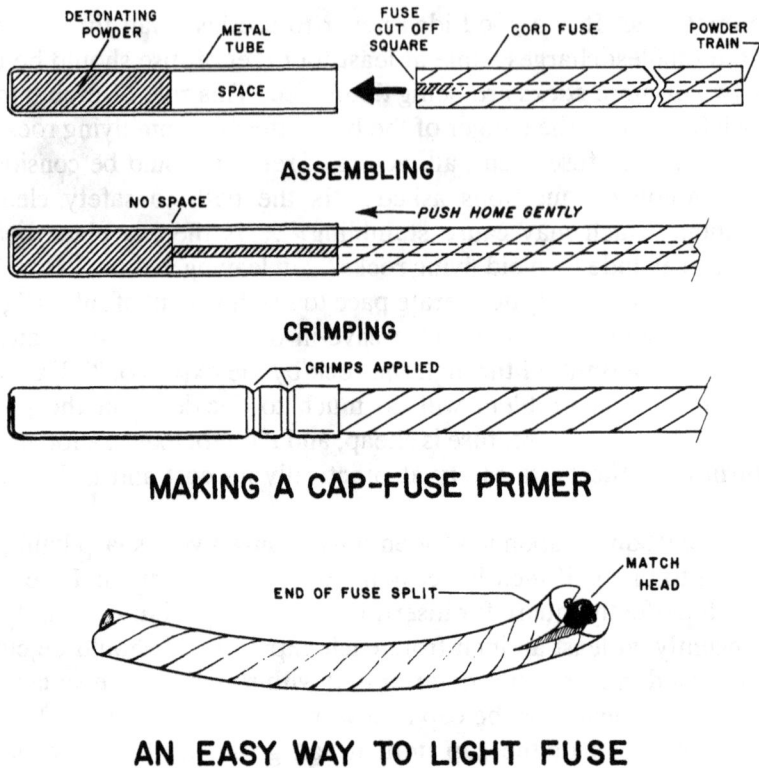

FIGURE 22. Making a primer for powder fuse is a simple operation but must be done carefully. When the fuse is inserted in the cap, use a straightforward motion — do not twist. Be sure to use a sharp knife to cut the fuse since this will make for easier insertion in the cap.

match; place the head into the slit end of the fuse until it rests directly against the powder train. The head will be held in place by the elasticity of the fuse. Now light the head with another match or with any open flame. It will flare up briefly and will be followed immediately by a long thin hissing flame of pale purplish color generated by the burning black powder of the fuse train. Burning black powder gives off white smoke and there will be little doubt as to proper functioning of the fuse when it is lighted.

Caps are inserted into dynamite sticks by first making a hole using a pointed rod or dowel of wood of slightly larger diameter than the caps to be used. The cap-fuse primer is then slipped into the opening provided and thus rests directly against the explosive. Holes should be as nearly

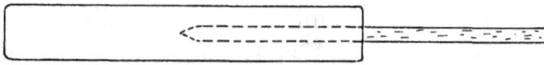

STEP I.-MAKE HOLE WITH WOODEN DOWEL

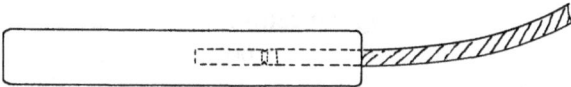

STEP 2.-INSERT CAP AND FUSE

END PRIMING

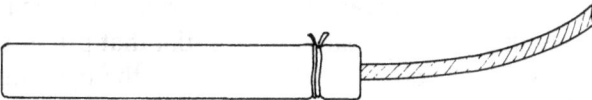

STEP 3.-TIE END OF STICK WITH STRING

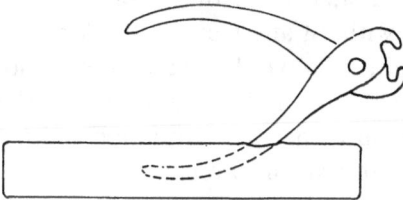

STEP I.-MAKE CURVED HOLE WITH CRIMPER

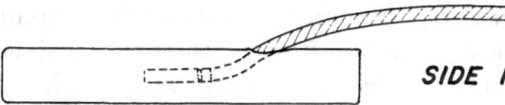

SIDE PRIMING

STEP 2.-INSERT CAP AND FUSE

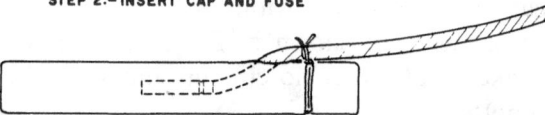

STEP 3.-TIE STICK, THEN TIE FUSE TO STICK

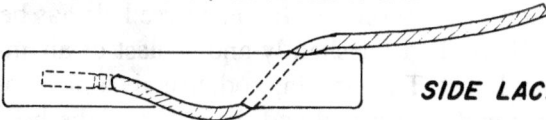

SIDE LACING

TYING NOT NECESSARY IN THIS METHOD

FIGURE 22a. The method illustrated at the top is useful when the stick of dynamite does not require tamping. Where tamping or pushing the charges into boreholes is required, one of the methods illustrated in the lower drawings must be used. In any method of inserting primers, the object is to provide maximum protection for the sensitive detonator cap by placing it as close to the central axis of the stick as possible.

along the centerline of the dynamite stick as possible; several ways of doing this are shown in Figure 22a. A single stick of dynamite which does not require tamping or pushing in order to seat it in desired position may be prepared by pushing the wooden rod through one end so that a cavity is formed along the central axis of the stick. The fuse-cap primer is then gently inserted until it bottoms in the hole. One end of the stick may be wrapped with twine to prevent pulling out the fuse while loading in the hole. This is the method illustrated in the upper drawing of Figure 22a. However, if sticks of dynamite must be tamped or pushed home with a tamping rod, it is essential that primers be inserted into the sides of the sticks so that both ends of the dynamite sticks are square and free of protrusions. In this way, the tamping rod can be placed against one end of the stick while the other end can rest against the bottom of the borehole without any fear that the primer cap may be accidentally set off or that the fuse will be cracked by bending. Several methods of side priming are shown in Figure 22a and are equally satisfactory. In order to be sure that the cap is located exactly in the center of the dynamite stick, it is strongly recommended that the curved handle of the dynamite cap crimper pliers be used to make the desired curving hole into the side of the stick. No matter how the stick is primed, the cap must be in the center of the explosive mixture so that it will receive the fullest protection from pressure or abrasion while being loaded into the borehole. Electric caps are treated differently because the wires are flexible and can be wrapped around the stick in a half hitch after the cap has been seated within the stick. Several methods of handling electric primers are shown in Figure 22b. For cut fuse, no liberties can be taken and under no circumstances should the fuse be bent sharply or knotted.

Prior to loading any hole, *all* loose chips of rock must be carefully scraped out by using the spoon rod. If compressed air has been used for drilling, the drill is backed off slightly and a blast of air introduced to clean out chips and dust. The tamping rod, usually a piece of cylindrical wood and *never metal*, is inserted and the depth of the hole measured. Dynamite equal to two thirds of the hole length is prepared for loading and one of the sticks is primed as described before. Since dynamite works best under confinement, some miners slit the sides of unprimed sticks to permit the plastic explosive to spread against the walls of the borehole as the sticks are firmly pressed home with the tamping rod. After sticks are in place and tamped firmly but never roughly, stemming

INSERTING ELECTRIC PRIMERS

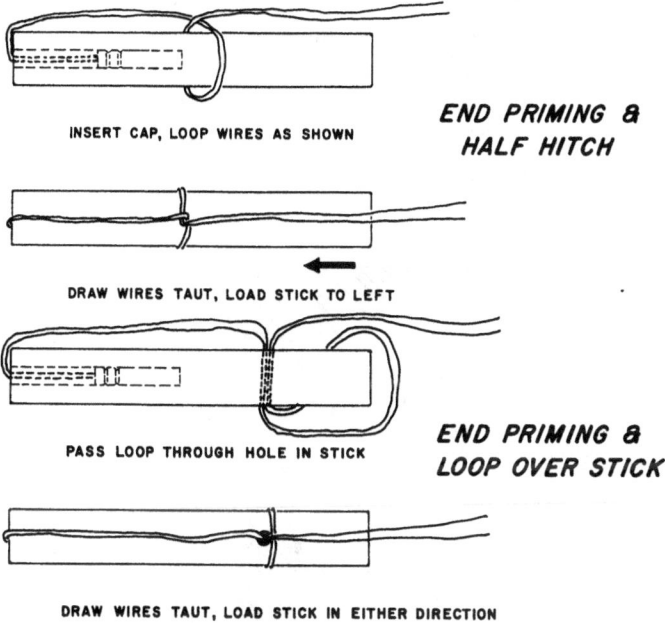

INSERT CAP, LOOP WIRES AS SHOWN

*END PRIMING &
HALF HITCH*

DRAW WIRES TAUT, LOAD STICK TO LEFT

PASS LOOP THROUGH HOLE IN STICK

*END PRIMING &
LOOP OVER STICK*

DRAW WIRES TAUT, LOAD STICK IN EITHER DIRECTION

FIGURE 22b. Because wires are far more slender than burning fuse, electrical detonator caps can be inserted in dynamite sticks and kept from accidentally pulling out by either of the wrapping methods shown here. The lower method calls for punching another hole in the stick but is almost foolproof in respect to pulling out caps. In the upper method note that the stick must be loaded in the hole in the proper direction, to be sure that the half hitch does not slip off.

of clay and sand mixed, damp clay, earth, or finely crushed rock, is fed into the hole and progressively tamped until the exit of the hole is reached. The best stemming material is damp clay and sand in a mixture of one part clay to two parts sand. Only enough water is added to this mixture to make it stick to itself; it must not be wet. Stemming materials must not contain any large sharp fragments of rock. During this operation, care must be taken not to bend, kink, or tear fuse or wires. A good tamping job results in a more powerful explosion because less gas escapes from the borehole and the remaining dynamite is confined just long enough to develop maximum detonation velocity.

If a single borehole is being charged with a number of sticks of dynamite, the usual practice is to measure the depth, taking 2/3 of the length as that to be filled with explosive. In a train of several sticks, the stick next to last contains the blasting cap. For example, if three sticks are loaded, the center stick will contain the cap; if four sticks are put in, the hole will be loaded with two sticks, then the primed stick, and then finished with the last stick. This method of loading initiates the explosion near the exit of the hole so that the explosion wave travels toward the remainder of the dynamite, compressing it and making it more efficient in its explosive action. This sequence of loading is shown in Figure 23.

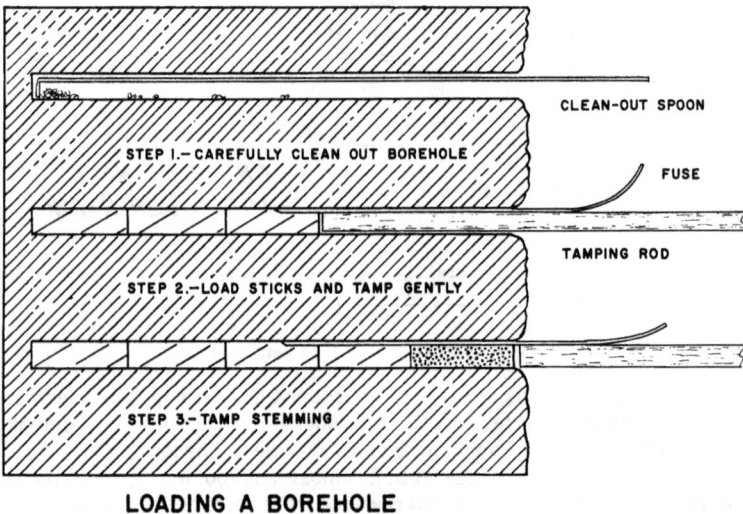

LOADING A BOREHOLE

FIGURE 23. It is absolutely essential that the borehole be cleaned as thoroughly as possible to reduce the possibility of jamming the dynamite sticks in the hole, tearing paper wrappers, or rubbing fuses and wires leading to detonators. It is best to load one stick at a time, seating each firmly with pressure from the wooden tamping rod.

In places where drilling is not possible dynamite can be used quite successfully if one selects the right kind of crack or crevice in lieu of a borehole. If a crack is seen which promises to detach a large mass of rock, it may be enlarged by chipping in a selected spot with a bar or hammered gad. A stick of 60% dynamite is then cut in half with a sharp knife upon a wooden board, and the paper wrapping removed from one of the halves. Care must be taken to avoid touching the explosive itself with bare hands. This precaution is advisable to prevent headaches and heart stimulation from the nitro-glycerine, which, in some persons, is absorbed in sufficient quanties through the skin to make itself felt. A small wooden rod or stick is used to press the dynamite very gently into a wad at the bottom of the hole directly over the crack, in the method illustrated in Figure 24. A fused cap is cautiously inserted into the top and the rest of the hole filled with clay or mud. The blast resulting from this charge will deepen the crack and shatter the rock enough to permit additional chipping by bar or gad until a cavity is made sufficient in size to accommodate one or more sticks of dynamite. It is possible in this way to make surprisingly deep holes which serve nicely instead of drilled holes for blasting away rock. The technique described is similar to that of "mud capping" in which a cone of dynamite sticks is placed upon a large boulder or slab, covered with mud or clay, and detonated. The cap

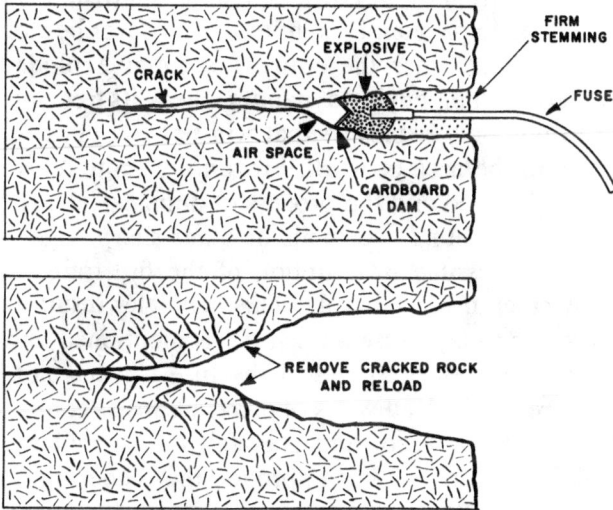

ENLARGING A CRACK

FIGURE 24. In the upper illustration, the plastic explosive from a dynamite stick is removed and gently pushed into a wad against a piece of cardboard folded into a vee an inch or two from the close of the crack. The purpose of the vee is to concentrate the explosion into a jet which penetrates deeper along the crack and makes it a simpler task to enlarge the crack for an additional explosive charge. It is important that only the tip of the cap be inserted in the explosive as shown. If firm stemming is not available, the cap and fuse must be supported by a forked stick or some other means to prevent it from tilting and falling out. After the first explosion, the cracked rock shown in the lower illustration is chipped out by prybar until sufficient space is provided to accommodate a charge large enough to blast the rock apart. No metal instruments or tools of any kind must be used in the method illustrated here, however, a flat piece of wood is satisfactory for applying the loose explosive.

is always inserted in the very tip of the cone so that the explosion wave travels toward the rock where it concentrates in a shattering blow. Additional ideas on how to use dynamite in loose form for removing rock will suggest themselves, but it is important to remember that unconfined explosive placed upon rock merely dissipates its violence into thin air, seldom doing more to the rock than to clean it off thoroughly.

Safety Hints

It is a good idea never to take along more dynamite, fuse, and caps than can be reasonably used. Storage is always a problem, especially where children or passers-by may discover dynamite and caps and, through ignorance, set off an explosion. Dynamite should never be stored close to caps, even in the field, since the entire stock may explode if a cap is accidentally set off. When buying dynamite, check its freezing properties and attempt to buy only explosive that will not freeze at the temperatures prevailing in the area of work. Frozen dynamite must be thawed 'out before it can be used and the process of doing so is very dangerous. Fuse should never be hung over nails or other sharp edges which may cause kinking and possible interruption of the fire train. Cold fuse is brittle and may crack if bent sharply. This may later result in wetting of the fuse powder and may cause a misfire. As mentioned above, always cut off an inch of the exposed end of the fuse if it has not been used recently. Never reuse the lead wires of electric caps as connecting wires; they may be cut or damaged, and may fail to transmit the electrical pulse. If a misfire occurs, do not approach the scene until at least 30 minutes have elapsed. Never attempt to dig out the charge lest the cap be struck by tools and detonated. Instead, carefully remove stemming from the top of the hole with a wooden tool or spoon, until the charge is in view. Make up a new cap-fuse assembly, insert in a small piece of dynamite and place in position against the charge in the borehole; cut fuse to proper length and refire. Always give plenty of time for fumes of an explosion to clear away; inhaling fumes may result in severe headaches or even unconsciousness; in closed quarters, as in mine tunnels, at least an hour may be necessary. Finally, buy a blaster's handbook, study it carefully, and also know the laws and regulations governing the use of explosives wherever prospecting or collecting is to be done.

3

Rock Classes and How to Recognize Them

Up until the beginning of the nineteenth century, mineral deposits were found almost entirely by accident. However, in that century, students of geology and mineralogy began to realize that mineral deposits just didn't "happen" and that actually there were important connections between *kinds of rocks* and *kinds of minerals*. As this realization grew, prospecting began to be more scientific and mining companies interested in developing the hidden wealth of the earth's crust turned more and more for advice to professionally trained geologists. However, even today when so much is known about the vital relationships between rocks and the mineral deposits found in them, many full-time and part-time prospectors do not take the trouble to learn more about rocks. The same can be said for the thousands of amateur mineral and gemstone collectors who enthusiastically take part in field trips or try a little prospecting on their own, but like as not fail to come home with much more than aching backs and bruised knuckles.

Even within well-known mineral occurrences, such as quarries and mines where much bare rock is exposed, a great deal of time can be wasted by searching over rock formations which simply cannot contain anything of value. In the field, where all rocks are just as Nature left them, the problem is far worse. How then does knowledge of rocks help in finding ores and minerals or the cavities within rocks where fine crystals grow? First, many rocks contain valuable minerals in quantities too small to be of practical value, but if the proper conditions are met, these valuable minerals could occur in worthwhile concentrations. Example: diamonds occur only in rocks known as kimberlites. Not all kimberlites contain diamonds, but certainly if one knows what kimberlite looks like in the field, it would be to his benefit to examine its outcrops *most* carefully. Second, some rocks seem to attract ores of metals, especially when they are in contact with igneous rocks. Example : limestones often contain valuable metallic ore deposits when next to granite-like igneous rocks. Third, some rocks often contain cavities lined with splendid crystals, sometimes gemstone crystals. Example : basalts containing cavities lined with crystals of amethyst, zeolite minerals, and many others; also pegmatite pockets from which most of our aquamarine, tourmaline, and other valuable gemstones are obtained. Finally, a knowledge of rocks can also steer one away from rocks which very seldom contain anything of value. Example : sandstone.

The lessons of geology are clear and it is foolish not to take advantage of them : to be successful in hunting for minerals and gemstones, the collector and prospector must know not only the minerals themselves but the rocks in which they are most likely to be found. He must also learn what minerals make up the various kinds of rocks and the rock formations which appear favorable for mineral deposits. The next several chapters will therefore devote themselves to this all-important aspect of collecting and will attempt to explain what the most important kinds of rocks are, what they look like when met with in the field, what minerals may be found as "float" or as "indicators" of mineralization, and finally the structure of mineral deposits themselves so that they can be intelligently dug up without ruining a great many fine specimens.

BELOW THE SURFACE

Most of us are convinced that the ground we walk on is perfectly solid. Every day we use such expressions as "solid as a rock" to show how much we believe this. Yet can the crust be really as solid as it seems when we read about earthquakes and erupting volcanoes, and the destructive tidal waves which follow? All of these natural disasters show that our "solid" rocky crust is really not so solid after all. There seems to be no reason to think that it will not continue to shift and buckle in one place or another for billions of years to come.

There are several reasons why the crust is not perfectly rigid, not the least being that the interior of the earth is plastic, perhaps like soft iron on the point of melting, while the outside, the only part which we can see for ourselves, is always being sculptured by rain, wind, and the gases in the atmosphere. To be realistic, we should think of the crust as a flexible layer of stone resting in a delicate state of balance on a yielding, almost liquid core. In Figure 25, which has been drawn to scale, the thinness of the crust is readily apparent, as is also the fact that it forms only a very small part of the enormous mass of mineral matter which we call our earth.

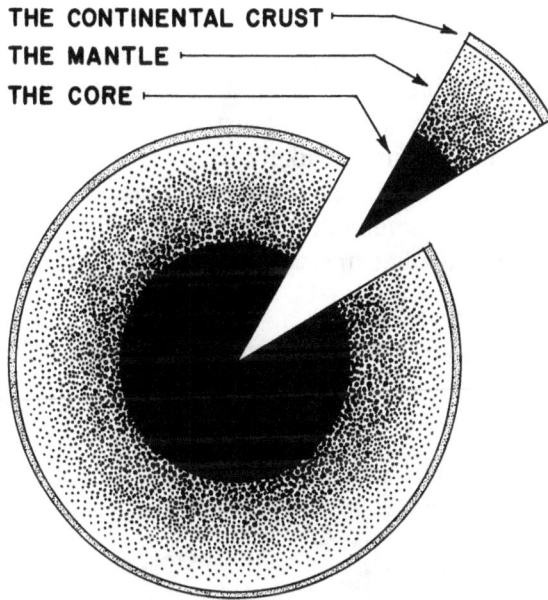

THE CONTINENTAL CRUST
THE MANTLE
THE CORE

THE EARTH

FIGURE 25. Cross section of the earth. The continental crust is a mere 20¼ miles in thickness while its average density of 2.84 is very close to that of common granite. The mantle is about 1782 miles with a density considerably greater, that is, 4.93, while the core with a radius of 2157 miles is densest of all, about 10.93. The greater densities toward the center are believed due to an increase in iron-nickel content.

Any slight disturbance of the balance between crust and core results in shifting and readjustment. As slight as these readjustments may be, they nevertheless result in earthquakes and volcanic eruptions along weak places in the crust. Will the balance ever be perfect? Probably not so long as earth keeps her atmosphere, for it is the atmosphere which whittles away high mountains, slowly to be sure, but without let up. Over millions of years, enormous quantities of rock are converted into crumbling grains of sand and particles of clay which wash away into low places far removed from the mountains themselves. Much of this debris eventually finds its way into lakes and seas which may be thousands of miles away. One needs only to stand on the banks of the Mississippi in New Orleans to see tons of fine mineral matter discoloring the water and moving swiftly toward the Gulf of Mexico a few miles downstream. This disintegrated and pulverized rock probably came from the ancient Rocky Mountains and indicates that they must have been far higher and broader than they are now.

When enough rock has been removed from one place on the crust and deposited elsewhere, the balance of crust on core is seriously thrown out of kilter and huge sections are likely to crack and buckle along giant fissures. New mountains will be formed, some places will be raised above sea level and others submerged, and the stage set for another cycle of erosion leading to a further upset of the balance and so on. Unless the

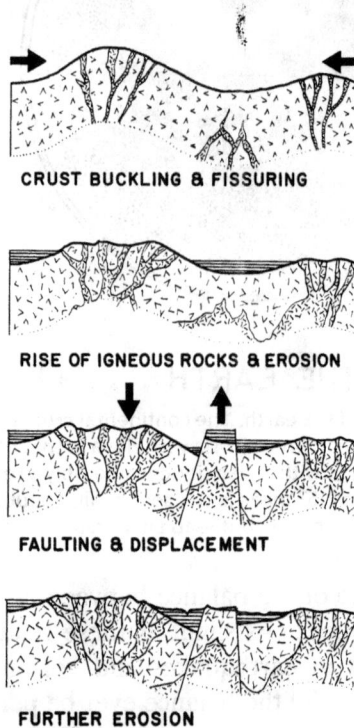

CRUST BUCKLING & FISSURING

RISE OF IGNEOUS ROCKS & EROSION

FAULTING & DISPLACEMENT

FURTHER EROSION

FIGURE 26. Buckling and sculpturing of the earth's crust. Cycles such as shown here may be repeated many times. Severe wrinkling resulted in intrusion of igneous rocks and also in the formation of sedimentary rocks because of erosion. Metamorphic rocks formed from enormous pressures and high temperatures developed in layers of material far below the surface.

earth's atmosphere should vanish, leaving conditions like those on the moon, changes and upheavals of the crust will continue. No doubt these vast upheavals occurred in the early stages of earth's development and account for the presence of certain rocks in places one would not expect to find them, for example, limestones which were originally formed on sea bottoms appearing on top of high mountains, such as in the Alps and the Canadian Rockies. A cycle of crust movements followed by erosion and a repetition of the cycle is shown in Figure 26.

THE FORMATION OF ROCKS

The easiest and most sensible way to talk about rocks is to divide them into classes according to how they were formed. The original rocks of the earth, formed directly from molten mineral matter billions of years ago, are called *igneous* rocks, the word itself meaning "fire" in allusion to origin. At the beginning, only igneous rocks were present in the crust but no sooner had they cooled then they began being attacked by rain and gases of the atmosphere. The debris resulting from this destruction washed into low places, as shown in Figure 27, and sorted itself into beds of clay, sand or gravel, depending on how fine the particles had become. The finest material found its way into lakes and seas but heavier or coarser material settled in stream and river beds somewhere along the way. Much mineral matter dissolved in the water eventually reached the oceans where it contributed to the "saltiness" of originally fresh sea water. Early sea organisms learned how to use dissolved minerals to make skeletons and shells for their bodies. When overtaken by death, these minute organisms, and larger ones too, fell to the sea floors to help build up the steadily accumulating layers of slimes, silts and oozes. In time, ocean and sea floor deposits reached such great thicknesses that bottom layers began to press together into solid masses creating another great class of rocks known as the *sedimentary* rocks. Here again the word sedimentary is descriptive because rocks of this class are solidified *sediments.*

Sometimes sediments became so thick that the pressure upon lowest layers created considerable heat. As a result of this heat, not to mention that which worked its way upward from the earth's interior, and as a result of pressure, new rocks were formed which little resembled the starting material, while older sedimentary rocks and even igneous rocks were subjected to the same transformation. Heat and pressure could also be applied by igneous material forcing its way into rocks already solidified. Sometimes the changes were so drastic that early geologists were often hard pressed to recognize the original material from which such re-created rocks were formed. Because of their distinctive nature, it was decided to call them *metamorphic* rocks, the word itself meaning "change in form" for this is exactly what happened to them. The general relationship of the three great classes of rocks are shown in the block diagram of Figure 27.

To review, all rocks fall into three great classes, according to how they were formed: igneous, sedimentary, and metamorphic. However, within each class there are so many varieties that it is necessary to divide them still further. Some subdivisions take into account special methods of formation, others the special mineral or minerals which are characteristic of the rock concerned. The reasons for subdivision of rocks within the great classes will become plain during the following discussion of the most important kinds.

ROCKS AND MINERALS COMPARED

Before going on, it is important to compare rocks and minerals to be sure the differences between them are clearly understood. In terms of raw material, that is, the stony material of the earth's crust from which all rocks and minerals form, there is no difference, since all of it comes from the same source, but in terms of bulk and the individual minerals which together make up this bulk, there is a great difference.

For example, *limestone*, a very common sedimentary rock, is composed, for all practical purposes, of one mineral—*calcite*. Because limestone forms over large areas and makes up important layers in the earth's crust, geologists consider it a *rock*, but on the other hand, the calcite which makes up the rock is considered to be a *mineral*. One is therefore a building block in the crust while the other is a particle within the building block itself.

Compared to the massive mixtures which we call rocks, minerals are true compounds, in the sense that the chemist uses the word. That is, they are combinations of elements such as *silicon* and *oxygen* in quartz, with specific proportions of each element, and forming distinctive crystals with distinctive properties. These properties permit us to identify minerals no matter where they are found, and in many rocks where the mineral grains are large enough to examine, we are able to identify the rocks because we can identify the minerals within them.

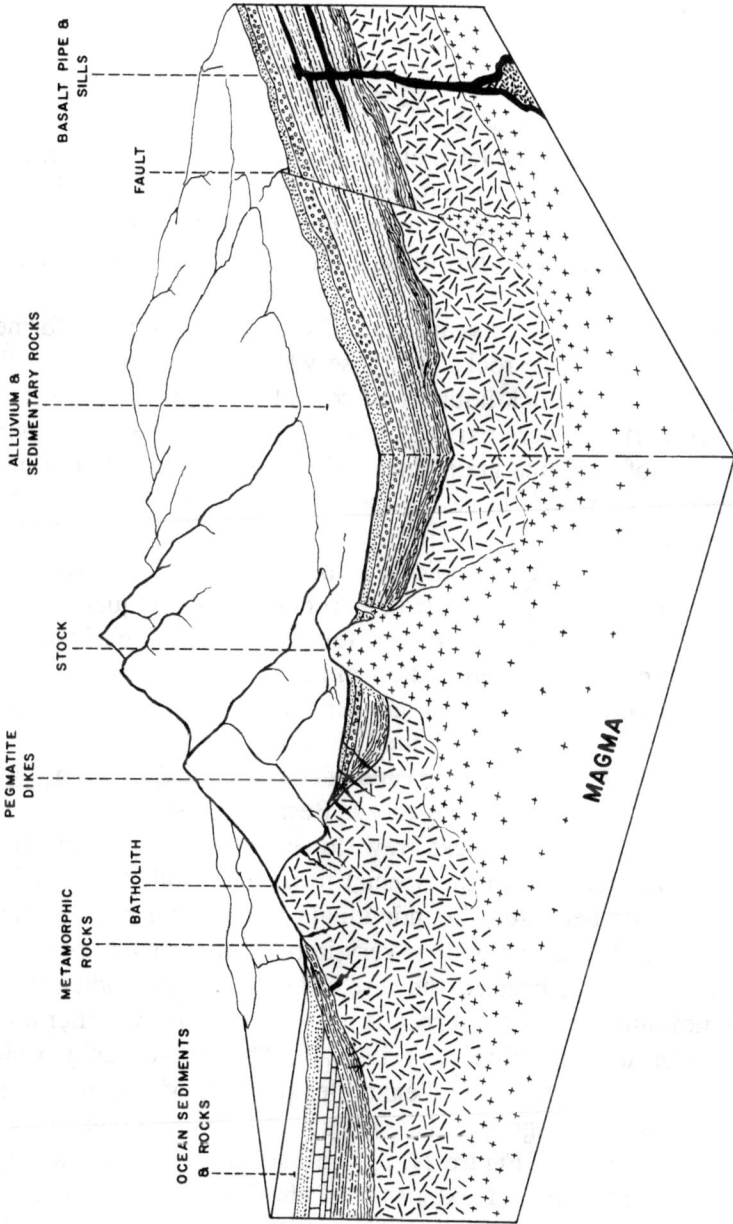

FIGURE 27. A block diagram showing a section of the crust with its three classes of rock. The upthrust portion of the magma, called a batholith, forms the spine of the mountain chain. Eroded portions have settled into layers on both flanks to form sedimentary rocks near the surface, and metamorphic rocks at greater depths.

Thus, to sum it all up, minerals are specific compounds which make up rocks, but the rocks themselves are the large building blocks of the earth's crust.

IGNEOUS ROCKS

Geologists place all rocks which were molten at one time or another in the igneous class because it is entirely possible that sedimentary and metamorphic rocks could have been engulfed by molten mineral matter or changed by heat and pressure to such an extent that they cannot be told from true igneous rocks.

Within the igneous rock class are several sub-classes for rocks formed in special ways. *Extrusive* rocks are those which poured out upon the surface of the earth as thick liquids and cooled very quickly because so much of their surfaces were exposed to the atmosphere. Rapid cooling results in rocks of very fine grain since individual minerals do not have much chance to grow into large crystals. On the other hand, *intrusive* rocks, as the name implies, are those which squeezed their way into cracks or crevices in already solidified rocks. These too cooled very quickly but not as quickly as extrusive rocks and consequently their grain size is generally somewhat larger. Lastly there are the *plutonic* or deep rocks, which receive their name from Pluto, the Greek god of the underworld, in allusion to their origin far under the surface. Plutonic rocks are now believed to have formed near the boundary between the mantle and the crust (see Figure 25) and of course cooled far less rapidly than either extrusive or intrusive rocks. Because of slow cooling, the various minerals on plutonic rocks grew slowly and developed into large crystals. In some cases, as in the special formations called *pegmatites*, which will be described later, the individual crystal grains reached sizes as much as several feet across. It is very important to remember these differences in grain size because they are often very helpful when trying to identify not only what kind of rock is involved but also whether it is a sedimentary or metamorphic rock instead. The photographs which appear on later pages show many examples of rocks within each great class and illustrate how "graininess" varies in the several kinds of rocks.

In the block diagram of Figure 27, plutonic rocks are represented by a *batholith*, a bulging upward extension of the huge mass of plutonic material underneath known as the *magma*. An example of an intrusive rock formation is shown in the *stock*, while the basalt *pipe* on the right hand side is extrusive. If samples of rocks from each of these formations could be examined, the grain sizes would vary from coarse for the batholith rocks, to medium for those from the stock, and fine for the basalt rock comprising the pipe.

Chemical Composition of Igneous Rocks

Studies of the nature and composition of igneous rock samples from many places in the world reveal the startling fact that practically all of the crust contains no more than *eight* elements: oxygen, silicon, aluminum, iron, calcium, sodium, potassium, and magnesium. In varying combinations and proportions this mere handful of elements makes up nearly 99% of the igneous rocks of the crust, with fully half the weight being taken up by oxygen alone! Because the minerals *quartz, feldspar, pyroxenes, hornblende* and a few others are composed almost entirely of these eight elements, it is no wonder that these minerals are so abundant in igneous rocks. If the amateur mineralogist learned how to recognize just these few mineral species alone, he would be well on the road to recognizing many igneous rocks in the field. In the next section, the principal igneous rock minerals are described and the reader is urged to get study samples to prepare himself for recognizing them in the field.

Igneous Rock-Forming Minerals

For all practical purposes, only seven minerals or mineral groups make up the major portion of the species usually found in igneous rocks. One of them, quartz, is composed entirely of oxygen and silicon while all the rest contain much of both of these elements plus others in the group of eight elements referred to above. Iron and magnesium are present in several minerals and mineral groups, and such are therefore called the *ferromagnesian* minerals, from *ferro* for iron and *magnesian* for magnesium. Almost all ferromagnesian minerals are dark in color, usually in various shades of dingy green, olive, brown or black, and the general color of any rock containing them depends on how abundant they are. Consequently rocks containing large amounts of ferromagnesian minerals are called *dark* igneous rocks while those lacking them are called *light* igneous rocks. The general coloration of igneous rocks is of great help in identifying them in the field. The more important rock-forming minerals are listed below.

PRINCIPAL MINERALS OF LIGHT COLORED IGNEOUS ROCKS

Quartz.   Colorless, milky, gray, brown; glassy to greasy luster.

Feldspars.   Mostly opaque white but also pink, red, gray; dull porcelain-like luster when partly decomposed but glassy luster when fresh. Potassium feldspars include *orthoclase* and *microcline;* plagioclases refer to a feldspar series containing varying amounts of sodium and calcium and include *albite, oligoclase, andesine, labradorite, bytownite* and *anorthite.* Perthite is common in pegmatites and is an intergrowth of potassium feldspar and albite.

Feldspathoids.   Compositionally very similar to feldspars, includes: *nepheline, leucite, sodalite* and *cancrinite.* Mostly white or colorless but *sodalite* sometimes blue or pink, *cancrinite* sometimes yellow; luster greasy to glassy. Easily altered on surfaces to white opaque coatings.

PRINCIPAL MINERALS OF DARK COLORED IGNEOUS ROCKS

Olivine.   Usually dark green, also yellow, olive, black; glassy to greasy luster; often in rounded, easily crumbled masses.

Pyroxenes.   Black, dark green and brown colors predominate; luster glassy to dull; sometimes sparkling reflections noted on cleavage planes; also metallic or bronzy reflections. Includes *enstatite, hypersthene, augite, aegerine.*

Hornblende.   Generally dark green, also black; dull to glassy luster; sometimes sparkling reflections noted on cleavage planes.

Biotite Mica.   Dark brown to black; flaky; sparkling.

In addition to the minerals listed above, many other species are found associated within various kinds of igneous rocks but always in small amounts and for this reason are called *accessory* minerals. The most common are tabulated below.

COMMON ACCESSORY MINERALS IN LIGHT COLORED IGNEOUS ROCKS

Muscovite Mica.   Silvery to pale or dark brown; flaky and sparkling; large "books" in pegmatites.

Apatite.   Colorless, white, also pale blue, green, pink, brown; greasy to glassy luster; soft; sometimes transparent.

Sphene.   Brown grains of strong luster; transparent in thin splinters.

Zircon.   Very similar in color and appearance to sphene; heavy.

Fluorite.   Colorless, pale green, blue, purple; often transparent; good cleavages; glassy to greasy luster; heavier than other minerals of similar appearance.

Corundum.   Colorless, white, brown, blue; strong luster; very hard; heavy; bronzy luster often noted on brown varieties.

Magnetite.	Dark gray to dead black; luster dull to somewhat metallic; heavy; magnetic.
Ilmenite.	Similar to magnetite but more steely gray; slightly magnetic.
Pyrite.	Bright brassy yellow; metallic luster; frequently coated with rusty films; brittle; heavy.
Pyrrhotite.	Less yellow than pyrite; metallic luster but frequently coated with gray to green powdery material; magnetic.

Extrusive Igneous Rocks

Volcanoes often pour out lava which cools so quickly that minerals have little time to grow into large crystal grains. In fact some lavas cool so rapidly that no crystals form at all and the rock then resembles a dark

FIGURE 28. Two forms of obsidian. On the left is ordinary black obsidian from Mono Craters, California, showing the characteristic pitch-like conchoidal fracture. On the right is a mass of frothy perlite formed from the alteration of solid obsidian but still containing several nodules of unaltered obsidian, or "Apache Tears" as they are known in the western United States; material from near Superior, Arizona. *Courtesy Smithsonian Institution.*

colored glass. *Obsidian* is a very fine example. When freshly broken, obsidian looks like shattered roofer's pitch and is quite unmistakable in appearance as can be seen from Figure 28.

Obsidians may be smoky brown, gray, greenish, or filled with swirls of brown and black material, but black is by far the most common color. Most obsidian is translucent on thin edges but some is transparent even through half-inch sections. The generally dark colors of obsidian are surprising, since the chemical composition of obsidian is much like that

FIGURE 29. View of Obsidian Cliff in Yellowstone National Park. The rudely columnar material is honeycombed with spherical masses of silica, some of which are open in the centers (lithophysae). Because obsidian weathers rapidly, the cliff material appears whitish rather than black. *Courtesy U. S. Geological Survey.*

of granite or rhyolite, or a mixture of the light-colored minerals feldspar and quartz. Although the best examples look like broken bits of tar and are therefore among the easiest rocks of all to identify, other kinds, called *pitchstones*, are duller in appearance and less easy to recognize. However, even pitchstones show traces of the shining luster and conchoidal fracture so characteristic of the purer material.

Obsidian is easily attacked by weathering and is soon penetrated by many cracks along which chemical change, or *alteration*, proceeds until the entire mass becomes scaly and porous. Figure 28 also illustrates this type, called *perlite*, and shows how the original solid obsidian has almost vanished leaving only a few cores of unaltered material. These cores, when released by weathering of the perlite, supply the transparent nodules known among gem cutters as "Apache tears." The rapid weathering of obsidian causes even fresh material to take on white coatings which are a far cry from the shining black surfaces of newly broken material. Figure 29 shows the famous Obsidian Cliff of Yellowstone Park which is all obsidian but seems light gray in color. It is not until a sample is broken open that its true nature is evident. Incidentally, this cliff is also the source of rare silica minerals from within small spherical gas cavities found in the obsidian. An example of obsidian containing such cavities is shown in Figure 35.

Obsidian is found in large quantities in North America, from the Aleutians through western Canada, into the western United States, and south into Mexico and Central America. It has not been found east of the Mississippi River. From the collector's standpoint, obsidians are of little interest but gem cutters use much of the better kinds for various lapidary projects.

Obsidian-type lavas sometimes contain so much gas while still in the fluid stage that the rocks become frothy and solidify as sponge-like masses which are sometimes so light they can float on water. Many volcanic regions, as in the Alaska Peninsula and the Aleutian Islands, betray their volcanic origin by the rounded masses of pale brown or gray *pumice*, as this rock is called, which litter lake and ocean beaches. Pumice, volcanic ashes and cinders, are often blown or washed into beds of *tuff*, an example of which appears in Figure 94 in Chapter V. Being light and porous, tuffs are easily permeated by solutions carrying silica, and, when hardened, become important sources of quartz gemstones. An example of silicified tuff is shown as No. 3 in Figure 30, while another type of far greater porosity is shown as No. 4 in the same figure.

Where volcanic flows of the same general composition as obsidian cooled more slowly, very fine-grained crystalline rocks resulted. These are called *felsites*. Rocks of this type are pale in color, opaque, and so fine in texture that it is impossible to see the separate crystals even with a hand lens. Many felsites can be easily mistaken for hardened clays or fine-grained sedimentary rocks and it is often necessary to examine samples under a high-powered microscope to be sure of their nature if nothing further can be told about them in the field. In appearance,

FIGURE 30. Fine-grained volcanic flow rocks. No. 1 is *hornblende andesite* from Mount Shasta, California. Sharp prisms of black hornblende are sprinkled uniformly throughout a groundmass of pale gray andesite. Specimen No. 2 is *rhyolite* from Babacomari Canyon, Cochise Co., Arizona. In this example, white feldspar crystals of small size are imbedded in soft porous material of brown color. No. 3 is *indurated volcanic ash* which has been stained by infiltrations or iron minerals resulting in beautiful bands and whorls of pink, red, gray and olive. This specimen, better known as "wonderstone" to amateur gem cutters, is from Martin Creek, Nevada. Specimen No. 4 is *liparite tuff* from Zacatecas, Mexico, and consists of a porous fine-grained groundmass of volcanic ash in which are imbedded larger fragments of pumice-like material. Specimens average 4 x 3 inches in size. *Courtesy Smithsonian Institution.*

felsites show smooth but dull fracture surfaces which look like those of broken porcelain. The color ranges from pale gray to many shades of red, brown, or even green, but very dark colors are unknown. Several felsite rocks are shown in Figure 30. In addition to forming large flows on the surface, felsites are sometimes found as small thin sheets intruded into other rocks, as in some of the older formations of the Appalachian Mountains, however, felsites are most common as lava flows in the western United States.

Although any fine-grained light colored igneous rock can be called a felsite, it is customary to apply a special name when the composition is known. Thus a felsite having the composition of granite, that is, feldspar and quartz plus a little mica or hornblende, is called *rhyolite*. An example of rhyolite is shown as No. 2 in Figure 30. A felsite rock similar to rhyolite but without quartz is called *trachyte:* another is *latite* which also is without quartz but contains two kinds of feldspar instead of one. Rhyolite, trachyte and latite are abundant in North America and often appear as large flows in some of the western states. Valuable ore deposits are found in some of them as well as useful quartz and opal gemstones.

FIGURE 31. Rhyolite showing well developed joints; note the light coloration of the rock. Scene in Harney Co., Oregon. *Courtesy U. S. Geological Survey.*

The field appearance of weathered rhyolite is shown in Figures 31 and 32.

Since igneous rocks cool at different rates, some minerals frequently begin to grow into well-formed crystals before the rest of the liquid mass solidifies. Such crystals often show sharp faces and if of different color from the rest of the rock provide a pleasing contrast and pattern. Rocks of this sort showing a sprinkling of large crystals in a groundmass of

FIGURE 32. Rhyolite-tuff eroded into cones and cavities. North foothills of the Palmetto Mountains, Esmeralda Co., Nevada. Cavities are places within the rock mass where weaker material eroded faster than elsewhere. Again note the light coloration. *Courtesy U. S. Geological Survey.*

fine-grained rock are known as *porphyries* while the large crystals themselves are called *phenocrysts*. Not being much different from the rocks previously described, they are simply called *rhyolite porphyry*, *trachyte porphyry*, etc. Porphyry texture is common in many kinds of igneous rocks. Several porphyry specimens are shown in Figure 33.

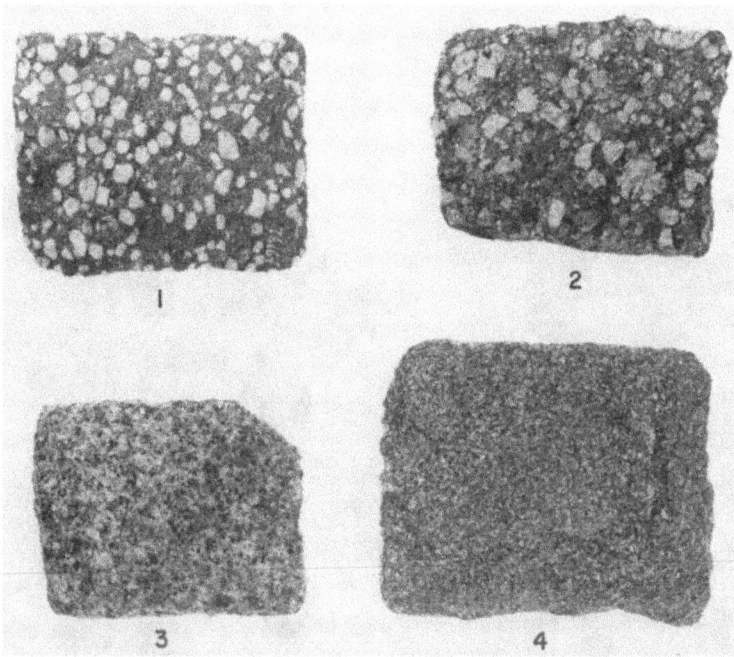

FIGURE 33. A group of igneous rock samples. No. 1 is *dacite porphyry* from Clear Creek, Shasta Co., California, showing well-formed white feldspar crystals, in a fine-grained groundmass of greenish-brown material. No. 2 is *quartz porphyry* from White Mountain Notch, New Hampshire, showing feldspar phenocrysts in a groundmass which contains considerable quartz, hence the name. No. 3 is *gabbro* from near Chester, South Carolina; the distinct grains are green and gray in hue. No. 4 is *diorite* from south of Cherry Creek, Madison Co., Montana; as compared to gabbro the grain size is considerably smaller; color; dark greenish-gray. The largest specimen illustrated measures about 4 x 3 inches. *Courtesy Smithsonian Institution.*

Another rock similar to those just described is called *andesite*. It is also a hardened lava and may be of pale gray or red color. It differs from other lavas by containing mostly plagioclase feldspar with one of the dark ferromagnesian minerals such as pyroxene or hornblende. Andesites are often prophyritic in texture as shown in the handsome example illustrated in Figure 30. Andesites weather rapidly and become brown or reddish-brown upon their surfaces due to the decomposition of the iron-containing dark minerals. An example of weathered andesite is shown in Figure 34. Thick flows are common in many places in the western United States, some of which are noted for commercial deposits of gold and silver.

Another important group of fine-grained extrusive rocks are known as the *basalts*, or, to the quarrymen who blast them down for crushed rock,

FIGURE 34. Andesite is easily weathered, as can be observed in this scene where only hardened vein-like sections stand upright above portions which have disintegrated into soil. South of Clayton Valley in the foothills of the Palmetto Mountains, Esmeralda Co., Nevada. *Courtesy U. S. Geological Survey.*

as "trap" rocks. Basalts are very dense, heavy and fine-textured rocks of dark gray, dark greenish-gray or black color. The principal minerals in them are gray plagioclase and black pyroxene with some accessory olivine and magnetite. None of these minerals is light in color and naturally neither is the rock. Some kinds are porphyritic and show distinct crystals of olivine, augite, plagioclase, hornblende or biotite. An example of basalt is shown in Figure 35.

Basalts are common in the western United States as widespread horizontal sheets and in the eastern United States as thin sheets intruded between sandstones. Figure 36 shows several diagrams of basalt intrusions; sheets lying more or less horizontally are known as *sills* while those nearly vertical are known as *dikes*. Basalt flows often develop shrinkage cracks on their upper surfaces due to rapid cooling. As cooling

FIGURE 35. Volcanic Flow Rock Specimens. No. 1 is *basalt* of almost black color from near Petaluma, California. An opening is partly filled with white chalcedony. No. 2 is black *obsidian* filled with spheroidal cavities called lithophysae. The latter contain micro crystals of rare forms of silica and other minerals. Specimen from Obsidian Cliff, Yellowstone National Park. No. 3 is very dark gray *diabase* from Sugarloaf Mountain, Boulder Co., Colorado. Diabase and basalt are very similar in appearance, however, diabase usually shows lathlike crystals considerably larger than the very small crystals found in basalt. *Courtesy Smithsonian Institution.*

progresses, the cracks work downward until some sections of the flows may be divided into numerous five or six sided columns with remarkably straight sides. These columns separate easily and create spectacular "postpile" cliffs like those shown in Figure 37. This vertical jointing of basalt is so prominent a feature that it provides a valuable recognition feature for the collector or prospector in the field. Another fine example appears in Figure 93.

Other basalts show signs of their once having been fluid. In some flow layers may be seen ropy or twisted structures, gas bubble cavities stretched in one direction, and large ball-like masses, as if some lumps of partially-hardened lava had been pushed along by lava which was still fluid. Basalt of this type is known as *pillow basalt*, and is of interest to

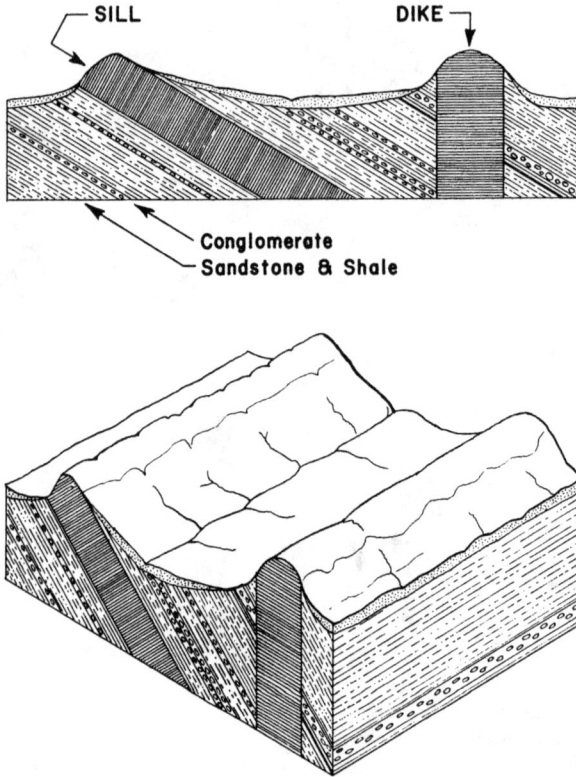

BASALT DIKE AND SILL

FIGURE 36. Basalt intruding sedimentary rocks. The horizontal or nearly horizontal body is known as a *sill* while the near-vertical body is called a *dike*. Prominent
cliffs and ridges often result from weathering or glaciation of these formations because basalt is usually more resistant than the softer sedimentary rocks.

collectors because open spaces between the "pillows" are often lined
with wonderful minerals. These cavities are the favorite home of the
zeolite minerals and many other species such as amethyst and prehnite
which are even more colorful. Still other basalts contain many round or
oval gas cavities in otherwise solid rock and are then called *amygdaloidal
basalts*, the name being derived from the Latin for "almond" in
reference to the shape of the cavities. Openings in amygdaloidal basalts
are often filled with agate and amethyst, and it is from weathered basalts

FIGURE 37. Two photographs of the Devil's Postpile National Monument located near the San Joaquin River, Madera Co., California. This is a splendid example of basalt which formed a plug in the throat of a volcano and, in cooling, contracted into the geometrical columns shown. The upper photo is a general view while the lower photo shows a close-up of some of the columns. Partial development of columns is common in many basalt flows but seldom as perfectly as this; compare the partial column development in the basalt of the Prospect Park Quarry shown in Figure 100. *Courtesy U. S. Geological Survey.*

of this kind that most of our supplies of these gemstones come. An amygdaloidal basalt is illustrated as No. 1 of Figure 35, and in Figure 112.

Intrusive Igneous Rocks

There is little difference between extrusive and intrusive igneous rocks except that intrusives cool more slowly and develop coarser grain. *Diabase*, a very common intrusive rock, is almost the same as basalt but is coarser in texture and frequently porphyritic. Its principal minerals are again dark, i.e., plagioclase and pyroxene, while its accessory minerals magnetite and olivine are also dark in color. However, the texture is distinctive because of the long flat crystals of plagioclase feldspar or pyroxene which criss-cross in every direction. Diabases may be gray, green or black in color but are mostly dark greenish-gray. Because they cooled more slowly, few diabase intrusions show columns but they may contain many cracks which tend to divide the rock into large squarish blocks. A close-up shot of diabase in Figure 35 shows the distinctive appearance of this rock; compare it with the photograph of basalt in the same figure.

Diabase sills are common in the western United States and also in the eastern states and in Canada. The Palisades of the Hudson as well as many other similar cliff-like formations in the eastern United States are diabase and, from many quarries opened in them, furnish fine mineral specimens similar to those found in basalt. However, angular cavities such as found in pillow basalt, or round cavities as in amygdaloidal basalt, are rare, and such minerals as are found usually occur in cavities along joints (*see* Figure 102).

Plutonic Rocks

Plutonic rocks stem from huge puddles of molten rock formed at great depth. Some are of stupendous size, which fact can only be appreciated by recalling that large mountain chains such as the Sierra Nevada and the Rockies are mere bulges on much larger plutonic masses underneath. Vast formations of this kind, or batholiths, appear to have pushed their way close to the surface by buckling and melting rocks above them, or by filling huge rents in the crust. Offshoots of batholiths are smaller bodies known as stocks and generally consist of the same kinds of rocks. Both formations are shown in Figure 27.

Because of the size of plutonic masses, rocks within them tend to be even in texture and show few signs of flow such as we have noted in basalt. For these reasons and because of their hardness and durability, they are favored for all kinds of building and construction work. The uniform texture and even size of the grains are shown in Figure 38, where two important varieties are pictured.

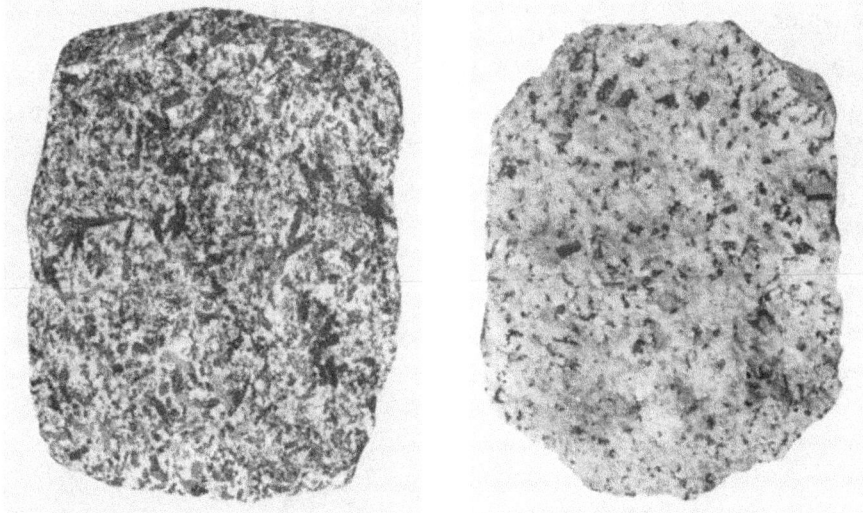

FIGURE 38. The granular crystalline nature of igneous rocks are well shown in photographs of *hornblende gabbro*, left, and *monzonite*, right. Note particularly the haphazard arrangement of individual crystal grains in both rocks, indicating that the parent bodies of molten material simply welled up from the depths and con- gealed without very much movement. In the left-hand photograph, the long lath- like crystals are very dark green hornblende while the smaller black specks are similar crystals broken across; some biotite mica is also present and, along with hornblende, contributes to the general dark coloration of this rock. In the right- hand photograph, the white groundmass is practically pure quartz while the black specks are hornblende and biotite mica. Both specimens from Yosemite National Park, California. *Courtesy U. S. Geological Survey.*

Perhaps the best known plutonic rocks are the *granites*, and scarcely any town or city is without buildings or other structures made of this durable stone. The light mineral in granites and allied rocks is most often feldspar, the gray mineral is quartz, while the black specks are usually biotite mica, hornblende, or some other dark ferromagnesian mineral. Depending on the relative amount of each mineral present, the general color of granite may vary from white to pale or dark gray, from pink to red, or may be evenly spotted with black on white. The textures of granite are shown in several examples in Figure 39. Although the grain size usually ranges from about one-sixteenth inch to one-half inch, the individual grains in the special types known as pegmatites may be several feet across. Because pegmatites are very fruitful sources of rare and unusual minerals as well as of fine mineral specimens and gemstones, a full discussion of them will be reserved for the next chapter.

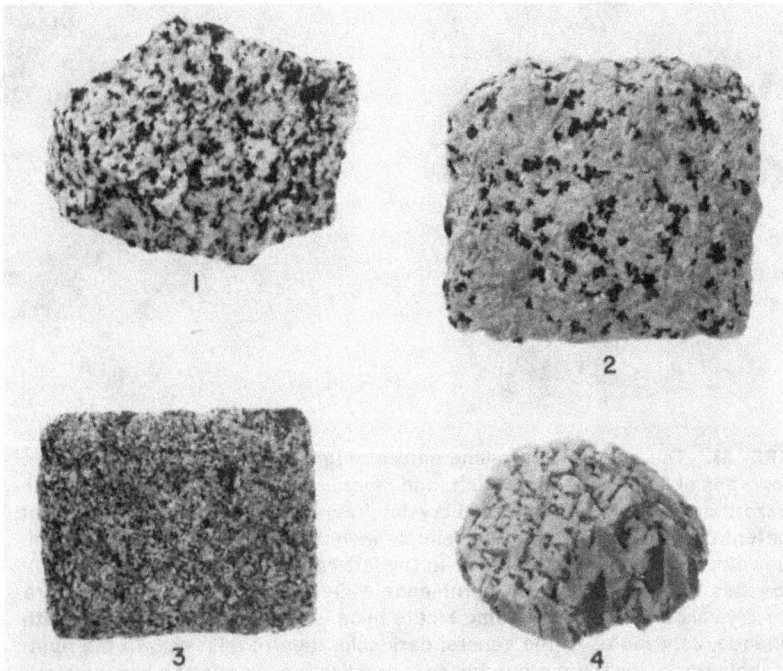

FIGURE 39. Granitic Igneous Rocks. No. 1 is *biotite granite* from near Davidson College, North Carolina. The dark spots are biotite mica while the white areas are a fine-grained mixture of feldspar and quartz. No. 2 is *syenite* composed of pale gray feldspar spotted with black biotite mica; there is no quartz in this rock. No. 3 is *granodiorite* from Coyote Hills, Oregon. The general color is gray due to the abundance of dark colored ferromagnesian minerals. No. 4 is *graphic granite* from a pegmatite near Portland, Connecticut. The major portion of the specimen is pale tan feldspar spotted by angular rods of gray quartz. Size of specimen No. 2 is 4 x 3½ inches. *Courtesy Smithsonian Institution.*

Granite without quartz is a light-colored rock known as *syenite*, but since there are all degrees of granite from normal granite to granite poor in quartz, the dividing line is not sharp. This is true of many kinds of rock and it often becomes a matter of personal choice as to what a rock should be called exactly. Syenite is shown in Figure 39 and from this illustration it can be seen that it isn't much different from granite in appearance.

Although the rock called *nepheline syenite* has been given a name similar to syenite, the name is rather misleading because this rock contains not only nepheline as an important mineral but also a ferromagnesian mineral, and often sodalite and cancrinite in addition to feldspar. Nepheline syenites outcrop in Arkansas, Ontario, and in British Columbia. Some interesting and handsome minerals come from all three areas; the outcrop at Magnet Cove in Arkansas is specially noted for rare and unusual minerals, and fine blue gem-grade sodalite occurs in quantity in the nepheline syenites of Ontario and British Columbia.

Other granite-like rocks are *monzonite*, shown in Figure 38, and *granodiorite*, shown in Figure 39. Slight changes in the amount and kinds of feldspars found in them, as well as in the quartz content, distinguish them from ordinary granite. *Diorite* is another plutonic rock which many geologists class with the granites because of its origin, but it is generally much darker in color than the others because it contains mostly gray plagioclase feldspar and one or more dark ferromagnesian minerals, with little or no quartz. A specimen is shown in Figure 33. Diorites are widespread and abundant, especially near large masses of granite, however, they usually form much smaller rock formations such as sills and dikes. The rock known as *gabbro* is closely related in every way to diorite but contains almost as much of the dark ferromagnesian minerals as of feldspar and is therefore very dark greenish-gray. Specimens of gabbro appear in Figures 33 and 38. Gabbro is found in California, especially near the Sierra Nevada and the Peninsula Range, in the region around Lake Superior, and in several of the eastern states.

The beautiful gemstone labradorite is found in a very coarse-grained type of plutonic rock known as *anorthosite*. The lovely flashes of intense color which arise from polished specimens come from large grains of labradorite feldspar of which the rock is almost entirely composed. The dark minerals which appear between the grains of feldspar are pyroxene and magnetite.

Because of their uniform grain, granites and granite-like rocks form characteristic weathering features which enable outcrops to be easily recognized even from a considerable distance. However, some kinds tend to decompose rapidly and thus form rounded outcrops largely covered with topsoil resulting from separation of the grains. In high elevations where weathering is less severe, granites create spectacular cliffs and jagged mountains; however, in the eastern part of the continent few granite outcrops are prominent because of the planing action of the ancient glaciers which once spread over wide areas and leveled off what might have been high mountains.

Several rather uncommon plutonic rocks will wind up our discussion of igneous rocks. The term *peridotite* is used by geologists to include several closely related rocks in which the mineral olivine, whose gem variety is known as *peridot*, is an important part. When olivine is by far the most abundant mineral, the rock is called *dunite*. *Kimberlite* is an unusual kind in which the olivine has been altered into serpentine; it frequently contains bright green gemmy grains of enstatite, clear red pyrope garnet, considerable phlogopite mica, and sometimes fragments of chalcedony and quartz. This hodgepodge is even more unusual for the fact that it sometimes contains diamonds and indeed is the only rock known in which diamonds do occur as a regular constituent.

Kimberlite often forms peculiar cylindrical bodies known as "pipes" and it is in such formations in Africa and elsewhere that diamonds are found. Kimberlite pipes outcrop in New York State, Kentucky, Arkansas, and in a small area near the junctions of Arizona, New Mexico and Utah, but diamonds have only been found in the pipes near Murfreesboro, Arkansas. Kimberlite and other peridotites weather rapidly, so rapidly in fact that for a time in the diamond mines of South Africa it was the practice to place freshly-mined kimberlite on the surface to expose it to the elements. In a matter of months it had disintegrated so thoroughly that it could be washed without preliminary crushing.

SEDIMENTARY ROCKS

Rocks of this class owe their existence to the breaking down of previously formed rocks. It seems scarcely possible that tough rock can be destroyed by the same elements of our environment which we cope with every day of our lives and think little about doing so. Yet the air we breathe carries oxygen, carbon dioxide, and water vapor, all of which attack rocks under the proper conditions. Many minerals combine with oxygen to form compounds which are less able to resist weathering, while carbon dioxide dissolves in water and turns it into an acid which in turn greatly speeds up the process of destroying minerals or converting them into other compounds. Even ordinary water adds its destructive effects by washing away decayed rock particles and exposing fresh material for new attacks. Furthermore, rainwater penetrates into every crevice and pore of exposed rocks, and by changing into ice during cold spells, exerts enormous pressure which enlarges cracks and provides room for more water to enter. To a lesser extent, the wind also wears away rock by picking up sharp grains of sand and hurling them against outcrops and crags, thus slowly but surely eating them away. But perhaps the most important function of the wind is that of sweeping in fresh supplies of atmospheric gases and rain to carry on the combined assault which eventually destroys even the hardest of rocks.

Where water is always present, as in warm muggy climates, rocks decay even faster since warmth and moisture promote chemical reactions and encourage heavy growths of vegetation. Rootlets penetrate into the smallest openings in rock, prying them apart as they grow larger, and when the plants eventually die and rot away, the acids in the rotting vegetation further attack minerals in the rocks. From Virginia southward in the Piedmont Region of the eastern United States, the destructive effects of climate and vegetation can be seen everywhere the ground is exposed. Many road cuts and ditches expose what seems to be solid rock but at the touch of a pick it crumbles away into dust, completely destroyed by the powerful acids seeping downward from the vegetation above. In some places, this decayed rock reaches depths of thirty feet or more and requires no more than a pick and shovel to remove. Deeply decayed rocks such as this are called *saprolites* and are abundant wherever the proper conditions for their formation are present. It is not difficult to imagine how easily this material can be washed away by a heavy rainfall.

Another important way in which rock is destroyed occurs when large spreads in temperature are the rule. For example, in desert regions, where it is not unusual for the temperature to plummet from broiling in the day to freezing at night, rocks receive very severe shocks from alternate expansion and contraction. In time, surface layers are weakened and begin to crack along the edges of the mineral grains. As expansion and contraction continues, pieces of rock fall off the surface and even large slabs peel off like the skin of an onion. A striking example of such peeling can be seen near Atlanta, Georgia, where the perfectly round top of the famous Stone Mountain represents only a part of a much larger original mass of granite. Another splendid example is the section of Half Dome in Yellowstone Park appearing in Figure 40.

FIGURE 40. A striking example of spheroidal weathering of granite. A near view of Half Dome overlooking Yosemite Valley in Yosemite National Park, California. From a distance Half Dome looks smooth but, as this near view shows, the rounded surface has been caused by the peeling off of enormous sheets of granite. *Courtesy U. S. Geological Survey.*

Once rock crumbles it remains only for water, wind, or ice to carry away the debris. Of these agents water is the most effective because it washes away fine particles, dissolves those minerals which are soluble in water, dashes large pebbles and boulders together in turbulent mountain streams, thus breaking and grinding them up, and finally dumps its mineral burden into lakes, seas, and oceans where extensive deposits form upon the floors. Wind, on the other hand, is not very effective in transporting mineral matter unless the particles are small enough to be carried aloft. However, as the enormous windlaid silt deposits (*loess*) of China show, and to a lesser extent, our own "Dust Bowl" in the west central states, it can do a great deal of work. Loess formed many thousands of years ago is sometimes found in the United States, as the example in Figure 41 shows. Ice sheets and glaciers in some of our higher mountains are still active in transporting destroyed rock but the ancient glaciers which once covered much of Canada and the United States did far more to alter the face of the continent. Several examples of their destructive effects appear in Figures 42 and 43. Under the irresistible planing action of large masses of ice, even the strongest of rocks must give way. The odds and ends of rock, sand, and clay known as *till*, are thickly distributed over Canada and the United States and many thriving sand and gravel businesses reap their profits from the raw material left by these ancient ice masses.

Because sediments seek their own level, rocks formed from them are always bedded in parallel layers or *strata*. This feature isn't always easy to see in small exposures or in places where the beds are tilted by some previous upheaval of the crust, in fact, in some areas, the beds may not only be tipped nearly to the vertical but may also be bent or folded, or even sheared and offset in *faults*. Nevertheless this parallel bedding or *stratification* is the most useful single means for the collector or prospector to recognize sedimentary formations. A very good example of stratification is shown in Figure 44. Other valuable hints as to sedimentary origin are plant and animal fossils, petrified wood, ripple marks, and waterworn pebbles or boulders within the formation.

In fine-grained sedimentary rocks, a magnifying glass is helpful in distinguishing rounded grains of sand or very small fossils and thus prevents confusing these rocks with similar-appearing igneous rocks. Limestones often show few outward signs of origin but sometimes the fossils within them contain silica which is resistant to weathering and therefore stand out in relief on exposed surfaces. Some fossil collectors accomplish the same result by taking samples of limestone suspected of containing fossils and immersing them in a weak solution of muriatic acid to dissolve the calcite.

The Formation of Sedimentary Rocks

There are several distinctive ways in which sedimentary rocks form; some are simple and some are complex, but all are worth knowing because each contributes to our understanding of this great class of

FIGURE 41. Steep-bluffed topography provided by deposits of wind-blown silt known as *loess*. Note how rainwater dribbling over the edges cut narrow grooves in the face of the bluff. In time, the bluff will be divided into a series of towers and pinnacles similar to the "badlands" topography of some arid regions of the western United States. Scene near Carroll Hotel, Vicksburg, Mississippi. *Courtesy U. S. Geological Survey.*

FIGURE 42. A U-shaped valley formed by the gouging action of a glacier which filled this depression millions of years ago. Looking from Red Mountain Pass, south of Ouray, Colorado. *Courtesy U. S. Geological Survey.*

rocks. Each process results in typical minerals; some are no more than the original minerals from decayed rocks, but others are brought into being by chemical activity within the beds.

DISINTEGRATION. In this process, durable minerals simply fall away from disintegrated rocks and are carried by water or wind into their final resting places in sedimentary beds. Aside from being made smaller by rolling, rubbing and fracturing in stream beds, they are very little changed. The final size of the particles depends upon the hardness and toughness of the minerals themselves, or if some native metal like gold is involved, on how well the pieces are able to resist the pounding they will receive. Precious stones and precious metals are most commonly obtained from gravel beds formed in this way. Among common minerals, quartz is most abundant in sedimentary beds formed by rock disintegration. The following minerals are also typical of such deposits and the rocks created from them: feldspar, mica, garnet, tourmaline, kyanite, staurolite, zircon, magnetite, ilmenite, rutile, cassiterite, chromite, gold, platinum, diamond, corundum (ruby and sapphire), topaz, beryl and chrysoberyl.

DECOMPOSITION OF MINERALS. The most abundant products of this process are several clay minerals which form large and small deposits in fresh and salt water. Several clay minerals may be found together but others occur only in deposits formed under special conditions. Feldspars alter into the clay mineral kaolinite; ferromagnesian minerals and obsidians change into montmorillonite, while the clay known as illite is most common in sea bottom sediments. In addition, quartz dissolves to some extent and furnishes silica which can be carried by water into the tiniest pores of sedimentary rocks. The following minerals are typical of sedimentary rocks containing decomposed or altered minerals: kaolinite, montmorillonite, illite, chlorite, quartz, opal.

PRECIPITATION. Extensive limestone beds were formed millions of years ago by particles of limey matter precipitated from sea water by primitive organisms. Some beds are virtually pure calcite but others contain clay and quartz brought in as silt by strong currents. Some calcite is also precipitated from mineral springs or within caves but these are always very small deposits compared to the very large sea bottom beds. The following minerals are commonly found in sedimentary beds formed through precipitation: calcite, aragonite, dolomite, quartz, and opal.

EVAPORATION. Fresh water bodies with no outlets, such as Great Salt Lake in Utah, keep receiving mineral matter from the streams which

FIGURE 43. Rock planed smooth by glacial action. In the photograph, the grooves point toward the observer and indicate that this was the direction of travel of the ice mass. Scene near Clinton, Worcerster Co., Massachusetts. *Courtesy U. S. Geological Survey.*

flow into them. Because there is no way for the water to escape except by evaporation, the "saltiness" of the water increases until a point is reached where the dissolved minerals settle upon the bottom and sides of the basin. The "dry lakes" of California are further examples of this

FIGURE 44. Perfectly stratified gypsum shales near Hanksville, Utah. The tower and pinnacle forms created by weathering and erosion are typical of sedimentary rocks. *Courtesy U. S. Geological Survey.*

process. Geologists believe that large expanses of sea water were trapped in ancient times and subjected to rapid evaporation which eventually formed huge beds of salt and other minerals. When sea water is overly saturated, the first mineral to precipitate is calcite, followed by gypsum or anhydrite, ordinary salt, potassium salts, and finally magnesium salts. Many of these minerals are now found as separate strata in sedimentary beds. The following minerals formed by evaporation are also found in such beds: carnallite, sylvite, polyhalite, langbeinite, thenardite, celestite, glauberite, mirabilite, kernite, borax, tincalconite, ulexite, dolomite, nahcolite, trona, strontianite, colemanite, boracite, etc.

OXIDATION OF IRON AND MANGANESE. Enormous deposits of iron ore and many small deposits of manganese ore were formed from the action of oxygen upon iron and manganese compounds dissolved in water. The most important minerals resulting from this process are: goethite, hematite, pyrolusite, psilomelane.

REMOVAL OF OXYGEN. Minerals in solution can also be robbed of their oxygen and thus form new mineral compounds. This appears to have happened in the depths of the ocean and in coal deposits. The following minerals are believed to have formed in this way: pyrite, marcasite, sulfur, siderite.

Rocks Formed Through Disintegration and Decomposition

Gravel beds whose pebbles are cemented together form the rocks known as *conglomerates*. The individual pebbles may range in size from one-quarter inch to ten inches in diameter but sometimes large boulders

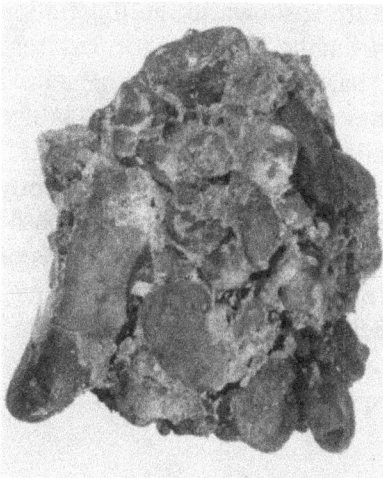

FIGURE 45. Pebbles cemented together similar to that shown here form *conglomerates*. This example is from an extensive bed in the Rocky Mountains. *Courtesy Smithsonian Institution.*

FIGURE 46. The field appearance of conglomerate is often unmistakable. In this instance, large rounded pebbles are not only prominent in those portions of conglomerate still standing, but also are abundant in the slopes below the formation. Scene in Iron Co., Utah. *Courtesy U. S. Geological Survey.*

are present also. Spaces between pebbles are filled with sand and clay and the whole is cemented together with calcite, quartz, iron oxides, or sometimes mixtures of several of these minerals. A conglomerate cemented together with calcite is shown in Figure 45. As a rule conglomerates are not very strong and outcrops are usually littered with many loosened pebbles. The pebbly nature is shown in the illustration of Figure 46. *Sandstones*, as one can tell from the name, are formed from beds of sand in which the individual particles are firmly cemented together. Because quartz is the most common material of sands, it is also the most common mineral found in sandstones. However, many sandstones also contain small amounts of other minerals which frequently impart dark colors. Various shades of yellow, red, brown and purplish-red are due to iron oxides such as goethite and hematite. Two kinds of sandstone, including a colored type, are shown in Figure 47. Sandstones cemented together by quartz are extremely durable but those cemented with calcite weather easily and crumble away. Sandstones are often very uniform in texture, even in thick beds, and consequently form mag-

FIGURE 47. Two examples of *sandstone*. Specimen No. 1 is pale gray sandstone from near Panguitch, Garfield Co., Utah. No. 2 is banded pale red, brown and tan sandstone of fine and uniform grain from Peoa, Summit Co., Utah. The dull luster of sandstones is well shown in these photographs and is due to the fact that sandstone breaks *around* the individual grains instead of through them, as is the case in quartzite (compare Figure 61). *Courtesy Smithsonian Institution.*

nificent cliffs with steep sides. Good examples occur in many places in the southwestern United States, particularly in the Grand Canyon area, as shown in Figure 48, and other lesser canyons in Utah, Arizona, New Mexico, etc. Aside from a few exceptions, as in the uranium and petrified wood deposits of the Colorado Plateau and the quartz crystal veins of Arkansas, sandstones are apt to contain nothing of interest to either the collector or prospector.

Cemented particles finer than sand are called *shales*, or sometimes *siltstones*, if the material was silt to begin with, or *claystones* if the material was clay. Shales are often very smooth in texture, split easily along layers, and, when containing much organic matter such as ancient leaves, twigs, wood, etc., become rather dark in color. A shale originally containing many leaves is shown in Figure 49 while Figure 50 shows an exposed shale bed. The lower resistance to weathering of shale as compared to sandstone is shown in Figure 51. In this figure the undercut portions are shale while the prominent portions consist of the more resistant sandstone. Shales formed from sea beds or formed near coal

FIGURE 48. A series of sedimentary beds beautifully exposed in the north wall of the Grand Canyon opposite Garnet Canyon, Coconino Co., Arizona. Formations include Bright Angel shale, Moah limestone, Temple Butte limestone, Redwall limestone, and the Supai formation. Far below the strata shown lie basement gneisses and granites of much greater age. *Courtesy U. S. Geological Survey.*

FIGURE 49. Soft, gray, earthy shale containing numerous plant fossils from Conception Bay, Newfoundland. Specimen size 4 x 3 inches. *Courtesy Smithsonian Institution.*

beds contain pyrite, marcasite, amber and jet. Borate minerals are found in shales in the Calico District of California. Since shales often contain many impurities and foreign substances, it is customary to describe them more accurately by using a special adjective. For example, a dark shale containing carbon is called *carbonaceous* shale, shales containing petroleum compounds are called *bituminous* shales, and so on. The more common adjectives are: *ferruginous* (containing iron), *micaceous* (containing mica), *calcareous* (containing calcite), *siliceous* (containing quartz), *arenaceous* (containing sand), *argillaceous* (containing clay), and *fossiliferous* (containing fossils).

Argillite is a clay shale which is much like ordinary shale in appearance but is denser and harder because it has been compressed more. Some authorities class it as between shale and slate, the latter being a very much compressed shale of much greater hardness and actually belonging to the metamorphic class of rocks.

FIGURE 50. Faulted and folded shales on Kayaderosseras Creek, northwest of Ballston, Saratoga Co., New York. The original horizontal position of the shale beds has been drastically disturbed but the parallel banding typical of sedimentary rocks is still preserved. *Courtesy U. S. Geological Survey.*

FIGURE 51. Alternating layers of sandstone and shale at the crest of the Santa Monica Mountains, Topanga Canyon Road, Los Angeles Co., California. The differences between shale and sandstone in respect to resistance to weathering are shown very clearly here; the rapidly disintegrated shale is far more easily broken up and washed away. Note how the sandstone overhangs the shale streaks. *Courtesy U. S. Geological Survey.*

Rocks Formed Through Precipitation

By far the most important rocks formed by this process are the *limestones*. Almost all limestones are composed of just one mineral, calcite (calcium carbonate). However, some limestones contain quantities of the magnesium carbonate, known mineralogically as dolomite, and then are labeled as *dolomitic limestones*. If dolomite is very abundant, the rock is simply called *dolomite*. Traces of shells and animal skeletons, sometimes perfectly preserved, are abundant in *fossiliferous limestones*. Certain varieties show interesting patterns and are much prized for ornamental work as polished slabs for walls, pillars and counters. Shells corals, and the stems of crinoids, an ancient relative of the modern starfish, are also common in limestones, however, most limestones are completely featureless masses of fine-grained texture, showing few visible signs of fossil life. Colors cover a wide range. Most limestones are gray to blue-gray, but others are almost pure white, pink, red, or even black. Several types of limestone are shown in Figure 52. Unusually compact kinds, called *crystalline limestones*, are formed by water carrying calcite in solution and filling all open spaces in the rock. Some crystalline limestones resemble marble, a metamorphic rock formed from limestone, but can be distinguished by the fact that fossils are never found in marble. A typical specimen of marble is shown in

Figure 52 for comparison to a sedimentary crystalline limestone shown in the same illustration.

Because of their compact nature, ordinary limestones and dolomites tend to split along joints at right angles to the beds and thus form steep spectacular cliffs. Being easily dissolved by water, some weather into curious twisted and jagged masses which are often so picturesque that small pieces are popular for putting into rock gardens. On a larger scale, the action of water on limestone creates many fascinating caverns and

FIGURE 52. Limestone specimens. No. 1 is soft porous *limestone* of buff color from Utah. Iron-bearing solutions migrated through pores and concentrated at various points to form brown circular patches. Specimen No. 2 is *marble* from Baltimore Co., Maryland. This pure white rock showing sparkling cleavage planes is the end product of strong metamorphism of ordinary limestone and consists of practically pure calcite. No. 3 *limestone* resembles marble when polished but has not been subjected to intense heat and pressure; this rock therefore shows extremely fine grain, and if fossils were originally present will also reveal these when sections are polished. No. 4 is weathered *limestone* from Glacier National Park, Montana. This specimen shows banded structure due to the precipitation of calcite by algae. Differences in porosity cause some of the bands to dissolve more readily than others and bring about the etched appearance. Specimen No. 1 measures 4 x 3 inches. *Courtesy Smithsonian Institution.*

FIGURE 53. A limestone "sink" in St. Louis limestone near Bowling Green, Kentucky. Roof collapse in a cavern beneath the point now marked by the pond caused the formation of a crater-like depression or sink; in some cases, sinkholes remain open and afford access to the caverns beneath. *Courtesy U. S. Geological Survey.*

FIGURE 54. The weathering of the Siyeh limestone on the road below Granite Peak in Glacier National Park leaves a plain record of the origin of this rock. The swirled and contorted weathered surfaces indicate that the calcium carbonate of this limestone was deposited by ancient algae, freshwater plants whose descendants still live in many streams and ponds of North America. When freshly broken, the Siyeh limestone is gray in color. The white streaks at the lower left of the photo are pure calcite introduced later by solutions. *Courtesy U. S. Geological Survey.*

sinkholes in regions underlain by this rock, as in Kentucky, Virginia, and many other places. Figure 53 shows typical terrain in limestone country, including a sinkhole where the roof of a cavern has fallen in.

An important feature of limestones which helps to recognize them in the field is their tendency to develop dusty white coatings wherever bare rock is exposed. However, some kinds contain enough iron minerals so that the coating is rusty rather than white. Perhaps the most certain way to recognize limestones is to watch for fossils which stand in relief upon weathered surfaces. A good example of the etched surface of a fossiliferous limestone is shown in Figure 52, and another in Figure 54. In both examples, the curious curled ridges are due to the deposit of calcite by plant life known as algae.

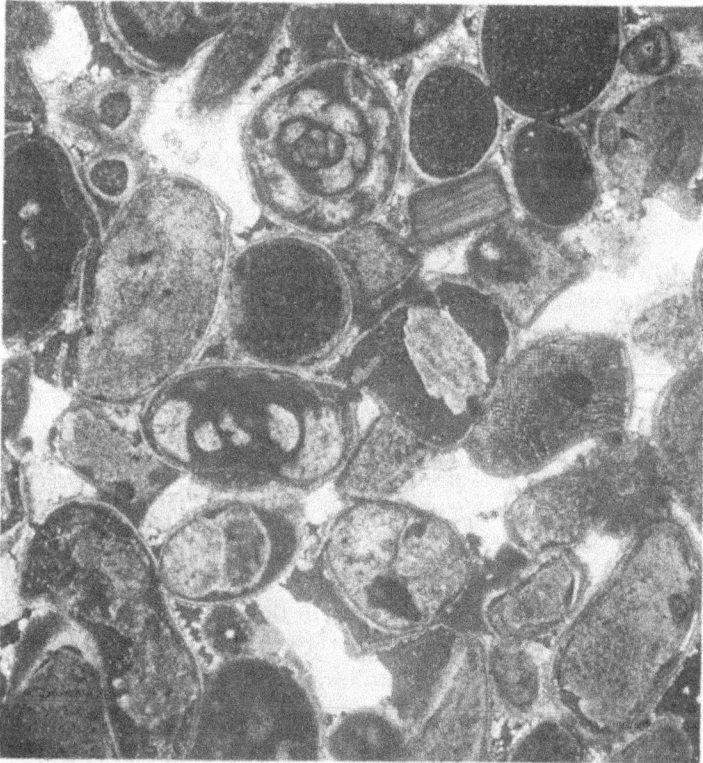

FIGURE 55. Indiana *oolitic limestone* section greatly magnified to show the animal organisms responsible for the small spherules or oolites typical of this popular building stone. Indiana limestone closely resembles a fairly coarse sandstone because of the oolites which might be mistaken for nicely rounded sand grains, however, its softness and violent bubbling under acid treatment soon prove it to be otherwise. *Courtesy U. S. Geological Survey.*

Ordinary limestones and dolomites are found in every state of the Union and in many provinces of Canada, but the largest beds occur in the broad valley of the Mississippi River and nearby areas in the Appalachian Mountains and Rocky Mountains. Some states such as Indiana and Kentucky are almost entirely underlain by limestones. Although ordinary limestones seldom contain interesting or valuable minerals, cavities are sometimes found in them in which splendid crystals of fluorite, calcite, barite, celestite and gypsum line the walls.

Oolitic limestone is a peculiar porous kind which consists entirely of small spheres of calcite. Each sphere has formed about the skeleton of a minute animal organism as shown in the enlarged photograph of Figure 55. Oolitic limestone is found in a broad area in the southern part of Indiana, where its uniform texture and easy workability cause it to be extensively quarried for building stone. *Tufa* or *calcareous sinter* is a spongy limestone precipitated from hot spring waters and is the material forming the terraces of Mammoth Hot Springs in Yellowstone National Park. An example of tufa in the process of forming is shown in Figure 56. A more solid variety of tufa is known as *travertine* and is extensively employed for interior decoration of buildings. Translucent and very dense limestone deposited from cold springs is known as *onyx marble*, or *calcite onyx* while a similar material found within caverns is called *cave onyx*. Calcite onyx is very popular for interior ornamentation as well as for manufacture of carvings, book ends, table and counter tops, vases, etc., however, its drab cousin, cave onyx, is very seldom used except to make up paperweights and other small souvenir items to be sold to visitors to famous caverns. Except for calcite onyx, limestones deposited by springs are entirely without interest to the collector.

The large amounts of silica found in limestones and other precipitated sedimentary rocks are believed to come from minute sea organisms which used silica instead of calcite to build their skeletons. In places, silica from such sources accumulates in definite bands or beds, causing the formation of a strong, hard rock known as *chert*, or smaller masses of silica, generally called *flints*. Flint and chert are both composed of silica in the form of chalcedony, but flint is generally more compact and more translucent. Some beds of chert furnish good material for gem cutting and occasionally good specimens of quartz crystals are found within cavities in this rock. A shattered and re-cemented tan-to-gray chert forms extensive beds in the famous lead-zinc mining region at the junction of Missouri, Kansas, and Oklahoma, and is noted for the

FIGURE 56. Calcareous tufa being deposited by waters of a spring heavily charged with calcium carbonate. The resulting rock is spongy and weak, and when dry, white to pale tan in color with powdery coating. Although this material may resemble some light-colored volcanic rocks from a distance, local inspection usually shows that deposits of calcarous tufa are limited to patches seldom over several hundred feet across. Scene on Cement Creek, Gunnison Co., Colorado. *Courtesy U. S. Geological Survey.*

presence of numerous angular cavities lined with splendid crystals of sphalerite, calcite, galena, marcasite and dolomite. Chert colored by iron oxides is often called *jasper* but this term is usually reserved for impure chalcedony formed by precipitation of silica from hot waters associated with volcanic activity.

Rocks Formed Through Evaporation

Evaporation of ancient seas led to the formation of large beds of *gypsum*, *rock salt* and *anhydrite*. In the United States, beds of salt over several hundred feet thick occur in Michigan, New Mexico, and in other states, while gypsum is so common that commercial deposits seem to be near every large population center. Gypsum is the raw material from which plaster of paris and plasterboard are made. Rock salt is familiar to everyone in its refined form but is most extensively used in chemical and manufacturing industries. Anhydrite has no significant commercial use.

Gypsum is usually colorless or white but impurities sometimes cause it to assume hues ranging from gray to yellow to pink. Ordinarily it is fine to coarse-grained in texture but extremely fine-grained material (*alabaster*) and fibrous (*satin spar*) types are known. Although found in splendid crystals in a number of mineral deposits, massive gypsum rarely furnishes good mineral specimens; however, good grades of alabaster and satin spar provide material suitable for carving into ornamental objects. Rock salt, or halite, as it is known mineralogically, resembles gypsum when in massive form but can be told from the latter by its salty taste. Like gypsum it seldom provides good mineral specimens; however, some clear crystal pieces sometimes contain movable bubbles of water and gas and are prized on this account.

Gypsum, rock salt and anhydrite are easily dissolved by rain, leaving outcrops deeply furrowed or even reduced to low rounded hills marked only by an absence of vegetation. Seams of these minerals enclosed in sedimentary rocks are often deeply undercut by water trickling over them, forming peculiar cliffs with many deep horizontal grooves as shown in the photograph of Figure 44.

In a somewhat different class from the ordinary beds of gypsum, rock salt and anhydrite derived from drying up of sea water, are the borate minerals which form deep beds beneath the dry lakes of California and Nevada. The beds beneath Searles Lake in California, and in other places in the same general region, provide not only commercial borate minerals but also many fine mineral specimens. The beautiful crystallized groups of colemanite, the satiny seams of ulexite, and many others from this area are well known to mineral fanciers the world over.

Rocks Formed Through Oxidation

The most abundant and important iron ores are sedimentary in origin. The red iron oxide, hematite, is the principal ore and is found as large beds in Minnesota and Alabama. Geologists believe that minute organisms in fresh water lakes and seas caused dissolved iron compounds to acquire oxygen and thus change into hematite or goethite which later settled to the bottom and solidified into iron ores. Goethite, a dark brown to yellow-brown oxide, is much less abundant than hematite and is the principal mineral in *brown iron ores* or *bog ores*. In the early days of iron-making in North America, bog ores were used by the colonists for their furnaces but supplies quickly ran out because deposits found in small bogs and marshes were limited in extent. Commercially important beds of manganese ore are believed to have formed in much the same way as the iron ores mentioned above. Aside from good specimens of the ores themselves, and occasionally accessory minerals found in openings in the ore, sedimentary iron and manganese deposits hold little interest for the collector.

Rocks Formed Through Removed Oxygen

Coal and rocks related to coal are largely composed of carbon compounds formed by decay of buried vegetation. It is believed that vegetable matter submerged beneath water was deprived of its oxygen by decay bacteria. Very little mineral matter in the ordinary sense of the

FIGURE 57. An eight feet thick coal seam at the Old Crawford Mine, thirteen miles below Glendive, Montana. The horizontal layering of this series of sediments is well shown here. Wherever exposed, coal and other sedimentary rocks rich in carbon provide unmistakable coloration, even from a considerable distance. *Courtesy U. S. Geological Survey.*

term is present in any coal. The starting material for all coal is believed to be *peat*, a spongy porous substance which forms beneath swamps and bogs from the remains of dead vegetation. All stages of solidification are known in the coal series, from poorly compacted types clearly showing woody plant remains, to hard shining black rock-like masses in which no trace of plant structure can be distinguished. A clearly exposed coal bed is shown in Figure 57. The most primitive coal is *lignite* or *brown coal*, containing much recognizable plant matter. *Sub-bituminous* or *black lignite* is darker and denser and plant remains are recognized only occasionally. *Bituminous* or *soft coal* is laminated and crumbly, and frequently contains pyrite and marcasite; plant traces are still present. *Cannel coal* is a special variety of soft coal but is very uncommon; it is even in texture and breaks with a conchoidal fracture. *Anthracite* or *hard coal* represents the final stage in the coal series. It is hard, dense, and shows no traces of plant origin. Since it occurs in rocks which have been subjected to considerable heat and pressure, some authorities consider it to be a metamorphic rock.

From the collector's viewpoint, the coal series are most unattractive; however, some fair pyrite crystals have been obtained from the coal mines of Pennsylvania, while jet is known from coaly sediments in Utah and elsewhere in the United States. Amber is often associated with lignite and some quantities have been obtained from sedimentary formations along the eastern seaboard of the United States as well as in Canada and Mexico. Lignite is easily recognizable because the plant remains in its beds look relatively fresh although dark brown in color and quite crumbly.

METAMORPHIC ROCKS

The third and last great class of rocks is labeled *metamorphic*, from the Latin word meaning to "change in form." It is applied to those rocks which have changed in important ways since they originally came into existence. Yet we know that practically every rock changes in some respect almost from the moment it forms. Where then is the dividing line?

To be truthful, the line is hard to draw in many cases, since many rocks merge gradually into the metamorphic class because of slight changes from layer to layer until the total change is quite pronounced.

This happens in sedimentary rocks perhaps more frequently than in igneous rocks because the latter originally formed from fire and pressure and thus are not likely to be changed much if subjected to heat and pressure again. However, sedimentary rocks which are laid down in deep layers, often show striking differences between the lowest layers and the top layers, with the bottom layers being far harder because of having suffered greater heat and pressure. Today, geologists fix the dividing line between metamorphic and non-metamorphic rocks at the point where any kind of rock is subjected to enough pressure, heat, and chemical activity to cause the original minerals to *recrystallize* and *new minerals* to form. In the process, the original texture of the rocks changes also.

A common example of what is meant by metamorphism is provided by the conversion of ordinary limestone into marble, the first being a sedimentary rock and the second being its metamorphic equivalent. Ordinary limestone is usually fine-grained and dark blue-gray in color, but after strong pressure and heat, enough to cause the original minerals to dissolve or melt, it is converted into a white glistening marble in which the crystal grains are large and distinct. During the process, impurities which were formerly present, combined with other minerals and part of the calcite in the limestone to form entirely new minerals such as wollastonite, epidote, garnet, etc. A typical grainy marble is shown in Figure 52 along with an ordinary sedimentary limestone to show how each differs from the other. These drastic changes are true metamorphism, that is, they cause new minerals to form and produce new textures in the rock.

Rocks are affected by metamorphism in two important ways. The first takes place along the edges of large igneous masses which push themselves into rock formations and make the latter intensely hot wherever they are in contact. For this reason, this process is called *contact metamorphism*. However, much more happens than a mere rise in temperature, in fact heating up the surrounding rocks is only part of the story. The most important changes take place as a result of hot vapors and fluids leaving the igneous masses and penetrating the surrounding rocks. Such vapors and fluids are often heavily charged with mineral matter, which by a series of chemical reactions causes a great many changes in the mineralization of the rocks invaded by them. How strongly the surrounding rocks are changed depends on how much heat and pressure is applied, how much mineral matter passes into them, and how susceptible the rocks themselves are to change. As mentioned before, limestones seem to be most easily changed while igneous rocks similar to granite are least changed.

In connection with metamorphism along contacts of igneous masses, one of the most important reactions which takes place is that of dissolving minerals in the rocks being invaded, and replacing these minerals by new ones entering from the igneous body. This exchange takes place particle by particle and the process is called *metasomatism* from a pair of Greek words which mean "to exchange at the same time." This process of exchange is extremely important because so many mineral and ore deposits owe their existence to it. In the block diagram of Figure 27, contact metasomatism is most likely to take place along the edges of the stock shown pushed into overlying rocks. More details on this process and the changes resulting from it will be given in the next chapter.

The second great process of metamorphism is called *regional metamorphism* because it takes place over wide areas from several miles to hundreds of miles across. As mentioned before under sedimentary rocks, the sheer weight of overlying formations can cause the lowest rocks to change considerably. This is one way in which regional metamorphism takes place. Another is when rocks are squeezed or buckled by movements in the earth's crust, or, in smaller areas, by being pushed upward by rising masses of igneous material from below. Of course, in the latter event contact metamorphism could take place too, but the most widespread result is regional.

Now to make some comparisons between the two processes:

Contact Metamorphism—involves small areas with the likelihood that drastic changes will take place in previous minerals and *new minerals will be added.*

Regional Metamorphism—involves broad areas with slight to strong changes in mineralization but *no* new minerals are added.

From the above comparison it can be seen that the greatest single difference between the two types of metamorphism is the introduction of new minerals in the contact process. In regard to appearances of rocks changed by these processes, it is not surprising to find that rocks in contact with igneous masses are so completely changed that they seldom resemble the original material. On the other hand, in regional metamorphism, the changes are generally much less pronounced and it is often possible to tell what kind of rock had been there before metamorphic activity started. Geologists found, for example, that certain minerals can form from other minerals only under certain conditions of heat and pressure. Finding such new minerals in metamorphic rocks therefore gives a fairly good idea of the previous composition of the rock.

FIGURE 58. Several common metamorphic rocks. The top-left specimen is a fine grain clay or *argillite slate,* of dark gray color, from Rock Mart, Polk Co., Georgia. The typical tendency to split easily is well known. The top-right specimen is *mica schist* of silvery color and glistening luster from near Woodstock, Vermont. The bottom specimen is *hornblende gneiss* from Jackass Creek Canyon, Madison Co., Montana. The principal light colored mineral is pink feldspar; pale gray quartz is also present. The dark minerals are abundant hornblende and lesser quantities of biotite mica. Specimen sizes average 4 x 3 inches. *Courtesy Smithsonian Institution.*

Special Identification Features of Metamorphic Rocks

Because of twisting, folding, bending and buckling, strongly metamorphosed rocks often show, first, a *distinct graininess* as in igneous rocks,
second, *long thin streaks* of minerals of contrasting color, and third,
foliation or the formation of many thin sheets within the rock which can
be easily split apart. These features show up clearly in several
metamorphic rock specimens shown in Figure 58. In the field, the
surface features of metamorphic rocks are less easy to distinguish from
igneous rocks since in effect, metamorphism tends to make the texture
very much like that noted in igneous rocks. However, some kinds which
are strongly foliated like *schist*, or decidedly streaked and banded like
gneiss, or show recognizable inclusions like the stretched out pebbles in
a conglomerate changed to *quartzite*, are unmistakable.

Metamorphic Rock-Forming Minerals

The characteristic minerals found in metamorphic rocks depend on the
starting materials in the rocks themselves, what minerals were added if
any, and how strong the changes were. Sometimes a single mineral or
several related minerals can only form under metamorphic conditions
and therefore when they are found in a rock whose nature is not surely
known, prove that the rock is indeed metamorphic. As a result of a wide
variety of ingredients which can be tossed into the metamorphic stew
pot, especially in contact metamorphism, it is not unusual to find many
interesting minerals within metamorphic rocks. On the other hand
when some rock such as sandstone which contains nothing else but
quartz is converted into a metamorphic rock, the result is bound to be
very plain fare because quartz merely changes its outward appearance
but not its composition.

The following minerals are typical of rocks which have been subjected
to increasingly severe metamorphism. Note that some minerals present
in one stage disappear in another.

The following minerals are commonly found in small amounts in
many metamorphic rocks: pyrite, pyrrhotite, magnetite, rutile, hematite, sphene, tourmaline. The following are *almost never found except in
metamorphic rocks:* grossular garnet, kyanite, paragonite mica, staurolite, talc, tremolite; this group of minerals should be memorized by
the reader because by recognizing one or more of them in the field one
may be certain that a metamorphic rock is being examined. The

MINERALS TYPICAL OF ROCKS IN VARYING STAGES OF METAMORPHISM

In Weakly Metamorphosed Rocks

Albite Feldspar	Epidote
Serpentine	Spessartine Garnet
Chlorite	Calcite, Dolomite, Magnesite, Siderite
Talc	Anatase, Brookite
Pyrophyllite	Brucite
Tremolite, Actinolite	Muscovite Mica

In Moderately Metamorphosed Rocks

Plagioclase Feldspars	Iolite
Potassium Feldspar	Almandite Garnet
Serpentine	Scapolite
Anthophyllite, Cummingtonite	Calcite, Dolomite
Hornblende	Ilmenite, Corundum, Spinel
Muscovite, Biotite Mica	Forsterite
Epidote	Idocrase
Kyanite, Andalusite, Staurolite	

In Strongly Metamorphosed Rocks

Plagioclase Feldspars	Almandite Garnet
Potassium Feldspars	Scapolite
Wollastonite	Calcite
Pyroxenes, Hornblende	Ilmenite, Corundum, Spinel
Iolite	Forsterite
Andalusite, Fibrolite	

following are especially common in *metamorphosed limestones:* andradite garnet, grossular garnet, corundum, graphite, pyroxenes, spinel, tremolite, wollastonite.

Metamorphic Rocks

Gneisses form from many kinds of rocks, depending on how severely the latter were affected by metamorphism. Offhand, they look like granite and in many cases this resemblance is not accidental because granites are sometimes converted into gneisses. The principal feature of all gneisses is parallel banding with streaked coloration, with or without folds or sharp curves due to buckling. Light colored streaks or bands of feldspar and quartz often alternate with dark streaks of mica or ferromagnesian minerals, as shown in the bottom photo of Figure 58 and in the views of Figure 59. Gneisses are usually very hard and tough, like granites, and almost as useful for constructional purposes, although not nearly so uniform in texture nor as handsome. Moderate metamorphism of granite or rhyolite results in *granite gneiss.* Other granitic rocks form *syenite gneiss, diorite gneiss,* etc. Intense metamorphism of conglomerate, impure sandstone and impure quartzite sometimes results in granite gneisses.

Gneisses are more easily attacked by weathering than granites because the foliations permit water or plant rootlets to enter along many thin

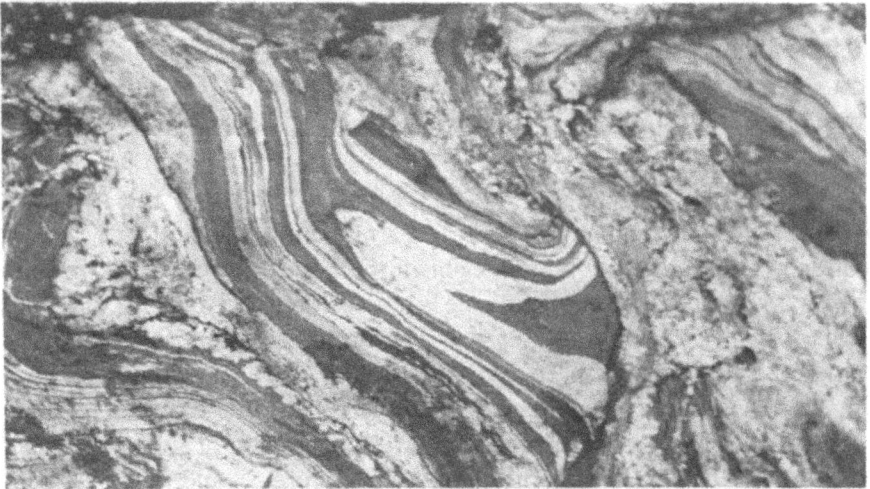

FIGURE 59. Two photographs of banded and folded *gneiss*, the upper being a view in Baltimore gneiss near Gwynns Falls, Baltimore Co., Maryland, and the lower taken near Gibbs Crossing, Hampshire Co., Massachusetts. Both gneisses show how dark ferromagnesian minerals concentrate in some bands and are absent in others, imparting the "zebra stripe" pattern so typical of this type of metamorphic rock. Both views show also the resistance to weathering of gneiss as compared to schist (see Figure 60). *Courtesy U. S. Geological Survey.*

flat crevices. In the field, gneisses can often be recognized by ribbed or ridged outcrops formed by the decay of portions which are less resistant to weathering while areas at the foot of outcrops are often littered by thin slabs of the more resistant material. Gneisses seldom contain anything of interest to collectors except quartz veins which sometimes open into crystal-lined vugs or very rarely contain native gold associated with pyrite. If gneisses are situated near large granite masses, they may be penetrated by pegmatites; any such pegmatites should be carefully examined because they so often contain valuable and interesting minerals.

Schists are similar in appearance to gneisses but the mineral grains are smaller and the rock is much more foliated and hence even more easily split. Mica is very abundant, in fact the most common variety of schist is known as *mica schist* because of the quantity of this mineral usually present. Mica schists often contain almandite garnet crystals, which may be as small as pinheads or as large as baseballs, formed into beautiful crystals or appearing only as rounded masses showing no crystal faces at all. A schist rich in muscovite mica is shown in Figure 58. The principal minerals found in schists are muscovite and biotite mica, quartz,

FIGURE 60. The ragged surface left by weathering and disintegration of schist is well illustrated here. In this view, taken along Kenton Road, Allegheny District, Sierra Co., California, a gentle fold is evident in the schist. Layering is also evident but is far more irregular than that noted in sedimentary rocks. Jagged, angular blocks are characteristic of fractured schist. *Courtesy U. S. Geological Survey.*

feldspar, chlorite and garnet. The presence of some unusually abundant accessory mineral leads to using such names as *tourmaline schist, talc schist, chlorite schist,* etc. Being far more easily decayed than gneisses, schists produce ragged, stained, dark-colored outcrops of very irregular outline surrounded by untidy litters of thin slabs or slivers of partly decomposed schist. Outcrops often sparkle with the reflections from a multitude of small mica flakes released from the rock by its decay. An example of a schist exposure is shown in Figure 60.

Sandstones, conglomerates and other rocks containing a great deal of quartz, change into metamorphic rocks known as *quartzites.* During change all pores are filled with quartz and the rock becomes denser, tougher, and very uniform in texture. Pure types show shining fracture surfaces which pass *through* grains of sand or pebbles instead of going *around* them as would be the case in unmetamorphosed sandstones or conglomerates. Less strongly compacted quartzites are decidedly grainy upon fracture surfaces, as shown in the examples of Figure 61. The conversion of sandstone or conglomerate to quartzite is gradual and it

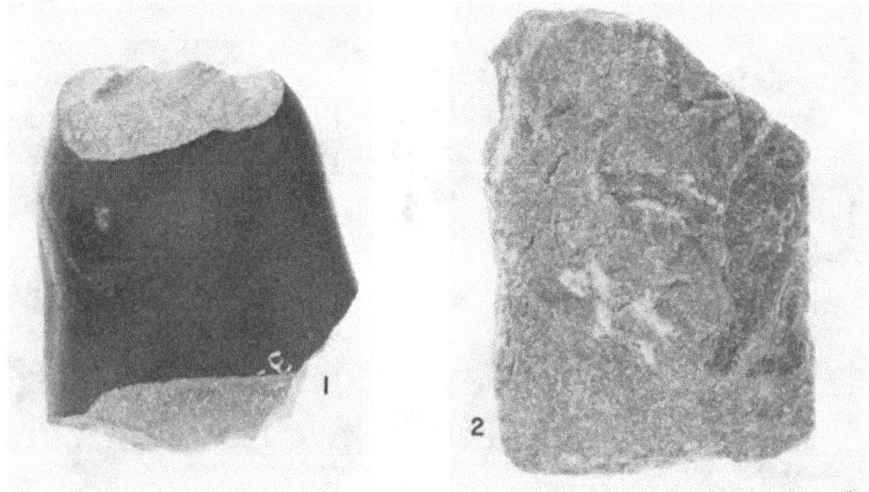

FIGURE 61. Two specimens of *quartzite.* Specimen No. 1 from the Tooele Valley, Utah, shows development of "desert polish" plus impregnation of iron and manganese minerals in the surface layers. Because of the latter, the exterior color is very dark brown while the true color is pale tan. Specimen No. 2 is pink quartzite from near Sioux Falls, South Dakota. Both specimens show graininess attributable to sand grains but luster and conchoidal fracture attributable to firm cementing by additional quartz. Compare with the sandstones illustrated in Figure 47. Specimen size of No. 2 is 5 x 3 inches. *Courtesy Smithsonian Institution.*

isn't always easy to tell which is which; however, if fractures pass through the grains or pebbles, the rock is properly classed as metamorphic rather than sedimentary. Quartzites range from thick dense beds of very pure material to impure beds which easily separate into thin slabs because of layers of inclusions such as mica, tourmaline, etc. Since quartz is extremely durable, quartzites weather very slowly and thus form steep bluffs and outcrops of angular blocks. Quartzite pebbles are very common in gravel beds. Mineralogically, quartzites are practically without interest to the collector.

FIGURE 62. An outcrop of slate near Perma along the Flathead River, Saunders Co., Montana. Of particular interest is the extreme regularity of the blocks of slate, which split along very flat and continuous planes. On the extreme lower left is the talus slope littered with flat slabs of slate. *Courtesy U. S. Geological Survey.*

The conversion of shale into its metamorphic equivalent, *slate*, results in considerable change in properties. Slate splits readily into thin slabs, a property which makes it useful for roofing and pavements. Common colors are gray and red. A slate sample is illustrated in Figure 58. With increase in pressure and heat, shale is converted past the slate stage into a rock known as *phyllite.* It is similar to slate in every way except that it is more easily split. Mica is an abundant and characteristic mineral in phyllite. Various states along the East Coast of the United States produce large quantities of slate, also the Great Lakes region. Slates and phyllites seldom contain anything more interesting to the collector than occasional quartz seams which may or may not contain crystal-lined openings. An outcrop of slate is shown in Figure 62.

The extensive hematite iron ore beds of the Great Lakes region were originally sedimentary but owe their present condition to metamorphic action. The first minerals deposited in the ancient sea floors from which the beds came were iron carbonate and iron silicate. Intense heat and pressure, plus water circulating through the pores of the rock, converted the iron carbonate into iron oxide (hematite) and changed the iron silicate into iron oxide plus silica. This combination formed the variety of quartz known as chalcedony and caused the formation of much jaspery rock known as *jaspilite*. Beds less rich in chalcedony consist of rock known as *taconite*. The removal of silica by the dissolving action of surface waters trickling to lower layers formed the extremely rich hematite ores which for many years provided the mainstay for the great iron-mining industry of Minnesota. Some excellent specimens of iron minerals and attractive ornamental materials have been obtained from these deposits.

From the collector's standpoint, the most important metamorphic rocks are the *marbles*, not the kinds which are found in large beds and used for buildings and monuments, but the marbles which occur next to igneous intrusions and formed from impure limestones. All marbles are usually uniform in texture, generally white or some other very pale color, and show no tendency to split in any particular direction. A typical marble specimen is shown in Figure 52. The grain size varies from fine to coarse. Some fracture surfaces are like broken lump sugar while others show single grains as much as an inch or more across. In general the fine-grained types are much preferred by quarrymen but it is the coarse-grained types which are most likely to contain good mineral crystals. Although marbles are abundant throughout the world, very few are good enough in quality to be quarried. Most marbles show numerous disfiguring streaks or are spotted with minerals which make them difficult to cut and polish.

Extensive marble deposits are worked in Vermont, Georgia, Massachusetts and elsewhere in the United States but few are worth examining by the collector for the reason that only the purest kinds are selected for quarrying. However, some deposits like those at Sparta, New Jersey, and at Riverside, California, are quarried for industrial applications and are noted among mineralogists for the wide variety of beautiful and interesting minerals found in them. The world-famous zinc deposits in New Jersey also occur in marble but the peculiar minerals found in these deposits were introduced and not part of the marble itself. In this and in similar deposits throughout the world, important ores and minerals yielding fine specimens find homes in marble in preference to other kinds of rocks. Although the special features of mineral deposits in limestones and marbles will be taken up in the next chapter, it is worthwhile saying now that all marble outcrops should be closely examined along their contacts with other kinds of rock in the hope that sources of minerals may be discovered. Contacts with igneous rocks should be looked for especially.

Another important metamorphic rock is *serpentine* in which the most prominent mineral is serpentine itself, and in some cases, huge masses of this rock consist of practically nothing else but serpentine. However, many serpentines also contain interesting accessory minerals in small to large amounts such as: hornblende, pyroxene, olivine, magnetite, and chromite. Chromite deposits in serpentine frequently provide a wide variety of other minerals including nickel minerals and the beautiful green garnet *uvarovite*. In commerce, serpentine is much used as an ornamental stone while the translucent and bright green variety known as *williamsite* is prized by gem cutters. Serpentines are abundant in the eastern half of North America, in northern California, and in Oregon. In places, important ores of chromium, asbestos, nickel and platinum are found in them.

Contact Metamorphic Rocks

Rocks intruded by igneous masses are often baked along the contacts to such an extent that for some distance around them the country rock is converted into *hornfels*. This type of metamorphic rock results almost entirely because of heat with very little chemical change taking place. However, some new minerals form and when some species is particularly abundant in the hornfels the rock is called *pyroxene hornfels, calc-silicate hornfels*, etc. Almost every igneous intrusion forms a hornfels envelope but its thickness can be as small as one inch or as large as a number of feet. The development of hornfels is most pronounced in shales, slates, impure limestones, and impure sandstones. A hornfels border in sandstone can be seen in the contact of sandstone to syenite in Figure 63. Changes due solely to heat are much less pronounced in granites, gneisses and similar rocks which were very hot themselves at one time.

The introduction of large amounts of mineral matter from igneous masses by means of escaping gases and solutions does much more than heat and pressure alone. The final changes depend most on the kind of rock being invaded, and, as remarked before, limestones are most easily

FIGURE 63. Intrusion of syenite into sedimentary rock near the Diamond Joe Quarry, Hot Springs Co., Arkansas. The syenite, light in color and fracturing in similar fashion to granite, is at the lower left while the sedimentary rock is at the upper right. Note that the latter is rudely stratified while the syenite shows no trace of stratification, as can be expected from its molten origin. The sedimentary rock shows evidence of baking, particularly in the band next to the syenite. In some similar situations, baking or *induration*, progresses so far that the intruded rock changes into jaspery material. *Courtesy U. S. Geological Survey.*

affected. Whenever limestones, or marbles, are involved, a special name, *skarn*, is applied to the zone next to the contacts in which a bewildering variety of new minerals may be found. Skarn minerals are most often silicates of iron, magnesium, and calcium, with the silica and iron coming from the igneous mass and the magnesium and calcium coming from the limestone or marble. Skarn minerals always appear close to contacts with igneous rocks and may be detected in outcrops by their tendency to weather less rapidly than the marble enclosing them. Outcrops often look warty or knobby because of this feature.

FIELD RECOGNITION FEATURES SUMMARIZED

Many rocks form such distinctive outcrops that it pays the collector or prospector to become familiar with their appearances. Some features are prominent even from a distance, for example, steep bluffs of light-colored sandstone, or conversely, of *dark* basalt, etc., but other features cannot be recognized except close at hand. The following table summarizes the features which are most distinctive and which can help out during field trips.

SUMMARY OF FIELD RECOGNITION FEATURES OF IMPORTANT ROCKS

Name	Distant Features	Close Features
	IGNEOUS CLASS	
Obsidian	Flattened flows with contorted surfaces.	Powdery white weathering surfaces; breaks like glass, splintery; spherical inclusions; commonly black.
Felsites	Flows common; rounded, bouldery or jagged outcrops; rusty color to almost white.	Extremely fine texture; even, dull fracture surfaces; porous; pale colors very common; phenocrysts.
Andesites	As above.	As above but darker colors and phenocrysts common.
Basalts	Sheetlike flows and dikes; perpendicular cliffs; "postpile" columns; also "pillow basalt" structure.	Weathered surfaces dark brown, gritty; dark interior colors; very fine grain; amygdaloidal.
Diabase	As above but columns less perfect or absent.	Coarser than basalt; lathlike crystals visible; more likely to contain fissure cavities than amygdaloids.

Porphyries	Like felsites.	Phenocrysts in felsitic ground-mass.
Granite Syenite Granodiorite Monzonite	Steep cliffs, rounded tops; domes; bouldery outcrops; right angle jointing; light color.	Generally light in color; "pepper and salt" patterns; uniform granular textures.
Granite- Pegmatite	White streaks on hills and mountains; upraised ribs of white rock.	Same minerals as granite but much larger grains; long black crystals of tourmaline often present, also mica books.
Diorite Gabbro	Similar to granite but outcrops often severely weathered; rounded brushy hills and knobs.	Generally dark color; uniform granular textures; often deeply weathered and crumbly; dark ferromagnesian minerals; many fine parallel striations on feldspar grains.
Anorthosite	As above but more resistant to weathering.	Coarser grain; blue reflections from feldspar; many fine parallel striations.
Peridotites Dunite Kimberlite	Rocky outcrops uncommon; rounded hills sparsely vegetated.	Glassy lustrous olivine grains; crumbly; outcrops often covered with blue-gray soil (kimberlite); gemmy grains of pyrope, enstatite and peridot.

Sedimentary Class

Conglomerates	Steep bluffs; much pebbly litter at bases.	Pebbles cemented together.
Sandstones	Often steep spectacular undercut cliffs; also buttressed mesas; parallel layering.	Sandy texture; herringbone banding within strata; evidence of water origin; petrified wood.
Shales Claystones Siltstones Argillite	Rounded or sloped terraces and benches; perfect parallel layering; gray color common.	Soft and clayey; shells, wood, fossils; gypsum, calcite, barite geodes; also quartz geodes; pyrite; marcasite balls.
Limestones	Perpendicular cliffs; sharp flat tops; perfect parallel layering; spectacular jagged mountain crests at higher elevations.	Whitish coatings but often gray to almost black interiors; fossils etched in relief; strata etched in relief; deep smooth sided fissures in moist climates fine to coarse grain; latter resemble marble; soft.
Tufa Travertine Onyx	Terraces; low flattened cones; ragged surfaces, often bare.	Crude onion-like layering in tufa and travertine, also many holes; onyx smooth texture, translucent, colored and banded; soft.

Chert	Steep low cliffs; sharp jagged blocks; fresh-looking; bedding not very distinct.	Conchoidal lusterless fractures; translucent thin edges; light colors; hard.
Gypsum Rock Salt	Strata severely rounded or undercut in bluffs; light color; efflorescence; plant life sparse or absent.	Irregular corroded weathering; fingernail scratches both minerals; gypsum crystals transparent, can be easily bent; salty taste of halite.
Coal Lignite	Dark bands or streaks in sandstone bluffs or terraces.	Black soils; pieces of coal; woody remains in lignite, also pyrite, marcasite masses, amber, jet.

METAMORPHIC CLASS

Gneiss	Like granite but shows some layering; more jagged outcrops.	Like granite but banding evident.
Schist	Ragged dark outcrops; layering often prominent and often uptilted.	Abundant mica, garnet; easily split; soft.
Serpentine	Outcrops often rounded, covered with sparse scraggly vegetation and grass.	Dusty light green coatings on weathered surfaces; jagged fracture surfaces; greasy luster, translucent on thin edges.
Taconite Jaspilite	Low terrain; not distinctive.	Hard; splintery to blocky when broken; gray-black steely hematite bands; brecciated; dull to bright red colors; heavy.
Quartzite	Steep bluffs; sharp squarish blocks; light color.	Glassy to granular quartz; pebbles broken through; hard; tough; sometimes slabby with mica on faces.
Slate Phyllite	Prominent hills, ridges, low cliffs with littered slopes; dark color.	Slabby fragments; perfectly parallel surfaces; silvery specks of mica; extremely fine grain; soft.
Marble	Rounded knobby vegetated hills; round boulders; dazzling white color.	Badly etched on weathered surfaces; uniform granular texture; bright twinkling fracture surfaces; knife scratches readily.
Hornfels	Not distinctive.	Baked clay appearance; jaspery texture and fracture.
Skarn	Gnarled pockety outcrops; light color.	Silicate minerals raised in high relief; coarse grain; cleavage surfaces broad and distinct.

4

How Mineral Deposits Form

Once the collector gains some knowledge of rocks, he is in a much better position to search for the mineral deposits which his neighborhood may contain. Faced with the problem of where to begin, he may well decide as some experienced prospectors do, that the best course of action is to get a geologic map of the area, and simply begin covering the ground in a systematic fashion. This is not a bad idea at all, if one has lots of time, but what if a mineral deposit is stumbled over? Would it be possible to recognize that it is something worth looking into? Unfortunately, most mineral deposits do not advertise themselves except by very small signs which take a keen eye to discern. Even these small signs are apt to be meaningless unless the hunter of minerals can fit them into a pattern which makes sense. But before he can do this, he must know what the pattern should be for the *kind* of deposit he is looking for, and this in turn means that he must also know the various kinds of mineral deposits before he can interpret the surface signs correctly.

From the geologist's viewpoint, there are many kinds of mineral deposits, but from the viewpoint of the collector of minerals and gemstones, there are really only a small number he could be interested in. It is the purpose of this chapter to show how the mineral deposits of interest to the collector were formed while the chapter which follows describes how they can be recognized in the field during collecting trips.

MINERALS CONCENTRATED IN MOLTEN ROCKS

Vast pools of molten rock far below the surface of the earth contain all of the elements which go to make up the rocks of the crust. This means that somewhere during the process of cooling, some of the elements join together to form one kind of mineral, then another, and still another, until all of the mineral matter is used up. Finally when the entire mass has cooled enough, it freezes into the solid rock with which we are all familiar. As pointed out in the previous chapter, if all the mass cooled quickly, the individual mineral grains would be small and the rock uniform in texture. However, we do know that this doesn't always happen and that somewhere in the underground pools certain minerals seem to collect in enough quantity to form rocks which are composed of virtually one mineral. This is the case with the anorthosite of Labrador which furnishes the beautiful specimens of labradorite so prized by collectors. Anorthosite is practically pure labradorite feldspar but it is puzzling to explain why it should be so pure and not mixed with other minerals such as one would expect to find in an ordinary igneous rock mass.

This problem concerned geologists for many years but after much study and looking for proof of theories in the rocks themselves, most geologists arrived at the conclusion that such concentrations come about through a process called *magmatic concentration*. These rather awe-inspiring words mean simply that certain minerals tend to collect in favored places in the subterranean pool of molten rock called the *magma*, and it is from the latter term that the process gets its name. Here is how the process works.

The first step takes place within the molten rock of the magma just as it is beginning to cool. As the thick mushy fluid slowly cools, a point is reached where the first mineral crystals start growing. Almost immediately they begin to rise or sink depending on how heavy they are compared to the remaining molten rock. Generally speaking, the dark ferromagnesian minerals such as hornblende and pyroxene are first to separate. If the cooling is slow enough, crystals of these minerals will drift slowly toward the bottom of the magma, forming layers which are composed of one mineral with some liquid material between the grains. If for some reason the magma is disturbed or squeezed, the concentrated portions could be squirted into cracks or rents in solidified rock along the edges of the magma. This is one way in which small igneous masses composed of practically nothing but one mineral are formed. This process is illustrated by a series of drawings in Figure 64.

While the heavier minerals are settling out of the magma, the temperature keeps dropping and other minerals crystallize. At about this stage very little uncombined material is left, in fact, the entire mass is now so stiff that it is no longer a liquid but rather a jumble of crystals

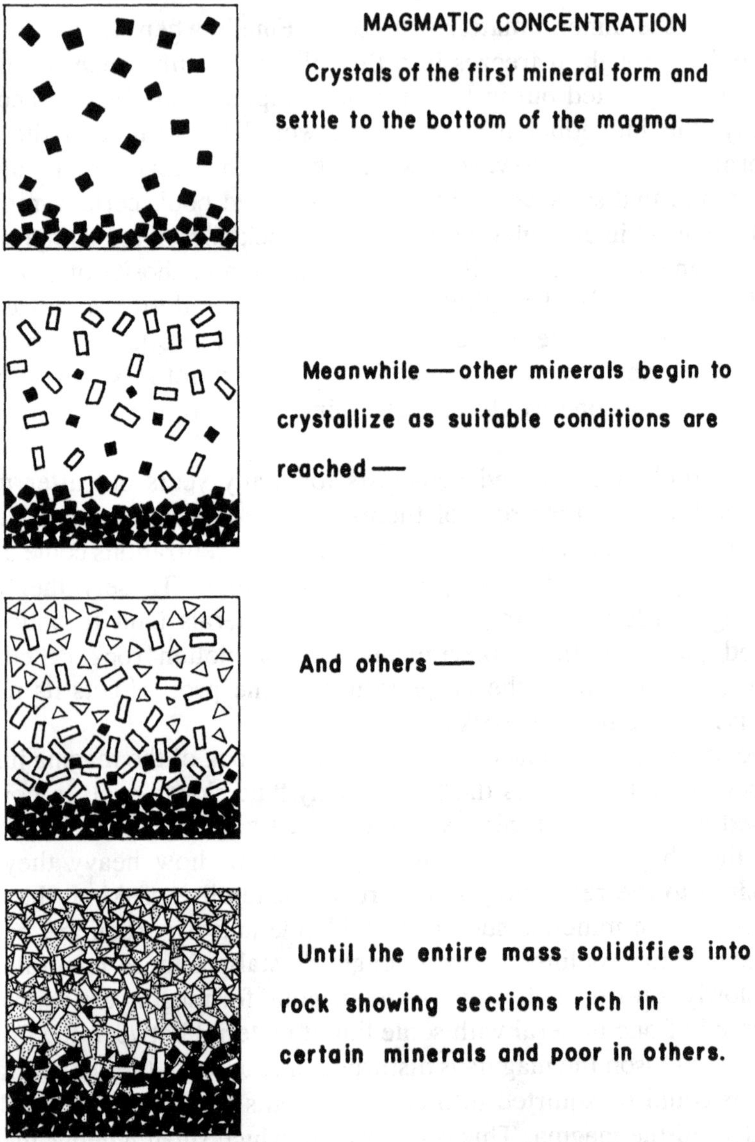

MAGMATIC CONCENTRATION

Crystals of the first mineral form and settle to the bottom of the magma —

Meanwhile — other minerals begin to crystallize as suitable conditions are reached —

And others —

Until the entire mass solidifies into rock showing sections rich in certain minerals and poor in others.

FIGURE 64. Schematic representation of magmatic concentration. Crystals forming at different times result in rocks of widely differing composition, although the original ingredients came from the same parent magma.

with some liquid left between them. However, by now this last bit of liquid becomes most important because in addition to some of the common silicate minerals of igneous rock, it also carries the very rare elements of the earth's crust which altogether comprise less than one percent of the total! Such scarce metals as beryllium, niobium, tantalum, thorium, tungsten and uranium are all concentrated in this precious remainder. This liquid, however, does not consist of molten metals by any means, but rather a mixture of the rare elements plus common silicates, plus superheated water. In many cases this fluid portion finds its way upward into fissures in overlying rock formations and thus forms a number of important mineral deposits.

There are several distinct types of fissure fillings, depending on the nature of the filling material. For example, if the material forced upward is mostly a mixture of silicates, the result is likely to be a deposit known as a *pegmatite* in which the principal minerals are the same as those found in common granite, namely feldspar, quartz and mica. If the material is mainly hot water carrying dissolved mineral matter, the deposit may be an ore vein containing metallic sulfides. Lastly, if the escaping matter is carried upward by vapors, the deposit may contain oxides of metals plus a variety of other minerals and it is likely that all of the fissure space may not be filled up completely.

Considering the kinds of deposits that can be formed from magmas, including those from the concentrated parts which escape from them, it can be seen why geologists say that almost all of our metals, except for iron, aluminum and magnesium, come from magmas. Even those veins which seem to have no direct connection to igneous masses are now believed to be derived from them although the sources may be buried far below and covered completely by overlying formations.

PEGMATITES

Now that pegmatites have been mentioned a number of times and the reader put off with several "wait until laters," it seems a good time to say something about them since they are one of the special kinds of deposits stemming from magmas. Pegmatites have often been called "giant granites" because the abundant minerals in them are exactly the same as those in granite except that each of the mineral grains is tremendously larger. As to the name *pegmatite*, it comes from the Greek *pegma*, meaning "joined together" in allusion to the fact that in such deposits, quartz and feldspar often form curious intertwined crystals known as *graphic granite*. A specimen broken across to show the pattern is illustrated in Figure 39, a polished specimen is shown in Figure 88.

Pegmatites are the principal source of feldspar used in pottery and abrasives, and of the sheet mica used in electronic equipment and for which there is no good substitute. Because of these two minerals principally, pegmatites all over the world have been prospected and mined for hundreds of years. In the early history of pegmatite mining, it was soon discovered that these deposits often contained rare and valuable minerals, some of which provided the only ores for niobium and tantalum (from the mineral columbite-tantalite), lithium (from lepidolite mica and amblygonite), and many splendid gemstones. Among the latter may be mentioned tourmaline, beryl (aquamarine, golden beryl and morganite), quartz in several varieties, spodumene, brazilianite, and a number of others. Quite aside from the commercially valuable minerals, pegmatites also contain rare minerals of interest to the collector, not to mention the beautiful perfect crystals of both rare and common minerals found in open cavities.

Not all pegmatites are favored with valuable minerals unfortunately; as a matter of fact, very few contain more than the standard feldspar, quartz and mica with perhaps small quantities of black tourmaline, garnet and beryl. While pegmatites of this type furnish excellent feldspar and mica when the deposits are large enough to be worth mining, they rarely attract much attention otherwise. Because of the few mineral species found in them, pegmatites of this type are called *simple pegmatites*. However, when a large variety of minerals is present, they are called *complex*, not so much because of the number of mineral species but because they formed in several distinct stages of mineralization, each of which provided possibilities for a greater variety of minerals to form. In complex pegmatites, as many as three or four stages occurred, and it is often possible for a skilled and observant collector to tell where each began and left off because of the changes in the mineralization. Many geologists believe that the first stage formed mostly feldspar, quartz and mica, from a concentrated thick fluid which cooled and crystallized into a simple pegmatite. However, if additional hot water solutions worked their way into the pegmatite, further changes took place depending on the temperature and pressure and what additional elements were introduced by the solutions. Water in itself is very effective in attacking minerals if it is working under high enough pressures and temperatures, as shown by quartz crystal growing experiments carried on in the past twenty years. Thus in complex pegmatites, not only did each separate stage bring in new minerals, but the hot water solutions also dissolved some which were already present and put their elements back into the water to recombine with others. Needless to say, the possible combinations are large in number and it is this which makes pegmatite minerals fascinating to the professional as well as to the amateur mineralogist.

Zones in Pegmatites

Because pegmatite material was produced in stages of mineralization, one of the distinctive features of the interior is *zoning*, or the arrangement of minerals in bands or layers corresponding to each wave. It is somewhat like the rings in a tree but far less regular, depending on the shape of the pegmatite itself. Simple pegmatites may have one or two zones while complex pegmatites may have as many as three or four. Zones are important to the miner or collector because of the tendency of certain minerals to appear in some zones and not in others. For example, in deposits containing commercial mica, only one zone contains the good mica usually, and it would be a waste of time to dig in other parts of the pegmatite when it isn't likely that mica will be there.

Since pegmatites were squeezed into cracks or fissures in colder surrounding rocks, a definite zone of small crystal grains is found next to the walls of the contact, their small size being due to quick chilling. This narrow zone is sometimes only a fraction of an inch in thickness but it may also be as much as several inches thick. It passes completely around the pegmatite like an envelope. Just beyond this band, toward the middle of the pegmatite, feldspar and mica occur as large crystals because of less rapid cooling. Sometimes this zone contains slender crystals of black tourmaline, garnet, and prisms of beryl in addition to the common minerals just mentioned. Still farther toward the center, all crystals are much larger in size with feldspar crystals sometimes reaching diameters of several feet. The final zone, and usually the smallest, is in the center and is called the *core*. In most pegmatites it is ordinary milky to gray quartz but may sometimes be smoky or rose in color. The quartz core ordinarily fills up whatever space was left after the feldspar crystals on either side of the pegmatite finished forming.

To the mineral and gemstone collector, the core is the most interesting part of the pegmatite because it is next to the core that openings or "pockets" containing fine crystals are most likely to be. A core and pockets along its edges is shown in the lower diagram of Figure 65. In some pegmatites quartz cores are single pods or lenses of solid

SIMPLE PEGMATITE

TOP VIEW OF OUTCROP SHOWING THIN
BORDER ZONE, A THICK WALL ZONE OF
FELDSPAR, AND A MASSIVE QUARTZ CORE.

CORE
WALL ZONE
BORDER ZONE

COUNTRY ROCK

COMPLEX PEGMATITE

TOP VIEW SHOWING A THIN BORDER ZONE
OF FINE-GRAINED FELDSPAR & QUARTZ, A
WALL ZONE ALSO OF FELDSPAR & QUARTZ,
AND SEVERAL INTERMEDIATE ZONES. THE
QUARTZ CORE CONTAINS POCKETS LINED WITH
CRYSTALS.

POCKETS IN CORE
INTERMEDIATE ZONES
WALL ZONE
BORDER ZONE

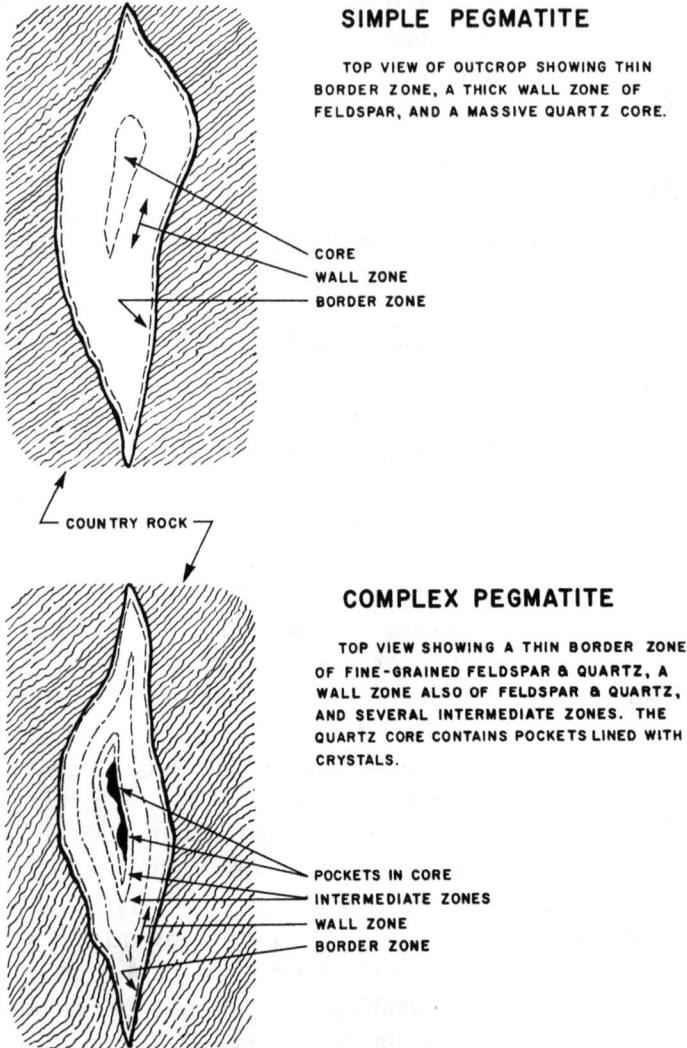

FIGURE 65. Schematic representations of simple and complex pegmatites. Zones are indicated by dashed lines, each zone representing a decided change in the character of mineralization.

quartz, but in others they may be long, drawn-out thin sheetlike masses or even consist of several thin cores strung out like pancakes with their edges touching. In simple pegmatites, beryl crystals often grow past the feldspar zones with tips extending into the quartz. As the crystals cross the boundary they frequently become clearer, show sharper and smoother faces, and sometimes contain good gem material.

The Shape of Pegmatites

Pegmatite deposits are often called *dikes* because so many are long and thin and also outcrop nearly vertically. Others are almost horizontal and are the then properly called *sills*. Still others may be cylindrical and called *pipes*, or shaped like *pods*, *lenses*, or split into *branches*. The shapes of pegmatites are limitless but as a general rule, the most common form is that of a thin sheetlike body. A number of typical pegmatite outcrops are shown in Figure 66, while the photograph in Figure 67 shows several small pegmatites exposed during erosion of the enclosing rock. Pegmatites range in length from several feet to thousands

PEGMATITE OUTCROP FORMS

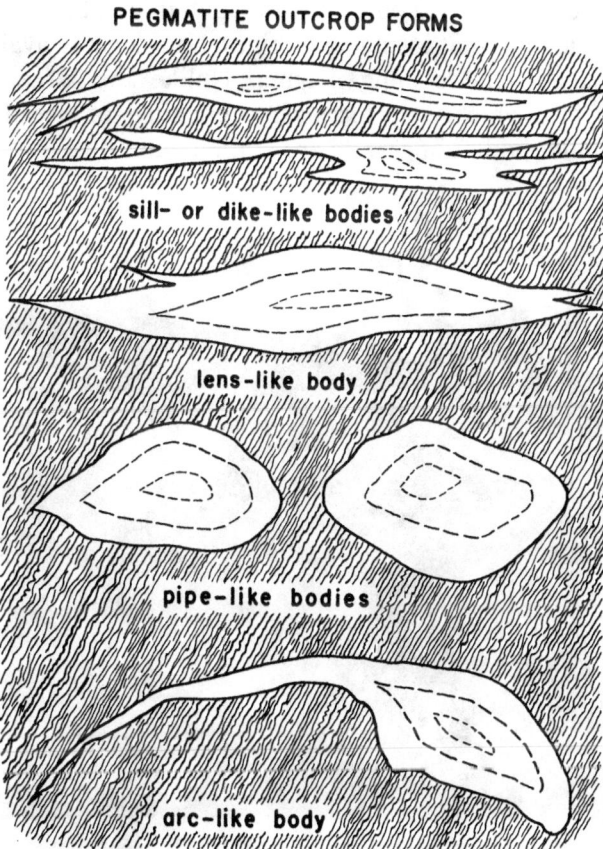

FIGURE 66. Pegmatites take many forms, some of the more common being shown here. In many cases, material is squeezed into country rock along weaknesses or planes of easy separation, as between layers or along faults or fissures. Zones are indicated by dashed lines.

of feet and in thickness from several inches to hundreds of feet. Not very much is known as to how deep they go, but those which have been dug up completely seldom go deeper than several hundred feet.

The pegmatites just described are the kinds most frequently found *around* the edges of large granite masses; however, a special type generally much smaller in size is common *within* granites and because the latter type is noted for pockets filled with splendid crystals of great interest to the collector, it will be described here.

Gas Cavity Pegmatites

Pegmatites formed within granite surround small openings believed to be gas pockets originally. Some granites contain great numbers of such openings, indicating that insufficient mineral matter was available to fill all the spaces in the cooling magma. Unlike the large pegmatites described before which were forced into openings in already solidified rock, the smaller bodies of granite are nothing more than coarse-grained

FIGURE 67. Pegmatite sills (horizontal white streaks) in dark diorite rock, with eroded fragments from another pegmatite body farther up the slope littering the foreground area. On the road from El Condor to Gavilanes, Baja California.

material surrounding the gas cavities. Wherever such openings occur, the minerals around the cavity have space in which to grow to perfection and it is such crystal terminations pointing into the pocket that the collector searches for.

Zoning along the edges of such cavities is very simple. There are no very fine-grained bands because there has been no rapid chilling. Actually all that happened in the formation of such pegmatites is that the normal size grains in the granite merely grew larger toward the gas pocket and reached their greatest size in the openings. In regard to minerals, the most common are again those most abundant in the granite itself, that is, feldspar and quartz. There is little doubt that the finest feldspar crystals occur in such deposits, especially crystals of the bright green microcline feldspar known as *amazonite*. Other minerals also of great interest are topaz and beryl, sometimes beautifully formed in crystals and of gem quality. In regard to size, openings are usually only several inches across but may be as much as a foot in diameter. A sketch of a typical pocket is shown in Figure 87. Gas cavity pegmatites are abundant in the red granite of the Llano Uplift of central Texas where fine topaz crystals have been found (see Figure 113), in red Conway granite in New Hampshire, also productive of topaz, and in the red Pikes Peak granite of Colorado noted principally for amazonite and smoky quartz specimens. It is remarkable that the granite most likely to contain gas pockets is much coarser in grain than most granites, and is also pink or red because of the presence of similarly colored feldspar.

Collectors in position to look for pegmatites are urged to examine them closely, bearing in mind the remarks made in this section and in the next chapter. Zoning features should be carefully examined because in outcrops they can point the way to the small core areas which are most likely to contain minerals of interest. Because some pegmatites stretch out for many hundreds of feet and are often partially covered by topsoil and brush, it pays to look for zoning features just to avoid a lot of needless digging or blasting in the wrong places in the outcrop.

DEPOSITS FROM GASES

From the day that the first geologist examined the gas vents, or *fumaroles*, of a volcanic region, it became apparent that hot gases and vapors escaping from below could carry surprising amounts of mineral matter. No doubt he saw that the throats of the vents were lined and sometimes almost clogged by growths of various minerals, in many cases the easily recognized bright yellow mineral *sulfur*. Today geologists believe that similar gases and vapors issuing from large masses or magmas of igneous rock far below the surface of the earth are largely responsible for the formation of the important ore bodies which surround them, or which are sometimes deposited many thousands of feet away. The process has been briefly mentioned in a previous section of this chapter.

Although gases cannot carry as much mineral matter as hot water solutions, they can deliver a great deal of heat into surrounding rocks, and, as we know, chemical reactions are speeded up when the temperature is raised. In respect to *how much* mineral matter can be brought into surrounding rocks, it is only a question of how long gases continue to escape into them. In many volcanic regions where fumaroles are active, gases have been escaping for centuries and do not look as if they mean to stop soon. It is obvious that over long periods of time, enormous quantities of heat, water, *and* mineral matter can be transferred.

In any event, escaping mineralized gases provide all the conditions needed for speedy chemical reactions and the formation of mineral deposits, that is, they bring in heat, raise the temperature and pressure, furnish water in the form of vapor, and supply mineral matter which is much different in nature from that already present. As the rocks are invaded by the hot gases, chemical reactions begin and accelerate as the temperature and pressure rise. More and more rock is changed as the minerals which are most easily affected give way. In their place grow new minerals which find the changed conditions to their liking. The rare elements previously trapped in the pores of the magma are now brought in, and having a place to crystallize and grow, fill the spaces left behind by the departure of easily destroyed minerals. As new elements come in, reactions take place between them and some of the elements which happened to be present in the surrounding rocks, thus creating still more new minerals until the entire zone around the igneous body becomes a hodge-podge of minerals found neither in the igneous rocks nor in the rocks next to them. This reaction around the boundaries is shown in the diagram of Figure 68. Mineralization is not always restricted to the exact edge of the igneous mass by any means; if fissures lead away from the igneous rock, they too can be filled with new minerals to distances of thousands of feet.

The exchange of new minerals for old in the contact zone next to an igneous body is largely carried on by the process of *metasomatic replacement* described in the previous chapter, that is, a particle of an existing mineral is dissolved and replaced by a particle of a new mineral. The process goes on as long as the proper conditions are present. Because this process is so pronounced along the edges of igneous bodies, it is called *contact metasomatism.* The effects of this activity are strongest in limestones and dolomites but much less in other sedimentary rocks. Almost no changes are brought about in igneous or metamorphic rocks. In limestones and dolomites, calcite and dolomite

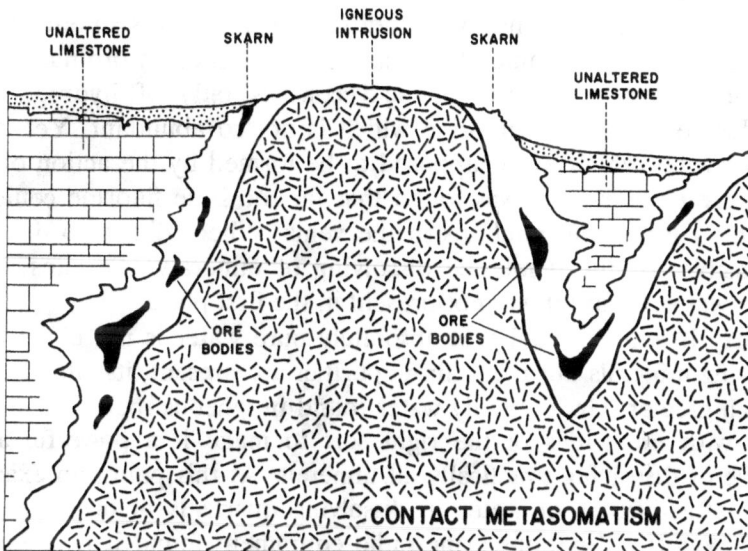

FIGURE 68. In this illustration, effusions from the igneous intrusion drastically altered the original limestone and formed a sheath of skarn rock surrounding the igneous mass. Small ore bodies composed primarily of various metallic sulfides formed within the sheath. Because of widely differing resistance of skarn minerals to weathering, outcrop surfaces are likely to be rough-textured.

are very easily affected and dissolve or decompose to make room for the new minerals in the *skarn* zone. Within the skarn may be small scattered metallic ore bodies, seldom farther than several hundred feet away from the contacts. Ores of copper, zinc, lead, tin and tungsten are common, while openings in fissures frequently furnish fine mineral specimens. The following metallic minerals are typical of metasomatic deposits: hematite, magnetite, ilmenite, cassiterite, pyrite, pyrrhotite, bornite, chalcopyrite, arsenopyrite, sphalerite, galena, molybdenite, scheelite, and wolframite. Common nonmetallic minerals include: corundum, spinel, fluorite, andradite garnet, grossular garnet, chondrodite, phlogopite mica, axinite, ilmenite, tourmaline and topaz.

DEPOSITS FROM HOT WATER

It is hard for us to believe that water, just ordinary water, can be the most powerful agent known in dissolving minerals. An older generation of geologists and mineralogists found it hard to believe too because they kept looking for mysterious "acids" which must have been responsible for dissolving large quantities of quartz and other minerals which appear so durable on the surface of the earth. One of their favorite suspects was hydrofluoric acid, a manufactured acid which is used a great deal in the glass and metal industries because it is so effective in dissolving metals and minerals which are not touched by ordinary acids. As a compound, hydrofluoric acid consists only of hydrogen, an abundant element, and fluorine which is not so abundant. Yet when mineral veins which were supposed to be formed by the action of this acid were examined, it was found that far too little fluorine could be accounted for in the minerals in the veins. Where did it go if it was responsible for the wholesale dissolving of minerals? The answer of course was obvious: it was not present in the first place.

Today it is recognized that absolutely pure water is not effective in dissolving minerals but if certain impurities are present, its effectiveness is much greater. Undoubtedly water found in igneous rocks is contaminated with impurities of the right sort to make it a powerful agent capable of dissolving practically all minerals. At this point, an example of the effectiveness of water in dissolving quartz is in order. During World War II, all nations using radio equipment found it necessary to obtain supplies of quartz crystals which had the property of keeping radio sets operating on exactly the right frequency. Most quartz was obtained from Brazil, and very little good material was found in North America. Accordingly a crash program was started to grow quartz from hot water solutions, using a "bomb" to hold the solution and to withstand the enormous pressures which were developed inside. Techniques were worked out successfully and it was found that quartz crystals several inches across could be grown in several months. The pressures and temperatures used could easily exist underground and it is not hard to imagine that under such conditions, water is indeed effective in dissolving minerals and depositing them elsewhere.

The action of hot water in dissolving and depositing minerals is called the *hydrothermal* process, "hydro" meaning water and "thermal" meaning at high temperature. Since a great deal of water is present in all igneous rocks, particularly in molten masses, it is extremely effective because it is both hot and working under high pressure. Much water escapes in the form of vapor and thus contributes to the speedy action noted in contact metasomatism in the section before, but a great deal begins very hot at great depths and gradually cools as it works its way upward toward the surface of the earth. As it cools, some minerals can no longer stay in solution and deposit along the way, but others remain until the temperature drops too much and they too must crystallize along the sides of the fissures through which the solutions are traveling. Eventually the entire fissure system is lined with minerals from bottom to top, starting with those which can exist even when the water is hot and finishing with those which crystallize from cool water.

Although there are all kinds of minerals in long fissures, reflecting the differences in temperature of the water which brought them up, some are characteristic of hot temperatures, some of medium temperatures, and some of low temperatures. A skilled geologist can tell from the minerals found in an ore vein just what the temperatures must have been to make it possible for those minerals to form. Not all minerals show the same degree of solubility in water however, and some species are therefore found in all sections of the vein because they can stay in solution at all temperatures. Many metallic ore minerals are found almost exclusively in hydrothermal veins along with the common minerals known as *gangue*. The following table lists some of the ores and common gangue minerals. The table is arranged according to the temperature of formation.

COMMON HYDROTHERMAL MINERALS

Ore Minerals	Gangue Minerals
HIGH TEMPERATURE	
Gold	Quartz (very common)
Cassiterite	Epidote
Molybdenite	Mica
Scheelite	Garnet
Wolframite	Topaz
Magnetite	Tourmaline
MEDIUM TEMPERATURE	
Gold	Quartz
Galena	Calcite
Sphalerite	Dolomite
Pyrite	Siderite
Chalcopyrite	Barite
Bornite	Rhodochrosite
Arsenopyrite	
Tetrahedrite	
Enargite	

Table cont'd. on next page.

COMMON HYDROTHERMAL MINERALS (*Continued*)

Ore Minerals	*Gangue Minerals*
	LOW TEMPERATURE
Pyrite	Quartz (often as chalcedony)
Marcasite	Calcite
Stibnite	Dolomite
Cinnabar	Aragonite
Native Silver	Adularia
Silver Sulfides	Opal
	Fluorite
	Zeolites (rare)

Hydrothermal Vein Deposits

Veins formed through hydrothermal processes often contain characteristic minerals in association. Knowing some of these associations is helpful in prospecting because of the possibility that valuable ores of gold or silver may be found in such veins, even though neither of these metals may be obvious in the outcrops.

GOLD QUARTZ VEINS. Native gold is found mainly in veins which consist almost entirely of milky massive "bull" quartz. A few sulfide minerals such as pyrite, chalopyrite and arsenopyrite are usually present in small quantities. The association of sulfides is so frequent that any quartz veins showing "rusty" outcrop coatings should be examined for gold, the "rust" coming from the weathering of pyrite.

GOLD AND SILVER IN COPPER VEINS. Small quantities of gold and silver are often found with veins carrying copper sulfides such as chalcopyrite, tetrahedrite, bornite, chalcocite, and also pyrite and some uncommon silver minerals.

SILVER IN LEAD VEINS. Practically all galena, the most common ore of lead, contains some silver, in some cases so much so that the silver brings in more money than the lead. Common associated minerals are sphalerite, pyrite, tetrahedrite, argentite, calcite, dolomite, rhodochrosite.

LEAD-ZINC VEINS. Lead and zinc minerals are very commonly found together in veins, especially in limestone beds. The principal minerals are galena, sphalerite, marcasite, chalcopyrite, dolomite, calcite.

COPPER-IRON VEINS. Although seldom used for ore, deposits of pyrite often contain the copper minerals chalcopyrite, chalcocite, bornite and tetrahedrite.

General Features of Hydrothermal Deposits

Hydrothermal solutions are under much pressure and easily force their way into an amazing variety of openings in rock, from pores too small to see to large openings such as fissures. The following are some kinds of openings and cavities in which deposits formed from hot water solutions may be found: pores between grains in rock, gas cavities in volcanic rocks, especially in basalt, shrinkage cracks caused by cooling of rocks, bedding planes in sedimentary rocks where thin openings may be found between the strata, and a large variety of openings in rocks brought about by such causes as bending, folding and buckling. Important ore deposits are sometimes found in the broken rocky rubble found along faults or within the throats of volcanoes. Two typical hydrothermal deposits are diagrammed in Figure 69.

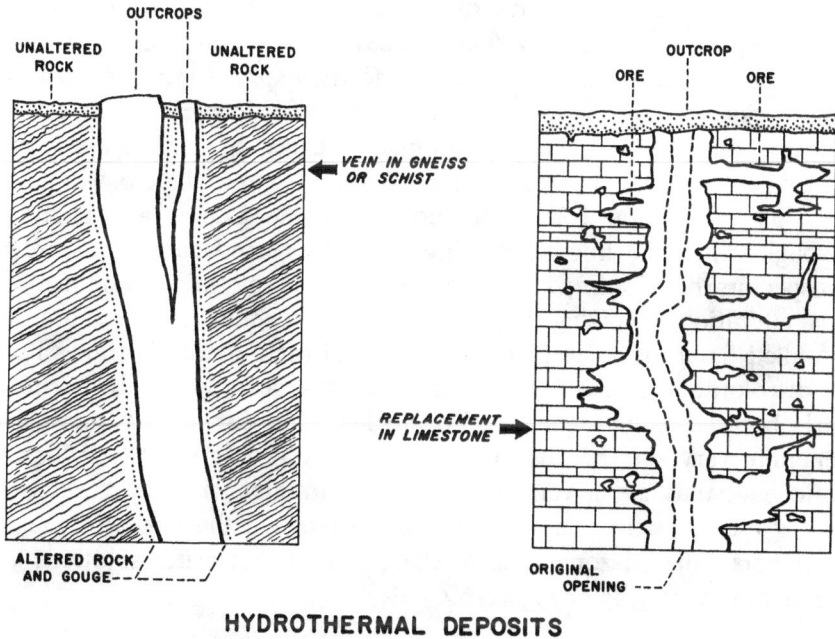

HYDROTHERMAL DEPOSITS

FIGURE 69. On the left is a sharp-bordered hydrothermal vein. Because of the resistance of gneiss and schist to chemical attack, only a thin zone of alteration, usually containing kaolin and sericite, separates the vein from country rock. In contrast, the ready solubility of limestone under similar conditions is shown in the illustration on the right. Ore deposited well beyond the limits of the original fissure and small masses may be found many feet away from the main body. The boundaries of the ore body are extremely irregular.

The nature of the rocks through which solutions pass is of great importance when it comes to providing spaces for minerals to form. Some rocks break more easily than others and thus provide more openings; limestone, in particular, is very brittle and also is so easily dissolved by water that small openings rapidly enlarge and hot water solutions are able to pass through even more quickly. As in contact metasomatism, it has been found that limestones and dolomites are much favored by hydrothermal solutions as places to deposit dissolved minerals. This is shown in the diagram of Figure 69 where much more limestone than originally lined a fissure has been eaten away by solutions.

The ease with which hot water solutions can penetrate seemingly solid rock is shown in the so-called "porphyry copper" deposits of the southwestern United States. In these deposits, hydrothermal activity brought enormous quantities of copper minerals into igneous rocks, depositing them in the very small spaces left between grains. Solutions apparently came up through fissures and then spread into the surrounding rocks, creating thousands of cubic yards of low-grade copper ore. Because such deposits can be mined cheaply by large-scale earth-moving operations, the resulting ores become profitable to work. Almost all rocks show some alteration along the fissures and channels through which the mineral-bearing solutions passed and some shrewd prospectors have learned to watch for the discoloration produced by this alteration, knowing that even if they cannot see any ore, an ore-filled fissure is some place nearby. Wall rock alteration shows itself by discoloration and softening, for example, rocks which are normally dark become much lighter in color and the discolored material is generally very soft because it has been changed into other minerals. Softened bands along vein walls often contain much sericite mica or one of the clay minerals, and such alterations are then called "gouge" by miners. Altered zones due to the effects of hot water solutions are shown in the drawing of Figure 69.

Banding in Veins

A striking feature of many veins is the parallel banding noted along the walls as minerals deposited in succession from solutions. If the solutions swept through the rock opening at a steady rate, banding is faint or absent, but if for some reason the solutions were interrupted, then banding is very pronounced. Quartz gangue often shows beautiful "comb" structure because crystals grew on the walls with their points facing inward like the teeth of a comb. Interruptions to the flow of

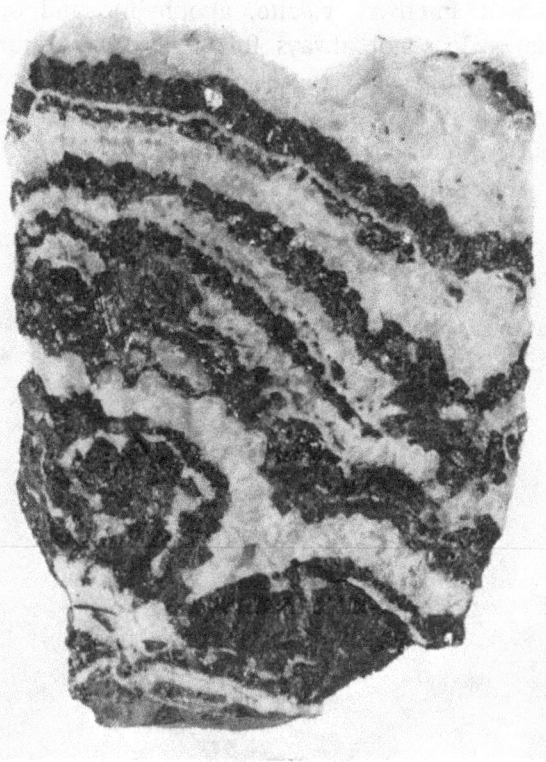

FIGURE 70. Comb structure in an ore vein. This ore vein section from the Rammelsberg District of Goslar, Germany, shows step-by-step deposit of dark brown sphalerite, gray galena, and white quartz upon the walls of a fissure. In the photograph, the portion nearest the bottom of the page shows part of the wall rock. Deposit of ore minerals and gangue began along this edge and worked inward toward the midline of the original fissure opening. Note the well-formed quartz crystals implanted upon sphalerite and galena and how they were later covered over by additional deposits. Size of specimen: 5 x 6 inches. *Courtesy Smithsonian Institution.*

solutions caused one generation of crystals to form, then another, and so on until the opening was completely filled. Figure 70 shows an example of a piece of vein filling in which the entire space is filled up with quartz with a little sphalerite. Sometimes cavities in fissures do *not* fill completely and it is in such openings that exceptionally fine mineral specimens are found. For some years, excellent specimens of this type, one of which is shown in Figure 71, have appeared on the market from Guanajuato, Mexico, where silver-bearing hydrothermal veins are commonly lined with amethyst, calcite, apophyllite and other attractive minerals. Quartz does not always form this way, unfortunately, and many quartz veins, especially those in which gold is found, are merely solid masses of milky material fit only for the crushing in stamp mills which is to be their fate.

FIGURE 71. Amethyst crystal specimens from veins. The large single crystal on the left is from the Four Peaks deposit in Arizona while the slab covered by numerous small crystals on the right is from a silver vein near Guanajuato in Mexico.

Replacement

In addition to filling whatever spaces happen to be available, hot water solutions also act like the gases mentioned in a previous section, that is, they take away minerals and put new ones in place of them. This is the *metasomatic replacement* process. It is a widespread process and its effects can be seen in many kinds of deposits besides ore deposits. In fact, replacement can happen wherever the proper conditions are met, whether it be in igneous, sedimentary or metamorphic rocks, and near the surface or deep below the surface. It is the process responsible for taking away the organic matter of wood and introducing silica in its place to form petrified wood. Not only is there an exchange of one substance for another but also no change in the volume or form of the original object. Examples of wood have been found, complete with outer wrinkled skin, which have been so perfectly replaced that it is possible to tell what kind of wood it was by examining a thin sliver cut from across the log. Replacement is also responsible for *pseudomorphs*, or crystals of one mineral replaced by another. In the process, the crystal's size, and all its faces are preserved perfectly but now it has an entirely different composition. Some examples of replacement are quartz replacing fluorite, quartz replacing calcite, cassiterite replacing feldspar, and native copper replacing aragonite. Partial replacement is also very common in pyrite and siderite crystals which are changed to goethite.

Because replacement is so penetrating, ore bodies formed by this process can be extremely varied in form. The most common types are massive deposits in which a great deal of rock is partially replaced, solidly in some areas and only in spots in others. Deposits in which the replacement is spotty are called *disseminated* deposits and are very common in many mining districts. If the rock as a whole contains enough ore, it may pay to mine all of it, subsequently crushing it to separate the very small grains of ore from the rest of the rock.

Ore bodies of the massive type are simple replacements of rock or replacements of other minerals. In many instances, veins, lodes and other fissure fillings are more or less completely replaced by new minerals which substitute for the old, or which even enlarge the original ore body by attacking and replacing the wall rocks. Good examples of replacement ore bodies of both massive and disseminated types are the copper ore bodies of Bingham, Utah, the molybdenum deposits of Climax, Colorado, and the extensive lead-zinc deposits of the tri-state district near the junction of Kansas, Oklahoma and Missouri.

WEATHERING AND MINERAL DEPOSITS

As mentioned in the previous chapter, weathering has two important effects, first, it breaks apart rocks by force, as for example in alternate freezing and thawing which cause weakening of the rock, and, second, it attacks rocks chemically, causing some of the minerals to be altered into different minerals. Actually each process seldom works alone and most weathered rock is attacked by physical *and* chemical forces working at the same time. In the section which follows, we will talk about the chemical effects of weathering because they are related to the processes we have just finished discussing, and in a later section about how mineral deposits are created by the physical side of weathering.

The principal agent of chemical weathering is rainwater, acting alone or with other substances which happen to be dissolved in it. From the atmosphere water picks up and dissolves carbon dioxide which is one of the common gases in the air. The same gas, when cooled and compressed, makes the familiar "dry ice" used for keeping food cold. When dissolved, carbon dioxide converts water into weak acid capable of dissolving minerals faster than pure water. Oxygen is also dissolved in water and it too can make the water more active chemically. Thus by the time water falls from the sky in the form of rain, it is a potent chemical agent, ready to go to work the moment it strikes the ground.

Within the ground, water picks up more acids from decaying vegetable matter, or if it passes through soil or rock containing decaying sulfide minerals such as pyrite and marcasite, it may easily become strongly acid and far more destructive in its effects. Perhaps because chemical changes caused by water cannot be seen readily, its real power is not fully appreciated. For example, the following chemical changes take place wherever water sinks into the ground:

- Carbonate rocks such as limestone and dolomite are dissolved, forming small to large caverns.
- Silicate minerals such as feldspar are changed into clays which wash into enormous beds.
- Quartz and calcite dissolve and redeposit in porous layers of sand and gravel, slowly converting them into rocks.
- Iron and aluminum minerals are concentrated and converted into useful ores.

Of special interest to the gemstone collector are the deposits of turquois and variscite which are formed by the process of weathering. Apparently weathering destroys surface rocks and releases the constituents necessary to form both minerals. These constituents are carried downward into seams by rainwater trickling slowly through the various rock formations, and, when proper conditions are met, begin crystallizing into turquois and variscite. Both usually form nodules or seam fillings in a variety of openings in rhyolites, trachytes, granites, and cherty limestones. In large seams, the tendency is for both minerals to

FIGURE 72. Granite boulders as shown here are common in many places in the western United States. Although they seem to be rounded from stream action, they are actually resting in the place of formation, having weathered to spherical shape by progressive peeling off of surface layers. Compare to the much more striking peeling shown on Half Dome in Figure 40. *Courtesy U. S. Geological Survey.*

form nodules imbedded in soft clay-like alteration material; however, in lower parts of the seams, or in places where the seams are very narrow, both minerals fill the openings solidly. So far as is known, none of the deposits of turquois or variscite have been mined so deep that the ends of the deposits have been met, but indications are that the deposits are probably not very deep since they form from the decomposition of surface material carried down by rainwater.

Thus it can be seen that water from the atmosphere is really a very powerful chemical agent, a fact worth remembering during the following discussions on mineral deposits formed through its help. An example of the utter decay brought on by water and weathering is shown in Figure 72.

WEATHERING OF ORE DEPOSITS

Probably no minerals do more to excite the wonder and admiration of collectors than the handsome specimens taken from weathered metallic ore bodies. Particularly colorful species, often perfectly formed in shining crystal groups, occur in the top zones of copper, lead, and zinc deposits. In such places are found deep blue azurite, malachite, as shown in Figure 73, pink or red velvety chalcotrichite, pale green, blue or yellow smithsonite, white glistening spears of cerussite, and many other minerals which reach peaks of perfection in the honeycomb cavities which penetrate the ore bodies.

All of the wonderful transformations which produced these minerals took place because of water. The drab massive sulfides of copper, lead, and zinc were changed through the agency of water into the treasured minerals described above, but all of this would not have been possible unless the water itself had not become chemically active as mentioned in the previous section.

Before an ore body can be drastically changed in its upper parts by the effects of weathering, it is necessary that it be situated in just the right place and in just the right climate. The first requirement must be for a supply of water but not too much. In very wet climates, a surplus of water results in dissolving and washing minerals away too quickly to permit the slow steady reactions which are needed to convert massive sulfides in the upper parts of the ore body into the desirable minerals mentioned above. In very cold climates, the reactions may be too slow or the ground below the surface may be permanently frozen, thus preventing any reactions at all. Even in places where proper conditions of climate are present, nothing happens if the deposit is located in the wrong place. For example, before water can trickle downward through the top of a mineral deposit, it must have some place to go. If the water table, or the level at which the ground is always soaked with water is too close to the surface, then water can only travel a few feet downward and reactions stop a little below this point. The ideal places for proper weathering of ore deposits seem to be very dry regions which verge on being deserts. Apparently in such regions, the water table is far below the surface and all of the ore body between the table and the surface is likely to be filled with the splendid minerals mentioned previously. Some geologists believe that the famous deposits of this type discovered in Bisbee, Arizona, and more lately in Mapimi, Mexico, were formed by the water table slowly sinking as the entire region became dryer.

Thus, as the water table drops, the water above trickles down slowly and carries on the chemical reactions which change the nature of the ore.

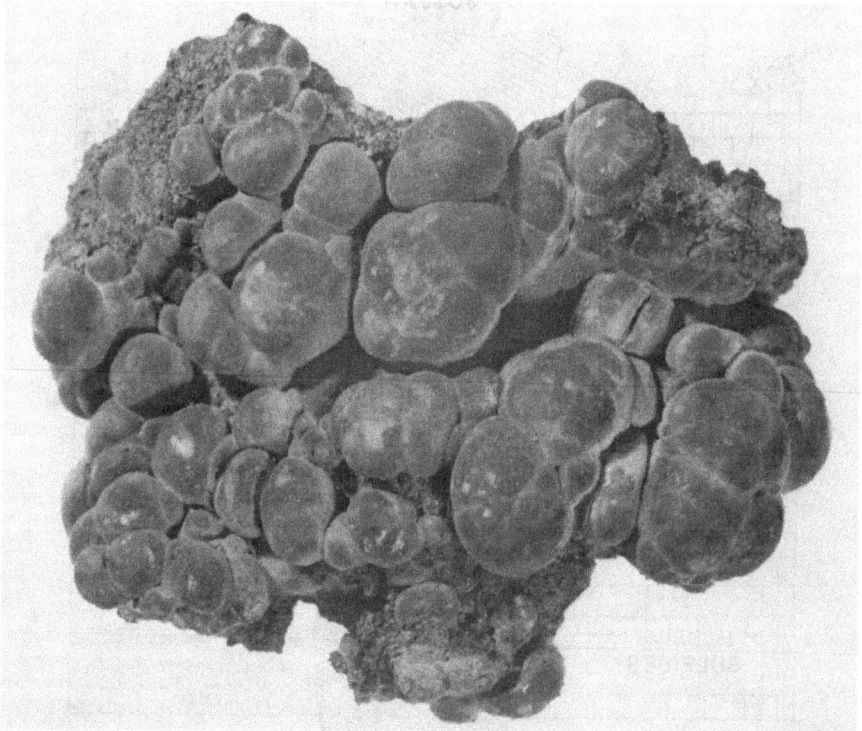

FIGURE 73. Malachite from Bisbee, Arizona. Each spherical growth consists of a multitude of needle-like crystals of malachite radiating outward from points upon the wall of a cavity in the oxidized zone. The featureless material upon which the malachite grew is porous *limonite*, usually of rich reddish-brown or brownish-yellow color. Specimen size 4 x 3 inches. *Courtesy Smithsonian Institution.*

WEATHERING OF COPPER DEPOSITS

Perhaps the finest mineral specimens from deposits of this type are collected from the upper parts of *copper* ore bodies and therefore this section will explain what happens when an ore body of this metal is attacked by weathering. A collector or prospector who is aware of how the process works is in a much better position to look for similar deposits or to select the places in old mine workings where weathered sections of the ore body may not have been completely removed. Figure 74 which shows an ideal weathered copper vein should be referred to during the discussion which follows in order to fix all points in mind.

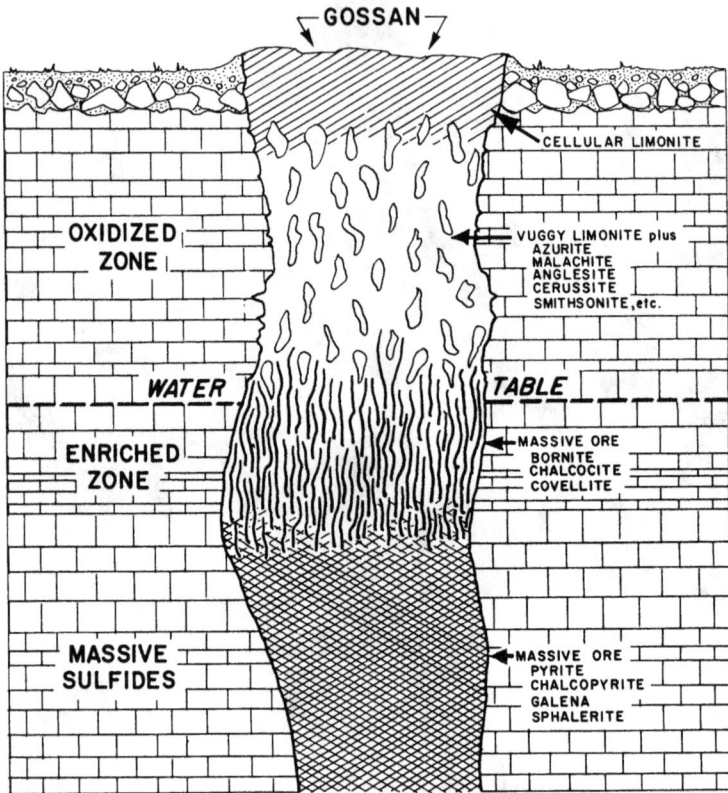

THE STRUCTURE OF AN OXIDIZED VEIN

FIGURE 74. An oxidized copper-bearing vein showing gossan, oxidized zone, the enriched zone, and the unaltered massive sulfides which form the original vein material.

Chemical reactions in the uppermost part of an ore body begin when the oxygen dissolved in water attacks iron pyrite, the common sulfide of iron. The absorption of oxygen by the pyrite causes it to change into another iron compound in a process called *oxidation*. Because so much oxygen is used up in the conversion of pyrite and other minerals in this section of the ore vein, the zone where it occurs is called the *oxidized zone*.

When iron pyrite is oxidized it takes up oxygen and water and changes into iron sulfate plus sulfuric acid. At the same time, quantities of iron oxide are produced and form spongy masses of bright yellow, red or brown *limonite*. Limonite is very abundant in oxidized zones and provides the matrix for many of the crystallized minerals which the collector treasures. At the surface, limonite remains in place as a spongy cellular mass, generally of dark brown color, and sometimes slightly upraised in respect to the surrounding ground level. This limonite mass is so characteristic of ores containing pyrite that old German miners gave it a name which persists today—"iron hat." The popular equivalent in the English language is *gossan*, a term coined by Cornish miners. Limonite masses, or gossans, are valuable indicators of ore bodies and whenever such cappings are discovered in the field they should always be looked into carefully, for they may lead to valuable deposits underneath.

Once iron sulfide is changed into iron sulfate, it dissolves readily in water and sets off a train of reactions with other sulfide minerals. Sulfuric acid, also produced in the oxidation of pyrite, reacts vigorously and accounts for many changes too. Each sulfide is attacked by iron sulfate and converted into a corresponding copper, lead, or zinc sulfate. All are soluble in water, except lead sulfate, or the mineral known as anglesite, which remains where it forms in small white lustrous crystals perched in cavities on limonite. Here are the conversions which take place:

CONVERSIONS FROM SULFIDES TO SULFATES

	FROM		TO	
Mineral	*Chemical name*		*Mineral*	*Chemical name*
Pyrite	Iron sulfide	→	Melanterite	Iron sulfate
Chalcopyrite	Copper sulfide	→	Chalcanthite	Copper sulfate
Galena	Lead sulfide	→	Anglesite	Lead sulfate
Sphalerite	Zinc sulfide	→	Goslarite	Zinc sulfate

Since the sulfates of iron, zinc and copper are very easily dissolved in water, they are carried downward from the oxidized zone, the solutions trickling through the massive sulfide minerals below. Because anglesite, the sulfide of lead is not easily dissolved, it is a common mineral in the oxidized zone but the others are relatively scarce. As the solutions carrying sulfates pass through or contact other minerals, further reactions set in and lead to the formation of new minerals. Copper sulfate is of particular interest because it reacts with calcite in limestone (calcium carbonate) to form azurite and malachite, both of which are carbonates of copper. It also reacts with chalcopyrite to form bornite, which in turn, when contacted by more copper sulfate, transforms into chalcocite.

Zinc and silver minerals take part in similar but less spectacular reactions, zinc sulfate reacting with calcite in limestone to form smithsonite or reacting with silica to form hemimorphite. Silver is generally found in copper, zinc and lead deposits as native silver but it sometimes reacts with minerals containing bromine and chlorine to form cerargyrite and enargite. Both bromine and chlorine minerals are common in arid regions and it is entirely possible that they were carried into weathered copper deposits by surface rain water.

Oxidized zones often reach considerable depths but many are very shallow, perhaps because the tops were eroded and disappeared. In any case, it has been found that the bottom limit of oxidized zones is always at the water table; if this level is deep, the oxidized zone will be deep also. The reason why oxidation stops at the water table is that the water descending from the surface loses its oxygen and without this vital element, the oxidation of sulfides cannot go on. In moist climates where the water table is only a few feet below the surface, oxidized zones are small but in arid regions with deep water tables, zones may extend several thousand feet below the surface. The limit set by the water table accounts for the sudden shutting down of copper mines which seem to be going along prosperously. In oxidized zones the ores are rich and not too difficult to remove and the mills are set up to handle this type of ore. However, when the bottom is struck, it often turns out that the massive sulfides some distance below the water table become too poor to carry the costs of deep mining, pumping of water, and different treatment of ore in the mills. Examples of this sudden shutdown are all too common. Many years ago, splendid copper minerals were produced by the copper mines in Bisbee, Arizona, then working in oxidized zones. For many years it seemed as if the supply of fine specimens would never stop, but the day came when one mine after another struck bottom and found they could not go on without losing money. From this point on, Bisbee specimens became scarce and today ardent mineral collectors who own Bisbee specimens cherish them dearly. A more recent case was in the Congo Republic, where copper mines famous for their enormous masses of malachite ran out of oxidized ores and are now producing only massive sulfides of little interest either to the collector of specimens or to the gem cutter.

Enrichment of Copper Ores

Although the chemical reactions which take place in the upper parts of the ore body do not reach below the water table because of the lack of oxygen, other reactions set in which cause the ordinary massive ores of the lower parts of the vein to become richer in copper. The zone just below the water table is therefore called the *enriched zone* as shown in the diagram of Figure 74. The principal mineral involved in the process is copper sulfate, which is produced in the oxidized zone and is carried by water into the sulfide ores below the water table. Copper sulfate then reacts with sulfide ores, adding its copper content to lean copper minerals and thus making them richer. How much enrichment takes place can be told by comparing the copper content of 34% in chalcopyrite, the most common sulfide ore, with the copper content of 66% in covellite, one of the new minerals formed by the enrichment process. In effect, enrichment takes away copper from the upper part of the vein and drops it off into the part below the water table.

Below the enriched zone (refer again to Figure 74) the unaltered sulfide minerals of the vein may be concentrated enough to make a profitable ore, however, there are many cases on record where such was not the case and mines had to shut down after the enriched ores were exhausted.

PRIMARY AND SECONDARY MINERALS

Ore body minerals in their original form are called *primary* minerals because they were created first and have not changed since that time. Those which result from the interactions described above, however, are called *secondary* minerals.

Before leaving the subject, we should point out that oxidation may occur in almost any metallic ore body, although for sheer variety and beauty of resulting oxidized zone minerals, copper ore bodies are unsurpassed. Nevertheless, ore bodies containing lead or zinc sulfides are capable of producing fine specimens also. Oxidized zones are found in many ore bodies throughout the United States, Mexico, and Central America, although the most spectacular specimens come from mines in the arid regions of the southwest United States and northern Mexico.

PRIMARY AND SECONDARY MINERALS OFTEN FOUND IN COPPER,
LEAD, AND ZINC DEPOSITS

PRIMARY MINERALS

Elements: native silver
Sulfides: pyrite, chalcopyrite, galena, sphalerite

SECONDARY MINERALS

Elements: native copper
Sulfides: chalcocite, bornite, covellite
Oxides: cuprite, goethite, tenorite
Halides: atacamite, cerargyrite, embolite
Carbonates: calcite, aragonite, smithsonite, cerussite, malachite, azurite, rosasite,
    aurichalcite
Sulfates: anglesite, gypsum, chalcanthite, melanterite, brochantite, antlerite,
    linarite, jarosite, caledonite
Molybdates: wulfenite
Phosphates: pyromorphite, vivianite, turquois
Silicates: quartz, hemimorphite, chrysocolla, dioptase, shattuckite, willemite

RESIDUAL DEPOSITS

The term *residual* refers to minerals left behind after rocks weathered
and disintegrated. The minerals remaining after the decay of rock may
be those formed by chemical action or those of such great durability
that they are not changed at all. Examples of residual deposits due to
chemical changes in the rocks themselves are: clay deposits formed
from the decomposition of feldspar in granite and other rocks; iron ore
composed of iron oxides formed from the alteration of siderite and
pyrite; and veins of opal and chalcedony formed from decomposition of
silicate minerals in serpentine. Examples of deposits formed from
durable minerals are gold and platinum and diamonds and precious
stones. Other examples could be given but the few above will illustrate
what is meant. A concentration of residual minerals is diagrammed in
Figure 75 while Figure 76 is a photograph of a residual deposit of
bauxite, an important ore of aluminum, formed by chemical breakdown
of overlying rocks.

It is important to remember that ores and valuable minerals remain
behind in residual deposits and do not wash away to settle elsewhere. A
residual deposit is usually a thin blanket of loose concentrated material
lying directly over the rock from which it formed.

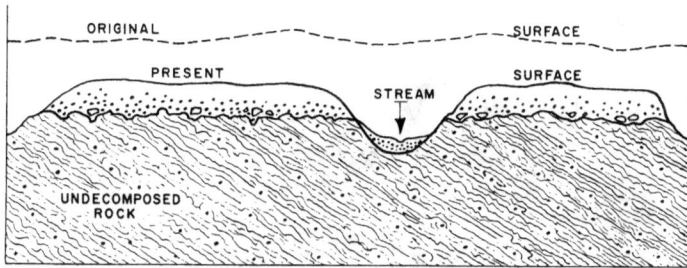

RESIDUAL CONCENTRATION

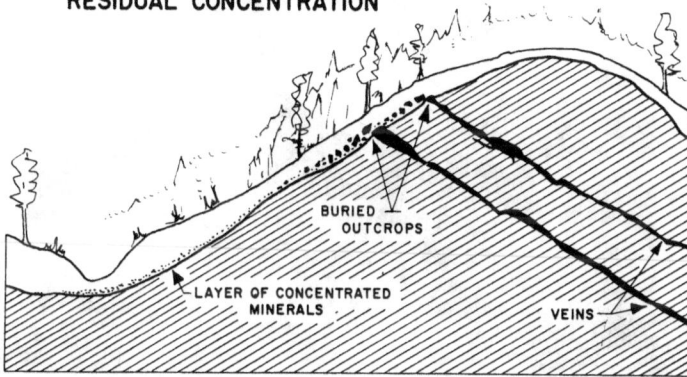

ELUVIAL CONCENTRATION

FIGURE 75. Two processes responsible for the formation of a number of valuable deposits. In the upper drawing, the black dots scattered throughout the undecomposed country rock represent a valuable mineral; however, the separate masses are too widely scattered for economical mining and it is not until weathering concentrates them in a layer beneath the topsoil and resting upon unaltered rock that it becomes feasible to mine them. In the lower drawing, concentrations of valuable minerals form in a similar process but downslope movement of soil containing the minerals as well as some disintegration and removal of less valuable gangue are involved.

MECHANICAL CONCENTRATION

The breakdown of rocks can be followed by residual deposits as described above, or by deposits formed through *mechanical concentration*. The term *mechanical* simply means that force of some kind is involved during concentration, that is, wind, water, or the movements of ice. When a miner uses a gold pan, he *mechanically* concentrates the gold flakes, but if he uses cyanide to collect the gold, he *chemically* concentrates it.

There are three important deposits formed through mechanical con-

FIGURE 76. Residual bauxite being mined as an ore of aluminum near the Sweetwater Branch, Andersonville, Georgia. The man is standing on a bed of bauxite four feet in thickness which has been covered by an overburden of sediments measuring about 20 feet in depth. *Courtesy U. S. Geological Survey.*

centration: *detrital, eluvial,* and *alluvial.* Detrital deposits are those which form from disintegrated rock, such as the broken material at the base of a cliff. Very little concentration takes place and the chief value of such deposits is that they give an idea of what minerals may be present high up on the slopes or cliffs. Detrital material forming a talus slope is shown in Figure 77. Eluvial deposits are really detrital materials in which a greater degree of concentration has taken place because of small particles being washed by rain or blown away by the wind. The heavier minerals, and usually the more desirable ones, creep downhill and settle toward the bottom, causing the lowest layers to become increasingly rich. By the time the process has been going for some years, valuable minerals tend to sink completely out of sight and may only be visible near the tops of slopes. Sometimes eluvial accumulations become so rich that they form profitable deposits. Detrital material slipping downhill and forming an eluvial deposit is shown in Figure 75.

FIGURE 77. A well-developed talus cone on the west wall of Canyon Creek Valley, Glacier National Park, Montana. Talus cones form at the base of deep vertical crevices in rock walls where slabs of rock falling from the sides funnel through the bottom of the openings. *Courtesy U. S. Geological Survey.*

When eluvial deposits form near the floors of valleys, particularly narrow ones, they are in good position to be picked up by rushing torrents and let fall in the third kind of deposits—the *alluvial.* Whereas the first two processes of concentration involved only the downslope movement of loose material, with or without the help of wind and rain, the alluvial process always involves movement by water. Concentration is much greater whenever stream action is involved, and of course the deposits formed by this process are far more important. The entire process of mechanical concentration is shown in the diagram of Figure 78.

If minerals are to be concentrated in the gravels of stream and river beds, several conditions must be met. First, the minerals must be heavier than most others in order to allow them to settle faster, and second, they must be durable. Minerals which meet these requirements are diamonds, sapphires, rubies, and many other gemstones, also magnetite, chromite, ilmenite, rutile, monazite, cassiterite, tantalite, columbite, and of course the heavy metals such as platinum, and gold. There are many other minerals which are both heavy and durable but those listed above are most commonly found in alluvial deposits.

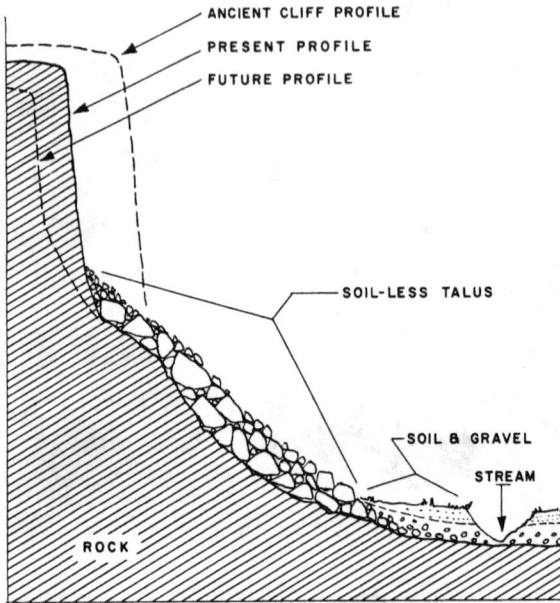

DEVELOPMENT OF TALUS SLOPES

FIGURE 78. Detrital material breaking away from a cliff forms steep talus slopes which may be prospected to determine if valuable minerals are present above.

To be effective in concentrating mineral matter in gravels, water cannot flow too rapidly or too slowly. If movement is very slow, all manner of rubbish will collect along stream bottoms in addition to desirable minerals, while, on the other hand, fast moving water will sweep everything before it and may leave nothing along the bottom except large boulders resting on bedrock and a few narrow streaks of gravel along the sides above the reach of all except floodwaters. Streams which change pace many times along their courses are most favorable for producing concentrations of minerals, since rapid stretches quickly erode eluvium along the banks while quiet stretches provide places for heavy minerals to settle. Ridge-like outcrops of rock crossing stream beds, or large boulders resting upon bedrock provide especially favorable spots for settling of heavy minerals. Deep crevices in bedrock and other cavities in stream bottoms also make efficient natural traps; however, potholes in which water churns violently are apt to result in crushing minerals to powder and causing them to be washed away entirely.

Within any stream valley producing valuable minerals, the possibility must not be overlooked that rich gravels may be found at many points besides the narrow strip along the present stream bed. Elevated terraces of gravel, frequently disguised by growths of vegetation, may be found along valley walls high above the present stream level. Such older gravels, left behind by deepening of the valley may contain as much in mineral wealth as the newer gravels. Furthermore, rich deposits may be found in long-abandoned watercourses often marked by snaking shallow depressions along valley floors and rows of bushes or trees.

Gold placers have been worked practically everywhere in mountainous regions of North America, even in the Appalachians, where considerable gold has been won from streams in North Carolina and Georgia. Diamonds have been found in the Appalachian gold gravels and also in similar gravels in the foothills of the Sierra Nevada. Sapphires have been recovered in large quantities from a number of placers in Montana; rubies and rhodolite garnets were once mined from Cowee Creek in North Carolina. In many places in Mexico, stream tin resulting from the disintegration of igneous rocks containing deposits of cassiterite and topaz has been recovered in considerable quantity from gravels along dry watercourses. Beach sands containing commercial quantities of gold were extensively mined at Nome, Alaska, while today rutile, ilmenite and monazite sands are concentrated by machinery in large-scale operations in North Carolina and Florida.

SOLUTION DEPOSITS IN SEDIMENTARY ROCKS

In a previous section of this chapter we discussed deposits formed from hot water solutions rising from heated masses of igneous rock. It was mentioned at the same time that sedimentary rocks, particularly limestones, often play host to such deposits. However, sedimentary rocks also contain mineral deposits, usually of very small size, created within them by the circulation of water at normal temperature. Mineral collectors are familiar with a number of them, such as the quartz-lined geodes found in shales and sandstones, the openings in limestone containing calcite, celestite, barite and fluorite, so common in Ohio and other states in which large beds of impure limestone occur, and the chert concentrations found in sedimentary rocks at Flint Ridge, Ohio, and in the Ozarks.

In general, solution deposits in sedimentary rocks are spotty concentrations, except in the case of cherts, which may form widely-distributed silica-rich bands in various layers of certain sedimentary formations. How silica or calcite or other minerals in sedimentary rocks chose to settle into certain spots has never been clearly explained. Some geologists believe that cavities formerly occupied by fossils later became filled by minerals deposited by slow movement of water within the rocks themselves. They point out how silica so often drifts toward fossils, animal and vegetable, and replaces them completely, or how pyrite sometimes replaces ancient snails and other forms of marine life. It is even more difficult to explain the larger cavities sometimes found in limestones which are lined with fine crystals of calcite, celestite, fluorite, etc., especially when such openings seem to have no veins leading to them. Since limestone is so easily dissolved, it is possible that the cavity could have formed by solution of the calcite and later filled with other minerals, but this still does not explain why the cavity is not connected to others, such as is the case with limestone caverns.

FIGURE 79. A recent view in the Arizona Petrified Forest National Park showing numerous silicified logs remaining upon the surface after enclosing sandstones had disintegrated and disappeared.

FIGURE 80. Silicified tree trunk in Ojo-Alamo sandstone east of Eagle Spring, Sandoval Co., New Mexico. The far greater resistance of the silicified wood to weathering is strikingly shown. Note the smooth rounded weathering surfaces developed by the sandstone. *Courtesy U. S. Geological Survey.*

A sedimentary deposit which has come to the fore in the last several years is worth a brief description, namely, uranium and vanadium in sandstones. The origin of uranium ores, as well as the vanadium ores which accompany them, in the Morrison formation of the western Colorada plateau region remains a mystery, but evidence points to introduction into the porous sandstones by circulating ground water. The richest concentrations are associated with remnants of organic matter such as petrified wood, other fossil vegetation, and fossil bones. Certain horizons seem to contain practically all available ores and the prospector therefore attempts to identify these layers and to follow them along the steep, towering cliffs characteristic of the plateau edges, until his detecting equipment records radioactivity. Lately, the gruelling routine of prospecting on foot has been short-circuited by enterprising individuals using light aircraft containing sensitive detection equipment. Outcrops in Morrison sandstones not only trigger detecting devices but also reveal themselves by brightly colored stainings of yellow carnotite, the commonest uranium mineral in the formation, bright green scales of autunite, and by other powdery deposits on the surface. Any kind of petrified vegetation or fossil matter found upon the surface or at the bases of cliffs is an encouraging sign. It is worth noting, in this connection, that the enormous quantities of high-quality silicified wood of the Petrified Forest and adjacent areas in Arizona, are weathered from similar sandstone formations. A view in the Petrified Forest appears in Figure 79. In this photograph enclosing sandstones have completely disappeared; however in Figure 80, also showing petrified wood, a large log can be seen still enclosed.

Other sandstones in the western United States are noted locally for containing seams filled with chalcedony, some suitable for gem-stones, dinosaur bone, also useful for lapidary work, silicified shells and other forms of quartz.

METAMORPHIC DEPOSITS

As explained in Chapter I, metamorphic mineral deposits tend to be widespread and low grade due to the nature of the rock-forming process involved and the raw material from which such rocks are formed. Some, like anthracite coal, are entirely useful, but others are little more than country rock in which valuable minerals, usually sprinkled throughout the mass, are somewhat concentrated and hence make the entire rock worth mining. Commercially important deposits include graphite, asbestos, talc, soapstone, ceramic materials, abrasive stones and powders, roofing slates, and sometimes gem quality garnet.

5

Field Features of Mineral Deposits

It is time to leave theory and turn to the practical side—how to recognize mineral deposits when you meet them in the field, and, perhaps even more important, where to look in them for valuable minerals or specimens for your collection. In effect, this chapter summarizes what has been learned before about rocks and the relationship of mineral deposits to them but now brings the lessons home to the practical side of field work that every collector and prospector must do if he is to be successful. Some information given before will be repeated but only when it is necessary to make points clearer.

In a previous chapter, we discussed rocks and what they looked like close at hand and from a distance. In this chapter, we will examine various kinds of deposits *close* at hand so that the places within them such as cavities, pockets, lenses, etc., most likely to contain the best specimens, will be recognized.

COMMON ROCK-MINERAL ASSOCIATIONS

Centuries of mining and mineral collecting experience shows that some minerals are so often associated with certain rocks that knowledge of such associations is of great help during field trips. Such knowledge also helps to identify a rock, or a mineral, when either one is unknown to the collector. For example, a collector finds a very heavy black mineral in a stream bed and by crushing it, notes that the powder becomes brown. He concludes that the mineral is *not* magnetite which crushes to a black powder, instead it is chromite which looks very much the same. If he has a magnet handy, the chromite also refuses to jump to the magnet as magnetite does. Having proved that the mineral is chromite, he can therefore expect that a chromite-bearing peridotite rock, possibly serpentine, is somewhere in the neighborhood. On the other hand, if he knows he is working in an area of serpentine rocks, and finds a heavy black mineral, he can almost certainly assume such to be chromite instead of magnetite.

It would be of even greater help to prospectors and collectors if associations were more numerous and more certain, but, unfortunately, so many minerals are found scattered so widely in many kinds of rock that only relatively few associations are truly reliable. A prospector may find well-formed quartz crystals in the soil of a hillside, yet this would tell him very little about the rock from which they came because fine quartz crystals come from cavities in many kinds of rock. However, if at the same time he found large feldspar crystals with the quartz, or perhaps pieces of black tourmaline, he can be sure that all of them came from a granite pegmatite.

Associations are therefore more than just one specific mineral for one specific rock, but also between *groups* of minerals and specific rocks, and the more that we know about them, the more likely we are to draw correct conclusions as to the kind of deposit the minerals came from. Some typical associates were given in Chapter III for the three broad classes of rocks and some important ones follow in this section, but complete lists will be found in any good book on mineralogy. In such books, the locality sections will often carry information like this: "Most commonly found in pegmatites associated with microcline, topaz and quartz." In this case, the mineral happens to be phenakite and the statement is taken from a standard textbook of mineralogy. Other statements as to associations are put down by the authors when these are helpful. Where the collector or prospector is uncertain as to what kind of deposit he has found, it is always a good idea for him to collect as many *different* minerals from the locality as possible, in order that he may leisurely study them at home and form conclusions as to what kind of deposit it could be. The same holds true for the rocks around the deposit, or rocks found in a general area.

Although it is impossible to put down all associations which have been recorded, the following table gives a few of the most important. The table is broken down into the three great classes of rocks, with columns in each for the rock type and the minerals or ores commonly found in them.

TABLE OF COMMON ROCK-MINERAL ASSOCIATIONS

MINERALS IN ITALICS ARE UNUSUALLY RELIABLE ASSOCIATES

Rock   Minerals or Ores

IGNEOUS GROUP

Felsite   Frequently host for sulfide ore bodies.

Rhyolite   Tin ores: cassiterite with topaz and tourmaline in Mexico; opal in cavities.

Trachyte   Turquois in altered trachyte; opal.

Basalt   Amygdaloidal types: native copper, quartz gemstones, massive datolite, etc.

                      Pillow basalts: angular and spherical cavities contain crystals of quartz, *zeolites*, datolite, prehnite, pectolite, etc.

Diabase   Silver, cobalt, nickel ores in Ontario; *zeolite* minerals, apophyllite, *prehnite, datolite*, in east U.S.A.

Granite   Tin, tungsten ores, cassiterite, scheelite, wolframite, black tourmaline and quartz; uranium and radium ores (pitchblende) in Great Bear Lake region, Canada; molybdenum (molybdenite); small pegmatite bodies contain crystals of feldspar, quartz, topaz, beryl, phenakite, fluorite, siderite, etc.; zircon.

Granite Pegmatites   Commercial feldspar, electrical grade muscovite mica; beryllium ores (beryl); tantalum ores (columbite-tantalite); lithium ores (*lepidolite, amblygonite*, etc.); cesium ores (*pollucite*); gemstones: *colored tourmaline, spodumene*, beryl, spessartite garnet, topaz, amazonite, moonstone, *rose quartz* (and other varieties of quartz).

Syenite   Gold in quartz veins in Canada; iron ore (magnetite).

Nepheline Syenite   Corundum; *zircon*, often in large crystals; *sodalite* and *cancrinite*.

Granodiorite Monzonite Copper ores ("porphyry" coppers) in southwestern U. S.; molybdenum ore (molybdenite) at Climax, Colorado; tin and tungsten ores in Nevada and California; gold, silver, zinc, and lead ores in many places; uranium minerals in monzonite near Marysvale, Utah.

Diorite   Copper, gold ores in many places; ilmenite.

Gabbro   Iron ores (magnetite, ilmenite) in N. Y. and Canada; native copper in Lake Superior Region; nickel-copper ores (pyrrhotite) at Sudbury, Ontario.

Anorthosite | Gem *labradorite* in N. Y. and Labrador; magnetite, ilmenite.

Peridotite | *Diamond, pyrope garnet* in kimberlite; *chromite; platinum;* nickel ores.

SEDIMENTARY GROUP

Conglomerate | Native copper, silver in Michigan; native silver in Ontario; quartz gemstones (chalcedony).

Sandstone | Uranium-vanadium ores in Colorado Plateau; native copper associated with basalt in Michigan, N. J., Conn., Mass.; quartz crystals, Arkansas; quartz gemstones (chalcedony, agate, petrified wood and bone); lead and zinc ores; mercury ores; barite, celestite, strontianite, calcite, gypsum, anhydrite.

Shale | Boron minerals in California, Nevada; jet, amber; pyrite, marcasite, gypsum, anhydrite in strata.

Limestone | Favorable for *sulfide* ore deposits in many places, especially lead, zinc, and copper ores; *galena, sphalerite, chalcopyrite; fluorite, calcite, barite,* in openings; decorative stones; quartz gemstones.

Chert | Lead and zinc ores: galena, sphalerite, dolomite, marcasite, chalcopyrite, in Tri-state District; quartz gemstones.

Saline Rocks | *Salt, gypsum, anhydrite* beds.

Lignite Coal | *Jet, amber,* marcasite.

METAMORPHIC GROUP

Gneiss | Often contains pegmatites; graphite; *andalusite; fibrolite; cordierite; almandite garnet;* corundum.

Schist | Often contains pegmatites; graphite; *almandite garnet; andalusite; staurolite;* corundum; serpentine; *talc;* jadeite.

Serpentine | Gem and decorative serpentines; *nickel ores;* mercury ores; *chrysotile asbestos;* magnesite; *brucite; chromite; nephrite.*

Quartzite | Sometimes host for metallic ores; quartz crystals in cavities.

Slate | Gold-bearing quartz veins common; quartz crystals in cavities; pyrite.

Phyllite | *Staurolite,* andalusite, kyanite.

Marble | Decorative stones; gem serpentine; metallic ore bodies; *brown tourmaline; phlogopite mica;* corundum and spinel, sometimes gem quality.

Contact Metamorphosed Marble; Skarn | *Andradite* and *grossular garnet;* graphite; *wollastonite,* etc.

IMPORTANCE OF KNOWING AREA ROCKS

Because of the all-important connection between rocks and the mineral deposits likely to be found in them, it is a very good idea for the prospector or collector to know ahead of time what rocks are present in the area he intends to search. If the area has not been studied by geologists and no maps are available, then reliance must be placed on recognizing rocks as they are met; however, much information on special areas is often available in maps and reports published by state and federal agencies and should be consulted whenever it is possible to do so. As recommended before, a small study collection of typical rocks should be obtained in order to learn the most important and most widespread kinds. However, if the collector or prospector knows the difference between igneous, sedimentary and metamorphic rocks, this in itself will be a great help. In any case, specific types of rocks found in the area can always be brought back for study and identification later.

SIGNS OF MINERALIZATION IN GRANITES

Because granites are usually so uniform in grain and texture, it is easy to prospect in them since changes in character due to mineralization are easily spotted. Granites of batholiths, like those which make the core of the Sierra Nevada in California, are hard, compact, and commonly pale in color. Terrain features show broad stretches of smooth unbroken rock alternating with places where the rock is split into blocks by joints and planes at right angles to each other. Enormous masses are often rounded into domes as in Yosemite Park (see Figure 40).

Generally speaking, weathering of any large rock mass of uniform composition and texture results in *sameness* of terrain, and because this is so it is often possible to look at surrounding areas which look the same and come to the conclusion that they must be the same kind of rock. In Figure 81, for example, showing an area of granite, the bold features and many bare exposures of rock are alike in all places. In this area, mineralization has not been strong and the rock therefore varies very little from place to place. Granite of this type is very unlikely to contain metallic ores or anything else of interest to the collector and should therefore be passed by.

However, granites which contain pegmatites or which have been strongly mineralized, fall apart quickly, forming smoothly-rounded hills

FIGURE 81. In relatively young mountains, granites and allied rocks form characteristic surface features marked by bold knobs of bare rock and large blocky fragments on talus slopes. Note the light color of the rock as compared to the dark green of the vegetation. In this photograph, taken in the Cottonwood Region near Silver Lake, Utah, the granitic rock is granodiorite. The lack of rounded, vegetation-covered hills indicates rock barren of mineral deposits. Compare to the general view of Mount Antero in Figure 82. *Courtesy U. S. Geological Survey.*

covered with reddish topsoil and supporting growths of brush or trees. Granites of this kind are often coarse-grained and crumble easily into sharp-cornered grains. Easy crumbling permits easy erosion by water and therefore the hills and rounded mountains develop shallow ravines which look like gentle folds or creases. The highly mineralized Mount Antero-White Mountain region of Colorado is a good example and is illustrated in the panoramic photo in Figure 82. Masses of harder and more durable granite may be included in easily decayed granite, and of course the terrain will be generally gentle but will also show bouldery outcrops or pinnacles pushing up much higher than the rest of the

183

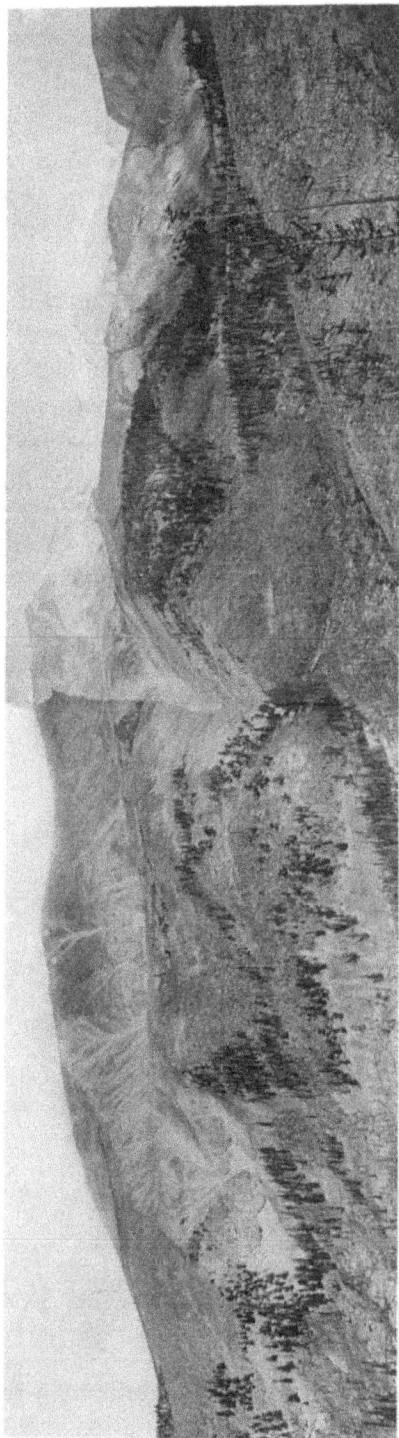

FIGURE 82. A famous collecting ground, the Mount Antero-White Mountain Area, Chaffee Co., Colorado. A composite photo taken from a point about 2½ miles west of the range toward a northerly spur. White Mountain appears in the center and Calico Mountain as a low dark ridge on the right. Mount Antero and White Mountain are granite and thus account for the prevailing light coloration but Calico Mountain is gabbro and allied rocks, and hence is considerably darker in tone. The easy weathering of the highly mineralized rock cause rounding of the granite and development of much surface debris. *Courtesy U. S. Geological Survey.*

terrain. Even in cases like this, the rule still holds that more easily disintegrated granite is more likely to be mineralized, while more durable granite means less mineralization. This is a very important rule to remember in field work because it applies to other kinds of igneous rocks as well as granite.

In the noted gem pegmatite areas of San Diego County in California, the connection between pegmatites and deeply-weathered rocks is so consistent that it is possible to ignore hills and mountains which show large areas of bare rock, since only those with smooth brush-covered slopes and very few outcrops contain pegmatites. In this county, granodiorites barren of mineralization are resistant to weathering and form hills covered with enormous round boulders of the type shown in Figure 83. A scene in the Ramona area of San Diego County is shown in Figure 84 to further illustrate differences between mineralized and non-mineralized areas.

FIGURE 83. Small boulders derived from granite occur when the parent rock mass is criss-crossed by a network of joints, as in this photograph taken in Gunnison Co., Colorado. Weathering agents creep along the joints, attack the sides and corners of the blocks, and eventually cause release of rounded boulders as in the upper left of the outcrop shown here. Compare to Figures 40 and 72. *Courtesy U. S. Geological Survey.*

The easy decay of granitic rocks is due to the alteration produced by mineralized gases, vapors, and fluids escaping from pegmatites or from upper portions of magmas. Alteration is sometimes restricted to narrow margins around pegmatite bodies but at other times, as in the red, coarse-grained granites of the Pikes Peak region in Colorado and near Conway, New Hampshire, the entire rock mass is made porous and crumbling. This disintegration is clearly shown in the photo of Figure 85, where only a few solid masses of granite remain after all else has crumbled away into soil. Disintegration due to similar causes occurs in other igneous rocks and results in terrain features of like character. From the standpoint of the prospector, distant views over granite or igneous rock areas are most rewarding because hills and mountains likely to contain mineral deposits· stand out against rugged crags and cliffs of barren rocks.

FIGURE 84. A general view near Ramona, San Diego County, California. Decided differences in weathering of underlying rocks are noted according to their composition. The foreground consists of easily weathered gabbros with some streaks of harder rocks, however, the crest of the hill in the background is granodiorite which displays greater resistance to weathering and weathers into rounded, boulder-like outcrops. The arrows mark mines in gem pegmatites. *Courtesy U. S. Geological Survey.*

FIGURE 85. A pegmatite outcrop opened up for microcline and smoky quartz crystals in the Florissant area of Colorado. Note the white quartz "float" above the pocket opening which led to intensive examination of the outcrop and selection of the exact point to begin digging. The white quartz is typical of the central core portions of pegmatites in this region and it is around such cores that pockets are most likely to occur.

SPOTTING PEGMATITES IN GRANITE

Decided differences in weathering, color, or in other surface features in granite terrain call for close examination for signs of pegmatites. Quartz is usually present in pegmatites and, being more resistant to decay than feldspar or mica, is also the most persistent float material. Massive quartz from cores is found as irregular blocks in float, usually of pure white color and sometimes with bits of cream-colored feldspar still imbedded. Pieces showing transparency or smoky coloration, or with attached fragments of amazonite, tourmaline, or other minerals, indicate origin worthy of a close look. On the other hand, transparent quartz *crystals* with sharp glistening faces *prove* origin within a pocket and should cause the collector to redouble his efforts to find the place from which they came. Although quartz is the most common float material, other species of pegmatite origin such as large flakes of mica, feldspar crystals, and tourmaline crystals should not be overlooked, for they too indicate nearness to a pegmatite body.

In level ground, quartz float fragments rest over the pegmatite from which they weathered and therefore give some indications of dimensions and direction of the outcrop. Only a piece or two of quartz may be present, as over a very small body, or a string of fragments extending over a distance of many yards, in the case of larger bodies. Still larger pegmatites may show masses of quartz several feet in thickness, deeply anchored in soil, and probably attached to the pegmatite. Long streaks of quartz should be examined carefully for signs of crystals since pockets ordinarily occur at only one point in the core, usually within the thickest portion, and much needless digging can be avoided by choosing the right place.

When a favorable outcrop or mass of float is found, its value is tested by trenching below the surface to expose the pegmatite clearly, if indeed there is one. This is best done by using a hand mattock or light shovel of the kind shown in Figure 9 to dig a narrow trench across the string of float. It must be remembered, however, that if the string of fragments is upon a hillside, some allowance for downward drift must be made, since all loose material in soil tends to work its way downslope because of rainfall and frost action. In still other instances, as in deep topsoils, fragments which weather from buried outcrops may not appear upon the surface until some distance below the true position of the pegmatite. The relation of float to outcrops on hillsides is shown in Figure 86. Digging is continued following the direction in which more fragments of quartz appear until hard rock is struck. The trench is then made long enough to show the entire cross-section of the pegmatite. The centerline along which quartz appears in a more or less continuous streak is then followed to establish the surface direction of the outcrop, and a close watch is kept for signs of crystals or openings. When a pocket is found, it will appear as a soft place filled solidly with topsoil and very likely penetrated by numerous plant rootlets. Ordinarily the filling is soft enough to be dug away with hands or very small tools such as knife-blades, screwdriver blades, and the like. Within the loose debris will be found well-formed crystals, which, however, may be so dirty that some scrubbing between the fingers is necessary to distinguish between crystals and lumps of dirt or rock.

In some pegmatite areas, particularly within the Crystal Peak area north of Florissant in Colorado, so much digging has gone on before that it becomes very difficult to decide whether quartz float really leads

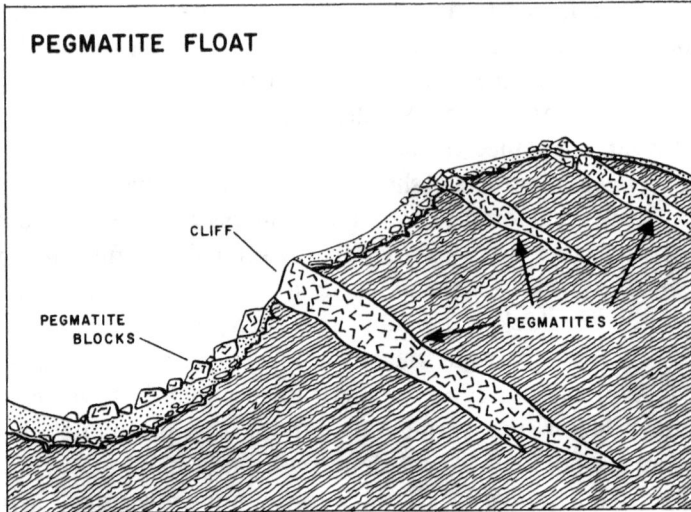

FIGURE 86. The relationships of pegmatite float to the outcrops from which such float came. In general, the steeper the slope, the more likely float is to be found considerable distances from outcrops. In some cases, as shown in the lowest pegmatite, the greater resistance to decay of pegmatite as compared to enclosing rocks results in the formation of prominent ribs or even small cliffs.

to an untouched pegmatite or merely represents rubbish cast out upon the surface by an earlier collector. Fortunately, older pits (of which there are hundreds) can usually be recognized as low depressions located uphill from the float. In this area, as well as in New Hampshire and other places where pegmatites abound, pockets are often marked by growths of shrubs or trees, which find the readymade pocket openings much better places for footholds than solid rock. Certainly every tree cannot be regarded as being potted in a pegmatite but it is only common sense that a tree is more likely to flourish in a pegmatite opening than elsewhere. Some large pockets have been found in Colorado and New Hampshire by shrewd collectors who closely observe the terrain for trees and shrubs apparently growing out of solid rock. In granite country, the alert collector not only pays attention to float but also to the patterns of plant life for any clue to underground openings.

SPOTTING PEGMATITE OPENINGS IN HIGH AREAS

At high elevations, such as in the Sierra Nevada of California or upon Mount Antero in Colorado, soil coverings are largely absent and make examinations of rock much easier in some respects, but much more difficult in others. Much of the rock containing pegmatites is buried beneath tons of broken debris which detaches itself from solid rock and forms steep talus slopes, dangerous and difficult to cover. If float is found, it is often impossible to track it to its source because it may have bounced downslope for hundreds or even thousands of yards. In situations such as these, the techniques of the famous Swiss mineral collectors come into play and prospecting is concentrated along the upper edges of debris slopes next to rock still in place. Walls and ledges are carefully scanned for marked changes in rock textures which may be due to pegmatites, with particular attention to changes in coloration, bedding, or the presence of any crevices or openings which appear to differ in some important respect from ordinary joints or parting planes. Shrubbery precariously placed upon sheer rock walls is always suspect and deserves examination if accessible. Attractive float found in talus slopes is certainly indicative of pockets above but if one is not equipped for mountain climbing, it is best to avoid the hazards of cliffs altogether and take to more level summit areas where the going is easier. Stretches of bare rock should be inspected as closely as possible because pegmatite openings are often disguised by fillings of rock fragments and soil in which alpine plants take root. By trapping sand and soil with their rootlets, plants gradually expand over the years until they completely cover considerable areas of otherwise bare rock with thin tenacious mats of vegetation. Swiss crystal collectors pay a great deal of attention to the evidence of plants, and justly so, for as has been said before, plants can seldom grow upon solid impervious rock; they do need crevices for roots.

PEGMATITE CAVITIES IN GRANITE

As mentioned in the previous chapter, small pegmatite bodies surrounding gas cavities are common in some coarse-grained granites. The rock around them is marked by crystal grains which grow larger as the opening in the center of the pegmatite is reached. Near the edges of the pocket an intergrowth of quartz and feldspar called graphic granite, usually forms a band completely encircling the opening and provides a valuable indication that a pocket is being neared. A section of such a pegmatite is pictured in the drawing of Figure 87, while the appearance of graphic granite is shown in the polished slab of Figure 88. The pattern of graphic granite is very characteristic of pegmatites in general, and in the case of small pegmatites, is also a reliable indicator that a

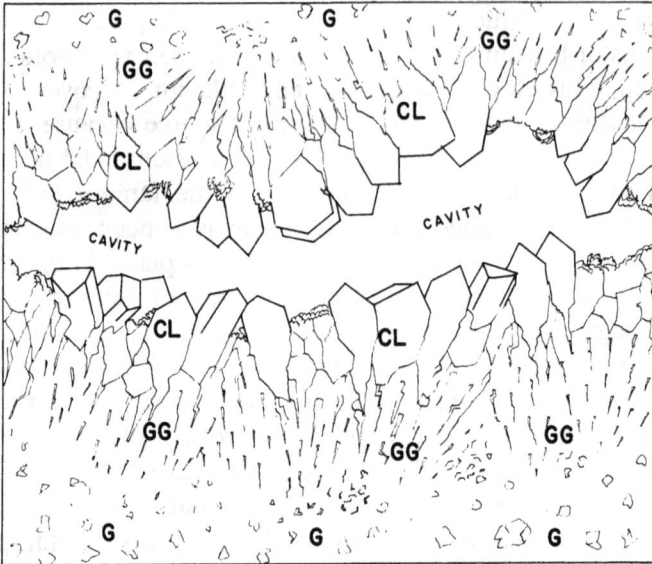

CL-CRYSTALS LINING CAVITY   GG-GRAPHIC GRANITE   G-NORMAL GRANITE

FIGURE 87. A drawing of a pocket in New Hampshire granite showing the abrupt change from ordinary country rock to graphic granite to the large coarse grains of feldspar and quartz lining the pockets and beautifully crystallized where room for development was available. This pocket measured about a foot in length and several inches deep.

pocket is somewhere nearby even though it cannot be seen. Just beyond the graphic granite, the single interlocked crystals of quartz and feldspar grow much larger and in a matter of inches the pocket itself is reached.

In some granite areas where gas cavity pegmatites are common, however, larger vein-like pegmatites also develop but are far less abundant. In such pegmatites, the coarse-grained mixture of feldspar and quartz is enclosed by bands of distinctive rock known as *aplite*. It is easy to recognize aplites because all are very much finer-grained than the granite itself, are very light in color when fresh, due to being admixtures of feldspar and mica, and break with a sugary fracture. Aplites appear as streaks within the granite itself but not always in connection with pegmatites; however, enough of them are found enclosing pegmatites with large pockets to make it worthwhile examining the ground very carefully wherever they are present. The pegmatites themselves are usually much longer than they are wide, which is *not* the case with the smaller kinds, and in fact resemble the extremely large pegmatites which supply commercial mica, feldspar, beryl, etc. Some

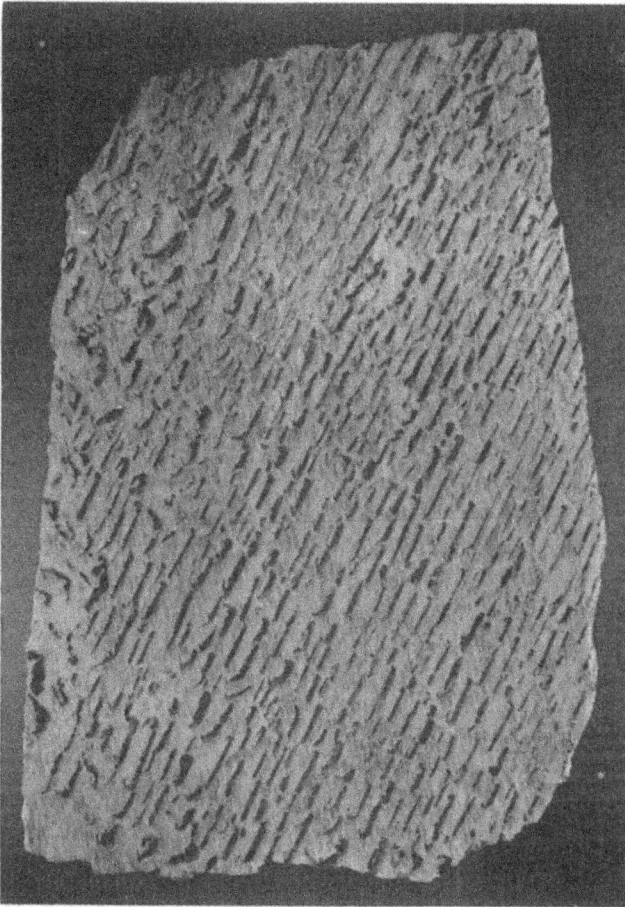

FIGURE 88. Graphic granite from Hybla, Ontario, showing the characteristic patterns formed by the intergrowth of feldspar and quartz. In this example, dark markings are smoky quartz and the lighter material forming the bulk of the rock is feldspar. Graphic granite is very common in granitic pegmatites and serves as a means of identifying them. *Courtesy Smithsonian Institution.*

geologists reason that long and narrow pegmatites entirely enclosed in granite originally developed around large gas cavities but were stretched out by internal movements of the granite while it was still plastic. In any event, the pockets in these pegmatites are also long and narrow and frequently filled completely with quartz, though many are hollow and therefore lined with perfect crystals. Some large pegmatites of this type have furnished the beautiful groups of green amazonite and smoky quartz coming from the Pikes Peak granite region of Colorado.

BATHOLITH FRINGE PEGMATITES

The largest pegmatites of all are found in the schists and gneisses which fringe batholiths. Some are enormous in size, dwarfing even the largest of their cousins occurring in granite. A number in the Black Hills of South Dakota, in North Carolina, and in Maine are of such size that steam shovels and trucks work entirely within the openings blasted into them. However, such large bodies are exceptional, and the majority range in size from only a foot in thickness and dozens of feet in length to perhaps ten to fifteen feet in thickness and several hundred feet in length. Although many are oval in outline, tear-shaped, branched, or bulged, the greater number are sheetlike bodies which therefore outcrop as thin streaks or ribbons. Figure 27 illustrates pegmatites fringing a batholith and shows them as formed in metamorphic rocks near the edges of the magmatic rock masses.

Prospecting generally follows the same procedures mentioned earlier for smaller pegmatites but greater size of batholith fringe pegmatites makes for greater prominence and easier discovery. Distant views often show large pegmatites as white streaks contrasting strongly to the darker color of the enclosing gneisses and schists, but such contrasts cannot be seen easily except in open or brush-free terrain. In heavily wooded regions, such as in Montana around the edges of the Boulder Batholith, in some places in Colorado, in New England, Canada, and especially in the Piedmont region of the eastern United States, outcrops may be completely invisible even from a helicopter, and prospecting can only be carried on by foot.

Unlike their smaller relatives in granite, fringe pegmatites often contain a great deal of mica which weathers from the rock and litters the ground around the outcrop with bright shining flakes. Large flakes of several inches across are very attractive signs of coarse-grained structure within the pegmatite and may mean the presence of commercially valuable book mica, perhaps also beryl and gemstones. Because feldspar and quartz resist weathering better than schists and gneisses, large pegmatite outcrops often stand above ground level and are therefore easily spotted. This feature is very pronounced in southern California where many pegmatites rise above surrounding brushy slopes as whitened ribs and ribbons easily visible from many miles away. However, this high degree of resistance to weathering as compared to enclosing rocks is not an unmixed blessing by any means, for many enormous blocks of pegmatite frequently break away from the outcrop and tumble downhill to make prospecting on foot a tedious and confusing job. In many cases, an outcrop which seems very distinct from some distance away, becomes a wild jumble close at hand, and the prospector is hardpressed to decide just where the pegmatite plunges into the ground. The causes for this can be easily imagined by referring to the diagram in Figure 86.

Outcrop features are vastly different in Canada, New England and in the Piedmont region. In these regions prominent raised ribs are the exception rather than the rule. In the first two mentioned, ancient glaciation smoothed or rounded all exposed rock and planed down all outcrops to the same general level. This is beautifully shown upon Plumbago Mountain in Newry, Maine, where the long climbing trail to the pegmatite quarries near the summit passes over fresh schist and gneiss planed smooth and polished to almost artificial perfection. Many small and large pegmatite veins and stringers are likewise reduced to the common ground level, showing perfectly all details of internal structure, somewhat like the gneiss exposures shown in Figure 59. Farther south, in the Piedmont region, glaciation has not been responsible for leveling outcrops but weathering has been far more intense and has accomplished the same result. The problems of prospecting are made far worse by a climate which encourages growth of dense vegetation on the deeply-decayed rocks. The terrain is gentle, as a rule, and very few rock outcrops of any kind are seen, in fact many pegmatites are found only because much mica appears in the topsoil over the pegmatite. In places where topsoil is very deep, very little feldspar or quartz appears upon the surface, and such pieces that do may be covered completely by underbrush and leaves. In higher hills of North Carolina, Georgia, and Alabama, rugged terrain makes prospecting an easier task because of better exposures, but in no area of the Piedmont is it as easy as it is elsewhere upon the continent.

EXAMINING PEGMATITES

Although large pegmatites are relatively easy to find, merely discovering one is not much of a trick unless the prospector or collector is able to look it over and form some ideas as to the possibility of recovering valuable minerals. This in turn requires the ability to recognize the various minerals which are common in pegmatites and the zones in the pegmatite likely to carry them. Therefore, the very first step in prospecting a pegmatite is to establish its limits, that is, its total length, its width, and the location of contacts all around the edges. A clear picture should now emerge as to the size and shape of the body, and should make it easier to spot those areas in the center or along the centerline where so many valuable minerals occur. In areas where pegmatites are covered with deep soil, or littered by rock fragments which do not come from the pegmatite itself, some clearing off may be necessary in order to obtain a good look. It is helpful to remember in clearing an outcrop that the size of crystals grains in any pegmatite *increases* toward the *center*, and conversely, *decreases* toward the *margins*. Thus if no idea can be formed as to the width of the pegmatite, topsoil can be cleaned off toward the direction of decreasing grain size until the contact is met. Doing this in several places will establish the general outline and size of the body. Once this has been done, it should be a simple matter to trench across the thickest portion to expose a strip of pegmatite from one contact to the opposite contact; further careful cleaning of the exposure will then allow identification of minerals and some judgment as to their value.

The following minerals characteristically occur in specific zones, and identifying them serves to identify the zone of the pegmatite, or, if the zone is known already, helps in looking for them; they are: mica, large crystals of feldspar, beryl, and quartz. In regions where commercial mica is known to exist, look for books of this mineral near the contacts. If much mica is present, the outcrop and surrounding areas are likely to be littered with numerous flakes split off from crystals, and from their size, a very good estimate can often be made as to commercial value. Books of mica do not occur everywhere along the contacts but mostly form concentrations or "shoots" in certain places. It may be necessary to uncover contacts along much of the margin to discover the favored spots where books form. Large feldspar crystals are found in zones toward the centerline, just past those where mica occurs, while beryl usually occurs farther toward the centerline and at the edge of the quartz core. Beryl crystals are frequently partly imbedded in core quartz and partly imbedded in adjacent feldspar. In regard to quartz, it almost always forms a core within the *thickest* part of the pegmatite (see Figure 65) but some bodies have very little quartz, or quartz only in the form of small disconnected pods. In pegmatites of regular form, the thickest part is usually midway between the ends and the sides, but in oval, tear-shaped, or even more irregular bodies, it may be necessary to pace over the entire outcrop to be sure where the thickest section

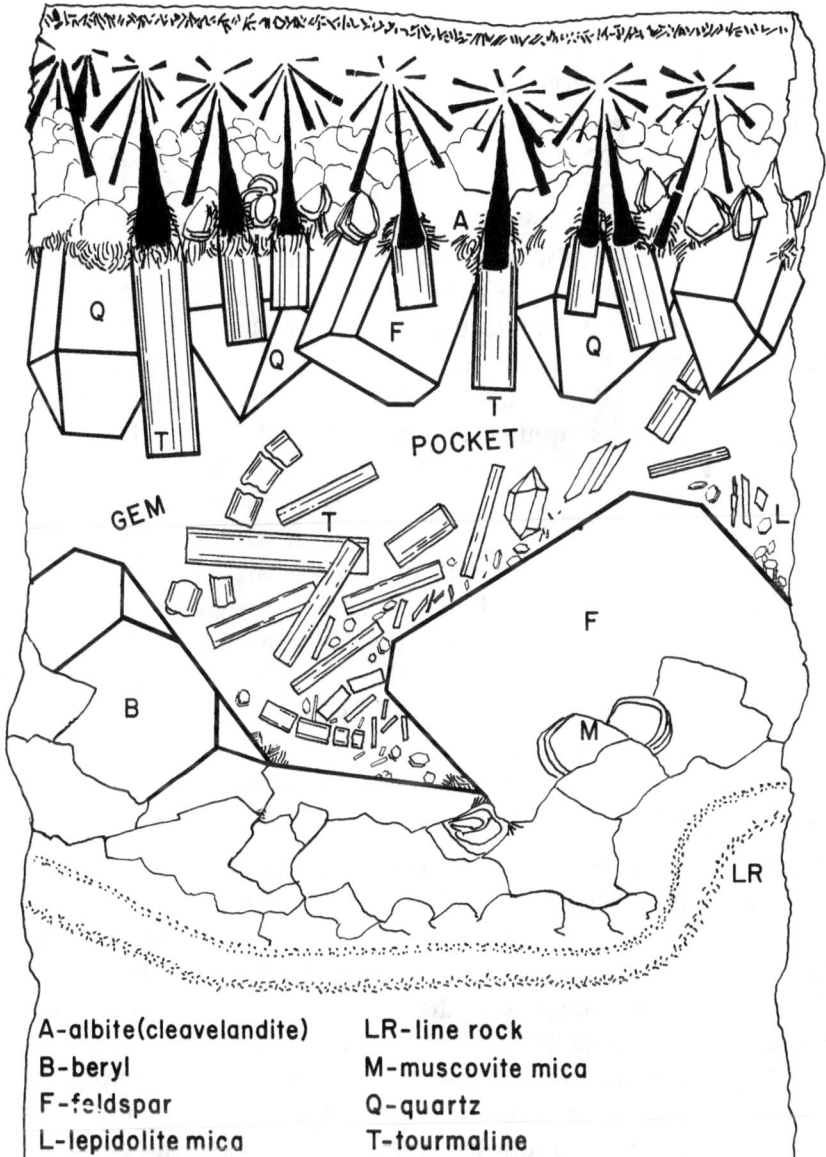

A-albite(cleavelandite)   LR-line rock
B-beryl   M-muscovite mica
F-feldspar   Q-quartz
L-lepidolite mica   T-tourmaline

FIGURE 89. A cross-section of a gem-bearing pocket in the Himalaya pegmatite at Mesa Grande, San Diego County, California. Although pockets of this type seldom exceed six or eight inches in depth, they extend considerable distances laterally and therefore provide enormous quantities of gem and specimens tourmaline as well as other desirable specimens. Compare with Figure 111.

actually is. In many cases, this close inspection is not needed because the greater resistance of quartz to weathering causes it to stand out above all other parts of the pegmatite. Quartz cores should be examined very carefully for beryl crystals and for signs of pocket minerals. Common core quartz is generally milky to white in color, sometimes rose-colored, gray or even smoky. A high degree of transparency is a favorable sign that pockets may be present.

The angle at which any pegmatite emerges upon the surface, or its *dip*, is important since it tells how the pegmatite should be mined. It has also been found that zones in pegmatites seem to be influenced by the position of the pegmatite during its formation, that is, a different type of zoning is found in vertical pegmatites as compared to those which are horizontal or nearly so. Those which are nearly vertical show evenly-spaced zones around the core, but those which are nearly horizontal show marked differences in zones and the minerals found in the zones from upper half to lower half. Many which are horizontal show development of thick bands of aplite in the lower portions, upon which rests the quartz core, with or without pockets, and above that, coarse-grained pegmatite. Well-developed aplite bands are characteristic of San Diego County pegmatites, especially in the Pala area, where narrow streaks of garnet and tourmaline in aplite cause the latter to be called *line rock*. The position of line rock is shown in the diagram of Figure 89.

Complex Pegmatite Outcrops

Due to the way they were formed, complex pegmatites are easily attacked by weathering and crumble away much faster than simple pegmatites. The repeated waves of mineralization which brought in new mineral matter also caused many cracks to appear between grains of quartz and feldspar, destroying the solid nature of the rock and making it easier for rainwater to enter. Many of the minerals formed within complex pegmatites are very easily destroyed also, for example, cleavelandite feldspar—a kind in which the crystals are thin brittle blades, easy to break at the slightest blow. Central parts of such pegmatites are particularly liable to be destroyed because of the formation of many small cavities and openings within the feldspar crystals themselves and the alteration of strong minerals into clay minerals. In fact, some portions are so rotten that it is often possible to dig them out with pick and shovel alone.

FIGURE 90. Outcrop of a granitic pegmatite at the Hercules Mine near Ramona, California. The pegmatite dips steeply toward the camera with its upper or "hanging" wall contact clearly exposed. Note that the upper part is jointed and disintegrating, indicating that pocket mineralization could be present. These favorable signs led miners to excavate a tunnel beneath in order to intersect the pocket zone indicated by the observer. The mineral sought was gem-quality spessartine garnet.

Another cause of weakness is the development of very large pockets which sometimes reach almost to the contacts on either side, making such sections of pegmatite nothing more than brittle thin shells. When loose material in such pockets slumps to the bottom or is washed away, the walls collapse inward. In regions where weathering has been severe, complex pegmatite outcrops sometimes develop double-wall ridges in which the stronger material along the contacts stands up to weathering but the softer material inside disappears. At other times, the difference between the contact material and that in the center is not so great and the outcrops may therefore show only thin crevices running down the centers. Since the midline is the zone most likely to contain pockets, all outcrops showing double-wall or split structure should be closely examined. Here again it is most important to remember that the hardest and most durable parts of a pegmatite are not likely to carry pockets, while the softest and most easily rotted parts are. Some of the features just described may be seen in the photograph of an outcrop of the Hercules Mine pegmatite near Ramona, California, shown in Figure 90.

Pocket Signs

In examining a pegmatite outcrop, it is important to judge accurately where to dig in order to strike pockets because pockets are not always so accommodating as to show up on the surface. Since pockets are almost always midway between the margins of the pegmatite in its *thickest portion*, it is first necessary to locate this part by the means described before, remembering that grain size of crystals is coarsest about the core. Next it is necessary to examine the minerals about the core and to decide whether they are indicative of pocket development.

A practical example is in order at this point. Suppose that a prospector or collector finds a pegmatite of several hundred feet in length and three to five feet in thickness. The entire outcrop is exposed. Slowly pacing its length, he notes two places where the pegmatite bulges and where mineralization differs in character from that observed elsewhere. In one of the bulges, large feldspar grains are present in the centerline but brief testing with a pick shows the material to be hard and tough. There are no accessory minerals. In the other bulge, however, feldspar in large grains is not only present but is accompanied by irregular masses of quartz and fine-grained gray mica while spaces between masses are filled with crumbling aggregates of cleavelandite. Brief testing with the pick shows considerable softness. Samples are removed from the heavily mineralized portion and broken open to expose fresh surfaces for a closer look. The gray mica is found to be actually lilac in color and is therefore likely to be the lithium mica, lepidolite. The quartz shows considerable transparancy while fracture surfaces display broad glassy areas. All of these signs point to intense mineralization and hence in all the outcrop this is the best place to dig.

Some pegmatite bodies of considerable length and narrow thickness may show many bulges, each with its inner zone of complex mineralization. Still others may show single continuous zones in which numerous pockets may be found scattered anywhere within such zones. The famous Mount Mica pegmatite in Maine and the equally noted Himalaya pegmatite in California show continuous cores of this kind and gem pockets were found in both over considerable distances laterally as well as in depth. The Himalaya Mine pegmatite, averaging only 20 inches in thickness and remarkably thin for its length, has been exposed for almost 500 feet in the main tunnel and shows evidences of pocket mineralization at fairly regular intervals throughout the entire distance. A typical pocket cross-section is shown in Figure 89. Compare this with the photos of an actual pocket shown in Figure 111. On the other hand, many pegmatites are known of tear-shape or pipe-like cross-section and in them pockets are found only in narrow zones within the centers.

The steps described above apply also to abandoned mines and quarries in pegmatite which often expose remnants of cores. In some quarries mined solely for feldspar, highly mineralized pocket areas were deliberately avoided by miners to prevent contaminating commercial feldspar with core minerals, since the product of the mine could be sold only in a specified state of purity. Even in old gem mines, the pursuit of pockets was not always guided by well-recognized principles and some workings show tunnels and drifts which look more as if the mineral sought was coal rather than some gemstone. For these reasons, it sometimes pays to examine old workings and to attempt to discover untouched core sections which could be mined profitably for rare minerals and gemstones. An old working in a sill of pegmatite atop Mount Apatite in Maine is shown in Figure 91; it still produces occasional pockets to the experienced and industrious collector.

FIGURE 91. A large sill-like pegmatite body atop Mount Apatite in Oxford County, Maine. The entire summit of this hill is pegmatite but because of glaciation, very little is exposed and the major portion is covered by topsoil and growth of vegetation. *Courtesy U. S. Geological Survey.*

Pocket Minerals

Immediately next to pocket openings are found certain characteristic physical and mineralogical signs, which, if followed, will lead to whatever openings happen to be present. Since pegmatites are weakest nearest to pockets, numerous cracks will be present radiating from the vicinity of pockets. Near the surface, this weakness often shows itself by complete rotting of the pegmatite so that an entire section of the outcrop may unaccountably disappear beneath the topsoil. Upon quarry or mine walls, however, cracks are not so noticeable and a close look may be needed to spot them. However, in such cases, cracks are often filled with bright pink or white pocket clays or very dark brownish-red clays. Where exposed to sunlight and weather, minerals such as quartz, lepidolite, and feldspar often lose their color and it is always a good idea to chip off a piece to see what the true color is inside. In respect to minerals, the kinds found next to pockets are so characteristic that they provide valuable clues as to the position of the pockets. The following minerals are most typical but not all of them may be in the same pegmatite:

Feldspar: large crystals of squarish cross-section with good faces toward pockets; faces are very commonly etched and corroded; crystals occasionally coated with minute scales of yellow-green mica, clay minerals, needles of tourmaline, or penetrated by sharp, well-formed crystals of quartz; rosettes of cleavelandite common between crystals or at their bases; graphic granite.

Quartz: changes from milky massive material to clear and glassy at pocket edges; colorless, smoky, smoky-yellow; sometimes capped with amethyst; fracture surfaces dull in luster and irregular in massive material, but bright and glassy in material next to pockets.

Cleavelandite: forms rosettes or radiated masses of thin white, yellowish or colorless and transparent blades; rosettes form spherical masses inside pockets; crumbly.

Lepidolite: masses of small pink to lilac scales; also larger scales and single crystals near pockets; perfect crystals are sometimes found in pockets.

Tourmaline: long black, rodlike crystals near wall of pegmatite and pointing toward the center; diameter increases toward center; numerous minute parallel striations on crystals within pockets; color often changes from black to green, red, pink, blue, etc., at edge of pocket; crumbly outside pockets but hard and firm at edges and within pockets.

Beryl: badly shattered pale green, yellow, blue crystals enclosed in quartz and feldspar at edges of pockets; long gemmy prisms of aquamarine inside pockets; also pink tabular crystals of morganite if lithium present in pegmatite; morganite crystals are often severely corroded.

Muscovite: crystals near pockets become yellow or green with silvery luster; if lithium is present, edges of books are often rimmed by lilac lepidolite; book size increases toward centerline; crystals sometimes present in pockets.

Clay minerals: include endellite, halloysite, kaolinite and montmorillonite; abundant in seams and crevices or filling small angular pockets; colors bright pink, yellow, white; surface clays are dark reddish-brown; deposits of light-colored clay on floors of pockets often cover fragments of quartz and gem minerals with brown clay filling remainder of space above floor deposits.

In addition to the principal minerals noted above, the following are found in lesser quantities in many complex pegmatites, most often in or about cores, or zones surrounding cores:

Amblygonite	Microlite
Apatite	Monazite
Arsenopyrite	Petalite
Autunite	Phenakite
Bertrandite	Pollucite
Beryl (aquamarine and morganite)	Psilomelane
Bismuthinite	Pucherite
Bismutite	Purpurite
Bornite	Pyrite
Cassiterite	Rhodochrosite
Chalcocite	Sicklerite
Columbite-tantalite	Siderite
Fluorite	Spessartite
Goethite	Spodumene
Helvite	Stibiotantalite
Herderite	Stilbite
Heterosite	Strengite
Heulandite	Topaz
Hureaulite	Triphylite
Lithiophilite	Triplite
Loellingite	Uraninite
Manganotantalite	Uranophane

PEGMATITE FAMILIES

Many prospectors and geologists have found that pegmatites seldom occur alone; if one is found it is almost certain that others are not far away. Such *families* of pegmatites show similar mineralization but not always to the same degree, some being simple and some being complex. Moreover, they tend to form parallel outcrops and may even dip at similar angles below the surface of the ground, as shown in Figure 92. In respect to mineralization, it is sometimes puzzling and discour-

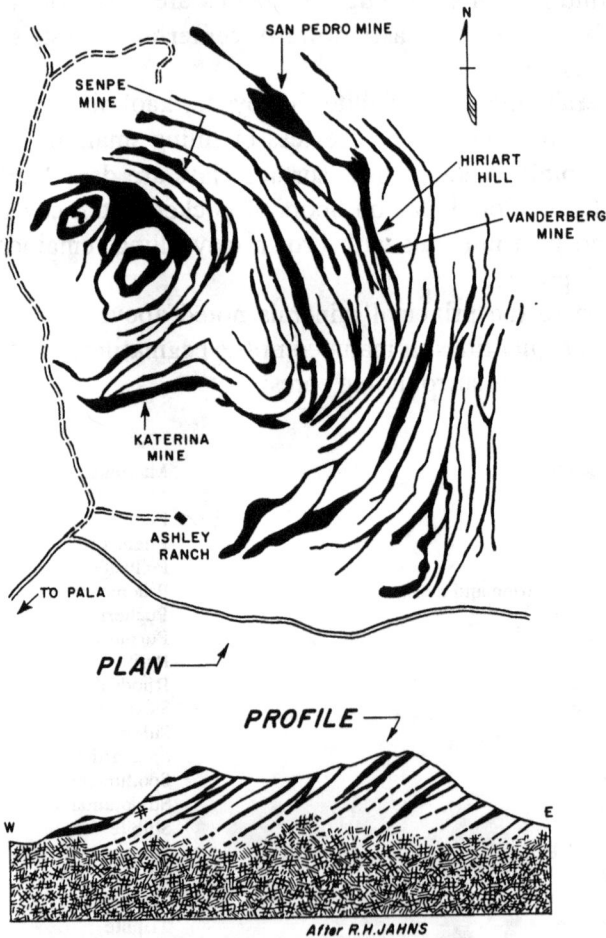

PEGMATITE FAMILY, PALA, CALIF.

FIGURE 92. The occurrence of a number of pegmatite bodies showing similar strikes and dips is illustrated in this figure which shows only part of the Pala pegmatite district. Other pegmatites are found on Pala Chief and Tourmaline Queen Mountain nearby. The mines shown on the diagram above have all produced gem spodumene and other desirable minerals from pockets. *Courtesy California Division of Mines and U. S. Geological Survey.*

aging when prospecting in such districts to understand why one pegmatite will be richly supplied with desirable minerals and another almost next to it may have nothing. This is common in San Diego County in California and in Oxford County, Maine, where certain world-renowned mines produced rare and valuable minerals, including gemstones, while pegmatites practically a stone's throw away were barren. Similar changes in minerals are noted in other pegmatite districts. From the prospecting point of view, this experience means several things, first, if a complex pegmatite is found anywhere in a district, other complex pegmatites may show up after careful search. Second, since simple and complex pegmatites often occur together, it is possible that complex pegmatites may still be found where only simple ones have been found before. A last worthwhile point is that the size of a pegmatite doesn't mean that pockets will be large or small or the mineralization will be simple or complex. Many large pegmatites have no pockets at all while others which are much smaller, contain many. For all of these reasons it pays to look at each pegmatite individually, and not assume that it cannot have valuable minerals because others near by do not.

SIMPLE AND COMPLEX PEGMATITE OUTCROPS COMPARED

Distant Features	*Close Features*
SIMPLE PEGMATITES	
Bold, continuous outcrops resistant to weathering; smooth-surfaced blocks; quartz core often large and prominent.	Lack of centerline disintegration; lack of pockets; simple mineralization: feldspar, quartz, mica, with or without pale yellow, green or blue opaque beryl; tourmaline sometimes present; books of brown muscovite mica often large and abundant next to contacts; hard; difficult to excavate with hand tools.
COMPLEX PEGMATITES	
Ragged jumbled outcrops, prominent in places, depressed or absent in others; "double wall" structure with centerline disintegration; blocks of smooth-surfaced aplite "line rock."	Centerline disintegration; often covered with growth of brush and saplings; vugs and small openings often present in zones other than centerline; black tourmaline in long crystals common; irregular masses of scaly lepidolite mica; small books of greenish or silvery muscovite mica; "rotten" areas in feldspar crystals; numerous cracks along centerline; often easy to excavate with hand tools.

QUARTZ VEINS NEAR PEGMATITES

Quartz veins are often found near pegmatites but whether they are related to the pegmatites is an unsettled question. Some geologists believe them to be nothing more than upward shoots from pegmatites far below the surface, with the quartz brought in by escaping hot waters. Others believe that such veins were formed at different times than the pegmatites and have no relation. In any case, it is true that such veins are to be found in some pegmatite districts but some may contain nothing but quartz, others mostly quartz with a little of the usual pegmatite minerals, and still others contain minerals unlike any found in ordinary pegmatites. A good example of this type of occurrence is in the Pino Solo district of Baja California, Mexico, southeast of Ensenada, where granite-type pegmatites are found as well as pure quartz veins and quartz veins containing such minerals as epidote, black tourmaline, and sphene. It is from the latter veins that the gem quality sphene of recent years has come. Farther north in the Gavilanes district, quartz veins contain scheelite, axinite, and clinozoisite.

In the Piedmont region, particularly in southeast Pennsylvania, and in the narrow belt underlain by ancient igneous and metamorphic rocks extending from Virginia into Alabama where pegmatites are present in great number, small quartz veins occur which frequently yield splendid rock crystal, smoky quartz and amethyst from thin flat cavities. Many of these bodies are almost pure quartz with very few accessory minerals but others contain enough feldspar to be considered pegmatites. The same general region is noted for gold-quartz veins which have been mined on and off for many years. The Mother Lode country of the Sierra Nevada in California furnishes additional examples of quartz veins containing gold and metallic sulfides, also quartz veins containing practically nothing else but quartz crystals in cavities, and still other veins close to granitic pegmatites in character.

Thus the fringes of batholiths or other granitic masses may provide various kinds of mineral deposits. Although the prospector expects to find only one type for which his particular district is noted, he must be prepared to apply his curiosity to any formation which strikes him as being the least bit out of the ordinary because the inconspicuous vein may be the one of greatest value.

URANIUM MINERALS IN GRANITIC ROCKS

Large deposits of pitchblende, the black pitch-like oxide of uranium, have been found in metallic ore veins in the vicinity of Great Bear

Lake, N.W.T., in the Beaverlodge area of Saskatchewan, near Central City, Colorado, and around Marysvale, Utah. Unfortunately, few distinctive signs of uranium mineralization appear upon outcrops except those associated with the alteration of other metallic minerals such as the pink of cobalt (erythrite) and the green of copper (malachite). However, certain oxidized zone minerals of uranium, namely autunite with its bright yellow color, and torbernite of vivid emerald-green color, may be present as earthy or powdery coatings or as very small crystals in crevices. Red hematite stains along the contacts are a feature of uranium-bearing veins in the Great Bear Lake region. In the Marysvale area, veins in fractured monzonite are oxidized in their upper parts and therefore show yellow autunite stains, blue-green torbernite stains, and yellow to greenish-yellow uranophane and schroeckingerite stains. Wall rocks in the vicinity of veins are altered to soft, clay-like minerals.

SULFIDE VEIN OUTCROPS

The most certain signs of sulfide ores in a vein outcrop are the abundant richly-colored stains which cover the outcrop and extend into country rocks for considerable distances, depending on how far they have been carried by water. Sometimes only the outcrop is covered, in which case the stained area clearly outlines the size and form of the vein, but at other times the stain forms a long veil below the outcrop, which from a distance seems to indicate a large ore body. Light-colored outcrops are most likely to be quartz or pegmatite but in either case indicate the absence of appreciable quantities of sulfide minerals. Iron sulfides cause limonite stains varying from deep red to brownish-yellow to dark mahogany brown. It is important to remember that very little sulfide needs to decompose to provide extensive staining and that one's hopes should not be buoyed up unnecessarily by discovering widespread discoloration until the source of staining has been found. Once the source is found, it is necessary to remove enough vein material to be sure that fresh rock is exposed for careful examination.

Rusty stains have been used by prospectors from time immemorial to locate sulfide veins, particularly quartz veins in which sulfides are commonly found with gold. Limonite recovered from within the vein or lying directly over the vein, must be examined most carefully for wires, platelets or small masses of native gold, since cavities within limonite are the places where gold is apt to be present in visible forms. If gold cannot be seen, some of the limonite can be crushed and panned to concentrate such gold as is present. Fresh quartz should also be removed from the vein to look for native gold or the tell-tale dark gray sulfides which often fill fissures in quartz. Native gold can be easily distinguished from all other minerals by a very simple test, namely, hammering to determine malleability. No other mineral of yellow color can be pounded flat or bent and twisted without breaking. In its behavior to hammering, gold is like ordinary lead.

Common Outcrop Stains

In addition to iron pyrite, other metallic minerals provide characteristic stains if not blanked out by limonite produced by decomposing pyrite. For example, manganese minerals decompose into sooty black oxides which cling to all kinds of rocks, forming coatings resistant to further weathering. Copper minerals announce themselves by altering into malachite and azurite which stain outcrops bright green and blue respectively. Azurite easily penetrates fractures in quartz causing it to take on an attractive pale blue color. In surface zones of copper deposits, chrysocolla, the silicate of copper, imparts an attractive uniform blue color to chalcedony which, if sufficiently intense, may cause the latter to become the prized gem material known as chrysocolla chalcedony. Nickel evidences itself as powdery, bright green to yellow-green incrustations of annabergite and garnierite, while chalcedony containing garnierite becomes the valuable gemstone known as chryso-prase. The oxidation of cobalt minerals creates an unusual and characteristic pink incrustation of erythrite or "cobalt bloom." Some of the famous Canadian cobalt-silver-lead deposits were noted for quantities of erythrite found upon outcrops or in zones of oxidation. Molybdenite alters into a bright yellow mineral which yields a conspicuous stain or incrustation.

Gossans

The continued accumulation of limonite over an outcrop of sulfide minerals eventually results in a more or less compact mass of gossan (see Figure 74). Masses of limonite are most fully developed over ore bodies in level or gently rolling terrain where surface waters do not carry away the decomposition products as fast as they form. Gossans are especially prominent and deeply developed in arid or semi-arid regions but may also be found in moist climates. In size, some equal the area of the outcrop and reach depths of from several inches to many feet, depending on how far oxidation extends. As mentioned in the previous chapter, gossans are exceedingly important indicators of sulfide ore bodies and each one found deserves careful inspection.

Gossans *by themselves* prove only one fact: that considerable quantities of iron sulfides were decomposed to form the capping. Whether copper, lead, zinc, gold, molybdenum or silver minerals were present in the original outcrop, and hence are present in depth, remains to be proved by a careful study of the gossan. This involves excavation of the gossan, extraction of masses of limonite, and close inspection of cavities for traces of other minerals.

The presence of copper in original vein material results in the direct precipitation of limonite within or over the outcrop, while the absence of this metal permits limonite to be more easily dissolved and redeposited elsewhere. Thus if the copper iron sulfide, chalcopyrite, was decomposed at the top of the vein, the gossan will more likely be of the same size as the actual vein, whereas if iron pyrite alone was involved, limonite resulting from its decomposition spreads over a considerable area and gives a false impression both of ore body size and of its exact location. The latter type of gossan characteristically develops geodes or cavities filled with shining black botryoidal linings of compact fibrous goethite. Some "bog iron" ore beds which look very much like sulfide gossans are found in low marshy places and are noted for containing large numbers of such geodes.

A prospector discovering a limonite-covered outcrop is certainly entitled to rising hopes, but at the same time he must recognize that the gossan may be formed from relatively valueless iron pyrite or may not even cover the actual outcrop. Ordinarily, however, gossans are situated directly over outcrops and serve to give fairly accurate ideas as to size and extent of ore bodies. Gossans capping quartz veins or ore bodies containing few minerals subject to decomposition, may be flush with the ground or even slightly upraised, but those formed over ore bodies rich in sulfides, tend to slump into shallow craters due to removal of minerals in the oxidized zones by the chemical processes explained in the previous chapter.

The type of underlying ore body is determined with some accuracy from minerals found in the gossan and from the nature of the cavities in the limonite. Minerals which tend to remain behind after chemical activity has done its work are: native gold, native silver, anglesite,

cerussite, smithsonite, and hemimorphite. In some cases, traces of
original sulfide minerals such as pyrite, chalcopyrite, galena, sphalerite
and others, may be found enclosed in quartz or shielded from complete
destruction by coatings of resistant minerals, but to detect them calls
for crushing samples of the gossan and then examining the particles
with a lens. Smithsonite, found very close to the surface as a rule, is an
excellent indicator of other metalic minerals, especially copper, because
it becomes bright blue or green if malachite or azurite were present
when it formed. In some deposits it becomes bright yellow from
greenockite, a cadmium mineral, or brown from inclusions of goethite.

Numerous small cavities in spongy limonite often give clues as to
minerals which were present in the original outcrop. A collector or
prospector familiar with crystal forms can determine what species were
present from the shape of the cavities. Characteristic "molds" are left
behind by cubes and pyritohedrons of iron pyrite, by thin platey
crystals of covellite, and by rhombs of rhodochrosite. Larger gossan
cavities are found in depth and contain crystal groups or velvety
incrustations of secondary minerals. Recognition of such species is far
more certain than guessing at the shape of gossan cavities and provides
enough evidence to be very sure of the nature of the ores below.

Metallic Ore Outcrops Without Gossans

The reader must not get the idea that all ore bodies are capped by
gossans. Limonite cappings form only through decomposition of iron
sulfides and if these are missing, or present only in small amounts,
outcrops will not be covered by gossans nor even discolored. In the
Mississippi River Valley lead-zinc region for example, outcrops lack
gossans altogether; instead the ores appear as partly-oxidized fragments
in topsoil, left behind by weathering of enclosing sedimentary rocks.
Cerussite, the common product of galena oxidation, is often present as
dusty coatings or as a cement caking together bits of rock and topsoil.
A little below outcrops are found masses of smithsonite of similar
character but more compact. Since ore of this region characteristically
contains very little pyrite or marcasite, limonite is not abundant and
such that forms over the years is carried away by surface water.
Oxidized zones tend to be shallow in these deposits but may extend
several hundred feet below the surface in channels dissolved in the
underlying limestone rock. In the Kentucky-Illinois area are found
fluorite veins which sometimes contain lead and zinc sulfides but again
lack gossans.

PROSPECTING CONTACTS

Zones between igneous bodies and those they invade are often marked by signs which can be read in the field. Knowledge of contacts is useful because ore bodies or deposits of commercially valuable industrial minerals often form at or near contacts. Since some degree of metamorphism occurs along all contacts, changes take place in the invaded country rocks depending on whether heat alone is involved or transfer of gases, vapors and mineralizing solutions in addition to heat. Thus contact zones may vary in thickness from several inches, as in rocks which are merely baked, to hundreds of feet, where extensive metasomatism took place. A contact between syenite and sedimentary rock is illustrated in Figure 63.

The principal field feature of all contacts is a decided difference in the appearance of weathered outcrops along both sides of the contact zone. Igneous rocks will usually weather to round, smooth outcrops but the invaded rocks develop very rough textures due to formation of new silicate minerals which do not decay easily and therefore stand out as bumps, knobs and bulges. If invaded rocks are limestones, the resulting marbles will wear away much more rapidly than the enclosed silicates and rough textures will be even more pronounced. Sandstones, shales, and other siliceous sedimentary rocks are not much changed except to be converted into quartzites, while igneous rocks are scarcely affected.

Other contact zone features are differences in height along contacts, as where one rock weathers much more rapidly than the other; differences in color, particularly if marble is involved; differences in vegetation, some plants preferring certain rock soils to others; and finally, development of small gossans or narrow zones of rusty discoloration due to decomposition of sulfides. Where rocks are clearly exposed, as in desert regions, shading or bleaching of basic colors in invaded rocks could be indications of nearby contacts even though the latter are covered by soil or debris.

In glaciated regions, the resistance of granites and other igneous rocks to scouring and abrasion results in terrain features which often emphasize the differences in rocks along contacts. For example, high, steep-sided ridges often prove to be granite, gabbro, diorite, or basalt, while strips of lower ground between them generally mean less resistant rocks such as limestone, shale, sandstone and the like. Such differences in erosion can be helpful in prospecting because they serve to identify rock types and narrow the search for contacts. In the field, the prospector may need to check a few ridges to be sure of the pattern of erosion but once this has been established, his task from that point on is made easier. In areas where many small igneous intrusions are abundant and enclosing rocks are of similar durability, differences in height will of course be much less and terrain of this type will be marked by many low hills or ridges. It is a good rule in prospecting to note any sudden change in topography because this may be due to a decided change in underlying rocks with development of possibly interesting contact zones.

Locating a contact is often made difficult by brush and deep topsoil, however, a contact zone can be roughly mapped out by pacing along a straight line crossing from one rock type to the other opposite, keeping a sharp lookout for signs of the contact. For this purpose it is easy to set up a landmark in each rock type and then stick to the straight line between them. The surface between is slowly and methodically covered, noting all changes in soil coloration, bits of float, changes in rock character and any other clue which will help to narrow the zone. In wooded country, blazes can be cut on trees to mark the way, or brush bent over along the path; in desert regions, piles of stone can be erected for the same purpose. If brook beds or washes are nearby, and if bare rock is exposed in them, direct evidence can be obtained as to the position of at least one of the rock types involved. Several traverses made on either side of the first serve to establish the trend of the contact zone and further examination of ground can take place along the axis of the contact. Preliminary work of this kind is very important if a prospector decides to stake a claim since it will insure that any ore body discovered will be on the centerline of the claim.

LAVA FLOWS

As a rule, lava flows are very simple in mineralogy because rapid cooling did not allow much time for formation of accessory minerals such as has been noted in the pegmatites of granitic bodies. In a few instances, however, hot water solutions brought in silica, zeolite minerals, calcite, copper and a number of other species which crystallized in openings or along seams. Despite the fact that important ore bodies seldom occur in them, examination of lava flows is worthwhile.

The easiest way to identify a lava flow in the field is to visualize it for what it is—an enormous outpouring of thick fluid. Some flows were more fluid than others and spread much like thick molasses spilled

FIGURE 93. A basalt sill clearly showing columnar structure exposed in the wall of the Yellowstone River Canyon near Tower Falls, Yellowstone National Park. Note that better weathering resistance of the basalt causes the sill to form a capping over the much less resistant volcanic ash deposits beneath.

upon a flat surface. In the field these appear as remarkably flat sheets with steep, cliff-like edges. All lavas are usually much darker in color than the rocks over which they spread. Especially large sheets of this kind extend over hundreds of square miles in Washington and Oregon; some reach thicknesses of several hundred feet. In the East, from Nova Scotia into the Appalachians of the eastern part of the United States, lava sheets formed sills of considerable thickness, squeezed in like sandwich fillings between red sandstones. A beautiful example of several thin sills formed this way in the Yellowstone Canyon is shown in Figure 93. Glaciation has exposed many eastern sills as long continuous low ridges, sloping gently on one side and ending in spectacular cliffs on the other where edges of the sills are exposed.

FIGURE 94. Tuff and cinder beds derived from the outbursts of the Irazu Volcano in Costa Rica are stratified much like sedimentary rocks but may be distinguished from the latter by close examination of the fragments. Ash beds of this kind frequently are permeated by silica which forms numerous small deposits of chalcedony gemstones. *Courtesy U. S. Geological Survey.*

Lava fields are often marked by several signs associated with volcanic activity, including cinder cones composed of small bits of lava and volcanic ash thrown out in the last sputtering phase of volcanic activity, and horizontal beds of light-colored ash washed into low places to harden into tuff beds as shown in Figure 94. Many of these look like beds of sand and actually formed the same way but a close look usually shows them to be made of brittle puffy bits of ash, or pumice, light in weight and easily crushed. Some lava flows are so recent in terms of geological time that they look as if they congealed only yesterday. In them, typical flow features provide unmistakable signs of origin. Some show contorted ropy lava known as *pahoehoe*, a name borrowed from the Hawaiians; others are rough and jagged or splintery in texture and are called *aa* lavas, again a Hawaiian term. Both types are pictured in Figure 95. Lavas poured out upon the surface are almost without interest to the collector because mineralizing gases, vapors and solutions escaped easily through many openings and thus had no chance to deposit minerals. A few lava flows, such as those at the San Carlos Indian Reservation in Arizona, and at Kilbourne Hole in New Mexico, provide nodules of gemquality olivine but this mineral was formed in the lava itself and not as a result of later mineralization. Peridot inclusions in basalt are shown in Figure 96.

Despite the general barrenness of surface lavas, all are worthy of examination because of the large quantities of silica introduced in adja-

FIGURE 95. Lava flows of two different types. The upper photograph shows the Kamooalii flow near the Kamakaia Hills, Hawaii and typifies the fluid type of lava known as *pahoehoe*. The lower photograph shows the cindery type of lava known as *aa* at the base of Lava Butte near Bend, Oregon. *Upper photo courtesy U. S. Geological Survey.*

FIGURE 96. Peridot inclusions in basalt along the northwest wall of Peridot Canyon, ½ mile above its mouth, San Carlos Indian Reservation, Arizona. Beneath the hammer head is a curving inclusion of peridot consisting of many loose small grains of clear material. *Courtesy U. S. Geological Survey.*

cent rocks by hot solutions arising from the same deep-seated magmas which provide the lavas. Soft and porous rock formations are frequently impregnated by silica which collects in seams and openings, or forms nodules in ash beds, or travels through sedimentary formations to replace vegetable matter, thus providing petrified wood, chalcedony, agate, jasper and opal. In some instances, entire standing forests were engulfed by lavas which burned out tree trunks but later supplied chalcedony, quartz and opal to fill cylindrical cavities in faithful casts of the original trees. Ash beds are rich sources of many quartz family minerals, especially large masses of jasper, seams of agate, and the odd spherical concretions known as *thundereggs*. The latter represent gatherings of silica at favored points within ash beds and, due to their far greater resistance to weathering, are found upon the surface in considerable numbers long after the enclosing tuffs have washed away. Thundereggs in rock and a polished example are shown in Figures 97 and 98. Other silica nodules and vein fillings as well as trunks of petrified trees weather out in the same fashion and may be easily spotted in barren terrain. It is more difficult to find such quartz minerals in wooded or brush-covered ground, but examination of stream or ravine beds will show them if they are to be seen anywhere because most are highly resistant to pounding and abrasion.

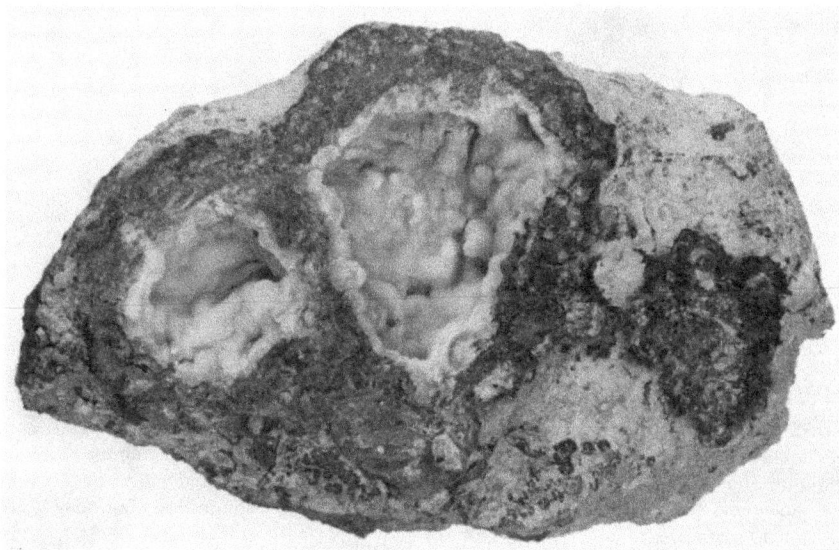

FIGURE 97. Chalcedony-lined nodules, popularly called "thundereggs," form within powdery volcanic material, in this case, a pale tan *perlite* found in abundance at Neveria, Durango, Mexico. When the perlite weathers, which it does readily, the nodules are released and found loose upon the surface of the ground. In the specimen illustrated, measuring about 9 x 5 inches, two well-formed "eggs" are joined together, while a third, toward the right, is joined by a thin band of silicified perlite. The color of the silicified portions is brownish-red while the chalcedony is very pale blue. *Courtesy Smithsonian Institution.*

Where lavas flow over sedimentary rocks, weathering and erosion create striking flat-topped mesas and table lands, rimmed by dark lava and supported underneath by lighter colored sedimentary formations. An example is shown in Figure 99. Slopes at the foot are the best places to look for minerals which may be present above. Formations in which lava beds are sandwiched between ash beds seem very favorable for finding chalcedony, agate, and opal gem material, including the thundereggs mentioned above. Thick flows one hundred or more feet

FIGURE 98. A "thunderegg" from near Madras, Oregon. The exterior is brownish-red silicified volcanic ash which has shrunk in the center to provide an opening for additional chalcedony. From the outside, such nodules are very plain in appearance, however, their spherical form is a reliable sign for recognition. *Courtesy Smithsonian Institution.*

deep deserve special attention because of the possibility of extensive mineralization within them. In many cases, such flows rested upon sedimentary rocks containing a great deal of water and mineral matter, which, upon heating, rose up through the lava and caused new minerals to form in whatever cracks or cavities happened to be present. Sometimes the richest mineralization is near the bottom, but most often it appears on top in the uppermost layers of the lava flows. As the lava is poured out or squeezed between sedimentary strata, gases within the molten rock tend to rise toward the top of the liquid mass, later providing openings for introduction of new minerals. This is believed to be the way in which many amethyst and agate geodes form.

Lava flows in Washington and Oregon furnish splendid opalized and chalcedonized wood, handsome banded and moss agates, and even precious opal from a few places in the eastern parts of these states. The famous precious opal of Nevada is taken from clay beds which are

FIGURE 99. An up-tilted lava flow exposed in the Prospect Park quarry in Paterson, N.J. The photo is taken in an easterly direction. Just beyond the trees is exposed the face of the flow and the steep drop into the valley of the Passaic River. Despite glaciation of this region, the flow stands high above the sandstones in which it is imbedded because its constituent basaltic rocks are harder and more resistant to weathering and erosion.

believed to be altered volcanic ash, while the equally famous cherry and flame opals of Mexico are dug from small cavities in trachyte and rhyolite flows.

MINERALIZATION IN BASALT AND DIABASE SILLS

As mentioned before, lavas squeezed into the layers of sedimentary rocks pick up minerals and moisture from the rocks around them and thus provide opportunities for new minerals to form in cracks and gas cavities. However, mineralization must have someplace to go and unless openings are provided, nothing happens. It is therefore necessary that the lavas themselves contain enough gases to create open spaces, or, lacking gas cavities, that large seams or cracks form along which mineralizing solutions can pass and deposit minerals in the walls of fissures. There are many differences among lava sills, some being completely barren and others being rich in cavities lined with fine crystals, while other flows show parts which are barren and parts which are rich.

FIGURE 100. Mineralized cavities in the basalt of the Prospect Park quarry in Paterson, N.J. The left photo shows ovoid cavities in solid basalt which typically are lined with fine prehnite while the right photo shows the much more abundant cavities which form between rounded masses or "pillows" of basalt. The width of the upper cavity in the left photo is about 18 inches. The cavity just left of center in the right photo is also 18 inches wide and about 6 inches deep. Cavities in pillow basalt commonly provide excellent specimens of zeolite minerals perched as crystals on drusy quartz (white), shown lining the cavities in the right photo.

Basalts showing column structure are completely barren of minerals and it is a waste of time to prospect them. However, some very thick flows show sections honeycombed with crystal-filled cavities, generally along the top layers, and bottom layers which are either columnar basalt or compact basalt with almost no cracks or cavities. Other sills show changes horizontally such that one part of the sill will be mineralized and another part some yards away will contain nothing at all. Variations of this kind are common in the basalt sills of northern New Jersey, especially in the famous quarry at Prospect Park shown in

Figure 99. In this picture, note how easily the rock is shattered, a sign of intensive mineralization along many hairlike cracks originally formed by fairly rapid cooling and shrinking.

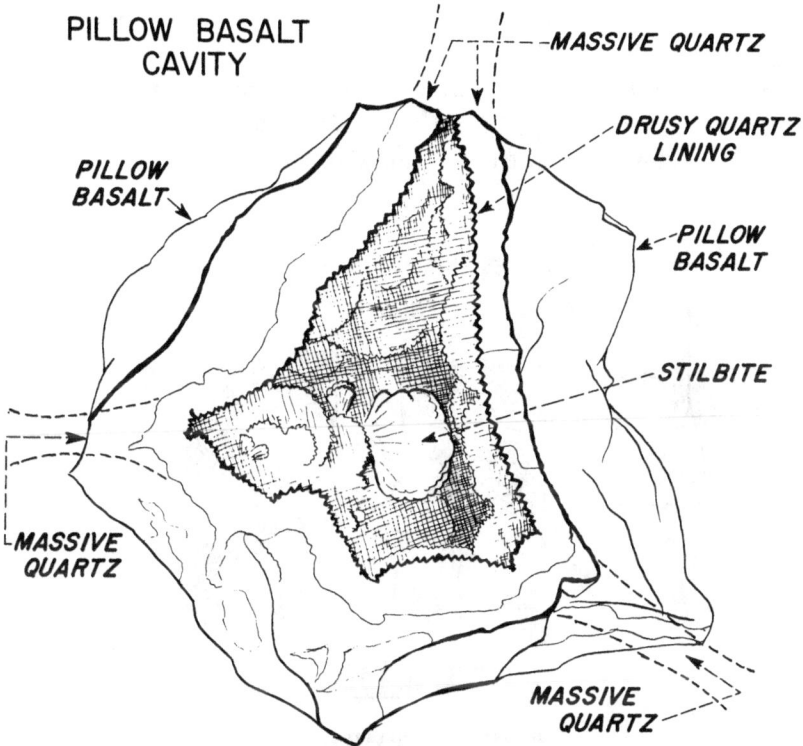

FIGURE 101. A typical angular cavity in pillow basalt from the Prospect Park Quarry (Vandermade), Paterson, New Jersey. This cavity formed at the intersection of several rounded masses or "pillows" of basalt. The basalt remaining on the specimen is greenish in color, much altered and very brittle.

In contrast to basalts, diabases do not contain nearly as many openings but such openings as may be present, may contain exceptionally fine mineral specimens. Diabase sills are generally thicker than basalt sills, and cool more slowly, thus giving crystal grains within the rock a chance to grow larger. The collector can often tell diabase from basalt because of this reason, the diabase showing distinct crystals of labradorite or hornblende while no crystals at all can be detected in basalt. Furthermore, because of slower cooling, diabase often breaks into large square or splintery blocks and does not show the ball-like

pillow structure so common in heavily mineralized basalts. Such mineralization as occurs takes place along vertical cracks in the rock which are
gradually enlarged by the passage of hot water solutions through them
until they are wide enough to form fissure cavities. Cavities in both
kinds of rock can be compared by their distinctive form, for example,
an angular cavity typical in pillow basalt is shown in Figure 101, while
a fissure cavity typical of diabase is shown in Figure 102. Both
drawings have been sketched from actual field specimens. Figure 103 is
a prehnite specimen taken from a pillow basalt cavity in a quarry near
Paterson, N. J.

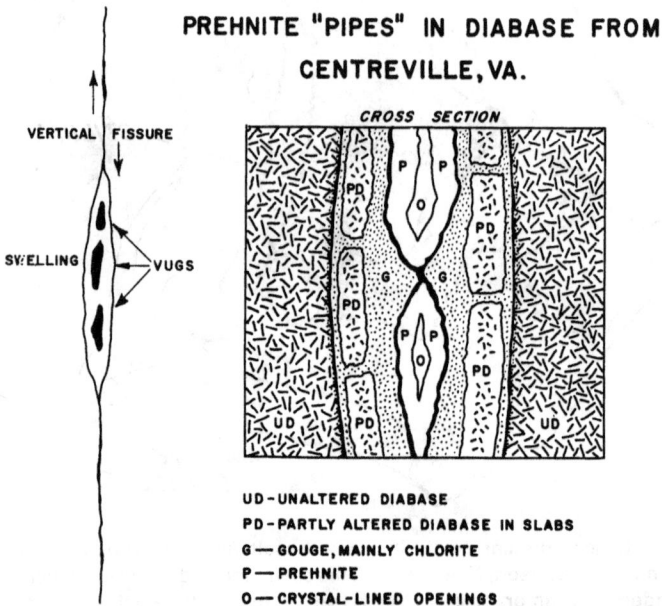

PREHNITE "PIPES" IN DIABASE FROM
CENTREVILLE, VA.

VERTICAL FISSURE

SWELLING   VUGS

CROSS SECTION

UD – UNALTERED DIABASE
PD – PARTLY ALTERED DIABASE IN SLABS
G — GOUGE, MAINLY CHLORITE
P — PREHNITE
O — CRYSTAL-LINED OPENINGS

FIGURE 102. A mineralized fissure in diabase containing pipe-like vugs lined
with prehnite and apophyllite of considerable beauty. In the quarry, near Centreville, Va., the diabase is broken into blocks by numerous vertical and horizontal
partings which greatly facilitate quarrying operations. It is along such a parting
that the illustrated fissure developed. Although the enclosing rock is extremely
hard and tough, it is possible to remove the prehnite because of the softness of the
chlorite filling. When the loose gouge material is taken out, it is easy to detach the
partly altered slabs shown along the sides and thus enlarge the fissure to gain
access within.

Field examination of basalt sills is not usually a difficult task because
structures favorable for mineralization are apparent even from some
distance away. The most favorable sills are of course those which are

crumbly and skirted by much talus material, while those least favorable are cliff-like outcrops. Many sills in the eastern United States and Canada, particularly in Nova Scotia, stretch for miles and provide readily accessible talus slopes at their bases. In fact, along the sea shore cliffs in Nova Scotia mineralized portions often occur so far up on cliff faces that direct collecting is impossible without danger to life and limb, and such specimens as are obtained are found in blocks of rock in talus. If sills are honeycombed with cavities from top to bottom, it sometimes pays to inspect the level areas on top for signs of exposed cavities. Many will be filled with soil but many still yield good specimens despite the dirt. In the event seams or nodules of chalcedony are exposed, they will not be spoiled by dirt and can be used as if coming from fresh unweathered rock. Because of the durability of chalcedonic gemstones, all streams and brook beds in the vicinity of any sill known to contain them should be examined closely for carnelian, a variety of chalcedony stained dark brown to various shades of dark brownish-red

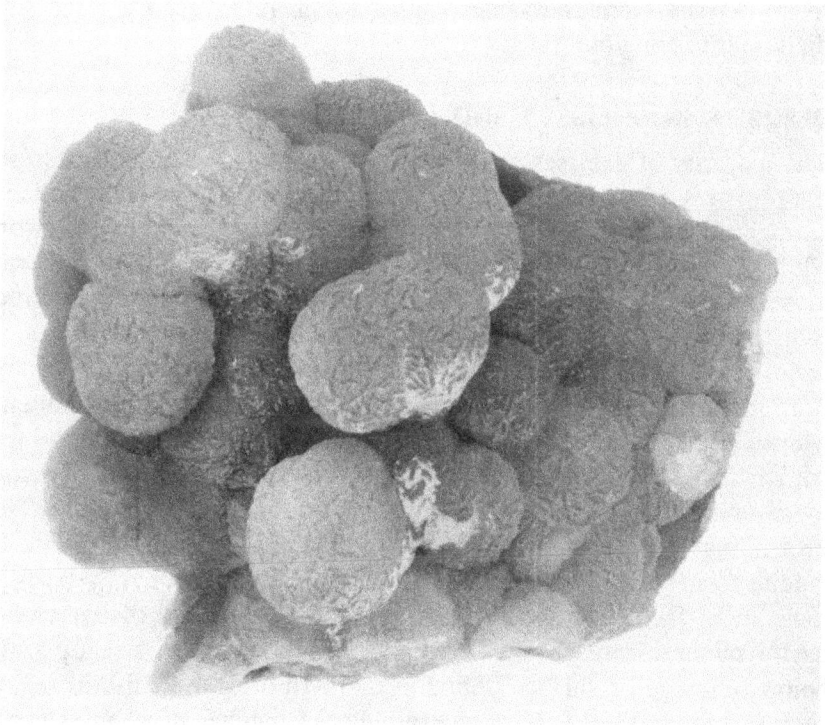

FIGURE 103. Growth of prehnite lining an angular cavity in pillow basalt; Paterson, New Jersey. *Courtesy Smithsonian Institution.*

by infiltration of iron compounds. Abundant iron is of course available from decomposition of iron-bearing silicates and magnetite or ilmenite which commonly occur in basalts and diabases. Geodes and nodules of chalcedony may also be found in such deposits but close inspection of gravels is called for because their rough pitted exteriors do not resemble in the slightest the material found within. Because basalts and diabases, locally called "trap rocks," are favorite constructional materials, numerous active and inactive quarries may be found in sills located near large population centers in the East and West. From them are obtained the majority of fine specimens of the species listed above, and if permission is obtained to collect in them just after a blast has been set off, richly rewarding collecting is often possible.

Basalt and diabase sills are frequently associated with copper mineralization in the Keeweenaw Peninsula of Michigan, where many tons of copper have been mined from deposits formed along sills intruded into conglomerates. In Canada, silver ores are often associated with diabase, as in the famous Cobalt district of Ontario, where rich ores are believed to be derived from the same magma which introduced a large sill of diabase into conglomerates.

DEPOSITS IN GNEISSES AND SCHISTS

The majority of gneisses and schists are completely without interest to the prospector looking for commercial ore deposits, but to the collector, enough minerals of interest occur in them to make examination worthwhile. In general, such minerals as may be valuable are considerably more resistant to weathering than the rocks enclosing them, although schist rots away much faster than gneiss because of its chlorite and mica. Exposures can be prospected rapidly until rotten or decayed portions are met with, or places where ribs or ridges stand prominently. Marked differences in weathering indicate decided changes in mineralization and call for closer inspection. Garnets are frequently found as loose crystals in soil derived from weathered rock or may be seen protruding like warts upon otherwise smooth outcrops. Nephrite and jadeite form sharp narrow ridges or bulbous masses or may be found loose in surface rubbish. Perhaps the simplest method of determining useful minerals present in these rocks is to examine stream gravels below outcrops or surface debris in talus. In arid or semi-arid regions, such as in the West, it pays to examine the patches of pebbles formed on the surface, where brisk winds have blown away sand and soil. Many pieces of excellent nephrite jade have been found in such places over a wide area in Wyoming and later prospecting has traced some to sources within gneisses and schists.

ALPINE TYPE VUGS

As long ago as the days of the Romans, the Alps of Switzerland and adjacent countries were known for the abundance of splendid minerals found in cavities or vugs in the highest elevations of the mountains. This reputation was established principally by the magnificent transparent quartz crystals which supplied practically all of the rock crystal used in lapidary or ornamental arts. Even today, after a period of intensive collecting dating back many centuries, new cavities are found by the mountaineers of remote villages who combine mineral collecting with regular occupations during periods of good weather from spring to fall. The mineral specimens collected by the "Strahler," as they are called, are taken to their homes to be painstakingly cleansed, assessed in value, and then sold to traveling mineral dealers from large cities, whence they eventually find their way into collections all over the world.

Although very few places with similar cavity minerals are known in North America, this may be due more to unfamiliarity with some of our highest mountains than with a real absence of vugs. Occasionally a find is reported from the Sierra Nevada in which the descriptions of minerals and their associates seem very similar to some found in the Alps. Can it be that the Sierra Nevada, parts of the Rockies, and many of the high mountain chains of Western Canada and Alaska do contain vugs of similar mineralization? It seems reasonable to suppose that in all this vast territory, hundreds of times greater in area than the alpine region of Europe, there must be places where conditions exist exactly like those which produce crystals in the Alps. In the hope that such may be the case, a brief description of Alpine occurrences and methods used by Strahler in prospecting are given to inform collectors of this possibility.

In Switzerland, the principal rocks containing vugs are granitic rocks, schists, gneisses, and to a lesser extent, syenites, diorites, gabbros, and amphibolites. However, vugs are most numerous in the first three mentioned types which incidentally are abundant in the highest mountain regions of North America. Several peculiarities of Swiss rocks are believed to influence cavity formation, the first being that all rock masses have been severely folded and subjected to regional metamorphism. Secondly, vugs seem to be most common in layers of rock with vertical "grain" or bedding. Swiss geologists believe that regional metamorphism developed fractures in which hydrothermal solutions traveled and dissolved mineral constituents along the way, re-depositing them in vugs. Vertical bedding is thought to be important because it gives rise to cracks which cut across the layering or "grain" and provide openings for solutions to pass. The combination of vertical bedding and horizontal cracks is so consistent that it seems beyond being an accident. These features are clearly shown in Figure 104.

The techniques used by the Swiss collectors in finding vugs and digging them out have been established by centuries of practical field experience handed down from father to son. The very first act on the part of the Strahler is to prospect only in rocks which are known to be productive; all writers on the subject stress the importance of this. Next, talus slopes are examined for signs of vug minerals beginning at the bottom and working up to exposed rock. All walls are carefully scrutinized for the tell-tale horizontal cracks which may lead to openings. The horizontal crevice which eventually provides the floor of the vug is known as the "Satz," or literally, the "seat." If a quartz vein is near a Satz, the collector notes if it bends and cuts across the rock nearby; if it does, this a very favorable sign. Many pockets are found within quartz veins, and it is this combination of horizontal crevices with quartz veins which leads to highest hopes on the part of the collector for he knows the best pockets occur where these signs are present. The exact place to chip or blast away the rock is guided by the depth of the crevice, the flow of water in greater amount at one point of the crevice than elsewhere, the presence of greenish chlorite and clay, and any sign of softness or discoloration of the enclosing rock indicating that it has been affected by hydrothermal activity. An exceptionally favorable sign is inward pinching, like the waist of an hourglass, of the country rock around the crevice. This is beautifully shown in Figure 104 where two vugs with well-developed pinching appear on the rock wall above the men. Inward deflection of rock becomes more pronounced as the cavity is neared and reaches its maximum at the opening itself. If quartz is present, as it usually is, its milky opaque character is lost and it begins to clarify or even becomes altogether transparent (this is true also in pegmatite pockets). A test of nearness to the opening is to strike the rock with a hammer; solid unaltered rock

FIGURE 104. Several Alpine vugs formed within severely folded and compressed metamorphic rocks. Each vug appears as a narrow disk-shaped opening at the places where the rocks are pinched in hourglass form. *Courtesy D. Jerome Fisher.*

gives a clear ring but partly decayed rock near openings gives out a dull muffled sound. As the cavity is approached, the country rock becomes softer and more bleached, with numerous cracks above and below which divide the rock into angular fragments, making it easier to remove. When the opening is penetrated, well-formed crystals are found within, with doubly-terminated crystals in floor deposits and matrix specimens on the ceilings. Most pockets are more or less filled with scaly masses of pale-green chlorite "sand."

A survey conducted some years ago among the mineral collectors of the Swiss Alps developed the interesting information that the following dimensions typified small to large pockets:

TYPICAL DIMENSIONS OF ALPINE VUGS

	Length	Width	Thickness
Small	1-2 feet	about the same	2"-8"
Medium	3-7 feet	2-3 feet	8"-28"
Large	10-16 feet	3-7 feet	20"-48"
Very Large	20-66 feet	10-20 feet	40"-80"

Note: The vast majority of cavities are small to medium in size; very few very large cavities have been uncovered, and when one is found it becomes a celebrated occasion carefully recorded in history.

The following rules of thumb have been developed by the Swiss collectors, based upon centuries of practical experience; some of them are good for us to remember too!

- Where a cavity is found, others will be found.
- Weathered rock is no good (in this case a diorite is referred to); cavities occur in granite and gneiss but the country rock must be hard and solid.
- A good collector must be a good observer; he must be able to follow productive rock wherever it leads.
- The more solid rocks form steep ribs or ridges; the softer rocks are cut through by brooks.
- The layering or bedding of the rock must be on edge (vertical).
- Rocks containing cavities are always steep-sided and cliff-like.
- A wise beginner takes samples of rock to an experienced collector to be sure he is prospecting in the correct type of formation.
- The type of rock is more important than the locality.

DIAMOND PIPES AND KIMBERLITE

Within all of North America, diamond is found *in-place* only in several kimberlite pipes near Murfreesboro, Arkansas, although hundreds of stones have been found in gravels in the Appalachians, in glacial debris around the Great Lakes from Wisconsin to Ohio and in many gold placers of the western slope of the Sierra Nevada in California. Although the Arkansas pipes are obviously the home of diamonds, the origins of the scattered gemstones found elsewhere remain unsettled questions, the best explanations lacking unanimous approval from geologists. Diamonds found around the Great Lakes were collected from points coinciding fairly well with the southern limits of expansion of the Great Glacier and for this reason, are believed to have been brought down from undiscovered sources in Canada. Appalachian and Californian diamonds are even less reasonably explained since they have been found at places hundreds of miles apart, and from country which has not been glaciated by large single masses of ice coming from afar.

As mentioned in a previous chapter, kimberlite is a soft, broken peridotite in which most of the olivine has been changed to serpentine. It is very easily decomposed during weathering and consequently never forms prominent outcrops, in fact, experience in Africa has shown that many kimberlite pipes actually weather to several feet below the prevailing terrain level, forming shallow circular pans or basins. The famous Williamson pipe in Tanzania was completely undistinguishable from the surrounding ground and only the chance discovery of soil which resembled the "blue ground" of Kimberley led to intensive prospecting on the part of Dr. Williamson, who eventually located the nearby in-place source. Mining of the Arkansas deposits was begun after the discovery of several loose stones, although a certain geologist some years before had recognized the nature of the pipes but did not succeed in finding a single gemstone despite careful search on hands and knees. Kimberlite pipes are also known in Kentucky and in the northeast portion of Arizona, however, nothing has been found in the Kentucky deposit except some very small pyrope garnets and fragments of green enstatite, typical of kimberlite rocks. The Arizona deposits produce considerable quantities of gem quality pyropes and very small clear peridots.

Potentially, all of the Sierra Nevada, and perhaps mountains farther north, are sources of in-place diamonds, as are some as yet undefined portions of Canada and the Appalachian Mountains; however, the very few stones that have been found do not point to extensive deposits but more likely to a number of very small scattered occurrences, probably in the form of kimberlite pipes.

Surface features of kimberlites are marked by shallow depressions but may also be marked by development of overburdens of iron-stained soils which in Africa are known as "yellow ground," in distinction to "blue ground" which is the unstained material below. Perhaps the best surface signs are numerous fragments of gemmy pyrope, enstatite, and peridot which are characteristic of kimberlites the world over. However, although they do identify the rock, they do not mean it is diamond-bearing. The unmistakable appearance of Arkansas diamonds in their rough state is shown in Figure 105.

SERPENTINES

Unlike kimberlites, serpentines are moderately hard and resistant to weathering but they do not compare to granites and other silica-rich rocks in the latter respect. Exposures are uncommon; most areas underlain by serpentine form rounded hills deeply covered by dark red soils. These soils often are actively poisonous to plantlife, especially in level, poorly-drained places, resulting in peculiar "barrens" covered by clumps of grass, scraggly and sickly trees of short stature, and thickets of poison ivy and brambles. Sometimes it is possible to plot areas underlain by serpentines accurately merely by noting surface differences in vegetation.

Serpentines contain chromite, native platinum, and ores of nickel. Chromite sand is often present in considerable quantities in nearby stream beds. In Canada, serpentines carry seams of chrysotile asbestos, which supply practically all of the asbestos used in industry. Similar serpentines with chrysotile occur in Vermont and along the Salt River valley in Arizona. The presence of chrysotile is a valuable recognition feature of serpentine in the event it cannot be recognized by other means. In addition to the ores and minerals mentioned, serpentines frequently contain lenses of nephrite jades, as in Alaska and California, and in the latter state additionally contain seams of massive idocrase or californite, and thin seams of garnierite-stained chalcedony (chryso-prase). Benitoite, a very rare gemstone known only from California, occurs imbedded in natrolite seams in serpentinous rocks. Translucent massive serpentine of good color is useful for ornamental stonework and to some extent in the lapidary arts.

URANIUM IN SANDSTONES

The most striking feature associated with uranium minerals in sand-stones and related sedimentary rocks is the display of vivid yellow, orange, and green colors upon outcrops. Such colors are very character-

FIGURE 105. A suite of Arkansas rough diamonds showing the brilliant silvery luster which characterizes this gemstone. The largest crystal shown is about three fourths of an inch in length. *Courtesy Smithsonian Institution.*

istic, few other minerals furnishing so pure or so intense hues. It was color more than anything else which first led prospectors to the numerous deposits which characteristically outcrop along steep canyon walls in the regional sandstones, shales, and conglomerates in the now-famous Colorado Plateau area of the United States. However, not all outcrops are so conveniently marked, uranium minerals in some being completely disguised by reddish or brownish coloration of enclosing sandstones. In such cases it is necessary to detect ore bodies with Geiger counters or similar detection devices. Nevertheless, color remains the most important aid to the prospector on foot.

Although primary uranium minerals such as uraninite and coffinite have been found within sandstones, they do not outcrop as a rule, and therefore the prospector sees only the secondary minerals of the oxidized zones resulting from their alteration. The most prominent secondary minerals and their colors are: carnotite, bright lemon yellow; tyuyamunite, greenish-yellow; torbernite and metatorbernite, bright emerald green; autunite and meta-autunite, lemon to sulfur yellow, and brilliantly fluorescent in yellow to greenish-yellow under ultraviolet light; uranophane, lemon yellow; and schroeckingerite, yellow to greenish-yellow, and also strongly fluorescent in bright yellow-green. All of these minerals appear as stainings or earthy incrustations, although some form very small platey or needle-like crystals. The already strong colors of autunite, meta-autunite and schroeckingerite are made even more intense in daylight because of fluorescence excited by the ultraviolet rays of the sun. Fluorescence excited by a handcarried source of ultraviolet light is of course unmistakable in darkness.

Sandstones containing uranium ores in the Colorado Plateau country are bedded horizontally with uranium-rich layers located some distance below rim rock. Typical terrain is shown in Figure 106. Most deposits prove to be thin lenses ranging from a fraction of an inch to several feet in depth and up to several hundreds of feet in width. Detached blocks of rock form steep talus slopes and provide rugged but accessible places to search. Many deposits show uranium minerals consistently associated with petrified wood in the form of logs, branches and twigs, but unlike the ordinary silicified wood found in the sedimentary formations of the Colorado Plateau region, most are far more decayed in appearance, less silicified, and are honeycombed with porous areas heavily stained with bright-hued uranium minerals.

FIGURE 106. Wasatch sandstones near the White River, Colorado. It is in such sandstones that uranium ores have been found. *Courtesy U. S. Geological Survey.*

PROSPECTING IN STREAM BEDS

The tremendous value of prospecting stream beds cannot be overemphasized. Layers of gravel and boulders represent samples of material gathered from surrounding rocks by natural processes and brought together in small areas for the inspection of the prospector or collector. Because only durable rocks and minerals survive stream pounding and abrasion, a process of natural concentration takes place which man with his best machines could scarcely duplicate. For these reasons, prospecting along watercourses should be one of the first activities of any person interested in determining the mineral resources of a valley and its surrounding higher ground.

In wide valleys with flat floors and shallow sloping sides, sediments may accumulate so deeply that only the lightest will appear on top, and it may be necessary to travel farther upstream to find exposures of gravel. On the other hand, gravels are often exposed to bedrock in narrow valleys with steep sides sloping directly to the central watercourses. Streams follow definite patterns of movement depending on the ground over which they flow; in deep soft sediments such as sands and clays they form serpentine channels which swing more wildly with the passage of time, until looped sections are cut off and beds become realigned. A classic example of a meandering stream is shown in Figure 107. In narrow valleys where lateral movements are restricted, streams descend in a more straightforward fashion but frequently undercut rocks on both sides by similar serpentine movements. In general, good exposures of gravel are found wherever streams take sharp turns.

FIGURE 107. Meanders in a stream called, appropriately, Crooked Creek; near Long Valley dam site, California. In time the loops of the stream will cut through at the necks, causing curved sections to be disconnected from the remainder of the stream. *Courtesy U. S. Geological Survey.*

Since the settling of heavy minerals requires water to flow at speeds appropriate to the size and heaviness of rock and mineral fragments involved, desirable minerals will be found only in portions of the stream bed where such conditions exist. For example, gold nuggets are so heavy in proportion to their size that they will settle in water flowing at a brisk clip but quartz pebbles, much less heavy for their size, will be carried farther downstream until more placid conditions are met and they too can fall to the bottom and stay put. Thus it is necessary to establish the pattern of water movement in any stream bed and, by taking panning samples from gravels at different points along the stream, determine the conditions which are favorable for settling of desirable minerals. Once the pattern has been established, other places along the watercourse which appear to repeat the pattern may be

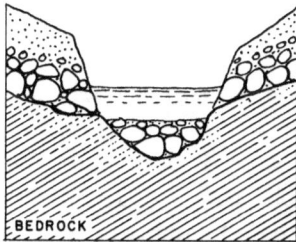

UPPER VALLEY STREAM
Steep sloping valley walls, in-
dented bedrock, large gravel.

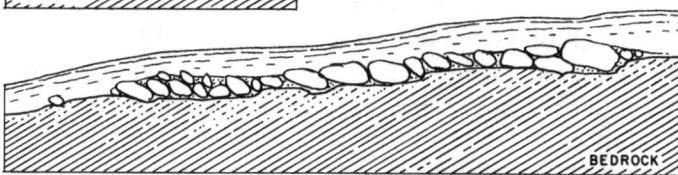

BEDROCK

BEDROCK

LOWER VALLEY STREAM
Deep layers of sand, gravel,
and boulders resting on bedrock

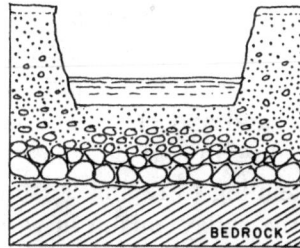

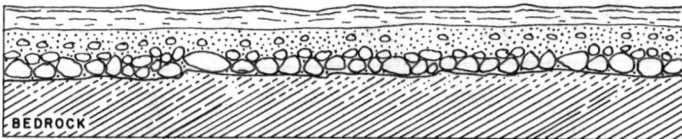

BEDROCK

BEDROCK

TYPICAL STREAM BEDS

FIGURE 108. In general, decided differences in the character of stream beds may be noted, depending on how rapidly the bed of the valley drops. Although consider-able gold or other valuable mineral may be introduced into an upper valley stream, it may find few places for lodging along the stream bed. On the other hand, lower valley stream beds may provide many resting places for valuable minerals.

examined for similar deposits. The character of stream gravels, depend-ing on stream velocity, is shown in Figure 108.

As any valley is ascended, the stream bed is lined with larger and larger stones and pebbles, because only the largest can withstand the faster flowing water. In upper reaches, sands, clays, and fine gravels are found less and less until they almost disappear in the narrow feeders which tumble down from valley walls. The pattern of alluvial deposits is generally as follows:

Lower Valley—Mostly sand, clay and topsoil; gravels are deeply buried and poorly exposed.

Middle Valley—More gravels are exposed but sands, clays and topsoils are most abundant in level places.

Upper Valley—Gravels frequently exposed; numbers of large boulders are present along the watercourse.

Feeders—Gravels and finer material scarce; many large pebbles and boulders in beds of streams.

Field Features of Gravel Beds

Because several erosion cycles may have taken place, it is often found that gravel beds vary considerably in composition from top to bottom according to the events which created them. For example, a thick bed of valley floor alluvium may show layers of gravel alternating with layers of sand and clay, each representing distinct periods of erosion, possibly due to radical changes in the climate. In times of heavy rainfall leading to raging currents, fine material will be torn from the floor of the valley, mixed in with the waters of the central stream, and will settle only in lower reaches where placid conditions occur. However, as the cycle of wet weather abates over the years, less water will flow through the valley resulting in a narrower stream which eventually shrinks to a size in keeping with the rainfall. As the flow of water lessens, fine matter will settle farther up the valley but since less of it is being carried along, the beds formed will be thinner. If another cycle of heavy rains begins, the same process will be repeated and all beds along the floor of the valley may receive another series of deposits on top of those already present. However, if the lower portion of the valley floor has been deepened by stream erosion, new material may be carried much farther downstream before quiet water permits settling. Thus it is conceivable that many variations can occur and a prospector should not be surprised at how changeable the character of any bed proves to be. Wide variations are noted mostly in lower reaches while upper reaches tend to reflect recent weather and therefore show normal type gravel deposits. A simple bed deposited during one cycle of consistent weather and rainfall generally shows large boulders with gravel filling spaces between them, resting upon bedrock, followed by smaller gravel, sands, silts, clays and finally topsoil. Figure 109 has been drawn to show such an alluvial deposit while Figure 110 shows similar features in an alluvial deposit of sapphires.

Due to variation in cycles of erosion, it is quite possible that useful minerals may occur only in one layer out of many, because rocks containing them were destroyed only at the time that layer was being deposited. Sometimes gravels are found resting upon decayed vegetation, representing flash flood conditions when brush and trees were suddenly covered by sediments from upper reaches. This kind of alluvial deposit is common in the thick beds of lower valleys but is rarely found in upper valleys where thin gravel beds do not support heavy growths of vegetation. Speaking in terms of geologic time,

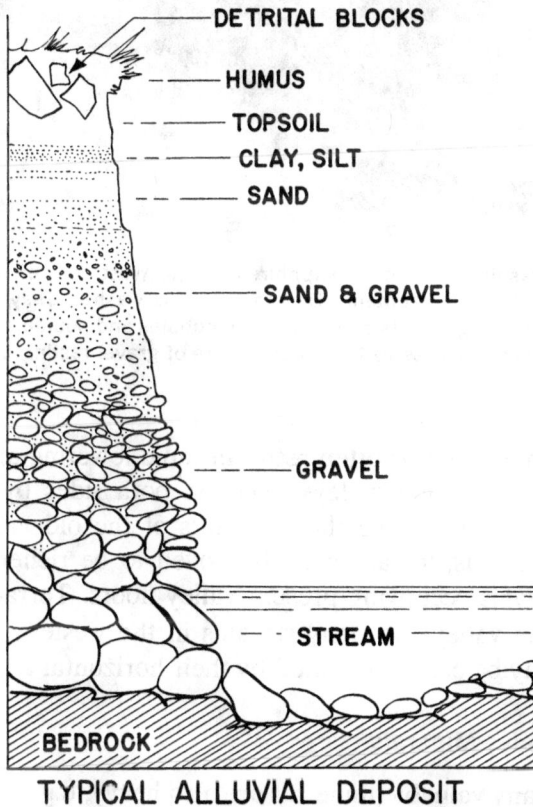

TYPICAL ALLUVIAL DEPOSIT

FIGURE 109. The vast majority of alluvial beds follow the pattern shown in this diagram. At the bottom, the largest boulders rest upon bedrock, followed by boulders of decreasing size. Still further above, pebbles and sand form additional layers. All masses of rock and particles decrease in size nearer the surface. If the alluvial bed is near steep rock slopes, angular blocks of detrital material are often found in or just below the topsoil.

FIGURE 110. Washing gravels for sapphires on the West Fork of Rock Creek southwest of Phillipsburg, Montana. Barren topsoil is washed away by hose to expose sapphire-bearing gravels beneath. Large pebbles and boulders are moved out of the way to gain access to the lowest layers of gravel resting on bedrock. *Courtesy U. S. Geological Survey.*

prolonged rainfall periods often result in rapid lowering of stream beds, resulting in steep-walled valleys lined on both sides by "marooned" gravel terraces representing the remnants of the old valley floors. In certain gold regions, terrace gravels proved to be richer in gold than the recent gravels occupying present valley floors. Terrace gravels are common in the valleys of many streams in the western United States where they may be easily identified by their horizontal tops.

Settling of Heavy Minerals

Because so many valuable minerals are also heavy, e.g., gold, platinum, diamond, sapphire, ruby, topaz, etc., the prospector seeks the lowest layers of gravel to test for their presence. Especially favorable sites are deep crevices, troughs or depressions in bedrocks, basins below water-falls, natural "riffles," as where bedrock forms ribs across the stream bed, behind very large boulders, and other places where sudden changes in stream velocity occur. Active potholes are not favorable for finding minerals of value because the grinding action of the pebbles destroys them. Although high density promotes rapid settling, size and shape of fragments are very important too. For example, a gold nugget will sink rapidly in fast water but a gold flake will flutter from side to side for many yards before it eventually finds the bottom. Even if the flake were shaped into a sphere, it would travel considerably farther downstream than a similar mass of gold much larger in size. For these reasons, it will be found that in any given stretch of water flowing at uniform speed, larger masses of heavy minerals will be found at the head of the stretch than at the foot.

Once a mineral drops to the bottom, deeper settling is promoted by the "jigging" action of water. Turbulent flow along the bottom causes pulsations which vibrate pebbles and permit them to yield to the slight but insistent pressure of heavier minerals seeking to drop to the bottom. In time, heavy minerals deposited on top of gravel will work their way downward, eventually coming to rest against bedrock if sufficient pulsating action separates the pebbles and permits passage between them.

Depending on the original size of any heavy mineral fragment, its toughness and hardness, and the violence and duration of stream action to which it was subjected, the final product may vary from a rounded grain of sand to a large smooth pebble or may show merely a few rubbed off corners. The diamonds found during gold washing in the Sierra Nevada and in the Appalachians often showed up in miners' pans as glistening smooth crystals with few signs of wear, attesting to the invincible hardness of this mineral (see Figure 105). On the other hand, quartz crystals subjected to moderate rubbing soon lose every trace of crystal faces and become oval or round pebbles pockmarked with small, crescent-shaped fractures. Sometimes very small crystals escape bruising by virtue of minute size, as in the case of zircons and garnets, which are often found in sands in amazing states of perfection. Gold and platinum are remarkably durable by virtue of their malleability, which permits pieces to be pounded without breaking apart. Consider how gold, found mainly within quartz, survives when the latter mineral does not Stream pounding is like ball or stamp milling, and works very efficiently indeed against quartz fragments enclosing gold. Crushed between stream boulders, quartz fractures easily but the gold within it bends, twists or flattens. In time, all of the quartz is broken off and only wires, plates or nuggets of gold remain.

Shrewd interpretation of the external condition of minerals and metals found in gravel can be of enormous help to the prospector and collector in tracking down sources. For example, finding quartz pebbles with considerable native gold in them shows that they could not have traveled far, as was explained above. In the same way, quartz crystals found in almost perfect condition also indicates that their source is very near. On the other hand, discovery of smoothly rounded pebbles of nephrite or jadeite may not be of much help because there is no way of knowing how large the original masses were and hence how much traveling was involved. In the case of very small grains, the perfection of crystal form is apt to be almost meaningless because small fragments of heavy minerals can slip so easily between larger pebbles without much chance of being crushed. It is interesting to note in this connection that beach sands along the eastern seaboard of the United States often contain well-formed crystals of zircon, monazite and rutile despite the fact that the nearest source must be in the Appalachians at least several hundred miles away. Other examples of external signs useful for determining sources may be mentioned but the above are sufficient to give the idea.

The following properties of minerals have a great deal to do with how they survive in stream gravels:

Hardness—Extreme hardness is favorable; crystals often show rubbing only on sharp corners. Examples: diamond, sapphire, ruby, chrysoberyl.

Toughness—Favorable. Moderately hard but very tough minerals such as nephrite, jadeite, and chalcedony are worn smooth but do not fracture into smaller pieces. Other examples: idocrase, serpentine, rhodonite.

Cleavage—Unfavorable, depending on number of cleavage planes and ease of development. Examples: topaz, mica, chlorite, calcite (reduced to smaller fragments).

Malleability—Favorable. Examples: gold, platinum, copper.

Solubility—Unfavorable. Examples: calcite and other carbonates, many sulfates, borates, etc., dissolve partly or completely in water.

Granularity—Generally unfavorable in coarse-grained rocks since many tend to separate easily along grain boundaries; very fine grain is favorable.

6

Collecting Practices

The techniques and practices described in the following paragraphs represent the experiences of many persons gained during hundreds of trips to a wide variety of mineral deposits. Other practices will certainly suggest themselves to the reader as he gains experience or solves problems connected with collecting in odd or unusual places. Throughout the discussions which follow, the greatest emphasis is laid on methodical, careful work, for the saying that "haste makes waste" is just as true in mineral collecting as it is anywhere else.

CRYSTAL CAVITIES

Two types of crystal formations are prized above all others: matrix specimens consisting of undamaged crystals perched upon sections of wall cavity material, and doubly-terminated crystals consisting of crystals entirely covered by faces. In each type, value depends on lack of damage, perfection of crystallization, color contrasts, arrangement, and many other factors which will be discussed fully in the next chapter. In cavities, matrix specimens are found attached to the walls but doubly-terminated crystals are found only in the center of the cavity since they require free suspension to develop on all sides. Some cavities contain only matrix linings but others, particularly in pegmatites, also contain small to large numbers of perfect and imperfect crystals lying upon the bottom imbedded in clay. Many pegmatite pockets, though discovered far underground, are filled with moist clays of white, pink, or dark reddish-brown color. Pale colored clays are related to pocket mineralization and are common in gem-bearing pegmatites, while dark clays are believed to form from the decomposition of country rocks and are brought in by ground water. In either case, clays may contain the finest crystals in the pocket and of course clay fillings must be very carefully

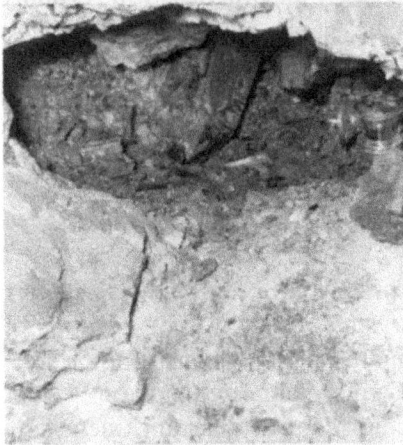

FIGURE 111. Entering a gem pocket of tourmalines at the Himalaya Mine, Mesa Grande, San Diego Co., California. The fabulously rich pegmatite of the Himalaya is shown here during operations in the spring of 1958. In the top photograph, the pegmatite measures only 23 inches in thickness while the gem pocket, located within the upper half, measures only 5 inches deep and 15 inches in length where first opened. In the close-up shown in the center photograph however, the pocket can be seen expanding both in depth and width as the compact filling of red clay and loose tourmaline and quartz crystals is removed. Quartz crystals appear hanging from the roof of the pocket while the jumbled mass of rodlike objects on the left side of the floor are actually hundreds of interlocked gem-quality crystals of pink tourmaline. In the bottom photograph, Elbert McMacken, Mine Superintendent at the time, is shown examining an exceptionally fine doubly-terminated crystal of tourmaline removed from the cavity. *Courtesy Elbert McMacken.*

A COLLAPSED PEGMATITE POCKET

A QUARTZ VEIN IN SANDSTONE

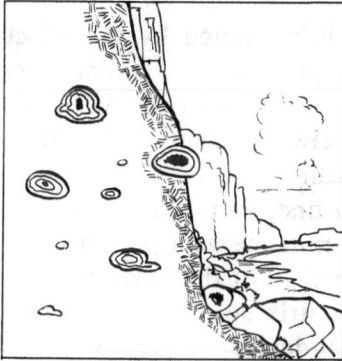

AGATE NODULES IN BASALT

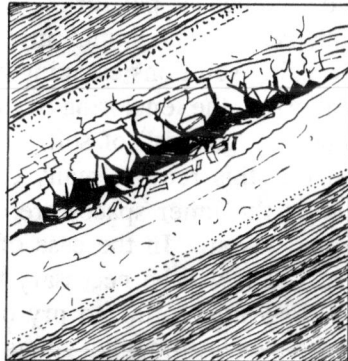

A GEM POCKET IN PEGMATITE

FIGURE 112. Several typical deposits yielding splendid matrix specimens as linings on cavity walls. Except for the cavities in agate nodules, which ordinarily do not contain loose material, all the rest may be expected to furnish doubly-terminated crystals in cavity fillings. The upper lefthand drawing represents small pegmatites in granite as from Colorado or New Hampshire. The righthand illustration represents a quartz vein in sandstone as in the Arkansas deposits. The lower lefthand figure shows nodules of agate in basalt as in the sills of Nova Scotia, while the opposite figure illustrates a shattered pocket in pegmatite as in California or Maine.

examined when the cavity is opened. The opening and cleaning out of a pegmatite pocket containing gem tourmalines is shown in the three photographs of Figure 111. In the first photograph, the rock next to the pocket has been carefully pried loose to provide access. In the second photo, the tourmalines and quartz crystals typical of such pockets can be seen imbedded in clay. In the last photo, a crystal is being wiped free of moist clay in order to judge its worth.

Cavities close to the surface, or actually exposed, may be filled with soil, clay, pieces of rock, roots and other rubbish. Despite this valueless filling, it must not be assumed for one instant that pocket crystals cannot be found lying loose beneath the trash. All such depressions should be carefully cleaned out and the material examined thoroughly to see if pocket crystals are present. In Figure 112, a variety of pockets are sketched to show the way in which openings occur in different formations. Except for the agate nodules in basalt, which like as not will remain in one piece or may not have any central cavities at all, all the other cavities are very likely to disintegrate and collapse inward if located at or near the surface. In some cases, if considerable space existed in the cavity to begin with, collapsed wall material and loose crystals will settle very deep and the collector must do much digging before he reaches "pay dirt."

Collapse of wall linings in pockets is promoted by the effects of mineralizing solutions escaping from the pockets during mineralization and altering the enclosing wall rocks. This results in very distinct partings or "gouges" of soft material between cavity linings and wall rocks. For this reason, many cavities can be very easily cleaned out providing the inner spaces are emptied first, so that the walls can be collapsed inward. In the case of the tourmaline gem pocket shown in Figure 111 it will be necessary to remove all of the loose crystals and clay before attempting to pry off the matrix specimens seen hanging from the roof. Although a gouge does not develop in pegmatite pockets as it does in many ore veins, a large number of cracks running parallel to the walls often provides the same result. Such cracks are shown in Figure 113 and in the lower right hand illustration of Figure 112. As a comparison, the amethyst specimen shown in Figure 71 has been removed from a gouge-lined vein similar to the upper right hand sketch of Figure 112. If it were not for gouges and cracks around pockets, the collector would have an extremely difficult time getting out specimens worth taking home. A thin gouge is characteristic of many ore veins and many veins containing quartz and amethyst crystals; such gouges also surround agate geodes and nodules in amygdaloidal basalts. In most cases, gouges consist of talc-like material which is usually sericite mica, chlorite, or some clay mineral formed from the alteration of wall rock. The shrewd collector always searches for gouge seams in order to exploit fully the weakness such seams represent.

FIGURE 113. An excavated pegmatite pocket in the granite of Mason County, Texas, showing firm granite above the pocket and the typical shattered pegmatite found surrounding the pocket. This opening yielded gem topaz crystals as well as quartz and feldspar crystals. J. W. Bishop prospect, two miles northeast of Streeter; photo taken in July 1913. *Courtesy U. S. Geological Survey.*

Opening Cavities

When a cavity is found, great care must be taken in opening it in order that no over-eager blow by a heavy tool damages the best matrix specimen, which, like as not, may be attached to the wall of the pocket nearest the collector. All dirt, clay, stones, and roots which in any way obscure the view are painstakingly removed to afford the best possible examination. Country rock immediately surrounding the pocket is inspected for cracks and where such are developed, blocks of rock are pried loose to obtain more elbow room for the attack upon the cavity itself. A small tool, such as a screwdriver or slender pick illustrated in Figure 15, is used to scrape away loose material and to probe the lining for loose wall sections. If such sections are found, they are carefully lifted away, using very slight leverage with small tools or prybars, or, preferably, removed by hand. In this way an opening is made into the cavity, which, with further clearing away of rubbish, should show the structure of the rock and the pattern of mineralization. Cracks which will permit further development with least harm to the crystals will also be revealed.

If the pocket is filled with clay or other debris, this material must be carefully removed as soon as the opening is large enough to admit the hand because wall linings cannot be collapsed inward unless there is empty space. In Figure 114, which shows the process of cleaning out a pocket, the removal of fillings always precedes removal of wall linings. Since fillings often contain splendid specimens, it is absolutely essential that they be examined as removed. If any crystals are present, do not attempt to pick them out at this time, but save the entire contents for leisurely washing and examination later. To prepare for this event, it is a good idea to have ready a sack or other container, or to go get one rather than take the chance of losing something of value. If nothing is available, clear off a place on the ground nearby, smoothing to a level surface, and place pocket material on this.

Clearing out loose pocket material calls for skill and restraint. Contents often consist of slender delicate crystals intertwined like jackstraws, sometimes easily visible but at other times so obscured by clay and debris that no sense can be made out of the jumble. Gentle work with the fingers is certainly the surest way to prevent breakage but great care must be exercised not to scrape or claw too energetically lest the fingers be deeply sliced by sharp splinters of quartz or other minerals. If in doubt, put on a pair of leather gloves. When as much loose material as possible has been removed with the hands, proceed to dislodge floor deposits with a small pointed tool or one which is hooked on the end. Delicate work will clear away loose material between crystals, revealing outlines and permitting extraction without damage. Large or long crystals found broken into sections should be saved for possible repair by wrapping immediately in newspaper. In this manner, cleaning out is continued until the narrowness of the opening prevents further access. In all cases, good lighting is vital and must be provided.

Deepening Cavities

Removing central pocket contents permits dislodging matrix specimens from the walls, which like the stones in an arch, cannot be dropped

REMOVING A POCKET

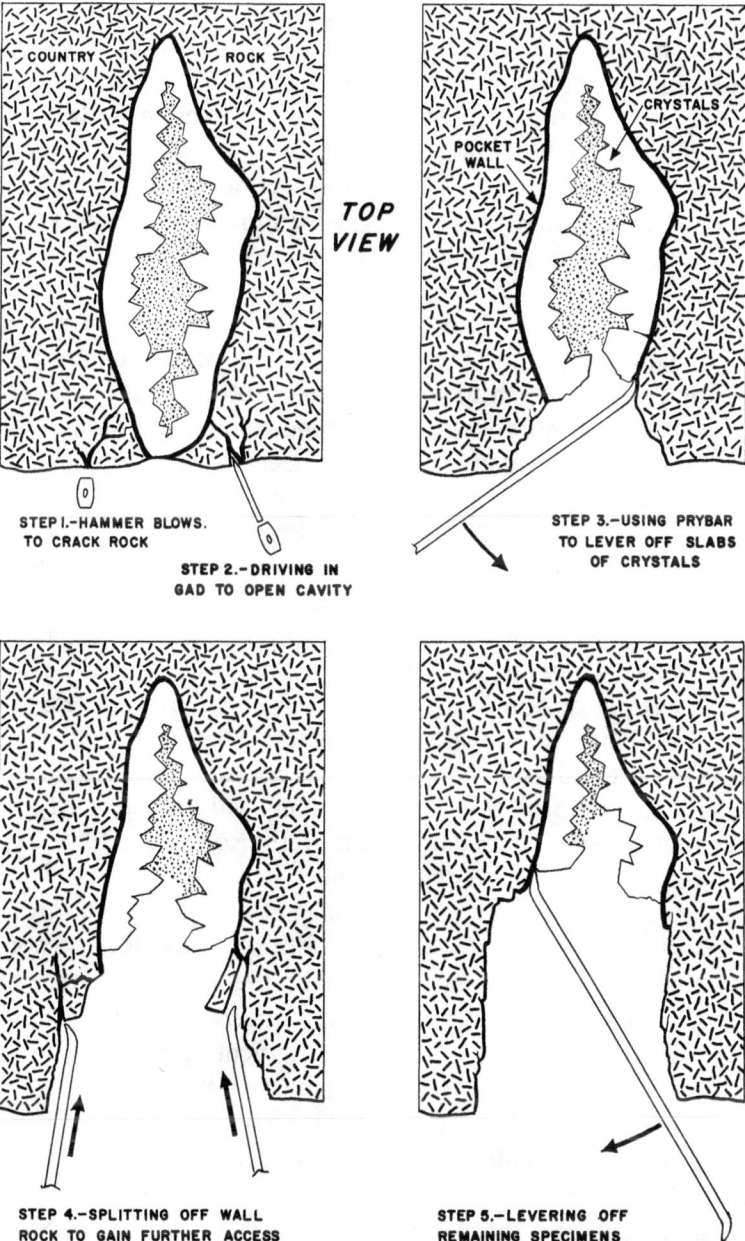

FIGURE 114. Opening, deepening, and removing the contents of a pocket. The loose material found within cavities of this type is represented by a series of dots. As work progresses, as much of this filling as possible is taken out to provide space for inward collapse of walls.

from their positions unless a keystone is taken out first. This is done by using a prybar at some point along the wall next to the opening, prizing between the base of the matrix and the country rock until the specimen begins to yield as shown in Figure 114. If there is a possibility that a wall section may drop and damage itself or other material below, the specimen may be held by an assistant or the pocket stuffed with newspapers or gunny sacks to cushion the section when it finally drops free. Once a section of pocket lining has been removed, others detach easily but the same care must be employed to prevent accidental dropping.

The procedure described above results in the removal of a ring or belt of wall linings nearest to the entrance to the pocket. Sometimes this affords enough elbow room to work deeper into the cavity to clear out more filling, take off more wall sections, and so on until the end of the pocket is reached, but usually it becomes necessary to remove country rock to make adequate space. This is done by carefully inspecting the rock surrounding the cavity for any signs of weakness and then exploiting this weakness with gads or prybars, or perhaps applying heavy blows with a sledge to create cracks if none are present. If there is the slightest chance that detached rocks or slipping tools may harm remaining pocket contents, the opening of the cavity should be closed off with newspaper or gunny sack stuffing, or even covered over with a knapsack if nothing else is available. In places where country rocks are too firm to yield to hand tools, it may be necessary to use light charges of dynamite to shake up the rock. Blasting will not seriously harm pocket contents, despite popular opinion to the contrary. However, the contents will be destroyed if the dynamite is foolishly planted in the pocket or so close to it that walls of the pocket are crushed inward. The author has observed many shots placed within several feet of pockets and has noted practically no damage to even the most delicate crystals. The so-called "broken" crystals frequently observed in crystal cavities actually show etch marks on fracture faces indicating prolonged chemical activity which obviously occurred many years before opening the pocket and firing a charge of dynamite. It should be remarked in this connection that Swiss collectors regularly use dynamite in opening pockets.

When a pocket reaches a depth of several feet, the process of removing country rock to provide elbow room often proves impracticable and further work is possible only with the tools and instruments which can reach inside. It is in such situations that the prybar known as the pocket robber comes into its own since its clever design permits removal of specimens from deep recesses when no other tool could do the job. Figure 114 shows how the pocket robber with its combination prying and piercing point can be used to lever out slabs of pocket lining or used to enlarge openings by scaling off sheets of country rock from the walls of the opening. It is possible when using a pocket robber of four feet in length to remove specimens from cylindrical or oval cavities only a foot across at the mouth but as deep as the tool itself. Since pocket robbers must be heavy to be strong, some skill is required in using them to be sure that exactly the right place is struck when the point is jabbed into cracks and crevices deep within a pocket. This skill comes only with practice and some specimens will inevitably be ruined before the knack is learned. It is sometimes helpful in seating the point to turn the bar over so that the point is directed toward the wall; in this position it has much less tendency to rebound and lodge within the pocket opening. After the point is seated, the bar is held firmly in position but rotated so that the point can act as a lever.

Sometimes in pockets that produce a number of fine matrix specimens, one section of the wall is about as well crystallized as another, but as a rule, there are one or two areas where crystals grow to special perfection or to unusual size. Obviously, careless cleaning out of a pocket with a heavy hand or a heavy tool may damage those sections to the point where possible museum specimens become nothing more than the kind apologetically described in sales lists as "slightly damaged," commanding prices far below that which their size would ordinarily call for. Seldom do large pockets with fine minerals come to the average collector in the course of a lifetime and it does not seem unreasonable to demand a little patience at such times. The author has seen many distressing examples of fine crystallizations utterly ruined by careless methods of extraction or by undue haste by collectors who should have known better. It is definitely best to work deliberately, carefully, and, if required, slowly.

QUARTZ VEIN CAVITIES

Quartz veins in gneiss, slate, sandstone and other rocks frequently open into thin lenticular cavities lined with fine crystals. In some cases, country rock is sufficiently softened by alteration to permit splitting along the junction between quartz and rock, but at other times, there is no visible evidence of cracks or planes of parting. If the rock is fresh, it may be virtually impossible to do more than detach separate crystals unless wholesale blasting is resorted to in order to obtain matrix groups. However, it is usually possible to separate matrix groups from enclosing rock by using a series of thin gads inserted along the junction of quartz and rock, as shown in Figure 115, about four to six inches apart. Each is seated firmly and then all are alternately tapped with a hammer, producing a split in the rock corresponding to the joint between quartz and stone. Because of the tremendous power developed by a number of gads acting at once, this technique may be used in other collecting situations where rather large masses of rock are to be split. Open cracks sometimes can be enlarged by the use of wedges also.

PILLOW BASALT CAVITIES

The angular vugs which sometimes form between rounded or egg-shaped masses, or "pillows," of basalt (see Figure 101) are generally lined with thick incrustations of quartz upon which are perched crystals of calcite, heulandite, stilbite, apophyllite and other minerals. As a rule, quartz vug linings are inclined to be brittle because they consist of a multitude of individual crystals which grow side by side at right angles to the cavity walls but do not adhere to each other strongly. For this reason some care must be used in extracting specimens. A saving feature is that the basalt immediately next to the quartz is commonly so brittle and so weak that it can be crushed or broken with small hand tools. In some instances, a gouge of dark green chlorite forms between the crystallized sheets and the rock, permitting easy separation once an opening has been made for lifting out the angular geode. Gray chalcedony is also common as a lining material, in which case it will be found next to the rock or separated from it by an incrustation of calcite. Since chalcedony is much stronger than other forms of coarsely-crystalline quartz, considerable pressure can be exerted during removal without much fear of breakage.

Other minerals such as prehnite, pectolite, natrolite, etc., are also found in basalt cavities and, when separated from the walls by chlorite gouges, can be easily pried loose by inserting thin gads between their bases and the rock upon which they rest. Unfortunately, the attachment is far more lasting in some cases, and if the specimens are worth the trouble the only remaining way to obtain specimens of value is to break

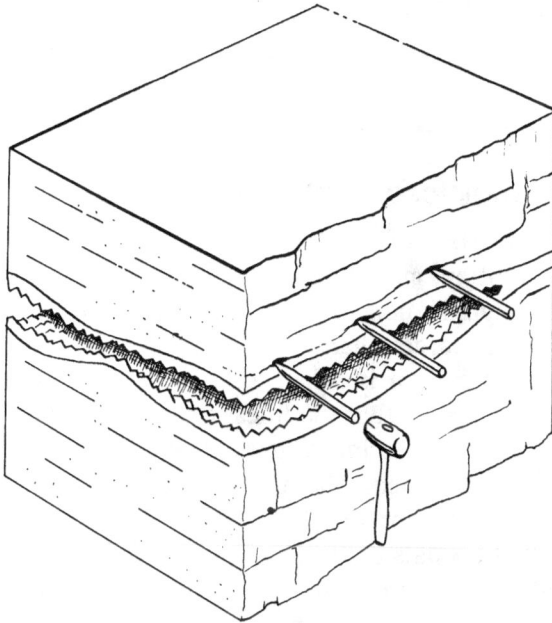

A SERIES OF GADS USED TO DETACH
SLABS OF CAVITY LINING

FIGURE 115. A series of gads inserted along edge of a crystal-lined cavity and alternately tapped to loosen large slabs of lining. This technique is very useful in many kinds of deposits containing crystal-lined cavities.

up the masses of basalt using heavy sledges. Where considerable quantities of gouge are present, look for loose crystals or mineral masses which frequently develop within the gouge.

AMYGDALOIDAL BASALT CAVITIES

Basalts lacking pillow structure but containing nodules of chalcedony, agate, thomsonite, chlorastrolite and other minerals, are difficult to collect from unless the rock has been deeply weathered. When loose nodules weathered from the basalt are picked up and the few still remaining in soft, partly-decomposed rock are removed, the only recourse for obtaining further specimens is to resort to blasting. This is the way much Mexican agate is being obtained now, and also thomsonite from Minnesota. After blasting, many nodules will pop out as the rock enclosing them splits, but others must be taken out by breaking up remaining blocks with sledges. Delicate hammering is required to remove thomsonite nodules because they split so readily. Blasting followed by hammer work is, incidentally, the method used to extract precious opal from trachyte at the Mexican opal mines.

RECOGNITION OF MICROMOUNT MATERIAL

An increasing number of mineral collectors are specializing in the collection, preparation, mounting, and study of extremely small crystals which require magnification to observe properly. When a crystallized sample, perhaps no larger than a pin head, is mounted upon a small pedestal in its own box, it is called a *micromount*. Fanciers of micromounts claim with justice that the finest crystalized material is also the smallest, and nowhere else in the mineral kingdom will so beautifully perfect crystals be obtained. The alert collector should therefore bear this in mind and, when opportunity offers, collect suitable micromount material as well as crystals of ordinary dimensions.

Micromount material is common in very small vugs, seams and other openings characteristic of ore veins of all kinds. In pegmatites, spaces between mica books and enclosing feldspar are often occupied by micro crystals while small openings surrounding crystals wholly imbedded in matrix often provide micromount material also. Especially fruitful sources of minute crystals are small cavities etched into large crystals of feldspar. All loose gritty or sandy material found within cavities or in gouges should be carefully washed and examined before it is decided to throw it away. A seven or ten power magnifying glass is handy to take along whenever small cavities may be encountered. Micromounts of rare minerals are frequently as valuable as fine specimens of common species thousands of times larger.

COLLECTING IN ELUVIUM

It is safe to say that the majority of quartz gemstones are obtained from various kinds of surface deposits where they remain behind long after enclosing rocks have decomposed. Other durable gemstones such as jade and rhodonite are also found in considerable quantity but their identity is frequently obscured by exterior coating caused by weathering. In many cases, coatings are characteristic of certain minerals, and when learned, can be used to identify them unerringly. Development of coatings depends largely upon the presence of moisture and whether the minerals are found exposed on the surface or buried in earth.

FIGURE 116. A desert flood plain in the Mojave Desert, northwest of Death Valley, California. Mount Whitney is on the left, the Ibex Hills are on the right. Millions of years ago, this area was subjected to heavy and prolonged rainfall which severely eroded the higher ground on either side of the valley. During this time, enormous quantities of alluvial material settled into the floor of this and neighboring valleys resulting in topography very typical of much of the southwestern United States. Due to a change in climate since the early period of erosion, very few changes are now taking place in this region. *Courtesy of U. S. Geological Survey.*

In desert regions, of the type shown in Figure 116, the absence of water lessens chemical activity and minerals tend to show little change. Gravel and sand deposits laid down by ancient floods are frequently without protective cover of vegetation with the result that winds blow away fine particles of rock, leaving larger pebbles and boulders exposed on the surface in pebbly pavements while wind erosion of sandstones commonly exposes logs of petrified wood. Minerals of fine texture such as chalcedony, jasper, chert, petrified wood, and jade are polished to astonishing smoothness by the continual pelting of wind-driven sand and silt. Curiously angular pebbles, called "dreikanters" from their three-cornered shapes, are believed to receive their peculiar scupture from sandblasting. The formation of dreikanters is shown in Figure 117

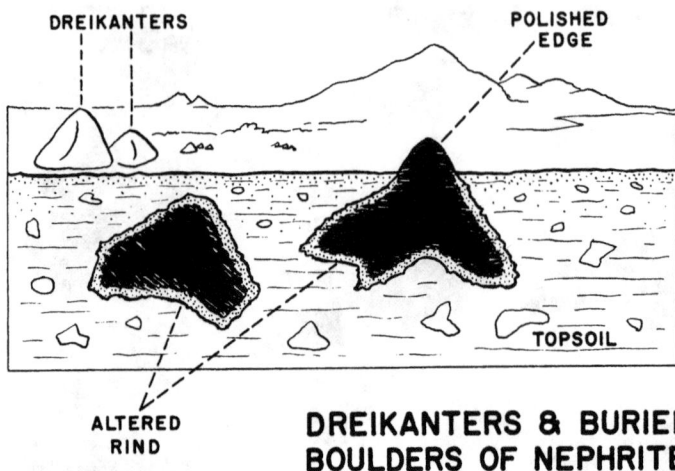

DREIKANTERS & BURIED
BOULDERS OF NEPHRITE

FIGURE 117. Smoothly wind-polished dreikanters resting on desert pavement. Buried boulders of jade are shown in the soil beneath. Note the altered material, or "rind," encrusting the buried jade in contrast to the polished protrusion of one boulder which has been exposed to the action of wind-driven sand. Compare also Figures 118 and 119.

FIGURE 118. The result of continuous sandblasting upon a large pebble of granite, This "dreikanter" measures 28½ x 18½ x 15 inches and shows the peculiar angles typical of surface pebbles subjected to prolonged blasting by wind-driven sand. Very fine-textured massive minerals or rocks such as jade and chalcedony assume high polishes as well as the peculiar forms shown here. *Courtesy U. S. Geological Survey.*

and a photograph of a large specimen appears in Figure 118. Pieces of jade and jasper in which soft and hard spots are present in the same specimen are even more fantastically carved, the jagged and pitted masses being prized by collectors because of their weird forms. Several weathered and sandblasted specimens of jade are pictured in Figure 119. A high degree of "desert polish" on gemstone pebbles of course permits easy recognition, and for this reason, flat, windy areas in desert and semi-arid regions are eagerly searched over by collectors. However, where some ground water is present, many pebbles receive tenacious coatings of black manganese oxides (see Figure 61) which adhere even when the masses are exposed on the surface. In such cases, it is necessary to chip off corners to test the material underneath the coatings.

In contrast, when ground water is abundant, it is surprising how deeply exteriors of seemingly durable rocks and minerals are altered or decomposed. This is shown strikingly in the arid regions of Wyoming, when polished jade fragments of natural color are found resting upon the surface of the ground while, just below, buried fragments bear not the slightest resemblance. Compare Figures 117 and 119 to see the differences. Some collectors found large jade masses in Wyoming with small exposed corners beautifully polished but the buried remainders coated with thick rinds of soft alteration material, dark red, grayish-green, or even white in color. As the word of finding jade in Wyoming spread, many collectors converged on the field eagerly searching for the prized green stone, in many instances walking over masses of dull-colored, uninteresting rock, which, had they only known it, were the jades they were looking for. Although a sure test for disguised jade boulders is to chip off corners with a mineralogist's pick, a better recognition measure from short distances is the pitted, corroded exterior, so characteristic of severely weathered specimens as shown by the right-hand specimen in Figure 119.

Burial in moist soil eventually affects all but the most resistant minerals, even agate, jasper, chert and other varieties of chalcedony are changed to some degree. Many forms of chalcedony are sufficiently porous to absorb solutions containing iron and manganese compounds which stain entire sections or produce bands, moss-like markings, and other internal patterns much prized by lapidaries. Collectors must be alert to the fact that beautifully-marked agates appear very common-place in the field. A good rule of thumb to follow whenever examining

FIGURE 119. North American nephrite specimens. The large slab in the background is dark green Alaskan jade showing several streaks of chatoyant grayish-green material near the top. Leaning against it is a slab of Wyoming nephrite showing a rind of altered material and small black specks scattered throughout the bright green unaltered material within the core. On the right is a rough partly altered specimen of similar material. The lower left and lower right specimens are also from Wyoming while the rounded pebble in the center is from a beach deposit in Monterey County, California.

surface material is to chip each kind of pebble and rock to form an idea of what minerals are present. It does not do to merely stroll over such places, expecting worthwhile specimens to be so conspicuous that one cannot help noticing them. If they were, they probably would have been picked up long ago. However, by sampling likely specimens it is possible to learn all the disguises which minerals assume in any particular field, and enable later trips to concentrate on materials likely to be worth keeping.

One of the most common disguises is whitening of exteriors, especially upon chalcedony gemstones. This is so universal that it deserves a
few words of description. Ordinary chalcedony is gray or blue-gray in
color, translucent, and more or less porous. For some unexplained
reason, chalcedony sometimes alters into a porous cellular material, the
change varying from a more or less complete replacement to partial
replacement in bands, or as a thin zone of replacement on the exterior.
So long as the porous material is saturated with water, it retains some
degree of translucency, but when thoroughly dry, it becomes very pale
tan, pink, or even dead white in color, and quite opaque. Thus, in the
famous agate fields along the Yellowstone River in Montana, chalcedony nodules picked up from the water are easily recognized for what
they are but those found exposed on bars or banks, or which rest upon
the surface of surrounding hills, may be more or less white and opaque
and of course far different in appearance. Many beginning collectors
visiting this area have been chagrined to learn later that the white
pebbles which they paid no attention to because they looked so much
like quartz pebbles were actually agate. In strongly-colored agates,
surface whiteness may not completely hide interior coloration or banding, and specimens therefore resemble ordinary jasper or chert except
for faint traces of banding. Those which are not broken and hence
show no banding, cannot be told from jasper without chipping. In some
cases, bandings weather at slightly different rates, resulting in some
standing in relief and imparting a ribbed or striated appearance to the
surface, however, close inspection is usually necessary to detect this
characteristic texture.

Tracing Float

Since eluvial material often travels but short distances from its original
rock, it is possible to trace it back by noting the abundance of surface
fragments and their distribution. Many deposits, metallic and non-
metallic, have been found this way. In general, when eluvial material is
carried from its place of origin, it suffers wear according to how far it
has "floated." If it has not been caught in a stream and rolled about,
angular corners will be present on fragments, sharper pieces indicating
nearer sources. The distribution of fragments upon the surface is also
helpful in locating sources, fragments tending to scatter more widely
the farther they move. By carefully examining the ground for addition-

al pieces, and noting along which direction the number of pieces seems to increase, by checking also for sharpness of corners, one may arrive very close to the place from which float weathered.

TRACING MINERALS IN ALLUVIUM

It is far more difficult to trace minerals found in alluvium because rounded pebbles give little hint as to how large they originally were and hence how far they have traveled. Prospectors seeking gold were faced with this difficulty but developed techniques which were based upon good common sense and were often rewarded by finding a valuable deposit somewhere upon the slopes of a valley. Since gold seeks the lowest levels of gravel beds, prospectors began their campaigns by trying to find places where gravel banks were exposed to bedrock. When such places were found, the gold pan was unlimbered and charged with a shovel full of small gravel from next to bedrock. If gold appeared, the process was repeated at intervals upstream until eventually a point was reached where repeated trials produced nothing. Steps were retraced to the last productive point and careful sampling slowly continued upstream to determine as closely as possible, the exact point where the gravels ceased to contain gold. The next step was to see if any side streams were bringing in the gold, and if this was the case, to pan up some smaller stream until the gold trail led up a branch or perhaps to attractive float.

By such a sampling procedure, prospectors accomplished several things at once: (a) the establishment of a broad area underlain by gold-bearing gravels, and, (b) the establishment of a very small area in which gold-bearing ore deposits were likely to be found. This same procedure can of course be used for any mineral which occurs in gravel, especially for a species which is both durable and heavy. It is said that the famous blue Yogo Gulch sapphires of Montana were traced back to their source in an igneous rock dike in limestone by gold panners operating in the creek of the canyon shown in Figure 120. Being heavy, the sapphires turned up frequently in the concentrates and although unrecognized at the time, eventually so aroused the curiosity of one of the miners that he sent some off for identification. On the other hand, sapphires from the gravels of the Missouri River and Rock Creek in Montana, have not been traced to sources agreed upon as responsible for their formation. It is possible that original veins or dikes

FIGURE 120. The American Sapphire Mine in Yogo Gulch, Montana in 1912; view looking northeast across the gulch. The steep cliffs are limestone and this is the rock in which the sapphire-bearing dike is intruded. At the extreme right, as marked by the arrow, the narrow defile created by removal of the dike rock is still to be seen. *Courtesy U. S. Geological Survey.*

which contained them were completely destroyed by erosion and thus may never be found.

In any prospecting campaign such as outlined above, it is important to remember that natural concentration processes accumulate enough valuable minerals in gravel to make placer mining worthwhile, but the rocks from which these selfsame minerals came may prove to be so lean that it simply does not pay to mine them. An all too common impression of the inexperienced is that a fragment found in gravel means that "there must be lots more where this came from!" This may be true for eluvial material found as float but certainly not for material in stream gravels which represents the final product of a prolonged process of concentration.

Minerals in float are characteristically associated, as would be expected from their originating in the same deposits, but the assemblages of minerals vary with rocks of origin. The following table shows common associates arranged according to the kinds of rocks with which they are found. It will be noted that not all minerals survive weathering and consequently many which occur in surface material not far from deposits, do not appear in sands and gravels of nearby streams.

TYPICAL MINERALS FOUND ASSOCIATED IN ELUVIAL AND ALLUVIAL DEPOSITS

Rock Type	Eluvial Minerals	Alluvial Minerals
Granite	Pegmatite minerals; quartz; feldspar; mica.	Quartz; gemstones of pegmatites; sands contain black tourmaline, zircon, monazite, garnet.
Rhyolite Trachyte	Quartz, agate, jasper, opal, chalcedony nodules.	Quartz gemstones; also cassiterite, topaz. Sands contain garnet, black tourmaline, quartz, cassiterite.
Basalt Diabase	Prehnite, natrolite, pectolite, thomsonite, chlorastrolite, agate nodules, rock crystal, amethyst, peridot.	Pectolite, thomsonite, chlorastrolite, agate, quartz, copper; sands contain abundant magnetite.
Sandstones	Rock crystal, chalcedony, agate, silicified wood, bone and shells.	Same, plus quartz sand.
Limestones	Chalcedony, chert, agate, rock crystal.	Same.
Shale, Clay	Concretions containing calcite, quartz, barite, celestite; gypsum crystals and fibrous masses; marcasite nodules and spears; vivianite; petrified wood.	Silicified wood, quartz; sands primarily quartz.
Slates	Quartz.	Quartz, gold.
Serpentine	Serpentine, rhodonite, idocrase, chalcedony, jade.	Serpentine, jadeite, nephrite, idocrase, rhodonite, chalcedony, chromite, platinum.
Kimberlite	Pyrope garnet, enstatite, diopside, peridot, amethyst, chalcedony, diamond.	Garnet, amethyst, chalcedony, diamond.

TYPICAL MINERALS FOUND ASSOCIATED IN ELUVIAL
AND ALLUVIAL DEPOSITS (*Cont'd.*)

Rock Type	Eluvial Minerals	Alluvial Minerals
Gneiss Schist	Quartz, almandite garnet, andalusite (chiastolite), sillimanite, iolite, kyanite, staurolite, rutile; pegmatite outcrop fragments.	Quartz, kyanite, staurolite, andalusite, sillimanite, rutile, garnet, gold, corundum, spinel.
Marble	Quartz crystals; andradite garnet; tremolite; scapolite, diopside, brown tourmaline.	Same.

The following table lists the external appearance of some minerals commonly found in eluvium or alluvium.

TYPICAL EXTERNAL APPEARANCE OF MINERALS IN ELUVIUM AND ALLUVIUM

Mineral	Appearance
Gold	Bright yellow, metallic; corners rounded: often flattened or flaky; sometimes small fragments of white quartz attached.
Platinum	Steel-gray color; sometimes bright; nuggets inclined to be smoothly rounded and bean-shaped.
Copper	Green-stained branching masses or leaves in soil; irregular nuggets of dull brownish-red color in gravels.
Meteorites	Rusty, pitted; resemble iron; some show smoothly rounded hollows.
Cassiterite	Brownish cauliflower-like masses of "wood tin," often concentrically banded in dark red, brown, green, tan; some types appear black with peculiar silvery luster.
Columbite-Tantalite	Black grains and masses.
Monazite	Dark brown to honey-yellow grains; slightly silvery luster.
Zircon	Similar to monazite; often found as small sharp crystals.
Rutile	Dark reddish-brown to black; slightly silvery luster; crystals often rounded but show traces of striations.
Topaz	Crystals often recognizable but sandblasted on all surfaces; basal cleavage prominent; pale blue color sometimes noted.
Diamond	Sharp, smooth crystals; bright silvery luster; commonly very pale greenish or yellowish.

TYPICAL EXTERNAL APPEARANCE OF MINERALS IN ELUVIUM AND ALLUVIUM (*Cont'd.*)

Mineral	*Appearance*
Corundum	Some crystals often perfect; others show crystal forms but slightly rounded corners; some crystals deeply etched; ruby crystals striated with lines crossing at 60 degree angles.
Marcasite	Ball-like nodules and branching masses; gray to brown exteriors; metallic luster, pale yellow color when broken open.
Goethite	Forms brown films and layers in gravels; hollow round rusty geodes; gossans; the most common brown stain in soils, gravels, clay and surface rocks.
Pyrite	Bright crystals and yellow masses; also small sharp crystals in sands; often tarnished to bronzy or brownish colors; crystals often converted into brown goethite.
Garnet	Often mistaken for ruby but far more waterworn; almandite typically appears as ball-like masses and sometimes excellent crystals; common as red grains in sands.
Tourmaline	Sometimes crystals recognizable but most are severely waterworn; traces of striations often present; usually black.
Peridot	Glossy to sandblasted irregular grains and masses of typical color; some volcanic ashes contain sharp small yellow crystals.
Sillimanite	Very tough fibrous masses; silky luster; smooth surface.
Kyanite	Flat blue blades and splinters with waterworn edges; often transparent.
Staurolite	Dark brown crystals of typical form; also of clayey texture and pale brown color.
Andalusite	Dark brown cigar-shaped crystals of very rough surface texture; internal "cross" patterns typical.
Iolite	Dark gray masses of oily luster; distinctive dichroism.
Beryl	Rounded masses with smooth sandblasted surfaces; pale greenish, pale blue.
Quartz	Smooth, sandblasted pebbles; sharp-edged glassy fragments common in eluvium; milky "bull" quartz common in gravels; pebbles show typical crescent-shaped surface cracks; sometimes appears as good crystals.
Chalcedony	Smoothly rounded masses of gray or blue-gray color; white coatings common; traces of bandings sometimes noticeable; crescent-shaped surface cracks.
Agate	Similar to chalcedony but brown, red, yellow colors prevail; less translucent; bandings often prominent.
Chert	Smooth round pebbles and fragments; no banding.
Jasper	Similar to chert; often large masses; sometimes deeply pitted.

TYPICAL EXTERNAL APPEARANCE OF MINERALS IN ELUVIUM AND ALLUVIUM (*Cont'd.*)

Mineral	Appearance
Silicified Wood	Looks like wood; annular rings usually prominent; other silicifications such as shell, bone, coral easily identified on basis of form of original object.
Opalized Wood	Shining conchoidal fractures common; light colors predominate; brittle.
Pectolite	Tough fibrous masses; usually white but also very pale green, blue; pebbles smoothly waterworn with silky luster; slightly translucent.
Thomsonite	Unmistakable ring markings but lintonite variety looks like translucent gray-green jade pebbles of small size.
Chlorastrolite	Dull dirty-gray green exteriors; small rounded pebbles; patterns often noticeable in waterworn pebbles but absent in those freshly weathered from rock.
Sodalite	Masses weather to dull white coatings.
Idocrase	Smooth pebbles; translucent; dark green to pale yellow-green colors.
Serpentine	Smooth pebbles; very dark green color; often opaque yellow-green coatings on weathered outcrops.
Jadeite	Smooth pebbles; thick opaque decomposed layer on masses buried in soil.
Nephrite	Very smooth "desert polish" on sandblasted specimens; waterworn pebbles almost as smooth; generally green colors; partly translucent; buried masses often thickly coated with dark brown-red to gray-green to gray-white crusts; buried masses often deeply pitted.
Rhodonite	Waterworn masses show typical colors and veinings; exposed masses invariably black coated.
Tektites	Black to dark green deeply grooved pebbles; glossy to glassy in luster; some wrinkled like prunes; green tektites translucent to transparent.
Obsidian	Rough, pitted exteriors when waterworn; usually dead black color; conchoidal fractures very typical; numerous crescent-shaped cracks on pebbles; "Apache tears" usually smoothly rounded, transparent, and dark brownish-gray in color; outcrop material often coated with light gray to white opaque film.

Notes: Sharp crystals indicate extreme hardness, or, in the case of soft minerals, nearness to original deposits. Diamond, ruby, and sapphire crystals often travel long distances without appreciable wear. Desert polish is found on many moderately hard, fine-textured mineral aggregates and rocks; black coatings due to manganese oxides are commonly observed on many minerals besides rhodonite. All spherical masses with rough exteriors should be examined closely; many will turn out to be thundereggs or geodes. All colors are intensified and patterns made plainer by wetting specimens, using saliva if necessary.

COLLECTING IN GRAVEL AND SAND PITS

It is often possible to obtain excellent specimens of chalcedony, agate, jasper, and petrified wood in gravel and sand pits. In Iowa, the gravel pits on the west bank of the Mississippi River just south of Muscatine have produced Lake Superior agate for many years. Collectors obtain them by visiting washing plants during working hours. At such times pebbles are piled up on huge heaps by conveyor belts, and while they are still wet they provide an unparalleled opportunity for examination. Since large gravel is seldom useful to pit operators, many workings discard pebbles over a certain size, in this way providing material of possible interest to collectors. It is in such discards that large agates and sections of petrified wood are most likely to be found. Rainy days are best for collecting in gravel pits because all material is made more plain in coloration and marking.

Because gravel pits frequently penetrate several alluvial beds to reach gravel of the right size and composition, it is sometimes possible to trace useful minerals to some special horizon in which they occur more abundantly than elsewhere. Once such a horizon has been found, it can be examined closely for additional specimens wherever it is exposed in the pit.

COLLECTING ON DUMPS

Although the fact is not widely appreciated, collecting on mine dumps virtually borders on an art because very few dumps are uniform in character, and much if not all collecting effort can be utterly wasted by digging into places where only country rock has been thrown away. Very few mines work entirely within the confines of their ore bodies, and in some cases thin veins being followed by drifts and galleries produce less than 10% of the total rock removed. In other instances, productive periods of mining are followed by exploratory or development work wherein tremendous quantities of waste rock are removed to provide access to untouched ore bodies or to attack veins from lower levels. These relationships are shown diagrammatically in Figure 121. For these reasons it is highly important that collectors regard dumps in their true light and not begin digging in the first one met without some preliminary examination at least.

Old dumps are apt to be more fruitful than newer dumps for several reasons. Very often initial mining efforts were carried on by a lone

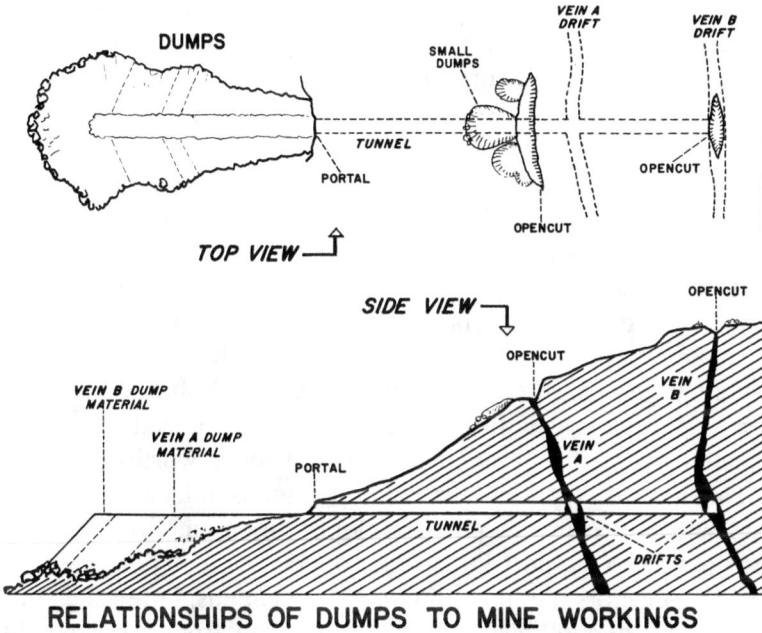

FIGURE 121. This illustration shows why mineral specimens cannot be found in every part of a dump. As can be seen, the tunnel driven to reach the two ore veins passed through barren rock; for this reason the dumps will be without interest except in the two fan-shaped layers containing material extracted from drifts along the corresponding veins. On the other hand, the small dumps associated with open-cuts near the top of the hill may contain considerable interesting material.

prospector or perhaps a small crew, short on equipment and money. To realize payable quantities of ore in the shortest period of time in order to carry on further mining on a larger and perhaps more profitable scale, it was often necessary to dig strictly within the ore body since every bit of country rock removed was so much time and effort wasted. Consequently older dumps contain material which miners did not consider worth saving, although today, with more efficient means of milling, such material may represent high grade ore. Furthermore, certain minerals of value frequently passed through the hands of the miners who knew well only those which experience had taught them to recognize, and those uncommon or rare species so prized by mineral collectors were tossed out upon dumps as of no value. Also thrown out were handsome specimens of non-ore minerals which any collector would be proud to own today. In still other instances, ores valuable now were useless then, for example, beryl in pegmatite. Many others could be mentioned, especially among radioactive minerals, but the point needs no further elaboration.

Frequently, in exploring old dumps surrounding old workings, one finds that initial mining areas were abandoned in favor of more advantageous places from which to conduct further mining. For example, as shown in Figure 121, an outcrop upon the summit of a hill may have been the site of the initial discovery, but later, when the property demonstrated its value and capitalization was provided for systematic exploitation, it proved much better to drive a tunnel into the base of the hill to make mining more efficient. It is obvious that newer dumps from the lower tunnel may contain much waste rock but the old upper workings, particularly if they were sunk into oxidized ores, may be surrounded by small but rich dumps much more worthy of examination. The immediate area surrounding famous mines may be pockmarked with old prospect pits, developed upon small ore bodies too modest in size to support large scale operations but perhaps of great interest to collectors in search of mineral specimens. Often such pits are filled with soil and rubbish which has slumped from the sides during the passage of time, but a little spadework may uncover small veins or ore bodies containing fine specimens if not payable quantities of ore. Debris of this kind cast out from small workings is likely to contain valuable specimens for another reason, that is, original topsoil made it difficult for old miners to see what they had, just as it does for modern collectors.

As a rule, large dumps are easily discovered, although they may be so overgrown by brush and trees that only the general form and the presence of large masses of sharp angular rock at the bottom of the slopes permits certain recognition. Small dumps may be completely obscured but it is possible to identify them by remembering the essential feature which all dumps possess—a level top along which ore carts traveled on tracks to dispose of their loads. In fact, around any old mine workings, it pays to investigate all level stretches of ground which look as if they may have been used as track beds because miners often found it more convenient to create track beds from dump material, rather than wasting hand labor by cutting into banks or slopes for fill, as is done today. At mining localities which have been visited by generations of collectors before him the shrewd collector often discovers totally untouched dumps. Common sense and the ability to visualize the problems which faced early miners can do more to guide collecting efforts than all other factors, except possibly sheer luck.

Remembering that miners needed places to dump valuable ore for hand sorting and sacking, it also pays to detect level areas near old workings which perhaps served as ore storage or sorting platforms. In most cases, these will be found close to office buildings or bunk houses, or near shafts and tunnels. Surface signs may be completely obscured by growths of grass or brush but the level nature of the ground may provide the necessary clue. There is always an excellent likelihood that surface layers of earth in such places may provide specimens of rich ore, or masses of ore and gangue which were deliberately discarded. If sorting took place in sheds, some valuable material may be found on the ground beneath floors where it dropped through crevices between planks or through knotholes. A story is told in the West about a gold mining ghost town which in its heyday was thriving enough to support a branch office of the U. S. Mint. The floor of the office was covered with rude planks containing the usual slight spaces between them. A clever prospector of later years happened upon the building and recognized the fact that gold *could have* filtered through the cracks in the floor. Accordingly he tore up the planks and proceeded to pan the top six inches of soil beneath for gold. It is said that he was richly rewarded for his trouble.

The age of dumps can be judged by discoloration and decomposition of rocks as compared to obviously fresher material of more recent origin, also by overgrowths of vegetation, and by smoothing of the sides brought about by the gradual slumping of loose material over larger rocks. The presence of trees of substantial size, say from six to twelve inches in diameter, indicates ages of from 25 to 50 years although it is difficult to judge age of trees accurately except by cutting them down and counting rings. The areas beneath trees and stout growths of brush are somewhat better places to dig as a rule because matted roots offer real discouragement to all save determined collectors. Poison oak, poison ivy, brambles, and other poisonous or disagreeable plants are also splendid places to search providing the collector is not unduly sensitive or has some way of clearing off such brush without paying the usual penalties.

Dump structure follows patterns which may be determined by careful examination and the application of common sense. In general, a beginning dump consists of a cone-shaped pile of debris with its apex at the mouth of the mine tunnel or other opening leading into the ground. The front is rounded just as a pile of sand would be rounded if it is created by pouring a dribble of sand through a small opening. As mining proceeds, the dump is extended forward, as shown in Figure 121, maintaining the same rounded front but creating a steep-sided ridge behind, whose length depends on how long it remained feasible to continue dumping material ahead. Sometimes a single tunnel was served by a single dump, but if the dump became excessively long, too much time was wasted in pushing an ore cart out to its extremity and another dump was then begun alongside. Thus there may be several dumps and it is a puzzle to discover which came first. In any event, dumps are a record of the history of the mine from beginning to end, through rich streaks to lean, and from profitable work to "dead" work. If careful prospecting along the dumps reveals the pattern, collecting efforts can be confined strictly to those sections likely to contain good material. Once such "streaks" are discovered, the collector digs into the dump, following the old rule that if a valuable specimen is found others may be found also.

It is important in digging into dumps to remember how material got there. As an example, consider a mine in which pockets of rich ore or crystals are found from time to time, possibly a mine like the Himalaya at Mesa Grande in California, famed for its gem tourmalines. If a pocket were discovered and cleaned out, the rubbish around it would not amount to a great deal in any case and would perhaps fill one or two mine carts. Thus, upon the dumps, this material, the most likely to contain overlooked tourmalines, quartz crystals, and other desirable minerals, would form a thin circular sheath over previous dump material. Many years later this thin streak may be discovered along the sides of the dump and encourage digging to uncover the remainder. However, if the dump is penetrated straight in, the "pay streak" will be gone through in a few inches and only rubbish will be encountered from then on. On the other hand, if it is remembered that the material must have formed a thin covering over previous dump material, it will become apparent that the streak must be followed in a curving path horizontally, and a sloping path vertically corresponding to the conical shape of the original dump. Furthermore, if it is also remembered that the largest masses of rock roll to the bottom, on any dump, that the next largest settle some place on the flanks, and that the fine material is arrested near the top, digging can be confined to the level most likely to contain the objects of search. Small crystals should be looked for within a few feet of the top; if matrix specimens are wanted, these may be found in the middle levels; but if large blocks which may contain streaks of solid ore or perhaps small crystal-lined cavities are looked for, they must be at the bottom.

If possible, collectors should acquaint themselves with the mineral associates for which any mine was noted before searching the dumps. In a copper-lead-zinc deposit, for example, in which oxidized ores provided the handsomest specimens during early mining, it is hopeless to seek such ores upon a dump composed of solid blocks containing massive sulfides, since these must be derived from below the original oxidized zones. Similar valuable clues may be detected in other mineral deposits, especially pegmatites in which secondary minerals nearest the core are characteristic and conspicuous. In the area shown in Figure 121 for example, the ability to recognize ore minerals obtained from either of the veins helps immeasurably in deciding where to dig in the dump.

Dumps are washed clean during heavy rainfalls or deeply grooved by gullies, and it is especially profitable to examine them immediately afterwards. Places recently dug up by other collectors are also worthy of notice after a heavy rainfall. If water is available in quantity, consideration should be given to washing down dumps known to contain quantities of specimen material or crystals. In many cases, old shafts and inclines are filled with water and it is not difficult to hitch up a portable gasoline engine pump to supply the necessary suction and water delivery. This operation works best with two persons, one to direct the hose and the other to examine material as soon as it has been washed. More elaborate arrangements can be made for sluicing and screening if desired. Pumps suitable for the purpose can often be rented at reasonable rates from equipment rental agencies in larger cities.

COLLECTING IN MINES

Regardless of how attractive the prospect of collecting in mines appears, it must be remembered that dangers lurk everywhere, more so in older mines abandoned for many years. Dangers from cave-ins vary according to the country rock through which galleries and tunnels pass, some rocks being so solid and so unaffected by atmospheric agents that they need no support whatsoever. However, other normally strong rocks may be sheared and crushed and apt to collapse at any moment once supporting timbers are destroyed, while still others disintegrate rapidly wherever exposed to air. Indications of crumbling or imminent collapse are piles of small rubbish or sandy material along tunnel floors. It is safe to say that such debris accumulated after the mine was abandoned, otherwise such weak places would have been shored up by miners to protect themselves. Dangerous settling often reveals itself in buckled timbers, which, if otherwise sound, will still furnish some degree of strength, but if rotten, leave no doubt that the rock above is precariously poised on the verge of collapse.

Wood props, supports, lagging, planks and ladders must not be depended upon to hold unless tested first by tapping with a hammer. Solid wood gives forth a musical vibration but rotten timbers crush under the hammer blow or emit only a muffled dead sound. Because of the warmth and moisture present in most mines, wood seldom lasts for more than a few years, unless specially treated to prevent decay. A hazard incidental to the rotting of wood which should be watched for is the development of atmospheres deficient in oxygen and rich in carbon dioxide, especially in mines in which no natural cross-ventiliation exists. Any dimming of carbide flames or quick extinguishment of match flames, or sometimes a "sour" smell or taste in the air, indicates fouling, and a hasty retreat should be made to better ventilated areas.

Good lighting is essential to safe underground exploration. All movements must be slow and deliberate, and one always should be sure of footing ahead. Innocent-looking "puddles" of water may turn out to be entrances to flooded raises or shafts, while inclines and ore chutes never seem as precipitous underground as they really are, possibly because poor light and lack of a natural horizon make it difficult to judge true steepness. All walls and ceilings should be examined methodically for signs of imminent collapse, and timbering tapped for soundness as progress is made underground. Extensive workings should not be explored without bearing in mind the possibility of becoming lost. If doubt exists, marks should be left upon walls to guide the return to daylight. Carbide flames make excellent soot marks on rock walls and timbers if held close to the surfaces.

Many old mines are visited frequently by professional collectors who have become thoroughly familiar with underground workings and know where to dig or blast for specimens. For the beginner out for the first time, however, it is extremely difficult to make head or tail out of the rock walls which everywhere face him. For this reason, it pays to discover beforehand as much about the mine as possible, at least to know what kind of ore body was being followed, since this information may help in confining search to most promising areas. It sometimes helps to proceed to the farthest reaches to seek out places where work was carried on last because freshest exposures of rock and ore should ordinarily be available there. Close study may show remnants of ore, the nature of the enclosing rocks, and other features which may help in prospecting remaining portions of the mine for overlooked leads and pockets. Dust, dirt, and mud often cover walls and make examinations difficult, requiring frequent use of the pick to chip off fragments of fresh rock. Fissures, cracks, and soft altered sections are inspected carefully in case they may lead to veins or pockets.

It is useful to remember that straight tunnels generally represent accessways since few ore deposits arrange themselves in flat bodies like beds of coal, amenable to wholesale excavation. On the contrary, highly irregular galleries and winding, twisting tunnels or "gopher holes" signify following of ore bodies and should be the places deserving of closest scrutiny. In such excavations walls, ceilings, and floors offer the best chances of finding valuable specimens in overlooked pockets or leads. Close examination of floors is also called for because ore or specimen material dropped during mining may have been trampled over and eventually covered with dirt and debris. In many mines, empty spaces left by excavation of ore are "backfilled" with waste, to avoid the expense of hauling to the surface and dumping, and these provide additional places worth looking into.

On the outside of the mine, vein outcrops often provide small but rich ore bodies which had to be left in place due to abandonment of opencut work and shifting to underground work. As a rule, opencuts following narrow veins or small ore bodies are continued only so long as caving of walls presents no problems. However, it is the general practice to shift to underground mining as soon as the ore body proves its worth, in order to take advantage of the natural support offered by rock left in place above. Therefore it is sometimes found that much of the outcrop is left undisturbed from just above entrance tunnels to original prospect pits higher up and perhaps some distance beyond. The probable extent of outcrops can be judged by examining ceilings in uppermost underground workings. Attractive sections can be located fairly accurately by reference to fixed points such as mine entrances, and then projected upwards to the surface to corresponding points near prospect pits. Outcrops are seldom prominent, however, and can be expected to be covered by soil or vegetation.

PROSPECTING AND COLLECTING WITH ULTRAVIOLET LIGHTS

During World War II many valuable deposits of scheelite, the principal ore of tungsten, were found by prospectors equipped with portable ultraviolet lights. The bright blue, blue-white, or pale to bright yellow glow excited by UV served to detect scheelite when ordinary visual examinations failed to distinguish this mineral from associated species of similar appearance. In many cases, scheelite occurred in small grains scattered through rock, forming profitable ores, but nowhere was it so concentrated or crystallized in such large masses that the attention of the prospector would be attracted to such places in daylight. A number of uranium minerals also fluoresce, notably autunite, meta-autunite, and others. Although the accepted method of prospecting for radioactive minerals involves electronic detecting devices, ultraviolet lights may be very useful on occasion. Aside from economic minerals, many species fluoresce in vivid colors and are prized by collectors on this account, some collectors even going so far as to assemble large exhibits containing as many varieties and species as possible, which, when excited *en masse* by ultraviolet light, create astonishing and beautiful spectacles.

Fluorescence is excited in minerals by irradiation with light rays past the purple end of the visible spectrum, hence the name *ultra*violet. Such rays are not seen by the human eye but their presence in sunlight shows up in sunburning and tanning of the skin. The usual way of obtaining ultraviolet without distracting visible light is to use a special quartz lamp containing mercury and the gases argon, neon, and helium. The small introduced droplet of mercury vaporizes and glows, emitting rays extremely rich in ultraviolet. A very dark-colored screen which practically eliminates visible light and lets only ultraviolet pass through is placed over the lamp. The lack of visible light has caused such lamps to be called "black lights." Although lamps meant for use at home are plugged to household current, portable field lamps are supplied with batteries to produce the necessary electrical current, as shown in Figure 122. Many models are available for home and for field work from small to large size.

FIGURE 122. Battery-powered ultraviolet light rigged for field work. This photo was necessarily taken in daytime to show all features of the equipment. *Courtesy Ultra-Violet Products, Inc., San Gabriel, Calif.*

Fluorescence is a variable property in many minerals; some specimens glow as if lighted from within, others only feebly, and still others not at all. In some species, fluorescence is known to be related to the presence of small quantities of impurities, but in other species causes are not quite so well known. A few minerals phosphoresce as well as fluoresce, or, put another way, the glow continues for some time after the ultraviolet light has been shut off. The following minerals are noted for striking fluorescence; some are valuable ores but others are only of interest to collectors.

In the field, portable lamps are generally carried about in the evening when distracting light from the heavens is at a minimum. However, there are many difficulties and dangers involved in prospecting at night, and wise persons usually examine likely areas in daytime, observing special hazards such as ravines, gullies, etc., and then return at night to those places most likely to be mineralized, keeping in mind hazards discovered in daylight. Another popular method is to prospect in daylight, taking along a black cloth hood to provide the necessary darkness when observing fluorescence. Still another method places a flexible hood over the lamp itself with a peephole above to view a rock surface suspected of containing fluorescent minerals. The eyehole also is shielded so that when the device is pressed against the rock surface no outside light will leak into the space under observation, either from under the hood or from next to the eye. Many mine and quarry dumps are regularly examined by fluorescent mineral collectors using one of the techniques described above. In a place like the Buckwheat Dump of the Franklin mine of the New Jersey Zinc Company at Franklin, New Jersey, where vividly fluorescent willemite and calcite are the prizes, the vast majority of material is non-glowing and much rubbish can be taken home unless tested on the spot.

FLUORESCENT MINERALS OF INTEREST TO PROSPECTORS AND COLLECTORS

Mineral	Fluorescent Colors	Remarks
Amber	Yellow, yellow-green	Common in lignite seams.
Apatite	Yellow to orange	Many specimens do not fluoresce.
Aragonite	Yellow, green red, white	
Benitoite	Deep blue	Strong glow.
Calcite	Red, pink, blue, orange, yellow; pale green, etc.	Red often vivid; many specimens do not fluoresce.
Colemanite	White	
Corundum	Ruby: dull to vivid red; sapphire: yellow, orange, red	Some rubies glow brilliantly.
Cupro-scheelite	Yellow, greenish-yellow	Strong glow.
Diamond	Blue, green, red, orange	Pale colors and weak fluorescence; most do not fluoresce.
Fluorite	Yellow, blue, green	Fluoresce better under long wave UV.
Gypsum	Green, pale yellow	Most specimens do not fluoresce.
Opal	Pale green, yellowish-green	Sometimes bright.
Petroleums	Greenish, yellowish	Sometimes bright.
Powellite	Yellow	Often associated with scheelite.
Quartz (agate chalcedony)	Greenish, yellowish	Many specimens do not fluoresce.
Scapolite	Purple, pink, yellow	Wernerite often glows vivid yellow.

Mineral	Fluorescent Colors	Remarks
Scheelite	Blue, pale yellow, white	Vivid; fluorescence is a reliable test.
Spinel	Red	Only red spinels glow.
Willemite	Green	Vivid; brown specimens do not fluoresce.
Wollastonite	Blue-green, yellow	Not all specimens fluoresce.
Zircon	Orange	Often bright glow.

URANIUM MINERALS

Mineral	Fluorescent Colors	Remarks
Autunite	Greenish-yellow	Vivid.
Meta-autunite	Yellow, greenish-yellow	Vivid glow.
Metatorbernite	Pale green	Faint.
Schoepite	Yellow-green	
Schroeckingerite	Yellow-green	Bright.
Torbernite	Green	Faint.
Uranophane	Yellow-green	Moderate to faint.
Zippeite	Greenish, yellow-green	Vivid.

Alluvial beds and stream gravels suspected of containing scheelite, ruby, or other fluorescent minerals of value, can be easily prospected at night. Opal, which often fluoresces bright yellow-green to pale yellow, may be detected in eluvial deposits and perhaps in certain sedimentary beds, such as those containing precious and uraniferous opal in Virgin Valley, Nevada. Fluorescent minerals also show up well on quarry walls or upon the walls of mine tunnels, and it is recorded that some mines originally opened for other minerals proved to contain payable veins of scheelite when underground workings were examined by ultraviolet lamps. In other cases, fluorescent minerals known to be associated with valuable ore minerals may lead to deposits of these ores if prospecting is done at night. Minerals formed through alteration of primary uranium ores frequently fluoresce vividly, or cause thin films of opal to fluoresce by being incorporated in this mineral. Such fluorescence upon the walls of pegmatite quarries and mines may lead the prospector to accumulations of primary uranium minerals which may be buried beneath several inches of rock and not ordinarily visible. Detailed prospecting and identification procedures for fluorescent minerals may be found in Sterling Gleason's *Ultraviolet Guide to Minerals* (D. Van Nostrand Reinhold Co., N.Y., 1960). This book is easily the most complete work on the subject.

PROSPECTING AND COLLECTING WITH RADIOACTIVITY DETECTORS

Minerals containing uranium and thorium give off invisible particles due to the fissioning of some of the uranium and thorium atoms. The human body and its organs cannot sense these particles and it is necessary to detect radioactivity by using electronic instruments. The most widely used devices are called Geiger and scintillation counters; both are capable of detecting fission particles and give the operator some indication of nearness to radioactive minerals by flashing light signals, sound "clicks," or readings on a meter.

Prospecting in any area begins by checking the "background count," or the radiations which are always present everywhere upon the earth's surface. The level of the background count is noted and from then on it is disregarded except when there is a decided increase. Because some radioactivity is present in all rocks, changes may be noted as one rock type is left for another. Granite and its related rocks give off more radiations than dark colored igneous rocks, while black shale and rocks rich in phosphates give off more than sandstones or limestones. By carefully noting such changes, it is possible to detect crossing boundaries between rocks. The best readings on counter instruments are from exposed rock because soil tends to absorb radiations. In all cases, the instrument must be held at a constant level above the surface since distance affects the readings and changes in carrying height may cause misleading indications of radioactivity. When the counter records an increase in radiations several times over background count, closer examination is made of the area by systematically covering the ground and attempting to localize the source. Sharp rises and drops indicate small concentrations while gradual changes indicate radioactive minerals spread over more rock and probably far less rich. Consistent counts over four times background call for very close examination and removing samples for later testing. Detailed prospecting techniques are very ably explained in a number of books currently in print, several of which are listed in the bibliography in Appendix V.

In mineral deposits containing small concentrations of radioactive minerals mainly of interest to the collector, counters can be used to good effect. For example, pegmatites often contain a number of radioactive minerals, sometimes well crystallized, and valuable in themselves, or associated with other rare non-radioactive species which are also valuable as specimens. By examining dumps, quarry walls or floors, and other places where pegmatite is exposed, it is often possible to detect concentrations which have escaped other eyes. In many cases, small "nests" of radioactive mineral crystals or perhaps only irregular masses may be just underneath the surface of exposed pegmatite feldspar, and with a little chipping away of rock, some good material may be obtained. Pegmatite close to radioactive minerals is frequently discolored brown, gray, or even black, and serves to pinpoint the place where such minerals may be found.

FIELD PACKAGING AND TRANSPORT OF SPECIMENS

For obvious reasons, as much care is needed in packaging specimens in the field as is required in extracting them. Very few localities are directly accessible by auto, while many are so far from the nearest road that specimens must be packed out over considerable distances. Every step of the way jostles specimens, and steep trails or rough terrain invite falls which may result in ruining contents of packsacks unless these are packed securely. In the case of massive material, packaging is unimportant except to prevent sharp corners from digging holes in the sacks and thence into one's shoulders.

An excellent idea is to gather all specimens in one place before leaving a collecting locality, then to examine them under good light and to discard those which are worthless. At the same time, large blocks consisting of small useful portions attached to valueless matrix can be cobbed to reduce them to more manageable proportions. Beginners tend to take everything, but professional collectors, knowing from experience what is desirable, are far more discriminating. Some common sense of course must be used in deciding what to keep and what to throw away, especially if strange mineral species are encountered. These may turn out to be so rare or so unusual that considerable demand exists for them. If too much material has been collected to pack out on one trip, a second or third trip can be made, or the remainder of the specimens hidden away for later pick up. In any case, too many specimens crowded into one bag result in damage to the specimens or in a staggering load which may cause stumbling or falling.

One of the easiest obtainable wrapping materials is ordinary newspaper; smooth magazine paper is far less suitable and should not be used. A generous handful of newspaper, folded over, fits nicely into a packsack and weighs very little. At the locality it is immediately useful not only for packaging but for spreading on damp or rocky ground to protect the knees and elbows when digging, or to provide clean places upon which specimens can be laid as they are collected. When slightly damp, newspaper is easier to wrap and fits better into spaces between projecting crystals which are too delicate to trust to ordinary dry paper. Newspaper tends to shred during hiking and for this reason it is a good idea to take along a number of small cloth sacks in which a few well wrapped specimens can be stuffed tightly. Sacks of this kind can be made from the legs of old trousers or from the sleeves of shirts, by sewing up one end and fitting the other with draw strings. In case no newspaper is available, emergency wrappings of clothing can be used; it is better to sacrifice the comfort of a shirt temporarily than to ruin an outstanding specimen for lack of protection. Grass and leaves are also useful but can easily be worked loose. Some collectors regularly use damp clay to coat delicate crystal groups to prevent damage, even when newspaper is available. In the case of unsorted pocket contents, as from cavities in pegmatites, it is always best to fill several sacks with the material as it comes from the pockets for cleaning and leisurely examination at home rather than to attempt selection in the field. Otherwise too many small but fine crystals or rare minerals are certain to be overlooked.

Loading of packsacks to insure safety of contents is an art in itself. One must not only guard against damage from accidental falls but must prevent wrapped parcels from rubbing against each other. Last but not least, the load must afford maximum comfort to the shoulders destined to carry it. If two persons participate in the trip, it is often desirable to place all specimens in one packsack and reserve the other for tools and other objects which may damage specimens if placed in the same sack. In any event, specimen parcels must be packed tightly to prevent shifting or jiggling while walking, and this may be possible only by stuffing all of them into one bag. As a closing remark, it should be mentioned that severe and damaging vibrations can occur in automobiles also, and the task of preserving specimens is not over until home has been reached.

A Note on Knapsacks

Knapsacks are indispensable wherever much hiking or transport of tools and equipment are involved. It is extremely annoying to carry heavy objects in the hands for any distance, especially if rough terrain is being covered. It is therefore much better to use a good knapsack, lashing bulky objects on the sides or back if they cannot fit inside. For light loads, small surplus ammunition knapsacks made from green-dyed cotton canvas are very useful but because they lack bracings on the

back or pads for shoulders, they soon become very uncomfortable if
heavily loaded. The best kinds of knapsacks consist of stout canvas
covers with stitched pockets and compartments stretched over light
steel or wooden frames curved to fit the back. For comfort, bearing
pads are provided for places where the sack rests on the small of the
back and also underneath shoulder straps.

7

Preparation of Specimens

The final preparation of specimens is often fully as important as finding them for very few are so bright and clean that they are ready to go into showcases or be put up for sale "as is." Practically all need washing at the least, while others require scraping, trimming, bathing in chemicals to remove stains and discolorations, or other treatments designed to reveal their true beauty. On the other hand, for reasons to be explained later, some cannot be touched and must be left in the condition found. In this respect, a few purist collectors claim that any treatment of mineral specimens is uncalled for because the natural state is the most desirable state. If they were to follow their own rules strictly, they would surely wind up with very drab collections indeed, for even clay and dirt, substances as natural as the minerals themselves, could not be washed off. Actually the objection is to excessive treatment which all too often results in specimens which obviously look artificial. A "best" treatment exists for practically every class of specimens but it isn't always easy to find, even for experienced collectors and connoisseurs. Mineral dealers whose livelihoods depend on sales to all sorts of customers, from novice to expert, are generally conservative in respect to cleaning. They rightly judge that the sparkling "flashy" specimens will sell themselves, while those which could be improved by careful cleaning will attract the experts who have the vision to recognize a good specimen underneath natural grime and who, in any case, prefer to do the cleaning themselves.

An important consideration in deciding upon which treatment to take and how intensively to carry it out is whether the material to be removed is essential to the mineralogical value of the specimen. For example, rusty stains upon quartz crystals are extremely common in cavities found near the surface and are undoubtedly due to the infiltration of iron oxides from the decomposition of iron-bearing minerals above. Such stains are not only very commonplace but actually foreign to the mineral in question and every right exists to remove them by chemical treatment. On the other hand, identical accumulations of rusty iron oxides in the oxidized zones of copper-lead-zinc ore bodies are characteristic and essential, providing as they do the matrix for other minerals; and of course they cannot be touched without destroying a vital feature of the mineralogical association. In other instances, overgrowths upon crystals cause cleaning problems even more difficult to solve, as when cookeite coats tourmaline crystals, or minute phenakite crystals form tiny clusters upon beryl which may be made somewhat unsightly as a result. In each case the collector must decide if the basic crystal improves so much in appearance by removing the coating that the loss of the mineral associate is more than compensated for. As a rule, removal of rare minerals associated with others less rare is considered poor practice, but the removal of very common minerals, such as calcite which often forms gangues or coatings, is acceptable. All factors contributing to the value of specimens must be considered before settling upon a course of action. A little later in this chapter, a discussion will be given of the features which make a good specimen and which serve as guides in deciding what treatment, if any, should be given.

WASHING AND PRELIMINARY EVALUATION

Extremely dirty specimens may be washed with an ordinary garden hose, using a low pressure stream if specimens are somewhat delicate, or a high pressure jet if they are unlikely to be damaged. Care must be used in hosing to support specimens so that they cannot roll over and damage themselves. Extremely fragile minerals such as tufted natrolite or very fine hairlike crystals of millerite cannot be washed at all for fear that even the gentlest rinsing will break them off. Water-soluble minerals cannot be washed with ordinary water but may be carefully rinsed or brushed with alcohol or acetone. However, before proceeding with any treatment it must be determined if it is safe to use water or other solvents, including chemical solutions. The solubility of common minerals in water and acids is shown in Appendix I, and this table should be consulted before beginning any treatment.

Soil is readily removed by ordinary water but clay often adheres so tenaciously it may be necessary to use a high-pressure jet, or, if this could cause damage, first to soak specimens for a few hours in a bucketful of water to which a little household ammonia has been added. An excellent needle-spray jet can be made from a garden hose coupling by soldering on a flat brass plate in which a tiny hole has been drilled. The thin stream of water emerges at high velocity and is very effective for cleaning out dirt and clay from deep angular crevices. Figure 123 illustrates how this simple device is made. Small dental tools, wooden splinters or toothpicks, nail brushes, old toothbrushes and long-bristle brushes of considerable stiffness all prove useful during washing. Dental tools should be used with caution because they may scratch soft minerals or break off delicate crystals; it probably is best to avoid their use altogether when treating minerals softer than feldspar (hardness 6) and to rely upon brushes or thin splinters of bamboo to remove soil. Since clay tends to pack tightly if brushed vigorously, it pays to clean clay-coated specimens in a slow-moving stream of water, lifting off masses with splinters rather than trying to rub the clay off with brushes.

Cavity and pocket fillings, or other bulk material likely to contain small crystals or bits of valuable gemstones, require washing in buckets or upon screens to be sure that only worthless matter is flushed away. An excellent scheme employs a wide bucket or small washtub into which some of the material is dumped and then agitated with a vigorous stream of water from a hose. By tipping the bucket and carefully directing the hose to all portions of the material at the bottom, one ends up with a clean gravelly mixture which can be spread upon newspapers to dry and later examined at leisure. Large quantities of loose material may be processed in washtubs or upon screens supported by 2″ x 4″ wooden legs; however, the mesh size of the screen must be selected with due regard to the size of the crystals or fragments it is desired to save. Where heavy minerals are mixed with minerals of less

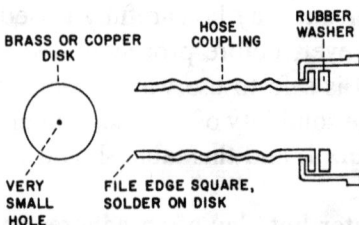

BRASS OR COPPER DISK   HOSE COUPLING   RUBBER WASHER

VERY SMALL HOLE   FILE EDGE SQUARE, SOLDER ON DISK

FIGURE 123. This effective cleaning device can be easily made up from an ordinary brass garden hose coupling. It can be put on or taken off readily.

NEEDLE SPRAY FOR CLEANING MINERAL SPECIMENS

density, it is easy to concentrate the former by using a cone screen or an ordinary kitchen sieve in the manner previously described in Chapter 2.

After initial washing, specimens are set aside to dry in order to permit realistic appraisal. Disappointments commonly occur at this stage because most specimens look much better wet than dry. Every defect upon surfaces of crystals, previously disguised by moisture, is now revealed and colors vivid under water become strangely dull. This is not true of all specimens, fortunately, but occurs often enough to make this cautionary note necessary. This is the time to inspect prizes and to determine what should be done with them. Some will require more cleaning, perhaps with chemicals, others may need careful picking, scraping or even trimming to make them more presentable. Still others, and it is hoped that this is a small number, should be thrown away as being of no value whatsoever.

TRIMMING

Specimens often require trimming for a number of reasons, the most important being to remove excess matrix, to make the outline more pleasingly proportioned, and to remove material from the bottom to make the specimen "sit up" well. For example, a small crystal-lined cavity in rock should be framed like a picture by removing matrix until the cavity is well-centered; if it is not, it will always offend the sensibilities of its viewers, though they may not know why, and will be less valued accordingly. Dimensional proportions are also important for the same reason: a long thin scraggly matrix will be less attractive than one which is more square in outline, and a specimen should "sit up" well for the simple reason that it is expected to look its best in a cabinet or showcase.

Naturally, trimming is not always feasible and each specimen should be studied carefully before one decides what is to be done with it. Thin cracks marking planes of imminent separation should be especially noted, because most unexpected disintegrations occur along them. It may well be that such cracks pass almost through the specimen and it would be best to leave it alone lest it break up into smaller, less desirable specimens. On the other hand, in the case of excessively large specimens which should be broken up, prying apart along pre-existing cracks is far safer than trying to split the rock by any other method. Perhaps the most important factor to consider in using this method is the nature of the matrix rock, which is generally far stronger than the crystals perched upon it. By virtue of its grain, the rock controls the direction of splitting. In many pegmatite matrix specimens, for example, the bases consist of graphic granite in which quartz rods form at right angles to the surface of the cavity upon which the crystals grew (see Figure 87). This structure makes it almost certain that splitting will divide any specimen through the crystals, a result which may not be desired. If it is not, then unwanted sections of the base must be removed with a diamond saw. All grained or layered matrix rocks can be expected to behave in similar fashion and in trimming one must take this into account.

Heavy trimming is best done by using a machine similar in principle to the old-fashioned George Washington printing press, consisting of a stout rectangular frame standing upright, through which passes a heavy screw shaft turned by a handwheel at the top. Specially hardened chisel or spear points of steel are fitted to the bottom of the screw shaft and to the opposite place on the bottom of the frame; as the handwheel is turned, tremendous pressure is applied to any specimen inserted between the points and fracturing results. The great advantage of such a device over hand trimming lies in its ability to apply far greater force under perfect control, precisely at the place required and with minimum shock to crystals. The latest models of rock trimmers use hydraulic jacks which can develop point pressures up to several tons. Figure 124 illustrates a fine machine designed for professional use and sold by Ward's Natural Science Establishment. With some ingenuity and invention, the amateur can devise trimmers from screw shafts or small hydraulic or mechanical jacks. Another possibility lies in using very heavy "C" clamps such as are used in machine shops or steel fabricating plants. Mounted in heavy bases and fitted with hardened steel points in lieu of the flat bearing pads usually furnished, they can certainly trim rocks of considerable size. Miniature screw-press trimmers have been made by various amateurs for trimming miniature and micromount specimens in which considerable delicacy must be employed to prevent jarring loose small crystals. Steel points can be made from carbon steel rod, ground to shape on a wet carborundum wheel, and hardened by the procedure described in the previous chapter. Old files can also be used effectively for this purpose. Machinist's vises are also easily adapted to specimen trimming but hardened steel points must be attached to the jaws in some fashion in order to apply pressure over small areas.

FIGURE 124. An extremely effective rock-trimmer utilizing a hand-pumped hydraulic jack for its motive power. Note that the operator is wearing a heavy leather mitt to protect the hand holding the specimen and plastic goggles to protect the eyes from flying chips of rock when the specimen parts in two. *Courtesy Ward's Natural Science Establishment, Rochester, N. Y.*

Hand trimming is a hazardous operation at best because so many slips can and do occur, but, with some practice and using the proper tools, very good results can be obtained. During trimming, it is vital to protect the eyes from flying chips by wearing a transparent plastic shield or non-breakable glasses (see Figure 124). Gloves, preferably leather, are a *must* for the hands. Though simple, the principles of trimming with hammers are not universally recognized. The most important principle is that the weight of the hammer must be proportionate to the weight of the specimen. If a small specimen of only a few ounces weight is struck by a mineralogist's pick, it is liable to absorb so much force that it will fly to bits, while at the other extreme, the same pick applied to a mass of rock weighing far more than the pick itself will probably do little except to make ineffectual pockmarks and dull its point. Ideally, hammer and specimen should be very nearly the same weight. This same principle applies to the use of chisels or gads, which must be proportionate in weight to the striking hammer. Another important consideration is proper support for the specimen while being struck. If a hand-size mass is being trimmed, it is grasped firmly but not tightly by the gloved hand and struck a short sharp blow. At the moment of impact, the specimen "rides" with the blow and thus absorbs all the force rather than transmitting part to the hand. One or two experiences with the sting passed along to the hand by an improperly held specimen soon convinces the collector to use both gloves and a light but secure grip.

Where projections or corners are being chipped off, the rules explained above do not apply, and much lighter tools and hammers can be used on heavy specimens. Where chisels and gads are employed, it is a good idea to cushion specimens on sand bags or loose earth covered by cloth, or even to hold them upon the lap, while both hands are freed to strike blows. It is not a good idea to rest specimens on hard surfaces during hammering because they may easily roll over and become damaged. Some collectors rest specimens upon blocks of lead because this soft metal grips the stone and prevents slipping, and at the same time distributes the shock so that unwanted fractures do not appear.

Chisels and gads are almost useless against solid rock but work very well along partly-developed cracks. At the start, the point of a chisel or gad is tapped lightly along a crack to cut a groove deep enough to permit the point of the chisel to exert maximum prying effect. When the groove is satisfactory, the chisel is held upright and struck a powerful blow to actually split the specimen.

Care in trimming is required to avoid unsightly marring which is almost impossible to remove or disguise. In some cases where blows must be struck upon the face of the specimen or on some spot which will be visible when the specimen is being exhibited, it is possible to protect the surface by inserting a small piece of plywood between stone and hammer head to receive the direct blow. At other times, a short piece of end-grain hardwood can be used in a fashion similar to a chisel, one end resting upon the rock where it is desired to break, and the other end struck by the hammer. Some collectors and dealers also use rubber or fiber hammers for shattering fractured masses of gem material in order to extract the clear and valuable pieces.

MECHANICAL CLEANING METHODS

It is almost impossible to remove every bit of clay or dirt by ordinary washing methods, and some additional work with mechanical methods may be necessary to remove remnants left in deep crevices. Because clay expands when wet and shrinks when dry, it is sometimes effective to let specimens dry thoroughly before attempting clay removal. When quite free of water, clay often loosens sufficiently so that a gentle prodding causes particles to drop out. Useful tools for this work include

FIGURE 125. Franklinite crystals in metamorphic limestone from Franklin, Sussex Co., New Jersey. In this photo, the typical octahedral habit of franklinite is well-illustrated along with the rhombohedral cleavage of the enclosing calcite. By chipping away the calcite with steel points, it is possible to uncover and place into prominent position crystals which ordinarily would be completely lost to view. Specimen size 6 x 4 inches; size of franklinite crystal: almost 2 inches in diameter. *Courtesy Smithsonian Institution.*

steel sewing needles mounted in cork, wooden, or metal holders, slender wires which can be bent to make hooks, and the wide variety of picking and scraping tools of stainless steel used by dentists. Bamboo splinters are excellent for cleaning hard-to-reach spaces because they can be split to almost any thinness and still retain stiffness.

Scaly masses of mica, calcite, or other minerals which coat crystals may be largely removed by the use of sharpened dental tools, of which a slender chisel-like instrument is particularly useful. Old razor blades serve the same purpose but most must be handled with caution to avoid cutting the fingers. Tourmaline crystals from gem pockets are regularly cleaned of cookeite by using the tools described, while calcite, a very common mineral coating, can be chipped away by pointed steel tools or electrical vibratory tools. Calcite can also be removed by hand rotary tools using ordinary steel points but even slight traces of other minerals will soon dull the points and render them useless. Practically all of the specimens from the splendid crystal groups of grossularite garnet, diopside, franklinite, rhodonite and many others which occur in contact metasomatic deposits have had overlying calcite painstakingly removed by a chipping and picking process. In the vicinity of the famous Franklin, New Jersey, zinc deposits, several local collectors were known for their skill in "developing" specimens of beauty out of drab masses of ore. The technique took advantage of the softness and easy cleavability of calcite which often covered desirable minerals. Small sharp steel tools were used to split off chips of the soft gangue; others permitted application of pressure, causing the calcite to crumble. Patient work removed almost every trace from around the crystals, leaving them standing in proud array. An example showing a minimum of this type of work appears in Figure 125. Although calcite is easily dissolved in dilute hydrochloric acid this solution attacks many other minerals, etching them slightly and dulling crystal faces. However, disfiguring powdery marks left by picking tools can be removed by brushing on a drop or two of acid, washing it away with ordinary water after it has done its work.

Very fine powdery deposits or incrustations can also be removed by brisk scrubbing with stiff brushes using thin slurries of pumice powder or carborundum grit, depending upon the hardness of the crystals being treated. Pumice is very useful because of the glass-like sharpness of its individual particles and the tendency to retain this sharpness as particles break down. Pumice has been used successfully in removing cookeite from pegmatite pocket minerals. Carborundum in sizes 400 and 200 is also useful provided it is not scrubbed too vigorously upon crystal surfaces of minerals less than quartz in hardness (7); for softer minerals, pumice powder is better. Ordinary toothpaste scrubbed vigorously with a toothbrush is also effective in removing thin films and incrustations because it contains a finely grained abrasive (generally feldspar).

Some years ago a technique was developed for removing soft matrix minerals from around crystals by using small chisels followed by sand-blasting. Careful work resulted in matrix specimens upon which the crystals stood in high relief. This method was most frequently employed for emphasizing the red tourmaline crystals imbedded in pale lilac lepidolite found in the Stewart Lithia Mine at Pala, California. A similar technique can be used today to remove disfiguring coatings, particularly those which can be lightly sand-blasted with soft abrasives. So long as the abrasive is softer than the crystals, there is no reason why it cannot work in special cases.

Ultrasonic Cleaning

For cleaning specimens with narrow crevices and recesses beyond the reach of ordinary tools, the modern ultrasonic cleansing bath is often the answer. The device consists of two basic units in one cabinet or separate units connected by a power cable. The electronic unit converts household current into pulsating power which is fed into one or more vibrating crystals attached to the bottom of a stainless steel tank. The crystals send ultrasonic waves into the tank fluid, where they strike the specimens and knock off adhering dirt and films. On all hard-surfaced materials, as metals, gems, crystals, and pebbles, excellent cleansing occurs within seconds to several minutes, depending on how tenaciously the dirt or film clings. However, on soft, resilient, or flexible materials, as coatings of clay, cookeite, or chlorite, removal is much slower and effective cleaning may require immersion from 5 to 60 minutes or more. The most striking effects are obtained on gem pebbles where the dirt is ingrained in numerous fine cracks or on mineral specimens which have been covered by dust and grime for years. Thin films of iron and manganese oxides are also removed from crystal surfaces, providing the specimens are left in the bath long enough. Particularly effective results are obtained on specimens consisting of masses of slender crystals where cleaning would be almost impossible by any other method.

Ordinary water may be used in the tank but its activity is greatly improved by adding detergents or ammonia, the latter for clay removal. Acid solutions may also be used, but if they attack the metal of the tank they should be poured into a glass beaker, which is then suspended in the water. The specimens can then be placed in the beaker. Because the vibrating crystals are attached directly to the tank bottom, nothing heavy should rest upon this area lest the crystals suffer damage. For prolonged cleaning, suspend specimens by loops of cord into the bath.

Cautions: intense ultrasonic vibrations can cause cracked specimen crystals to separate. Prolonged use of the unit also results in the water temperature rising to the point where it may be harmful to the specimens. Avoid dipping the fingers into the water, at least for long periods of time, while the unit is operating. It is believed that excessive exposure results in a painful joint condition similar to arthritis. However, most cleaning jobs take only a few seconds and short exposures are not harmful.

Cleaning by Tumbling

Another successful cleaning process for nodular minerals such as variscite and turquois employs tumblers to rub off clay coatings, exposing internal quality and hence making grading and pricing far simpler tasks. One Nevada turquois miner uses an old cement mixer for tumbling mine-run material. Ordinary sand and water are added to the rough nodules of turquois and the mixture is allowed to tumble for some hours at the end of which the charge is carefully washed to remove all traces of iron which may later stain the turquois. It is a simple matter at the end of a run to grade material according to color, pattern, solidity and other factors influencing price. On a smaller scale, gem tumblers are regularly used by dealers to process peridot grains from Arizona which are ordinarily so frosted upon their exteriors that it is difficult to tell internal quality. Similar treatment is useful for garnet pebbles, jade lumps, and other gemstones showing surface coatings or alteration.

CHEMICAL CLEANING METHODS

A number of chemicals are used regularly to clean minerals, either by directly dissolving undesirable coatings or by changing their chemical natures so that they can be dissolved. Water alone dissolves many minerals and must be used with caution, particularly against nitrates, borates, and sulfates. As a general rule, minerals susceptible to damage from water are those found in sedimentary beds where they were originally deposited by water, although a number found within oxidized zones of ore bodies are also susceptible, since water had much to do with their formation. On the other hand, minerals found within igneous and metamorphic rocks are generally unaffected but it is still a good idea to check the water-soluble nature of every mineral before proceeding with its washing. A table listing mineral solubilities in water as well as in other agents appears in Appendix I. It should be consulted before attempting any chemical treatment.

The effectiveness of water is greatly improved by adding one of a number of ordinary household detergents, most of which contain a wetting agent which enables water rapidly to penetrate the smallest pores and thus promote cleansing. Many substances lose strength when immersed in water and experienced collectors have noted this in connection with removal of coatings and incrustations, which become decidedly softer after soaking. The cause is partly chemical and partly physical and is promoted by wetting agents. Although ordinary detergents may seem harmless it must be remembered that they are chemically active and may cause damage to some minerals. It is not a good idea, for example, to soak metallic minerals such as sulfides in detergent-treated water for long periods of time unless previous experience shows no harm will result. After *all* treatments with detergent solutions, be sure to rinse specimens thoroughly in plain water to remove traces of detergent. This must be done also whenever chemical agents, including acids, are used. In any event, the general rule in washing or chemical treatment is to subject specimens to treatment only so long as appearances are improved; when there is no longer any noticeable change, it is time to stop.

Detergents often attack zinc-coated, or galvanized pails or buckets and are very active against aluminum containers; for this reason it is best to use containers made from polyethylene plastic. These are perfectly resistant to attack from all chemicals which the collector is likely to use, including the extremely powerful hydrofluoric acid.

Removal of Iron Stains

The most common cleaning problem is the removal of rust-like stains and incrustations of limonite, a yellow to brown earthy material composed primarily of the iron minerals goethite, hematite and jarosite. Goethite forms readily from iron-bearing minerals such as pyrite, chalcopyrite and siderite, and also from hematite, although both goethite and hematite may be found as coatings in the same mineral deposit. Where weathering or infiltration of surface water has been prolonged, goethite is usually found alone. Limonite stains are most successfully removed by soaking specimens in solutions of oxalic acid, citric acid, or ammonium citrate, while hematite stains are removed with hydrochloric acid, commonly known as muriatic acid. Oxalic acid is the best of the several agents mentioned for removal of limonite although hydrochloric acid will also work very well.

Oxalic acid is sold in white flaky crystals, put up in quantities from an ounce or two to as much as is wanted. It is available from paint stores because it is commonly used in certain painting processes, but it may also be obtained from druggists, although they charge more for equal quantities. Oxalic acid is an internal poison and a skin irritant, and therefore requires care in its use. It is not a violent poison unless solutions or dry crystals are taken internally and reasonable precautions in its use should suffice to prevent difficulties. Containers of powder should be stored out of reach of children, while the best way to avoid accidents from water solutions is to keep them someplace where no one can reach them and then throw them away after minerals have been soaked. Rubber gloves should be used to immerse and remove specimens.

Oxalic solutions are prepared by dissolving about a cupful of crystals in four quarts of water, changing the proportions up or down according to the size of the container and the amount of water. Crystals dissolve slowly in cold water but rapidly in warm water, and since all chemical reactions are speeded by heat, it pays to keep the solution as warm as possible without risking cracking of specimens. One successful way for doing this is to use a double-boiler arrangement similar to that shown in Figure 126, in which a large container full of plain water is kept simmering over a cook or camp stove and an inner container, resting on blocks in the hot water to keep it away from the bottom holds the specimens and the acid solution. In this connection, it is best to place specimens in a cool solution first, then raise the temperature afterwards to avoid the possibility of severe shock leading to cracking. When specimens are sufficiently clean, they may be transferred from the acid solution directly to the hot plain water to rinse off all traces of acid and

SPECIMEN — INNER BATH (ACID)

OUTER BATH (WATER)

GRILL

WOOD BLOCKS

BURNER

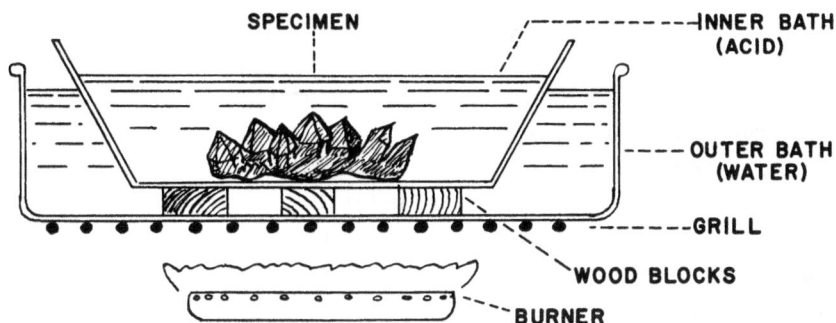

DOUBLE-BOILER ACID BATH

FIGURE 126. This arrangement is very useful for applying heat safely to acid baths because there is less likelihood of disastrous boiling over. The height of the burner flame is adjusted until the water bath is held at a temperature well below boiling point. Because of evaporation losses, it is necessary to add water to the lower bath from time to time.

iron minerals in solution. The plain water is then allowed to cool slowly until room temperature is reached; it is then discarded because it contains slight traces of acid.

Prior to immersing specimens, as much clay, dirt, and iron stains or incrustations should be removed as possible, since these will greatly prolong the operation and wastefully consume acid. As in all chemical reactions, a certain amount of oxalic acid is required to dissolve a fixed quantity of iron oxides, the reaction proceeding so long as enough acid remains in solution. For this reason, it is usually wise to use a generous container capable of holding plenty of solution to cover the specimens and to allow for evaporation losses. As chemical action proceeds, iron stains will begin to disappear, forming water-soluble compounds which stain the solution yellow. When the color becomes very dark yellow, a point is reached where so much material is in solution that danger exists of doing more harm to the specimen than good. Dissolved iron compounds could force their way into minute crevices where they would precipitate and stain the specimen a brilliant unnatural yellow. To prevent this, discard the solution and switch to a fresh batch, repeating the process as necessary. Cracks in quartz and feldspar, or pores in earthy or spongy minerals are particularly susceptible and great care must be taken to prevent stains which may be extremely difficult to remove later. In the event stains do occur, the best course of action is to make a fresh solution and re-treat the specimens.

Hematite stains or incrustations are almost impossible to dissolve with any common chemical other than hydrochloric acid (HC). This acid is obtainable in glass or plastic flasks from paint or hardware stores in concentrations of about 30%. It is generally pale yellow in color due to the presence of slight iron impurities; however, for mineral cleaning purposes it is quite satisfactory. Chemically pure or technical grades may be purchased from druggists but cost much more for equal quantities. Hydrochloric acid is much used by painters and masons for cleaning concrete walls and brickwork. Commercial acid is used "as is" for dissolving hematite but is greatly diluted for dissolving carbonate minerals.

In diluting acids it is extremely important that water should never be poured into concentrated acids. Even a drop or two in concentrated acid results in violent release of heat which causes the water to flash into steam and the acid to be spattered. The *proper way* is to pour thin streams of concentrated acid into cold water since the heat which is generated is promptly dissipated and no violent reaction occurs. This method is shown in Figure 127. The heat reaction mentioned above does not occur when crystals of oxalic acid are dissolved in water but is to be expected whenever hydrochloric, nitric, or sulfuric acids are diluted. Of all common acids, sulfuric acid is the worst in its behavior when being diluted.

As with oxalic acid, iron stains dissolve faster in warm hydrochloric acid and the same double-boiler arrangements may therefore be used to advantage. However, unlike oxalic acid, concentrated hydrochloric gives off acrid fumes and more so when warmed. This severely limits its use indoors not only because the vapors are offensive but because they actively attack wood, paper, and cloth, as well as metals. Steel tools exposed to acid fumes quickly rust and must be stored elsewhere if their bright finishes are to be preserved. If arrangements can be made to do acid treatments outside, the least possible hazard will be incurred but the bath must be isolated from children and pets. Hydrochloric acid is not particularly poisonous but will damage tissues as well as cause irritations of the eyes and lungs from fumes. For these reasons, inhaling of vapors should be avoided and all handling of solutions and specimens should be done with rubber gloves. If available, rubber aprons and plastic eyeshields afford good additional protection.

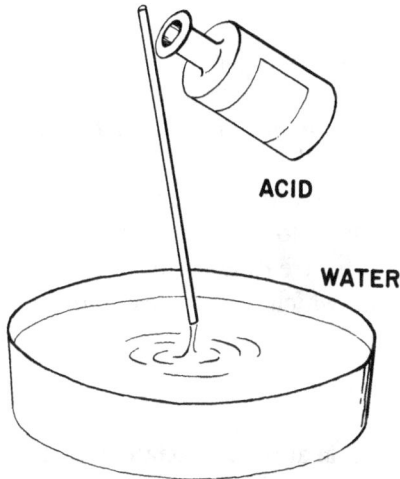

ACID

WATER

FIGURE 127. Using rubber gloves to protect the hands, the concentrated acid is poured into the water along the glass rod (hands not shown). This is the safest way to dilute acid.

THE SAFE WAY TO DILUTE ACID

Iron-stained minerals placed in hydrochloric acid immediately announce chemical activity by giving off deep yellow stains which gradually darken the solution until it turns almost red. The activity is much faster than noted in oxalic treatments and sometimes only a quarter of an hour is needed to clean off specimens which may take hours to do in oxalic acid. When solutions become very dark red it is time to change them. However, since much acid still remains which could be used for dissolving carbonate minerals, the solutions should be saved for this purpose. Procedures for washing off specimens are the same as outlined above for oxalic acid. If solutions must be discarded, they may be neutralized first by introducing chips of marble, limestone, or calcite; when bubbling ceases, all acid has been consumed and the solutions may be flushed down drains.

It must be emphasized at this point that the effectiveness of any acid against minerals depends not only upon its concentration but also upon its temperature and purity, and upon how finely-divided the mineral happens to be. For example, the majority of limonite and hematite incrustations are actually spongy or porous though they may seem hard and solid. This means that literally millions of minute surfaces are exposed to the action of acid, and, as these are attacked, even more areas are bared for further corrosion. For this reason, ordinary earthy stains are readily removed but thick incrustations or masses of pure goethite or hematite are so slowly corroded that scarcely any impression is made upon them. This is an extremely important point to remember in the use of any acid because it helps decide whether or not an acid treatment will be effective. Because of the much lessened activity of acids against solid materials, it is possible to clean large hematite and goethite crystals without destroying them although if the treatment is unduly prolonged, they may lose their fine natural luster. Calcite, for example, is very quickly attacked by hydrochloric acid used warm or cold, but perfectly solid crystals survive the treatment far better than massive forms such as marble or limestone which have many pores and crevices into which the acid enters.

Dissolving Carbonate Minerals

Hydrochloric acid is particularly effective against carbonate minerals, being universally employed to dissolve calcite enclosing crystals of other minerals. Dilute solutions of 5 to 10 per cent are most active and at the same time offer least chance of harm to other minerals which may be attacked by this acid to some degree. Because of the rapid action, solutions of hydrochloric acid need not be warmed when calcite is being dissolved; due to the absence of fumes the low concentrations permit solutions to be used indoors. However, some fumes do go off and the remarks made before about rusting of steel tools apply.

Calcite and other carbonates attacked by hydrochloric acid give off large quantities of carbon dioxide gas in the form of numerous minute bubbles which rise from the specimens wherever carbonates are exposed. Vigorous currents created by rising bubbles insure good solution circulation and no stirring or agitation is needed. Although the gas is quite harmless, large bubbles "popping" at the surface splash droplets of acid and it is necessary either to cover the container with a sheet of glass, which, however, must not be gastight, or to surround the container with pieces of newspaper to protect the table top.

Crystals of calcite, rhodochrosite, and dolomite, covered by whitish dusty coatings or by thin iron stains, or perhaps slightly marred or chipped, may often be much improved by quick dips in dilute acid. Minerals enclosed by calcite such as idocrase, grossularite garnet, epidote, and others characteristic of skarns or metamorphosed limestones may also be treated with this acid but are often attacked themselves and thus lose surface luster. It is best in such specimens to remove as much calcite as possible with steel tools and then rinse quickly in dilute acid to dissolve powdery calcite left in inaccessible crevices. Prolonged immersion is to be avoided because many specimens of the kind mentioned look perfectly solid but are actually held together by films of calcite and will fall apart if such films are completely dissolved. Close inspection of grossularite garnet specimens is particularly advisable because this mineral frequently forms a series of alternating calcite-grossularite shells which undermine and crumble when the calcite is dissolved completely.

Acetic Acid

Acetic acid, better known as the sour constituent of vinegar, is sometimes used for dissolving calcite because its action is less harsh upon associated minerals. For example, glacial acetic acid (28% concentration), obtainable from chemical or photo supply houses, dissolves calcite from dioptase but does not seriously harm this mineral as would happen if hydrochloric acid were used. Although acetic acid is not harmful in very dilute form, it is poisonous in strong concentrations and should be treated with care and respect. Avoid inhaling its fumes.

Sulfuric and Nitric Acids

Although commonly used for many purposes, these acids are only seldom useful for cleaning mineral specimens. Concentrated sulfuric acid (H_2SO_4) is a very heavy oily colorless liquid which has the property of extracting water from the air until it dilutes itself to 53% concentration. Thus if a small quantity is accidentally poured upon the floor or left exposed in a dish, it will quickly increase in volume and may even overflow or spread to a considerable puddle. On the other hand, dilute sulfuric acid loses water in a dry atmosphere until it also reaches a concentration of 53%. Bottles of concentrated acid must always be tightly stoppered to prevent absorption of water, while any acid spilled accidentally should be immediately wiped up and the spot flushed with water. It is a good idea never to fill bottles to the top but to allow some room for expansion in the event moisture from the atmosphere should find its way in.

Nitric acid (HNO_3) is also a colorless heavy liquid but is watery rather than oily in consistency, either dilute or concentrated. Unlike sulfuric acid, it fumes badly whenever exposed and therefore requires the same care in handling as explained above under hydrochloric acid. When attacking iron and other metallic substances it frequently gives off reddish vapors of nitrogen oxide which are extremely unpleasant to inhale and also quite poisonous.

Aqua regia is a solution of hydrochloric acid and nitric acid used for hundreds of years to dissolve gold. Almost any mixture of the two acids can be called aqua regia but the proportions generally used for dissolving gold are three parts by volume of concentrated chemically pure hydrochloric acid and one part by volume of concentrated chemically pure nitric acid. Platinum is dissolved in an aqua regia of nine parts hydrochloric and two parts nitric acid. If aqua regia is needed, only small batches should be mixed as necessary because it does not keep beyond several weeks. Sulfuric and nitric acids may be purchased in one-pound bottles from drugstores.

Hydrofluoric Acid Treatments for Silicate Minerals

Ordinary acids may be very effective against a number of minerals but their ability to attack silicates is very limited, and for this purpose hydrofluoric acid (HF) must be employed. This acid is a colorless solution of hydrofluoric acid gas in water. The gas is generated commercially by treating powdered fluorite with hot concentrated sulfuric acid. Solutions of various concentrations are extensively used in industry for cleaning metals, for creating other chemicals, and for etching glass. Because of its quick attack upon glass containers, this acid must be stored and shipped in lead vessels or in polyethylene jars and bottles. It is sold by chemical supply houses in one-pound or ten-pound plastic bottles.

Unlike other acids, hydrofluoric is *extremely dangerous*. Its action upon the human body is to destroy tissues very rapidly; it penetrates through the skin and is almost impossible to remove completely, continuing its work until severe blisters and wounds result. Furthermore it gives no immediate stinging or burning sensation when dropped upon the skin, and by the time it is felt, it has had opportunity to penetrate deeply. Needless to say, its fumes cannot be inhaled. It is possibly the most treacherous acid in common use and requires extraordinary precautions to prevent accidents and injuries; however, because of its effect upon silicate minerals, no reasonable substitute for certain cleaning operations is known.

Hydrofluoric acid is most useful for removing clay minerals, cookeite coatings, feldspar, and other disfiguring minerals from tourmaline, spodumene, beryl and topaz crystals. Because of its great penetrating powers it enters the smallest pores where other acids cannot reach—a decided advantage. Its action is best in dissolving porous or spongy mineral masses and is much slower against perfectly solid crystals. However, if the lustrous surfaces of crystals are to remain untouched, specimens cannot be left in the solution for more than an hour or so. As remarked before, the best way to prevent etching of crystals is to clean them of adhering material as thoroughly as possible to reduce time of exposure to acid to the minimum. In the case of gem-pocket tourmalines which are often partly or completely covered with porous talc-like films of cookeite, it is necessary to scrape off as much of this mineral as possible so that only the narrowest grooves and crevices retain traces. A quick dip in the acid bath will then dissolve the little remaining without dulling the brilliant natural finish of the crystals.

Since hydrofluoric acid has no effect upon beeswax, solutions of beeswax can be used to paint over portions of specimens which need protection. Ordinary gasoline, lighter fluid or acetone (the last is best), serve as solvents for the wax. To make up a solution, fill a small bottle half full with one of the solvents and add shavings of beeswax, shaking vigorously from time to time. When the solution is thick, paint over specimens and allow to dry. After acid treatment the wax can be removed by washing in solvent or melting and floating off the wax by simmering the specimen in hot water. By using wax it is possible to clean selected portions of specimens which contain minerals certain to be dissolved by the acid if exposed directly. For example, a pegmatite specimen of tourmaline, feldspar and lepidolite can be cleaned of cookeite by masking off the feldspar which is very readily attacked, and leaving tourmaline and lepidolite exposed. A brief dip in the acid will not harm the lepidolite before most of the cookeite has been dissolved. Further deposits of cookeite can then be removed by rinsing the specimen in clean water, drying thoroughly, and repainting the lepidolite. Further immersion will not seriously harm the tourmaline which is most resistant of the three minerals mentioned.

The safest way to handle hydrofluoric acid is to conduct all cleaning operations under a laboratory hood fitted with a positive air removal system which insures exhaustion of fumes. Since even the smallest drop upon the skin causes a painful sore, as much protection for the body should be provided as possible. Some kind of transparent face shield is necessary, plus rubber apron and gloves. If a regular laboratory hood is not available, the cleaning may be done outdoors well away from all objects and shrubbery, taking a position such that the breeze blows fumes away from the body. Containers for the acid bath must be polyethylene, the author having found an ordinary diaper bucket very useful, especially since a tightly-fitting lid is provided. A polyethylene cup fastened to a stick at least two feet in length is used to lower specimens into the acid and extract them after treatment. The bottom of the cup must be perforated with a number of holes to allow the acid to drain rapidly. Immediately upon removal of specimens, place them in a large bucket filled with water which is constantly being replenished by a running hose. Replace the lid of the acid container. Specimens should be left in rinse water for several hours at least because the acid penetrates deeply and time is needed to remove all traces. If specimens are full of cracks and crevices or consist of spongy material, it may be necessary to soak them for several days to be certain no acid remains. It is extremely dangerous to try to pour back acid into the bottle and therefore it is best to leave it in the bath, replacing the tight-fitting lid and, after washing off all exterior surfaces, storing the container some-place where it is *impossible* for anyone to tamper with it. If it is impracticable to safeguard the acid, then it should be neutralized and thrown away. Neutralization is accomplished by placing several lumps of marble, limestone or calcite in the bath, or pouring the acid out upon concrete where a vigorous bubbling will show it is reacting with carbonates in the cement. The waste material is then flushed with large quantities of fresh water. Since this acid, as well as others, is harmful to vegetation, fresh or spent acid and fumes must not be allowed to con-tact plant life of any kind.

A far less dangerous substitute for hydrofluoric acid is the chemical known as ammonium bifluoride (NH_4HF_2) which in water solution dissolves many silicates, although its action is much slower. This agent is used in etching quartz crystals destined to be sliced into electronic oscillators. It is purchased from chemical supply houses in wax-lined glass bottles containing white flaky crystals of the pure substance. Ammonium bifluoride in warm water liberates hydrofluoric acid and therefore the powder and solutions made from it must be handled with due caution; however, since the concentration of acid is much less, solutions do not emit fumes and are generally fairly safe to handle. Its slower action, however, causes an equal degree of attack on most minerals making it necessary to protect softer or more readily dissolved areas with wax. If wax is used, the solution of course cannot be hot. Quartz crystals coated with scales of chlorite or hematite may be treated successfully in this solution providing they are not allowed to soak too long.

Miscellaneous Chemical Treatments

Hydrofluoric acid and ammonium bifluoride quickly clean native metals such as gold, silver, and copper. These metals may also be cleaned with nitric and hydrochloric acids. However, for copper, an old formula should be used which is safer and just as effective. The solution used consists of twenty parts by weight of water, three parts by weight of rochelle salts, and one part by weight of sodium hydroxide or household lye. Dipping native copper specimens in this solution results in removal of the black oxides.

Another copper-cleaning solution is as follows. Stir together 70 milliliters of concentrated sulfuric acid and 90 milliliters of glacial acetic acid; in this solution dissolve 30 grams of sodium dichromate. Place the mix into a one gallon jug; add distilled water to fill.

Cyanide solutions may be used to clean gold, silver, copper, and silver-copper (halfbreeds), and compounds of these metals. Black coatings upon chalcopyrite crystals may be removed in a two per cent solution of sodium cyanide. *Caution: All cyanides are quick-acting poisons and must be handled accordingly.* Hydrochloric acid also cleans tarnish from sulfides, a one-minute dip in dilute solution usually being sufficient. Careful rinsing is needed afterwards to remove all traces of acid.

Tarnished native silver specimens may be quickly cleaned in a warm solution of one ounce baking soda (sodium bicarbonate) and one ounce table salt dissolved in two quarts of water. This solution must be placed in an aluminum pan to be effective. Cleaned specimens must be thoroughly rinsed in warm water to be sure no trace of salts remains.

Black petrified wood and brown tigereye can be bleached in laundry bleach or in oxalic solution. Manganese oxides dissolve in solutions of hydroxylamine hydrosulfate. To clean gypsum, use solutions of ammonium chloride. Clays are washed away more readily in household ammonia solutions.

PRESERVATION OF SPECIMENS

Minerals may impress us as being the most durable of all natural substances, yet it is amazing how many require protection from the atmosphere or even from ordinary light. A good rule of thumb which may be used to anticipate preservation troubles is to compare the environment from which any mineral was taken to the environment of the home. If differences are great, changes are sure to occur unless preservative action is taken. For example, minerals collected in damp places probably will not be harmed by washing or by keeping them in moist atmospheres, yet they may be harmed if kept in atmospheres which are too dry. On the other hand, minerals collected in desert regions may be seriously harmed by water or moist air because moisture is normally absent at the places where they were collected. Many species found in sedimentary rocks, in borate or salt deposits, and in oxidized zones of metallic ore deposits may lose or gain water when removed from their natural environments. They may be preserved by several methods, such as placing in air-tight jars or plastic boxes or by careful cleaning with alcohol followed by spray-coating with clear colorless plastic lacquer such as Krylon. At least three coats of lacquer are recommended, and great care must be taken to see that all surfaces are completely sealed.

Marcasite is particularly troublesome to collectors because it so readily alters when exposed to ordinary atmospheres. Many specimens develop networks of cracks containing a white powder of the mineral melanterite which continues to form at the expense of the marcasite until the entire mass crumbles away. The standard method of preservation calls for washing in ammonia water immediately after the specimens have been taken from the ground, to neutralize any acid which may be present, then drying in a warm place until every bit of moisture has been driven off. This is followed by the lacquer treatment described above. However, not all marcasite specimens crumble and some mineral dealers therefore put away newly-purchased specimens for several years, discarding those which disintegrate and selling those which survive.

Other species, especially native metals, metallic sulfides and sulfosalts, readily alter upon their surfaces by acquiring oxygen from the air or by being exposed to fumes or vapors which cause chemical reactions. A number of minerals are damaged by light rays which cause alteration or decomposition, or sometimes bleaching or changes in color. Silver compounds are especially sensitive to light because of the first reason, while a number of transparent species such as beryl, topaz and spodumene change color or lose color. The obvious way to prevent light damage is to keep such specimens in the dark, bringing them out only when necessary to show them. Although any kind of light is damaging to such minerals, the fastest and most drastic changes occur when specimens are exposed to direct sunlight. A table in Appendix II lists species which may receive damage from the causes described above.

REPAIR OF SPECIMENS

Accidentally broken specimens or those discovered in broken condition may often be repaired to advantage. However, no matter how well repairs are made, such specimens will not command prices as high as those obtained for sound examples of equivalent quality. Furthermore, disposing of repaired specimens without clearly indicating this fact to buyers is sure to damage the reputation of anyone found guilty of doing so; certainly specimens may be repaired and sold but never with the intent to deceive. As a general rule, specimens of common minerals are not worth the time and trouble needed to repair them, since the amount of money realized from their sale as "repaired" specimens is much less than that obtained from selling undamaged examples. However, rare species or exceptional specimens of common species are another matter and may bring good prices even when labeled to reflect their condition. As in cleaning and other treatments, the exercise of good sense is the best guide in deciding when to repair specimens.

Only specimens with clean unchipped fractures or cleavages should be repaired. If fracture edges are rubbed or chipped, which unfortunately is most often the case, lines of separation will be marked by a series of angular pits which glisten brightly because of the fresh material exposed in them. It is sometimes possible to fill these in with suitably pigmented material but this is a delicate and time-consuming task, which, like as not, merely emphasizes the artificiality. Only a glance is needed to see such specimens for what they are and most serious collectors will have nothing to do with them. On the other hand, fractures through the bases of matrix specimens, in which upper surfaces appear undamaged, may be repaired since the joints will not be conspicuous. Specimens damaged by rough treatment during removal from pockets are seldom repairable because severe cracking or pitting mar the surfaces and no amount of skill can improve them.

When a specimen is to be repaired, the first step is to clean all sections thoroughly to remove dirt and chips of mineral matter clinging to fracture surfaces. The pieces are then pressed together to see if a close fit is possible. Partly open cracks which cannot be closed by hand pressure alone are often found in large specimens, and it therefore is necessary to separate the parts deliberately, clean out the foreign material which prevents surfaces from matching, and then cement the pieces back together. When satisfied that all sections will fit together as closely as possible, prepare a supply of cement and have ready rubber bands or string to force the fragments together and hold them securely while the cement is setting. Broken pocket crystal fragments are often found which, though obviously belonging to the same crystal, cannot be matched exactly; examination usually shows fracture surfaces overgrown with additional mineral matter which was deposited *after* the original crystal broke apart. This is a very common occurrence in pegmatite pockets and of course the separate pieces can never be tightly joined together.

The choice of cement is governed by the nature of fracture surfaces, that is, whether they are rough or smooth, and by the color and the transparency of the specimen. Exceptionally smooth surfaces are difficult to cement because adhesives which dry hard do not adhere to them well. However, if the surfaces are interrupted by many offsets or ridges this roughness improves the total bond and permits the use of almost any kind of cement which is otherwise satisfactory. Clear and colorless crystals require cements which are also clear and colorless when dry, while colored minerals generally demand the use of cements pigmented to match. Actually, if fracture seams are extremely narrow very little cement will show upon the surface and the requirement for properly pigmented adhesive loses its importance. The most demanding situation occurs whenever perfectly transparent crystals such as rock crystal, topaz, beryl, tourmaline and others similar must be cemented, since it is usually possible to see the fracture surfaces within the crystals unless the cement matches both color and optical properties of the mineral. It is for the last reason that Canada balsam is very useful in repair despite its pale yellow color. One needs only to cement a broken crystal with ordinary colorless adhesive and another with balsam to see the difference immediately; whereas ordinary cement reflects light from fracture surfaces within the crystal, making the place of repair quite conspicuous, Canada balsam more closely matches optical properties and permits light to pass through instead of causing reflections. Some epoxy resins are better than Canada balsam because they do not deteriorate and become brittle with the passage of time.

Water-soluble cements of various types such as hide glue and vegetable glue should be avoided because specimens cannot be washed later without risk of falling apart. Colorless, rapid-drying plastic cements such as model airplane makers use are very good for repair of porous specimens but very poor for rejoining large crystals which are quite impervious and thus prevent evaporation of the solvent. If time is no object, however, such cements can be used and specimens left tied together for several weeks after which time most of the solvent will have escaped from within the seam. Since the solvent occupies space, some shrinkage occurs in cements of this type thus greatly reducing the strength of the joint. A good feature of this kind of cement, however, is that it is possible to buy small bottles in various colors. Glyptal cements are also very good for repair, drying to a transparent solid material of dull luster.

A very good water-soluble cement is a plastic-base thick fluid of white color, generally furnished in "squeeze bottle" containers, which dries to an inconspicuous, lusterless, colorless transparent film, highly resistant to water. It has the advantage that it can be thinned with water and introduced by capillary action into hairline crevices which would be impossible to fill otherwise. For this purpose, a drop or two is diluted with several drops of water until the cement is watery; it is then painted along cracks with a small pointed brush. Its penetrating action is greatly improved if the specimen is first soaked in warm water and then dried in a towel to remove excess water. For badly shattered specimens or those which promise to fall completely apart if any sections are removed, this cement is probably without an equal.

Canada balsam, as mentioned before, is good for transparent crystal repair. To be effective, however, it has to be "cooked" to drive off volatile substances which would otherwise keep it tacky for a long time. The process is a simple one, and merely consists of taking some cement from the bottle and warming it over a low flame in a shallow dish. The cement is heated as long as a small sample dipped up by a toothpick shows stickiness even when cool. When a trial droplet hardens to the point of brittleness the balsam is ready to use. During the time the balsam is cooking the specimen fragments should be warmed gently in an oven or raised to temperature in water which is heated until it is uncomfortably warm to the touch. In the latter method of heating, all water must be wiped off before cementing. By heating both specimen and cement, the thinnest possible layer of balsam can be applied to all matching parts, a very important consideration because an excess is unsightly and actually produces a weaker joint. As soon as the parts are united, strong pressure is applied with string wrappings to hold the sections together and to squeeze out excess cement. When the specimen is quite cold, the excess balsam is chipped off with a razor blade and the rest removed by brushing quickly with an alcohol-impregnated swab. Since balsam is soluble in alcohol, the swab must not be brushed over the joint longer than necessary.

Ordinary shellac is also very useful for cementing because it possesses good strength and is remarkably "sticky" even to the glassiest surfaces. Shellac dissolved in alcohol may be purchased in paint or hardware stores but suffers from being spotty in quality and often contains so much water that it never dries hard. It is best to buy some pure wood alcohol and a stick of shellac of suitable color and make up a small quantity of solution as needed. This is easily done by pulverizing part of the stick upon a clean hard surface and dissolving the powder in alcohol in a small, tightly-capped bottle. As with balsam, the shellac is applied to pre-warmed fragments which are forced together and tied securely. Since the little alcohol remaining must be evaporated, the specimen should be kept warm for several hours and then permitted to cool. If time is no object, the specimen should be left tied for several days.

Perhaps the strongest cements currently available are special plastics in liquid form which harden when mixed with small quantities of catalytic agents. Among them are the "epoxy" resins now being sold in small quantities to hobbyists for many cementing purposes. Unfortunately, most resins of this type are extremely thick at room temperature and it is very difficult to spread films thinly enough for neat joints. However, warming of specimens helps to make the cement more fluid and, in fact, is necessary with some types in order to hasten the "setting" action of the catalyst. Since no volatiles must be driven off, joints reach maximum strength as soon as the resin is hard. Directions furnished for their mixing and use must be followed to the letter to insure successful work.

CUTTING AND POLISHING SPECIMENS

Many minerals and their associates cannot be appreciated fully or studied properly unless specimens are sliced through and polished to show internal details. For example, from the outside whole nodules of variscite are among the drabbest of natural objects, but when cut open and polished they are transformed into beautiful specimens of greatly increased scientific and commercial value. The following features should lead to serious consideration of lapidary treatment:

Coloration—vivid hues, contrasting hues, etc. Examples: variscite, malachite, etc.

Patterns—interesting geometrical lines, patches, bandings, etc. Examples: agate, brecciated metallic ores, septarian nodules, etc.

Crystals enclosed in massive material—porphyry, graphic granite, dendritic silver, etc.

Inclusions in clear crystals—many kinds are found in quartz, calcite, etc.

Zoning in crystals—bands, veils, phantoms, or other features related to the enclosing crystals. Examples: amethyst zones in rock crystal, "watermelon" tourmalines, etc.

Zoning in massive ores—bands, concentric rings, etc., which show alteration, replacements, successive waves of ore deposition, etc. Examples: comb structures, massive sulfides, smithsonite, etc.

An increasing number of collectors; both amateur and professional; fully realize the advantage of preparing specimens in this manner and are now acquiring saw outfits for slicing as well as trimming specimens. Many still depend upon amateur cutters with whom they are acquainted to do this work for them, while others take advantage of the reasonable rates charged for such work by professional lapidaries who advertise regularly in the popular earth science magazines. Lapidaries will cut material into slabs, or will cut and polish at so much per square inch of sawed surface. Full instructions on the selection and use of diamond saws as well as other lapidary equipment is given in the author's *Gem Cutting—A Lapidary's Manual.*

From the commercial standpoint, sawing has several advantages, the greatest being that large specimens which cannot be sold except to museums, can be divided into many small specimens which are far more easily disposed of and indeed may bring more money altogether than would be possible otherwise. Furthermore, many damaged specimens such as single crystals of tourmaline or rock crystal containing inclusions, can not only be salvaged but perhaps sold at higher prices as polished slabs than as broken crystals.

8

Storage and Exhibit

A few serious collectors of minerals and gemstones keep their collection material in boxes or drawers, wrapped in paper, and hidden from view, but by far the larger number like to display their choice material or keep it handy to show visiting enthusiasts. However, before specimens are introduced in the collection, it is necessary to label and record them, decide on what kind of arrangement the collection should follow, stow specimens properly to prevent damage or to preserve them from harm, and finally select a number to exhibit at home or at shows. The following sections deal with these pleasantly time-consuming details, which are as important to many collectors as the actual field work involved in collecting the specimens themselves.

LABELING AND CATALOGING SPECIMENS

It is of greatest importance that specimens be labeled immediately after being collected, particularly in respect to locality. Nothing receives so cold a reception from the serious collector or museum curator as a specimen without a label or one which merely identifies the mineral and gives the locality in some very general way such as "Ohio," "Brazil," etc. Even a misidentified specimen can be put right, but no amount of mental effort will ever erase the doubt as to locality unless the person who actually found the specimen places the locality upon the label. It is just as important that specimens be identified by some mark placed upon them which can be matched to a label or to a catalog since specimens have a habit of becoming separated from their labels. The eminent American collector, Col. Washington A. Roebling, whose collection went to the Smithsonian after his death, always took the trouble to affix minute paper labels on his specimens which told not only the species name but the locality. Other collectors perhaps do not go this far but do take the trouble to at least apply a number somewhere upon the specimen which can be referred to a master catalog for full details.

Several methods are used for applying identification numbers and letters, the most popular and permanent being painted patches upon which numbers and letters are written in India ink and then varnished over. By using a fine crowquill pen of the kind that can be bought in draftsmen's supply houses, it is possible neatly and legibly to affix labels as small as a quarter-inch in diameter, as shown in Figure 128. Flat white quick-drying paint is best for the purpose, while ordinary colorless spar varnish does best for the preservative coating over the inked lettering. Do not use shellac.

Specimens ready for entry into the collection are examined for reasonably level spots upon which small patches of paint can be applied. Areas selected must not cover interesting features nor should they be visible when the specimens are placed in exhibit position. If no

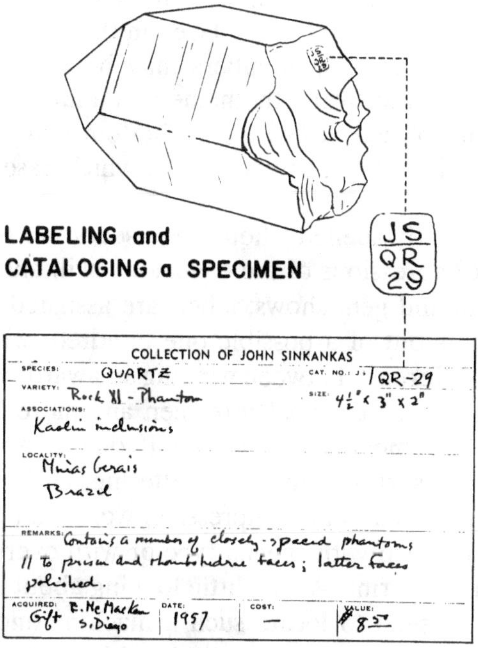

LABELING and
CATALOGING a SPECIMEN

JS
QR
29

COLLECTION OF JOHN SINKANKAS

SPECIES: QUARTZ   CAT. NO.: J-7 QR-29
VARIETY: Rock XI - Phantom   SIZE: 4½" x 3" x 2"
ASSOCIATIONS: Kaolin inclusions
LOCALITY: Minas Gerais
          Brazil
REMARKS: Contains a number of closely-spaced phantoms // to prism and rhombohedral faces; latter faces polished.
ACQUIRED: Gift B. McMackin   DATE: 1957   COST: —   VALUE: $8.50
          S. Diego

FIGURE 128. After a specimen is cataloged, either in a book catalog or upon a file card, such as shown here, the catalog number is printed in India ink upon a white patch painted upon the specimen in some inconspicuous place.

level places are available for the label, some can be made by rubbing flat spots with a carborundum stick or a steel tool. Some collectors use a little dab of plaster of paris which is flattened just before the plaster sets. The label paint is applied with an artist's oil painting brush of no more than one-eighth inch in width. The coating should be thick enough to cover the mineral underneath but not so thick that it takes too long to dry. After paint spots are dry, code letters and numbers are applied with India ink and, after a few minutes to permit drying, varnish or clear plastic lacquer is gently brushed over them. Entries in the catalog should be made at this time to be sure that the same code numbers are not issued twice.

If specimens are to be exhibited, small card labels are made up with the following basic information: species name, variety name, and locality. The usual size of labels is about 1¼" x 2" but larger labels may be used if they do not cause a cluttered appearance in the cabinet or case. Additional information usually supplied on larger labels includes the Dana System number as taken from Dana's "System of Mineralogy," preferably placed in the upper righthand corner, the mineral associates, and the chemical formula placed in the center just below the name of the mineral. Catalog numbers may be placed in the upper lefthand corner if desired, while the name and address of the collector or dealer is usually placed at the top or bottom margin unless specimens are to be exhibited in competition, in which case owners names are omitted.

Neat labels, correctly spelled, should be used at all times since they furnish important impressions of the collector's skill and workmanship. In modern mineral and gem shows, labels are assigned credits of from ten to twenty points out of a possible one hundred, with their quality often spelling the difference between winning an award or being an "also ran." Very few handwritten labels are seen any more because superb penmanship has become a lost art, and if one is not exceptionally skilled it is best to resort to printing or lettering. Ordinary typewriting is satisfactory but much more impressive work can be done upon electric typewriters fitted with special type or with oversize type which closely resembles bookprint. With a little looking about among business firms, it is often possible to locate such a machine and arrange for a number of labels to be made up. Beautiful and impressive labels can be prepared by use of draftsmen's lettering guides which come in a variety of sizes and styles of alphabets and numbers. Some practice is needed to do a neat job but the results are worth it. Excellent labels can also be made freehand by using ball-point or square-point pens but even more practice is needed, since nothing guides the pen point except the operator's skill. It helps in any freehand work to lay out horizontal and vertical lines in light pencil to serve as lettering and centering guides.

Keeping an accurate, complete catalog of items in the collection is far more important than most persons realize, for inevitably the time comes to dispose of the collection either during the lifetime of the owner or after his death. A good catalog supplies everything worth knowing about any specimen, including when, where, and how it was obtained, what price or what exchange was made for it, and details as to size, shape, color, weight, etc., which may be pertinent and which help to surely identify the specimen. A large ledger or looseleaf notebook may be used for the catalog, with ruled columns for standard information plus a "remarks" column for additional useful information. The author has devised as an alternative scheme to notebook-type catalogs, a card catalog consisting of standard 3″ x 5″ file cards kept in steel file card boxes. A typical card is illustrated in Figure 128. The printing shown upon the cards was done professionally at a very modest cost. With this system, a single card is generally used for a single specimen although several similar crystals or small specimens coming from the same locality can be entered on one card. The code system employs a combination of letters and numbers, the letters indicating the species and the numbers the specific specimens. The code designation is the same as that lettered upon the corresponding specimen. Since the back of each file card is blank, additional room is available for information which will not fit upon the front. If any specimen is disposed of, a duplicate card can be made up for the new owner and a note as to what happened to the specimen placed upon the original card. Dead cards are kept separately for reference to localities, prices, and other information which may be needed in the future. If specimens are acquired from prominent collections, the original labels should be specially asked for and attached to the new owner's label or to the catalog entry. Many specimens of ordinary caliber by modern standards are highly prized by collectors because of their historical associations.

ARRANGEMENT OF COLLECTIONS

There are a number of ways to arrange mineral collections in systematic and sensible fashion, but whatever method is finally adopted should enable the collector to put his hands on any specimen at a moment's notice. The simplest arrangement is an alphabetical one which makes it easy to go directly to any drawer whenever a certain mineral is called for. However, this system has no scientific merit since it does not put related species together. Nevertheless, it is often used just because of its directness, and where the collection being assembled is not a scientific one, it is certainly the best. Another method employed by many is to arrange species according to chemical classes, in other words, the way they are arranged in Dana's "System of Mineralogy." In this scheme, all elements such as gold, native silver, copper and so on, are put together in one drawer, oxides in another, sulfides in still another and so on. The drawback to this arrangement is of course that the collector must be able to tell within what class any species falls if someone asks him to produce a certain species. This is not always easy to do, especially if the collection is a large one. However, this problem can be overcome by refering to an alphabetical list of specimens showing in what drawer each is located.

Another scheme calls for arranging specimens according to locality, whether it be a single mine, ore deposit, a mining district, a county, state, province or other political subdivision. Thus there are collectors who specialize in acquiring minerals from single mines such as the Crestmore Quarry at Riverside in California; from districts such as Bisbee, Arizona; or Franklin, New Jersey; from counties such as San Diego County in California, noted for its many pegmatites and pegmatite minerals, and so on. A strong advantage of any locality collection is that its owner tends to become expert in the ore or mineral deposits of the locality, as well as becoming expert in the specific minerals and mineral associates. If the collection is carefully maintained with superior specimens being substituted for poorer specimens whenever the opportunity offers, it may eventually become both scientifically and monetarily valuable, for it is just this kind of collection that museums and universities are most anxious to acquire.

Because of the multitude of mineral species and the almost limitless number of their varieties, some collectors confine their efforts to single species such as quartz or calcite, to minerals of single elements such as "coppers" or "silvers," or to minerals of a single chemical class, possibly sulfides, sulfosalts, or phosphates, etc. Enough variety within each is available to keep even the most avid collector busy for a lifetime. Other collections can be made on the basis of metallic ore minerals, non-metallic commercial minerals, clay minerals, pegmatite minerals, minerals of oxidized zones, etc. There are a great many possibilities, some of which are listed below:

Size—micromounts, thumbnails, miniatures, hand specimens, cabinet specimens, museum specimens.

Locality—mine or quarry, district, county, state, etc.

General—all species, usually on the basis of attractiveness.

Chemical classes—elements, oxides, sulfides, sulfosalts, phosphates, etc.

Mineral groups—garnets, tourmalines, feldspars, zeolites, etc.

Single species—quartz, calcite, fluorite, gold, etc.

Metals—copper minerals, zinc minerals, etc.

Single crystals.

Twin crystals.

Inclusions—in quartz, feldspar, mica, etc.

Special mineral deposits—pegmatites, oxidized zones, basalt or diabase minerals, etc.

Commercial minerals—ores, clay minerals, refractories, etc.

Crystal systems—cubic, hexagonal, orthorhombic, etc.

Geodes, agates, thundereggs, jaspers, etc.

Gemstones, cut and rough.

ASSEMBLING COLLECTIONS

Although it is possible to accumulate a large number of the almost 2,000 mineral species now known to exist, the hopelessness of such a task for persons of ordinary means soon causes them to specialize along one of the lines listed above. Actually this is all to the good, for it is extremely difficult to find even professional mineralogists who are thoroughly familiar with the entire mineral kingdom, indicating that it is better to know a small field thoroughly than to know little about everything.

Once a specialized field has been selected, it remains to decide upon the size range within which specimens should fall. This decision is governed largely by the space available for storage and the money that can be spent on acquiring minerals which cannot be personally collected. As a rule, specimens over hand size increase sharply in cost, although the tendency these days when smaller sizes are popular is for dealers to sell large specimens for less than they should bring in proportion. In fact, many dealers do not trouble to advertise large specimens except to schools, museums, and a selected few private collectors who want large pieces and can afford to pay for them. Many dealers break up museum-size masses into considerably smaller pieces which are sure to sell. However, despite decreased costs, small specimens of perfect proportions and singular beauty are not easier to get than larger ones, particularly since the demand for them has increased. Another factor which makes collecting single-size specimens difficult is the fact that not all minerals are obliging enough to occur in made-to-order sizes. Some species habitually form nothing but minute crystals, suitable for the micromounter but hopeless for the miniature specialist. On the other hand, the micromounter is equally pressed in striving for a complete collection by being unable to obtain crystals of certain species small enough to match those in the rest of the collection. In any case, this all adds interest to the game of collecting by preventing any collector from ever acquiring the best of everything. There is always room for improvement.

Although experience is the best teacher, in mineral collecting as well as in other pursuits, it is possible to make her lessons a little less expensive by learning from other collectors who have been in the game for some time. Their own collections and their advice are invaluable in coming to the conclusions as to what represents top quality in specimens. It is very instructive to visit a school or museum collection with such a person, for he soon makes known which specimens he considers to be "upper crust" and those which are merely ordinary. By and large, good collections are assembled by discriminating persons who know enough about the minerals they collect to recognize quality when they see it. How much money is paid for a specimen is no guarantee of quality. Many collectors of more than ordinary means possess specimens which do not merit a second glance from true connoisseurs simply because the choices were not made expertly. Too often, size alone appeals to such collectors, and too often their larger specimens are mediocre in quality though superior in price. This is not to say that top-notch specimens can be acquired for a song, top quality must always be paid for, but poor quality need not be. A good collector must be tough-minded; he must not only know good material but must have the courage to get rid of specimens which do not match the quality of the rest of his collection. Mediocre specimens may be kept if they are the only examples of the species but when an opportunity comes along to obtain something better, it should certainly be taken. It is possible by starting with a modest collection of small specimens of good quality to work up gradually to a respectable collection of truly fine minerals. The process takes years but is worth the effort.

In respect to purchasing specimens, many narrow-minded individuals condemn the practice as being somehow unethical, although it is difficult to see how this is more reprehensible than buying a collection of phonograph records, books, stamps, coins, glassware, or antiques. Some claim that the only legitimate way to acquire a collection is by actually collecting the specimens or obtaining them through exchange. This may be a practical way if one lives in a collector's paradise filled with minerals of surpassing loveliness which other collectors the world over are eager to acquire but unfortunately most of us are condemned to live in regions which are not so well blessed, and we must, if dreary collections are to be avoided, spend some money to pay for the time and trouble of another collector who did the actual digging. Happily most collectors realize this and are perfectly content to pay rather than go without.

Many collectors who obtain extra material on field trips exchange them for species missing from their own collections, or sell the surplus to dealers. Exchanging often results in both parties getting something new, but all too often such transactions are disappointing. The best exchanges take place between persons who are knowledgeable of values and fair in their dealings, while the worst exchanges take place between individuals who are uncertain of prevailing prices or who place too high a value on specimens collected personally. It is human nature to prize highly personally-collected specimens since the memories of the cost and labor involved in getting them are still fresh in the mind and influence the valuation. Another factor which often results in boosting prices to unrealistic heights is the attitude of local collectors toward specimens found within their region. Thus, in some areas such as San Diego County, California, or the area to the west of Colorado Springs, Colorado, both noted for splendid mineral collecting, resident collectors vie with each other for every worthwhile specimen in order to improve their own local-area collections. This keen competition results in high prices being set upon good material which seem sensible and fair to local collectors but may seem unrealistically high to others. It is for this reason that dealers find it possible to sell Franklin minerals at higher prices to collectors around New York City, San Diego County pegmatite minerals to collectors in San Diego, and so on. In the final analysis, the best common ground on which to exchange is that of fair prevailing retail specimen prices. If each party knows his prices, he can state them in his letter, describing the specimens at the same time so that the other party can judge accurately what is being offered. If possible, exchanges should be for pieces of equal quality, or, put another way, a sackful of broken crystals should not be accepted for one small but perfect specimen. Sheer weight or volume of material exchanged is no exchange at all; the best exchanges are those in which a few excellent pieces are given for a like quantity and quality on the other side.

STORAGE OF SPECIMENS

Good specimens deserve and *need* good storage; they must be systematically arranged, each specimen in its own space, correctly labeled or otherwise identified, and protected from dust, dirt, excessive light and from the well-meaning but often destructive handling of those who neither appreciate their fragility nor realize their value. In this connection, a good friend of the author's tells a tale which is repeated here to illustrate how many persons simply do not know how to treat specimens and why it is necessary to prevent them from handling the more delicate ones.

The tale revolves about a kindly relative who was being shown the collection. A number of specimens were handed to her in turn and each received complimentary remarks. Perhaps gratified by the reception accorded them, the owner proudly handed her an especially fine piece, the upper surface of which was covered by numerous slender crystals of millerite. He was horrified a moment later to see her brush the back of her hand over the top to clear away the needle-like crystals which she mistook for an accumulation of lint, hair, and dust such as is found in obscure nooks and crannies even in the best-regulated houses. From this moment on, needless to say, the owner of the collection placed his prizes under lock and key and would only open the case to recognized experts.

Millerite is of course notoriously fragile but many other minerals are equally delicate and require the greatest care in their handling. If they are to be preserved, proper cabinets or cases are required, preferably with glass fronts which permit full view yet prevent handling.

Almost every collection includes "show" specimens of especially fine quality which should be placed in glass cabinets on permanent display, but in the main it consits of less attractive though scientifically important specimens which may be placed in closed storage in drawers or cases. Provisions for both kinds of storage should be considered when accumulating a collection. However, because larger specimens take up so much room, many collectors tend to limit the size of specimens to 2″ x 3″ or less. This permits acquiring a larger number of species yet does not result in being forced to clutter the tops of bookcases, shelves, and mantelpieces within the living spaces of ordinary homes where specimens become dusty or are knocked off during housecleaning. The least amount of space is taken up by micromount collections consisting of small bits of matrix, crystal groups or minute single crystals mounted on pedestals within 1″ x 1″ boxes. Hundreds of such boxes take up very little room when stored in a small cabinet fitted with shallow drawers. The so-called "thumbnail" specimens, as the name implies, measure no more than 1″ x 1″ x 1″ over-all, and again may be fitted into a very small volume. The usual arrangement calls for pasteboard or wood trays, with or without covers, which are divided into numerous small compartments. A tray a little over a foot across can contain forty or more specimens. The next standard size specimens are the "miniatures" which do not measure more than 1½″ x 1½″ x 2″ over-all, large enough to view easily without magnification, yet small enough to be easily stored and handled. Collections of this sort are ordinarily stored in special wooden cabinets which most collectors make for themselves or order from cabinetmakers. Exceptionally handy and compact cabinets can be made from old sewing thread spool cases, such as were used to store and display thread in shops selling dressmaking supplies. Old dental tool cabinets are particularly prized for mineral collections because of the number and variety in size of drawers, beginning with shallow drawers at the top and finishing with deep drawers at the bottom. A mineral collection of mixed-size specimens can be held very nicely in such a cabinet although provisions are needed to break up each drawer into compartments to prevent specimens from bumping into each other as drawers are opened and closed. It is strongly recommended that when the time comes to obtain storage cases, second-hand and antique stores be looked into, since they often stock old-fashioned cases which need only some cleaning up and refinishing to make them into practical, handsome cabinets.

Excellent storage cabinets for small specimens can be made at home from hard or soft wood planks plus plastic compartmented trays such as are used to store screws, nails and other small hardware items. The first step is to buy as many trays as are necessary, planning for a number which will fit vertically in an open-front case with just enough clearance between them to permit easy sliding in and out. The case is made of three planks of wood, one on each of the vertical sides and the third in the center to provide two vertical spaces in which the trays will fit. The back of the cabinet is covered with plywood, glued and nailed in place to provide the necessary strength and rigidity. The trays fit upon strips of aluminum angle or thin pieces of hardwood, drilled for screws. When completed, the cabinet shows two vertical rows of plastic

FIGURE 129. Sliding glass door exhibit cabinets; the two sections shown may be purchased separately. *Courtesy Ward's Natural Science Establishment, Rochester, N. Y.*

FIGURE 130. Table top cabinet for small specimens. Shallow drawers are compartmented with pasteboard trays which permit storage of specimens without fear of shifting and bruising. *Courtesy Ward's Natural Science Establishment, Rochester, N. Y.*

trays, each tray resting upon a pair of slides of aluminum or wood fitted to the inner walls of the case. If the clearance between trays is reduced to the minimum, very little dust or dirt will enter the cabinet. If desired, the front of such a cabinet can be fitted with a pair of hinged doors. Smaller, professionally-made cases of similar design may be bought from hardware stores.

Popular display and storage cabinets available from Ward's Natural Science Establishment are shown in Figures 129, 130 and 131. The glass cabinet is fitted with a lock and due to tight construction is fairly dustproof. The sliding drawer cabinets are designed to accommodate shallow pasteboard trays of standard size, several of the largest size or more of smaller sizes, but all fitting together snugly to prevent shifting. Most collectors devise their own schemes for preventing specimens from rattling or bumping within drawers, a popular method being to cut out strips of white pasteboard which are notched at regular intervals to permit criss-crossing and to break up the space into square or rectangular compartments. Others use standard size cardboard mailing boxes, one for each specimen, while still others employ white Styrofoam plastic sponge cut into blocks with each specimen pressed into the yielding upper surface to hold it securely in place. Whatever scheme is adopted, it is important to prevent excessive movement of specimens once they have been placed in compartments.

Compartment or drawer linings should be light in color to show specimens to best advantage. Especially fragile minerals may require some kind of soft resilient material upon which they can rest, both to prevent jarring and avoid scratching. Cotton is very good but is inclined to adhere to specimens; however, it can be covered with small squares of white tissue paper such as is used in department stores in lining boxes containing articles of merchandise. Small pads of cotton can be cut from rolls of surgical cotton to fit compartments exactly, or quilted rectangles of cotton used by women to remove cosmetics can be purchased by the box to accomplish the same purpose. To prevent linting, squares of cotton can be sprayed lightly with Krylon plastic spray which serves to cement the fibers together yet permits the cotton to retain resiliency. Styrofoam plastic sponge is very commonly used and has many advantages. It is soft enough so that specimens can be pressed into its surface, creating recesses which fit the underside contours exactly and holding specimens securely in the best display posi-

FIGURE 131. A storage cabinet for larger specimens. A door, hinged at the right, swings to cover the face of the cabinet. *Courtesy Ward's Natural Science Establishment, Rochester, N. Y.*

tion. It is especially desirable for single crystals, several of which can be pressed into the same block. Styrofoam can be purchased in blocks and sheets from firms which specialize in selling materials for window-dressing and for displays. It may be cut by an ordinary table-saw but the blade must be sharp to leave a good smooth finish. Some collectors cut Styrofoam blocks with razor blades, thin-bladed cabinet saws, or even jeweler's saws, rubbing the blocks to proper size and squaring corners on a sheet of sandpaper laid flat upon a hard surface. Blocks of an inch thick or so can be beveled in front for labels which can be cemented or pinned on with glass-head map tacks. Needless to say, Styrofoam is very popular for mounting specimens for competitive display.

SPECIMEN EXHIBITS IN THE HOME

The most spectacular and professional method of exhibiting specimens at home is to use glass-walled cabinets such as previously described and illustrated. However, if cabinets of this kind cannot be installed, it is possible to use smaller exhibit cases such as "shadow boxes" which look like ordinary framed pictures but are actually deep enough to accommodate several specimens or crystals. Such boxes are simple to construct out of quarter-inch plywood and suitable picture-frame molding but should have provisions for glass covers to keep out dust. Backgrounds are usually black velvet or some other kind of inconspicuously-colored cloth of non-shiny surface texture, or may be flocked or even painted with flat paint of low reflectivity. Specimens are attached by stout wire claws which are fastened firmly to the back; specimens should never be cemented in place. When a properly made box is finished, the specimens seem to float in air against a dull background which does not draw the eye away from the minerals themselves. Small but choice crystals and crystal groups or, possibly, cut and rough gemstones are extremely attractive when displayed in this fashion. Shadow boxes also have the advantage of blending into almost any kind of interior decor when tastefully designed.

Many collectors use Riker mounts for portable displays which can be passed from hand to hand. Riker mounts consist of shallow cardboard boxes, stoutly constructed, of about an inch in depth, fitted with glass-topped covers which press down crystals, gems, etc., into thick cotton batting and hold them securely in place. Covers lock in position with pin inserted from the sides. Several Riker mounts are shown inside the cabinets of Figure 129. If too many specimens are placed in them, however, the specimens tend to slide into each other and ruin the appearance of the display. Riker mounts are sold by mineral dealers in a variety of sizes, from small boxes several inches across to some about a foot in length. With a little ingenuity it is possible to make similar boxes at home; one kind used by the author consists of a frame of quarter-inch plywood backed with cardboard and topped by glass panels which slide in and out of grooves cut in the plywood. Instead of cotton, rectangles of Styrofoam plastic are cut to fit snugly with each small specimen or crystal pressed firmly into the foam.

Some collectors make up decorative items around their homes such as polished wood bookends on which crystal groups are fastened to provide both decoration and the weight necessary to make them function properly. Others have devised attractive lamps using large crystal groups as bases. Thin polished slabs of agate, chalcedony, chrysocolla chalcedony and other quartz family minerals have been used in lamp shades, as overlays on coffee tables and as transparencies cemented to glass panes for placing in windows. Coffee tables fitted with plate glass tops, or small corner tables with display space beneath the tops have long been popular items of furniture for collectors who like to show a few small choice items in this fashion.

EXHIBIT AND STORAGE OF GEMS

Because of their small size, gems lend themselves especially well to Riker mount displays, glass-topped coffee and corner table displays, and other shallow display cases. However, unless fastened properly, faceted gems will roll out of position while cabochons will slide back and forth; in each instance, damage to delicate edges and corners is very likely to occur. Groups of faceted gems may be held securely by pressing them into a block of Styrofoam, while cabochons may be tacked in place with small drops of colorless transparent cement (which can be scraped off later if necessary) applied to the backs. Cabochons may also be pressed into Styrofoam but the pressure must be applied gently through the center of each stone, to be sure each seats evenly.

A number of holders for faceted gems have been devised, among which may be mentioned the small blown-glass stands originally created for the gems of the Morgan Collection in the American Museum of Natural History in New York and later adopted for the new Mineral and Gem Hall exhibits at the Smithsonian Institution in

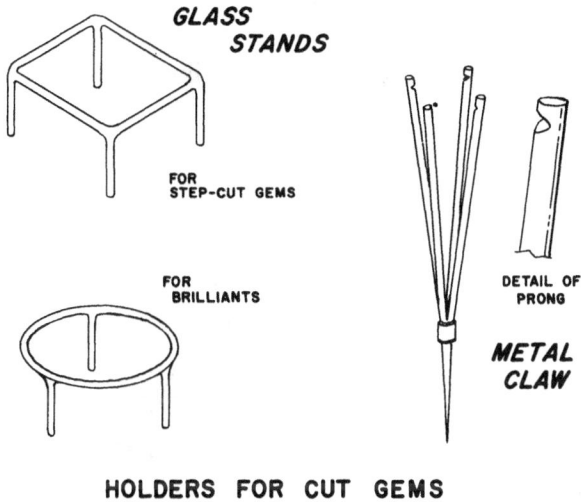

HOLDERS FOR CUT GEMS

FIGURE 132. The glass stands shown on the left are made from slender rods cleverly fused together. Being colorless and transparent they do not detract from gems displayed. The metal claw holder on the right is made from german silver wire or other metal of suitable springiness.

Washington, D. C. These consist of slender glass rods, not more than one-sixteenth inch in diameter, fused together to construct the stands; circles for brilliants are supported by three legs, others for step-cut gems are squares or rectangles with four legs. Several of these stands are shown in Figure 132. Although most collectors cannot handle glass, it is possible to make up similar stands from lengths of colorless transparent plastic rod, using a suitable plastic cement to join sections together. Stands of this sort are extremely effective in displays because they detract so little from the gems. There is no reason why such stands cannot also be made up for prized crystals and small mineral groups.

Other stands for gems have been made out of springy wire clips which are fastened into a sleeve and soldered in place, as shown in Figure 132. The bottom of the sleeve is fitted with a sharp pin so that the entire assembly can be stuck into the wood or plastic base of the exhibit case. One model uses rather thick wire for the clips, with small vee recesses filed near the tops into which the girdles of the gems fit. An even less conspicuous type has been recently made up by a friend of the author's in Vancouver, Washington, who employs discarded hypodermic syringe needles with their attachment fittings cut off and extremely fine piano wire prongs inserted into the central channels. The ends of the wire prongs are clipped off to the proper length and then bent over slightly to hold gems in place. All of these devices elevate gems above the floor of the exhibit case and provide strikingly handsome exhibits, particularly since light enters the gems from all sides.

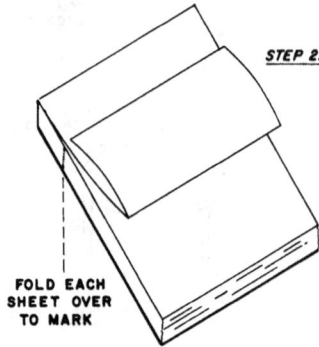

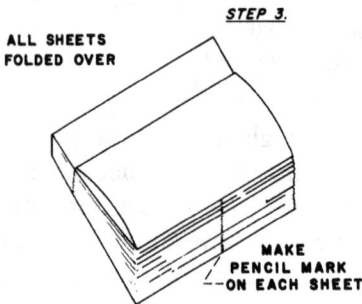

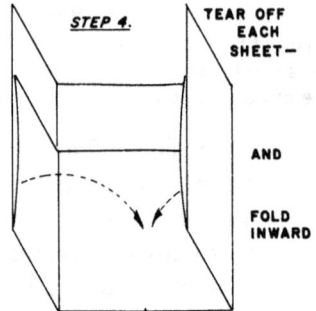

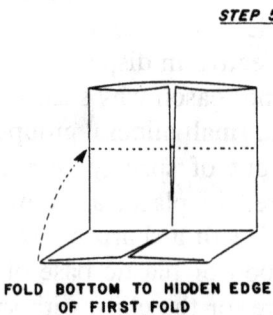

STEP 1.

PAD OF PAPER

MAKE PENCIL MARK

STEP 2.

FOLD EACH SHEET OVER TO MARK

STEP 3.

ALL SHEETS FOLDED OVER

STEP 4.

TEAR OFF EACH SHEET—

AND

FOLD INWARD

MAKE PENCIL MARK —ON EACH SHEET

STEP 5.

FOLD BOTTOM TO HIDDEN EDGE OF FIRST FOLD

STEP 6.

NOW FOLD TOP FLAP OVER AND DIAMOND PAPER IS COMPLETE. STRONGLY CREASE ALL FOLDS.

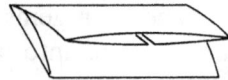

HOW TO MAKE DIAMOND PAPERS

FIGURE 133. By the steps shown above, ordinary paper in pad form can be converted very inexpensively into serviceable papers for storing gems and small crystals. The initial mark shown in Step 1 is made at a point slightly less than one-fifth of the paper length from the top of the pad. A little experimentation is needed to determine the exact places to fold papers but after a satisfactory paper has been made up, it can be unfolded and used as a model.

The storage of gems is best accomplished by using "diamond papers"—small rectangular paper packets which may be lined with thin tissue paper and fitted with small cotton pads to keep loose gems from shifting and rubbing against each other. Many years of experience have led to the adoption of a standard method of folding of these papers as shown in the step-by-step drawings of Figure 133. Although such papers can be bought in a number of sizes, it is far cheaper to make up your own from almost any kind of standard typewriter-size paper of good quality. The best paper is a fairly thin light-weight bond or airmail paper which folds easily yet is tough and long lasting. Standard bond paper when folded properly produces packets which are just large enough to contain the rectangular cosmetic pads of quilted cotton mentioned before. The shallow grooves impressed during the quilting process fit the pavilions of gems nicely. The papers just described have the merit of fitting upright in shallow cabinet drawers making them readily available for reference.

Diamond papers containing gems should be labeled with the species and variety of the gem, its cut, weight, and locality from which the raw material came. These facts should be entered in a ledger book or a loose-leaf notebook catalog, along with other pertinent data. Small, loose crystals, spare micromount material, and other small mineral specimens are also advantageously stored in diamond papers.

EXHIBITING AT SHOWS

The proud owner of a collection is naturally eager to display it, and this desire finds an outlet in the many shows which are held each year by various societies and federations of earth science clubs throughout the United States and Canada. Such shows encourage collectors to do their best to win prizes which, although they may be entirely without monetary value, publicly recognize the collector's efforts to become expert in some field of mineral collecting or lapidary work. However, competition is keen and less consideration is being given each year to drab or uninspired exhibits. As in any kind of competition, the desire to win is an extremely important factor, since it influences collecting activities during the remainder of the year and gives additional purpose to the hobby. Since shows are judged by experts, competitors soon learn what is considered top quality in collection material.

After some years of experience, a number of societies and federations have adopted standard rules governing competitive exhibits and provide set "yardsticks" for judging exhibits. A typical set of judging percentages for mineral displays is as follows: quality of material—45%, variety of material—20%, showmanship—15%, rarity—15%, labeling —5%, for a total of 100%. Judges are instructed to assign marks within the limits shown which when all added up give a total percentage. If the total falls within 85-100%, a first prize blue ribbon is awarded, if between 70-84%, a red second prize is given, and if the percentage falls between 60–69%, a white third place ribbon is awarded. Under this system, awards are given only if exhibitors deserve them and numerous instances are known where judges considered no displays to be worthy of top awards and accordingly made none.

From the above it can be seen that quality of material can earn the maximum number of points which is as it should be, however, many exhibitors make the mistake of detracting from top notch specimens by including mediocre or poor quality specimens, perhaps under the illusion that a large display is more impressive than a small one. Certainly, size of display is important but few expert judges are influenced by this factor alone, especially if so much is stuffed into the exhibit case that it becomes cluttered and confused. It is actually far better to include only the best specimens, striving above all for uniform quality and a neat, orderly presentation, with enough space around each specimen so that viewers may see it as an object apart. If the case seems too barren, it is a good idea to make labels somewhat larger or to install a placard in front which gives some information on the specimens, such as their mode of formation, special features, unusual crystal sizes, etc. A truly exceptional specimen may be placed atop a pedestal to draw attention to its importance. As to what constitutes quality in a specimen, the rules for placing values on specimens explained in the next chapter are good ones to follow in determining where each specimen fits.

Variety of material in mineral exhibits refers to species rather than to varieties of the same mineral. This factor rates a substantial judging percentage because it is more difficult to collect a number of equal quality specimens, each of a different species, than it is to acquire a number of uniform character of one species. This method of judging prevents an exhibit from containing too many specimens of one species, even though each specimen is truly superb. In exhibits of one mineral species, some sets of rules give nothing for variety but give as much as 35% for variety of associated minerals. In any case, variety indicates a broader knowledge in collecting and does much to influence judges in their marking.

Showmanship has become increasingly important in recent years and substantial percentages are always given to encourage exhibitors to provide more attractive cases. Some collectors protest any award for showmanship, contending that specimens should be judged strictly on their own merits. However, since shows are educational and are meant for the public as well as for the participants in some earth science hobby, it is important that laymen be attracted to exhibits. On the other hand, exhibitors must be very careful in "dressing up" cases that they do not do so at the expense of the objects being exhibited. Some exhibitors go so far as to employ costly satins, silks, and other fancy materials, artfully folded and draped until the insides of cases remind one more of coffins than anything else. It is rather ridiculous to see mediocre to poor material ensconced in such settings, and discerning judges are sure to think that if as much effort had been expended upon the objects themselves, the exhibit as a whole would have been much improved. On the other hand, the importance of showmanship must never be underrated, even if no judging marks are assigned, because every person is consciously or unconsciously influenced by such factors as neatness, cleanliness, good visibility and lighting, easy-to-read labels, and so on. These are the reasons why so much attention is paid to window displays in shops and stores, and why a thriving and important business has sprung up in window-dressing alone. Sloppy, unattractive exhibits subtly influence onlookers, and judges too, leading to unfavorable impressions of the skill of the exhibitor or casting doubt upon the value of specimens whose owner thinks so little of them that he is content to display them in poor surroundings.

Rarity is a factor that may or may not be assigned a judging percentage in competition, but it certainly exerts a strong influence. It is relatively easy to obtain good to excellent specimens of common minerals but rather more difficult to find a satisfactory example of a rare species, no less one of exhibit quality. Where a collection contains a substantial number of rare species, it indicates the expenditure of considerable time and effort on the part of the owner in tracking down and acquiring them, quite aside from any expense involved. In order to obtain some rarities it is necessary to leave standing orders with mineral dealers or with dealers who operate in mining areas where such species may be available. In other cases, certain species cannot be obtained except from dealers abroad, again involving considerable effort in the way of correspondence. Expert judges are aware of these difficulties and may be expected to view exhibits containing rarities with special favor.

In regard to labeling, the advice furnished in a previous section of this chapter holds good for competitive exhibiting. It must be emphasized, however, how important neat, clean, easily legible labels are to establishing a professional tone. Though specimens speak for themselves, labels speak for their owners and really give one of the very few clues available to the judges as to skill, mentality, and zeal of the person. Do not make the mistake of believing that specimens only are judged. Minerals are products of nature and any merits they possess are not to the owner's credit, but their identification, selection, and arrangement are, and it is really on these last counts that the judges' decisions are based.

9

Marketing Mineral Specimens and Gemstones

Mineral specimens and gemstones have been traded for centuries, but in terms of volume and value the trade in gemstones far exceeds that of mineral specimens. Under the unceasing demand for beautiful gems for personal ornamentation, precious stones such as diamond, emerald, ruby and sapphire have been and will continue to be produced, finding their way into well-established trade channels where they receive sorting, cutting, and setting into jewelry. Additionally, some gemstones such as diamond and quartz are used in industry and serve to keep alive mining enterprises which might be unprofitable if confined to gemstone sales alone. In contrast, buyers of mineral specimens are relatively few and far between, and when the demands of private collectors, school and museum collection curators, and others who want specimens are added up, the total is very little compared to the demand for gemstones. Furthermore, very few mineral deposits are ever mined for specimens alone as is the case for gemstones; the major supply comes as incidental outputs from ore-mining or even gem-mining.

The supply of gemstones at any time is therefore apt to be greater than the supply of mineral specimens, and because there are many more customers for them, it is generally more profitable to deal in gemstones than in minerals. Although a cut gem excites wonder and admiration, the same cannot always be said for mineral specimens, which to the uninitiated often evoke expressions of "how curious" rather than "how beautiful," while many specimens of purely scientific value impress many persons as being so much stone. Yet despite these inherent handicaps of some minerals, handsome examples, or those of some unique interest or scientific value, can always be disposed of.

SOURCES OF MINERAL SPECIMENS

Aside from a few regions such as the Alps of Europe or the granite areas of Colorado west of Colorado Springs, where mineral specimens have been systematically collected for many years, virtually all specimens enter the market as by-products of mines operated for metallic ores or industrial or gem minerals. Copper, lead, zinc and other metallic ore specimens are supplied exclusively from mines opened for these metals, usually through the efforts of miners who take out a few pieces every day until they accumulate a stock to dispose of to dealers. This is the way the famous Franklin specimens reached the market from "cellar hoards" and the way many currently abundant specimens reach collectors now. In pegmatite and stone quarries, however, many specimens are collected by private individuals who sometimes strike it rich on field trips and obtain so many specimens at one time that they find it profitable to dispose of extras to professional dealers. It is true that some collectors find and work small deposits for specimens alone but unfortunately the number of such persons is very small; although within all of North America there must be an enormous number of places where careful search should uncover additional deposits, perhaps too small to support formal mining but still extensive enough to warrant private work at a profit.

The usual method of obtaining specimens from commercial mines and quarries is by encouraging miners to set aside handsome pieces which can be taken out in small quantities at the end of each day's work. However, in precious metal mines this practice is strictly prohibited, since a hand-sized specimen of exceptionally rich gold or silver ore may contain enough precious metal to equal a day's wages, and removal without the sanction of the mine owners constitutes the unlawful practice known as "highgrading." Any specimens obtained by visitors nowadays are usually selected from "picking tables." Here rich ore is separated by hand from waste rock and gangue and shown to some mine official; he then gives permission for its removal from the premises or sells it in behalf of the mine for its actual bullion value. The problem of highgrading has always been a serious one in precious metal mines and various ways have been tried to prevent it, some with success but many without. It is obviously next to impossible in an extensive mine employing many persons to operate an internal detective agency to keep track of every miner, and consequently some mine officials look the other way when they know highgrading is going on, considering that the money received by the miner for his surreptitiously collected specimens is in the nature of a fringe benefit. Other mines recognize the futility of stopping collecting by miners and as gestures of good will actually permit them to collect during off-hours, especially where the metal value of the ore is low, though the mineralogical value of the specimens is high. This practice is perhaps more prevalent in Mexico than in the United States. In this connection, the system employed for many years in the famous tin mines of Cornwall, England, probably resulted in far more specimens reaching the hands of collectors than would have been possible otherwise, because each miner worked for himself in producing ore which he sold to the mine owners. The more efficient he was at his tasks, the more ore he obtained and the better he was paid. If in mining he came upon handsome specimens worth more than ore value, he could of course set these aside and sell them at higher prices to collectors.

Active underground mines seldom permit collecting by visitors due to interference with work in progress and the likelihood of injuries which the company may be unprepared to recompense with insurance. Many collectors express indignation that mines do not permit gathering specimens within workings and believe that if "waivers" of claims for personal injuries are signed that they should be allowed to collect. Unfortunately, waivers are seldom worth the paper they are written on because courts have held that persons cannot sign away their lives or their persons, especially if dependent wives and children are left without support. Although the collector himself may agree to hold the company harmless, he cannot agree for his dependents who may bring suit in their own behalf. In the present "suit conscious" atmosphere which prevails throughout the United States and Canada, it is no wonder that mines and quarries generally prohibit any kind of unescorted visiting or collecting.

On the other hand, in the case of abandoned mines it is often possible to obtain specimens from local collectors who are familiar with the workings, and who may consent to obtain more if a demand exists. This possibility is common in Mexico, where many mines for precious metals were operated under methods which would be considered wasteful today and were abandoned when rich "bonanza" ore played out. Yet smaller shoots or leads filled with vugs and cavities may still be found by careful search and exploited with hard work and dynamite. Mineralogically this is possible because handsomely crystallized speci- mens frequently occur in lean sections of ore bodies and were often by-passed by old-time miners in favor of solid masses of rich ore. A number of dealers take regular trips to mining communities in Mexico and in the Southwestern United States to arrange for local collection in abandoned mines.

Large open pit mines such as the Bingham Canyon mine in Utah, or some of the enormous copper pits of southern Arizona, are less likely to produce specimens because mining operations are almost completely mechanized and few miners work directly upon rock, as is the case in underground mines. However, during lunch breaks or after hours, some material may be collected by miners who take this opportunity to walk around and stretch their legs. Good light tends to make up for the lack of direct contact with ore and somewhat compensates for the lack of collecting opportunities. Many rock quarries are also highly mechanized and operations become little more than blasting down entire walls of stone and scooping up the material in shovels to waiting trucks for transfer to crushers. Again opportunities for close inspection are lack- ing, however, some good specimen material is saved nevertheless and eventually reaches the market. In pegmatite quarries, opportunities are much better for specimen collection because hand-cobbing is necessary to separate waste rock and contaminating minerals from feldspar, mica, and beryl. In the process, an unusually close inspection is made of all products of the mine and interesting minerals saved out for disposition by the owners or by the miners.

Many miners and quarrymen eventually become collectors them- selves, and frequently become expert in the mineralogy of the deposit in which they work. Such persons are among the most valuable allies of the collector and dealer, for they are in the best position to salvage specimens which would otherwise pass through the crushers. Within mining communities they are known by reputation and it is to them that dealers go on buying trips and through them make arrangements for the systematic stockpiling of specimens for the next trip. However, in mining towns where collecting by miners is officially banned, it is not easy for strangers to find specimens because of the natural suspicion which always attaches to unknown persons, and it usually proves that one or two regular dealers have the local market under control. However, excellent specimens may still be had, providing the necessary "leads" or "contacts" can be developed. One of the best sources for this kind of information is some official of the mine who, though unable or unwilling to stop collecting by miners, probably has excellent ideas of who among them may be doing collecting. It pays to inquire in stores, shops, and cafes frequented by miners. Once a direct contact has been established and fair business dealings engaged in, it is possible to expand the circle of acquaintances and assure a future supply of material. Company geologists, local science teachers, local mineral club members, or earth science instructors in colleges and universities nearby may also provide information on how to obtain specimens or whom to see.

THE MINERAL SPECIMEN TRADE

Regular dealers in the United States and Canada catering on a full-time basis to the needs of the mineral collector can be numbered on the fingers of both hands. At least a dozen others are known who either work part time as mineral dealers or specialize in minerals, though they may sell rough gemstones and other items of a related nature. A small number who originally began with the intent of selling minerals only have found it necessary to take on additional lines such as lapidary equipment, jewelry tools and findings, books, and so on, in order to continue in business. At least one dealer is known to the author who began exclusively in minerals but gradually changed the character of his business until now he sells no mineral specimens whatsoever. In addition, there are hundreds of small shops and businesses run from private residences. This splintering of the trade is in marked contrast to the situation which prevailed up to about 1930. Until then a smaller number of full-time establishments existed, but each was of larger size, and these dealers provided practically all the mineral specimens worth talking about. Perhaps the present multiplicity of shops is due to the rapid rise of the gem-cutting and jewelry-making hobbies, which now far exceed in number of members those devoted to mineral collecting alone. Greater leisure time, plus an increasing number of retirees who establish small shops in suitable climes, especially in the Southwestern United States, have done much to account for this rise. Praiseworthy enterprise has expanded the base of business but has made it more speculative than before, so that where the serious collector could once turn to several reliable dealers for specimens, he now is faced with many dozens, from a few who are enterprising and well-informed to many who really sell minerals as just another item of merchandise. The net result is that any collector seriously interested in expanding his collection to include as much variety as possible finds it necessary to shop around a good deal more. He must be sure that choice specimens in the hands of a small dealer are not overlooked. At the same time, however, the increasing number of part-time dealers has greatly encouraged activity by miners and collectors, who now have many more outlets for their specimens. A larger number of smaller shops also causes much greater public awareness of minerals, and without doubt does much to popularize earth science hobbies.

Dealers obtain specimens in several ways, changing methods to suit local conditions. Some doing business in those mining communities whose mines are famous for their splendid specimens tend to specialize in local minerals; eventually they become retailers to drop-in trade and wholesalers of local material to dealers in other parts of the country or abroad. Intimately acquainted with miners, they are in the best position to make firm arrangements for the systematic gathering of specimens. Another class of dealers includes persons who operate "rock shops" along arterial highways or in tourist resorts where brisk retail businesses prevail during summer but taper to practically nothing in off-seasons. Such dealers frequently close up shop during slack times and thoroughly cover well-known mining centers to obtain stocks for forthcoming tourist seasons. Many also conduct mail-order businesses to tide them over slack periods. A few dealers operate exclusively as mail-order businesses, finding that the time required to attend to drop-in trade far exceeds the money realized from over-the-counter sales and places too many restrictions upon their freedom. Dealers in this category are in the best position to travel extensively and amass large stocks of fine specimens which they have personally selected. On the other hand, dealers established in large cities usually find travel difficult and expensive and therefore obtain specimen stocks from other dealers or specialize in buying up entire collections, of which a surprisingly large number are put up for sale each year. Some establish enviable reputations for knowledge in mineralogy and fairness in dealings, and thus are kept informed of collections coming up for sale through pleased customers in schools and museums, or other individuals who hear about such matters. The final class of dealer comprises those who deal in minerals specimens on a wholesale basis only. These individuals do a great deal of traveling to round up large quantities of material which are purchased cheaply and sold with modest mark-ups so that retailers can add to their own profits and still make prices attractive. Since it isn't easy to obtain large lots of specimens exactly alike, wholesalers tend to limit their stocks to "standard" items, generally a mixed bag of massive material which can be broken up for small pieces to be used in student mineral sets or gemstone material suitable for cabochon work or for tumbling. Occasionally they stumble upon a large stock of specimens from an individual mine which are of good enough quality to warrant individual pricing and listing. Exclusively wholesale dealers generally do not advertise in the earth science magazines but prefer to send offers and price lists to retailers directly.

THE GEMSTONE TRADE

Up until the time the amateur hobbies of gem-cutting and jewelry-making became so popular, virtually all rough gemstones were traded within long-established commercial channels. The most important section of the trade dealt with diamonds, emeralds, rubies, and sapphires, the classical "precious stones," while another section dealt with stones of lesser importance, commonly called "semi-precious stones." Even today there are clear-cut lines of specialization in the trade, some merchants handling nothing but rough diamonds, others handling nothing but emeralds and so on, while still others make themselves expert in the gemstones produced by certain regions such as Brazil, Burma, or Ceylon. Since until recently the art of gem-cutting was known to extremely few amateurs, and no equipment except that of the traditional lapidary was available, the sudden development of amateur interest followed by a vigorous demand for rough material caught the trade by surprise and for a number of years no attempt was made to satisfy this new market. As a result, the vacuum was filled by amateur collectors turned dealer who collected locally-available materials such as agate, petrified wood, rhodonite, nephrite jade, and many other gemstones, and by vigorous advertising campaigns in the earth science hobby magazines, entrenched themselves in the gemstone business, where they remain today. However, very few of these dealers were able to command enough capital or become so familiar with foreign buying that they could take over any large part of the traditional commercial trade and as a consequence, long-established dealers still supply the major portion of gemstones imported from Brazil, Ceylon, India, Burma, and other overseas countries. There are signs that this situation is gradually changing, and some ex-amateurs are now entering this section of the trade and may, in time, become firmly established.

Thus the gemstone trade is clearly divided into two parts, one for supplying traditional gems for traditional jewelry, and the other supplying relatively inexpensive gem materials to amateurs. Although some overlap occurs, this division of markets still largely prevails and it is for this reason that mineral and gemstone collectors within North America have had difficulties in disposing of native gemstones to long-established firms, despite the very considerable merits of some local products, and have had to sell them to the host of smaller businesses catering to the amateur trade. Another factor which has caused native gemstones to be regarded with disfavor by long-established dealers is that it is seldom possible to mine them as cheaply as abroad where labor does not command so much in wages. This cuts down the profit margin and of course makes exploitation of native gemstones less attractive. Still another factor which dealers in traditional gemstones consider is the difficulty of introducing relatively unknown gem materials into the jewelry trade where customers are used to hearing such familiar names as topaz, emerald, sapphire, etc., and simply refuse to buy gemstones which bear strange titles. Because of these reasons, the best market for native gemstones remains the amateur cutter.

Dealers catering to the amateur trade obtain supplies of materials in much the same fashion that mineral specimen dealers obtain theirs, that is, from local collectors who make a part- or full-time business of searching for gemstones in alluvial or surface deposits, or who operate small mines. Again the tendency is for "rock shops" to specialize in selling local materials which the proprietors find themselves or buy from collectors who live nearby. Thus small highway shops along the valley of the Yellowstone River in Montana all stock Montana agate nodules found in the bed of the river, while shops in Wyoming carry nephrite jade found on the surface over a wide area in the southern part of the state. Dealers in large cities obtain materials by visiting known collectors in these areas or order stocks from local dealers within each gemstone-producing region. Foreign gemstones must be bought from dealers who have established overseas trade channels, and who generally furnish to retailers lists of rough gem material with wholesale prices low enough to afford a fair profit after retail mark-up.

OFFERING MATERIAL TO DEALERS

Practically all dealers advertise more or less regularly in the several earth science magazines such as *Earth Science, Rocks and Minerals, Lapidary Journal, Gems and Minerals,* and several others. An unusually complete compilation may be found in the special April issue of *Lapidary Journal* entitled *The Rockhound Buyer's Guide.* Almost every company and individual doing business in some aspect of the earth sciences is listed in this book-like annual. Many reputable dealers interested in maintaining high standards of business ethics have banded together to form an organization entitled The American Mineral and Gem Dealers Association, using as a symbol a small triangular device which each firm may use upon its advertisements and business papers. This association is glad to supply information to any person interested in doing business with member firms and will answer inquiries about disposing of mineral specimens and gemstones to dealers most likely to be interested.

Offers of material are first made by mail, explaining to prospective buyers exactly what it is that is being sold, what quantity is available, and what the prospects are for future supply. Dealers are apt to be more interested in a steady supply of material rather than a small quantity which is all that will ever be found. However, in the case of mineral specimens, mineral dealers usually entertain offers even for one specimen provided it is completely described and is something rather unusual. After initial correspondence, dealers ordinarily request samples but rightly insist that such samples be representative of the lot. The natural tendency to offer samples of the best quality must be curbed because it leads to false impressions of the quality of the lot as a whole and results in misunderstandings. If the collector or miner wishes to continue in business he cannot afford to antagonize dealers. In respect to prices, a following section deals with how prices are established, but it must always be remembered that dealers cannot afford to pay lot prices close to retail prices since they must make a profit too. Possibly the best sales are made when both the seller and dealer are fully aware of the going retail prices for the material in question and each is willing to settle on a figure satisfactory to both. Whenever possible, visits should be arranged, so that the dealer can be shown the quantity and quality of material being offered. It is for this reason that most collectors and miners attempt to find dealers doing business close to them so that the necessary travel is as short as possible, and the dealer is encouraged to come in the first place.

Sales to dealers may be made in one of two ways: outright sale of the lot, or on consignment. The latter method is often adopted by dealers who wish to take the whole lot but cannot scrape up enough money, or by those who are doubtful as to the popularity of the material and therefore do not wish to risk taking on a large quantity which may take years to dispose of. Because so much money may be tied up in stock if an entire lot is taken, dealers generally offer much less under this plan than they do when specimens or gem material are placed on consignment. Using the consignment scheme has certain drawbacks to the collector or miner: first, since the material does not belong to the dealer, he is not so strongly impelled to either care for it or to "push" it; second, if a dealer finds sales of the material slow, he may remove it from shelves and thus eliminate the possibility of further sales; third, in the rare event of a dishonest dealer, he may sell the material at a good price but claim that it had to be sold at a much lower price, thus reducing the amount of money due the owner. To eliminate the possibility of misunderstandings, it is necessary to inventory the material before the dealer takes it away, making up duplicate lists showing number of specimens or quantity of material, and agreed reimbursement to the owner. In this way the owner will have a record of what was furnished the dealer and can check on what has been sold at any time and what sums are due him. The consignment scheme, despite the disadvantages enumerated above, is a very popular one because the owner generally gets more money for his material, though he may have to wait longer for all of it to come in. At the same time, the dealer likes the arrangement because he does not tie up capital in stock and yet can make money by offering specimens at prices which assure him a fair profit for his trouble.

OFFERING GEM MATERIAL

Although the quality of mineral specimens is usually obvious at a glance, it is a different story when gem material is involved, especially if expensive transparent stock suitable for facet gems is being offered. Some miners and collectors offer gem material as "mine run," that is, an entire lot of all grades is offered for sale just as it comes from the deposit but free of waste rock or waste minerals. Prices asked must be much lower than for "selected" material, of course, but must still be high enough to reimburse the miner or collector for his work and expenses and afford a profit besides. Offering mine run material is popular because the miner need not take the time and trouble to sort out the lot while the dealer, if he is shrewd, examines the lot and visualizes how much of the stock is top grade material, how much medium grade, and how much might be disposed of as small specimen or tumbling material, possibly with a fine profit involved. It is rather a gamble but a popular one.

On the other hand, some mine owners or collectors prefer to sort through their mine run material, believing that more money can be realized by knowing exactly what grades of material are present and in what quantity. The decision to do so generally depends on the kind of material involved, for example, turquois which is apt to be uniform in quality from a particular deposit is often sold mine run but the contents of gem pockets in pegmatites containing gem tourmalines and a variety of other minerals, receives a careful cleaning and examination to separate beryls, quartzes and rare minerals which may be of no value for lapidary work but may be sold as mineral specimens. Also sold as mine run are such minerals as variscite nodules and Montana or Mexican agate nodules which cannot be graded for quality without slicing open each one with a diamond saw, a job which the miner or collector is usually unable or unwilling to perform.

Extremely valuable gem material such as fine emeralds, sapphires, opals, and good blue aquamarines may be sold to small dealers but it is probably best to offer them to long-established firms catering primarily to commercial gem-cutters since they are most likely to dispose of them and hence most likely to pay good prices.

SELLING DIRECTLY TO THE PUBLIC

If time and facilities permit, many small miners and collectors dispose of surplus material by advertising retail sales in the earth science magazines mentioned above. Advertisements range from small inexpensive classified ads costing no more than several dollars per insertion, to larger advertisements which take up part or all of a single page and may cost as much as $300 for a full page. Full-page ads placed in favored positions, i.e., inside front cover or back cover, usually cost more. To be successful, advertisements must briefly but clearly state what is being offered, quality and color, size, and of course cost. Advertisements *must not* mislead buyers in any way, especially by wording which implies quality much higher than actually available, or wording which leads buyers to believe they are getting a more valuable mineral when in reality they are not. For example, the term "California jade" was coined many years ago to describe a massive form of idocrase (vesuvianite) which superficially resembles some types of jade. Since jade is found in California, this term if used without qualification is definitely misleading to persons who are not well acquainted with California gemstones. Another practice which should be eliminated or held within bounds is affixing personal names to rather ordinary chalcedonies and agates which differ somewhat from usual material but really not enough to warrant new titles. For example, *myrickite*, after an old California prospector by the name of Myrick, was attached to a kind of jasper and is still used to label specimens of this material, however, it is a confusing term because in the science of mineralogy, new species of minerals are frequently named after some person and the suffix "ite" added. Yet "myrickite" is not a new species nor even a remarkable variety of quartz, and undoubtedly was coined solely for the sales appeal of a special name. It is far better to stick to naming unusual forms of gemstones after places or localities, or after an area in feature special to them alone, e.g., *Laguna agate*, after an area in Mexico from which fine agates are obtained; *flowering obsidian*, after the flower-like patterns found within it, etc.

Preparing attractive advertisements is an art but if one is unskilled in it, the aid of the magazine editor may be enlisted. He will be pleased to assist in wording ads in such a fashion that they will be absolutely truthful yet intriguing to the reader. Before any ads are worded, it is a good idea to go through the pages of the magazines and select advertisements which appear unusual or attract attention in some way. Good ideas for wording may be obtained in this fashion. Style in advertising is very important because each write-up must be pitched to the group expected to buy the material offered. Again the best way to obtain ideas on this score is to read magazine advertisements carefully, noting how wording changes according to whether the material being offered is inexpensive or dear. Many dealers adopt a "homey" style in all of their advertisements and even in their catalogs, working on the assumption that the largest customer group wants inexpensive material of good average quality. At the other extreme, dealers who sell high-priced merchandise may deliberately word their ads to suit the tastes of persons most likely to be in higher-income brackets and thus the group most likely to become customers. Insofar as "pulling power" of ads is concerned, most editors strongly advise making three insertions in three consecutive issues, claiming that one ad alone will attract customers who have already heard of the material being described and are just waiting for it to be advertised but will not claim the attention of those who need reminding or who need to think about the material before deciding to buy.

RETAIL BUSINESS PRACTICES

Although it is manifestly impossible to describe in full detail all aspects of conducting a retail business, whether it is operated from a home or from a shop, some comments are in order upon the more important practices which should be followed and some of the pitfalls to be avoided. The most important single requirement for conducting a business is to keep adequate records of all expenditures and all income, for it is only by comparing income with outgo that a businessman can determine whether his enterprise is succeeding or failing. It is astonishing how many persons neglect to keep even the simplest of records and it is perhaps this fact which helps cause so many small shops or mail-order gemstone and mineral specimen businesses to fail. Records alone are not enough however; persons intending to gain an income from retailing must cultivate what is commonly known as a "business sense," which implies (a) knowing their merchandise thoroughly, (b) knowing "going" prices of merchandise, (c) anticipating the needs of the market, (d) making good "buys," (e) stocking items for which steady demand exists, (f) getting rid of items which do not sell, and (g) cultivating "goodwill" by courteous fair dealings. In effect, any successful business implies that its operators know *what* they are doing and *how* they are doing.

In respect to bookkeeping, all transactions should be recorded. For example, in a mail-order business, such as the collector is most likely to engage in to dispose of small quantities of material, it is necessary to record orders in duplicate upon bills of sale. The white original slip, marked "paid" or "on approval" as the case may be, is sent to the customer, and the yellow slip, which is a carbon copy, is kept on file. Blank forms may be purchased in pads at stationery stores and overprinted with a rubber stamp of the name and address of the person doing business or may be ordered from professional print shops with printed headings. It is very important that all details be entered on the slips, including the date. When the order is filled, duplicate slips are set aside with the notation on them of when the order was filled and when the parcel was mailed. These slips are collected at the end of each week and the data from them entered in the master ledger. The slips are then filed for at least two years in case customers complain or tax authorities require re-computation of business expenses and income. Approval orders should be set aside until payment or return of merchandise closes the transaction. If payment is made, it should be entered on the duplicate slip and entered in the ledger on the date of payment.

Ledger books with vertical rulings can be purchased at stationery stores and used to keep account of expenditures and receipts. Expenditures for any month may be kept on the left-hand pages of the book while receipts can be recorded on the opposite or right-hand pages. Since the mind is notoriously unreliable in keeping track of all petty sums expended, it is a good idea to enter each expenditure as soon as it is made. At the end of the month, expenditures and receipts can be added up and compared to give an indication of the progress of the business; however, due to seasonal fluctuations in business, it may be necessary to wait until at least six months to prove a trend.

Before businesses are established, it is necessary to determine what municipal, county or state laws apply. Some municipalities do not permit regular businesses to be carried on from houses within areas zoned as "residential" while others do, and since laws differ it is necessary to ascertain local restrictions and comply with them. The same remarks apply in respect to licenses, which may be required not only by the municipality but also by county or state governments. Information on such matters can be obtained from city and county clerks, while state requirements can be obtained by asking county clerks for addresses of state offices concerned. At the same time that license matters are looked into, requirements for taxes should also be ascertained, since these may be imposed by every level of government from the municipality to the state to the federal government.

Whenever certain gemstones are sold, the United States government requires payment of 10% Federal Excise Tax imposed on the final consumer by the business firm making the sale. The following gemstones are taxable:

Amber	Lapis Lazuli
Beryl:	Nephrite
aquamarine	Opal
emerald	Pearl: natural and cultured
golden beryl	Peridot
heliodor (golden beryl)	Quartz:
morganite	amethyst
Chrysoberyl:	bloodstone
alexandrite	citrine
cat's eye	moss agate
chrysolite	onyx
Coral	sardonyx
Corundum:	tigereye
ruby and sapphire	Spinel
Diamond	Topaz
Feldspar: moonstone	Tourmaline
Garnet	Turquois
Jadeite	Zircon
Jet	

Federal Excise Tax is to be collected whenever sales of the gemstones listed above are made unless proof of exemption from tax is furnished. A retailer buying from a wholesaler or from another retailer can avoid payment of tax if he furnishes a certificate stating the name of his business, its address, and that the merchandise is to be resold, and that 10% tax will be collected and remitted to the Director of Internal Revenue for his tax district. Certificates must be kept on file by the party making such tax-exempt sales in order to furnish proof that a part of his sales income was not subject to tax. Copies of *Regulation 51—Retailer's Excise Taxes* can be obtained from local directors of internal revenue or from the Commissioner of Internal Revenue, Washington, D. C.

The rather intangible attitude of the buying public known as "goodwill" is best gained right from the beginning and then carefully kept up in all subsequent dealings. It is based primarily on fairness in dealings, promptness and courtesy in replies to letters, speedy dispatch of parcels and careful attention to insure that the customer knows the conditions of sale. It is a good idea to state conditions of sale upon sales slips, and to refer to the most important sales conditions in advertisements. Several conditions must be insisted upon, as for example not allowing the polishing of "windows" upon gem rough in order to determine internal quality, or not allowing return of material kept much after expiration of a specified approval period, generally five to ten days. However, most dealers allow steady and reliable customers to return specimens at their convenience, considering that the loss of specimen availability is preferable to the loss of a good customer. Gaining goodwill also implies knowing one's material, that is, being quite certain as to the identity of minerals and gemstones and certain of their relative quality.

Sending material on approval is a common practice but naturally some element of risk is involved in those rare cases when dishonest customers are encountered. Most businessmen do not send approval shipments to persons unknown to them and either ask for deposits, payment of the entire cost, or furnishing of credit references. Valuable parcels should be insured or registered, or if sent on time-limit approval, checked for arrival by the post office "return receipt" system.

Many dealers prepare and regularly issue catalogs which may be a few pages of mimeograph stapled together, or larger and more professional booklets. Costs are surprisingly high for almost any type of catalog and should be carefully looked into before going ahead with preparation. Very good catalogs can be made up inexpensively by the mimeograph method, with the dealer cutting stencils himself and then sending them to some firm in a large city which specializes in running off as many copies as are wanted. Because of costs of preparation and postage, most dealers charge a small sum for their catalogs refundable with a purchase over a certain amount, usually $5.00. One-of-a-kind items such as mineral specimens should be listed in inexpensive catalogs to save costs, but better catalog construction should be used when customers can be expected to re-order from them many times in the future.

PLACING VALUES UPON SPECIMENS

It is always a good idea to place fair market values on specimens for the following reasons: (a) it is necessary if specimens are to be sold by the collector through advertisements or through some retail outlet, or in quantity to a dealer, (b) it helps to make the private collector a better judge of values when buying specimens he cannot collect any other way, and, (c) it places values upon collections which will guide a widow, friend, or relative in disposing of collections in the event of death. The reasons first given are obvious but the last is seldom thought of by collectors who should know better. Perhaps everyone dislikes thinking of death but it is something all of us must face at one time or another. Many splendid and valuable collections or even smaller ones accumulated by persons who had advantageous access to certain mines or mineral deposits have been given away by ignorant relatives who cared nothing for minerals, or who threw them out upon the dump heap as being just so many "rocks." If a collection is valuable, provision for its disposal after death should be made, the best way being to label, catalog, and evaluate specimens carefully as soon as they are acquired. If so much cash is paid for a specimen, this amount should be entered in the catalog, because specimens seldom decrease much in value with the years, and many increase greatly.

In arriving at the fair market value of any specimen it must be remembered that many minerals have basic values regardless of other merits. For example, gold, silver, and platinum are worth so much per ounce as metals, depending upon purity, and it would certainly be foolish to sell precious metal specimens for less than their bullion values. This rule is also applied to gemstones such as sapphire, ruby, beryl, topaz, and many others. Each specimen collected should be viewed accordingly and if it contains some commercially valuable mineral, a weighing or an estimate should be made to determine how much. This provides the basic value to which other values may be added, for factors such as beauty, crystallization, size and so on.

The most attractive and most scientifically valuable mineral specimens are those which display crystals, and accordingly the highest prices are paid for them. The supreme specimen from the viewpoint of the collector and connoisseur is a matrix, tastefully studded with perfectly formed, undamaged crystals, large enough to be impressive. The micromounter demands similar perfection on a minute scale, while the collector of thumbnail or miniature specimens asks for the same in proportion. An ideal matrix specimen is also well-formed; it cannot be odd in profile, unless this oddity adds to its value, and it must have its crystals arranged in such a manner that everyone observing it is struck with its beauty.

In all crystals, whether on matrix or single, lack of damage along edges and tips greatly increases value, especially if the mineral is notorious for being extremely fragile or brittle. Thus a mashed-down ball of natrolite needles commands practically nothing as compared to a similar mass upon which all needles of the mineral are erect. Very common minerals such as calcite and quartz displaying damaged crystal edges are virtually worthless, however the quartz species is sometimes comprised of gem material such as amethyst, smoky quartz or citrine and may be valuable on that account. Other factors which increase crystal value are smoothness of faces, with the best examples being extremely flat and glassy in polish; transparency, if the species occurs in transparent form; vivid coloration; presence of rare faces; and of course, size. Detached crystals are generally worth much less than matrix specimens, especially if broken off, however, doubly-terminated crystals are worth far more depending upon perfection and the other factors mentioned above. Twinned crystals, small but perfect groups of crystals, crystals growing in odd forms or clusters, and other unusual features in specimens increase value also.

Perfection of crystallization often adds astonishingly to the value of an already valuable mineral or metal. For example, a splendid octahedral crystal of gold which may be worth only $15.00 in bullion could easily command a hundred or more dollars as a specimen. Even common smoky quartz crystals may leap greatly in value over the basic worth as raw gem material because of perfection and transparency, a fact well shown by the prices demanded and received for Swiss smoky quartz crystals. In similar fashion, exceptionally large crystals of a species well-known for ordinarily producing very small individuals may command very substantial prices.

The number and size of crystals upon matrix also strongly influences price. For example, a dolomite matrix upon which many small cubes of galena are sprinkled is worth far less than a specimen of similar size covered by only two or three much larger galena crystals, perfection of crystals being equal in each case. Grouping of crystal individuals is important too in respect to whether crystals are huddled together, scattered about, or present only on one end. The most important considerations here are personal preferences and tastes.

Rarity of any species almost automatically increases the value of its specimens, in many cases even examples showing no crystals at all being worth considerable money as scientific reference material or as source material for rare elements. In this class are pollucite which is in demand for cesium, tantalite-columbite in demand for tantalum and niobium, and a number of others. Increased value due to rarity also manifests itself in the pricing of a limited number of specimens obtained from a mineral deposit of very small size. Some of the splendid orange crocoite crystals and crystal aggregates from Dundas, Tasmania, provide an example of such high prices; this species, not common anywhere, was found only in the upper levels in a certain mine at Dundas. When the orebody penetrated by these levels was exhausted, no more crocoite was forthcoming and the result was that later demand for specimens gradually forced prices upward. On the other hand, in the case of species typical of large rock formations such as pillow basalt, high prices probably will never be realized for any except the very few truly outstanding specimens, because as one producing quarry shuts down, another is opened elsewhere, tending to feed a steady supply of new material into the specimen market.

Value is also affected by minerals associated upon the same specimen such that color contrasts, patterns or placement of crystals increases the attractiveness. In some instances, associations are valued because they tell something of the mode of formation. Plain quartz crystal groups from pegmatite pockets are not generally known for their beauty but if sprinkled over or penetrated by tourmalines, beryl crystals, or topaz crystals, their value immediately rises to a much higher plane, and certainly if such crystals are gem quality, the price will be higher still. Associates which also affect price are species which penetrate or are included in crystals of other minerals, with quartz most often being the host mineral. Thus rutile needles or bright pyrite crystals in quartz, gold, silver, and many others, may all appear included within clear crystals and bring for them a much higher price than otherwise possible for plain crystals.

In summary, many factors come into play in the valuation of specimens and the shrewd collector takes as many of them into consideration as possible before settling upon prices. Advice on the prices of commercial minerals and metals is obtainable from state or provincial mining bureaus; these bureaus do not buy or sell or establish prices, but they can tell where such information is obtainable. Gemstone prices may be found in a special table in the author's *Standard Catalog of Gems*, or in numerous advertisements in various popular earth science magazines. Many companies advertising in these magazines distribute price lists and catalogs, and these should be sent for to obtain a sense of prevailing values. Mineral specimen dealers also advertise and issue catalogs but it is more difficult to compare qualities and values of our own material against that offered through advertisements. Ideas of value are best obtained through practical experience acquired by visiting private collectors and commercial dealer displays, or by visiting museum collections to appreciate what "top" quality means in relation to mineral specimens. If selling to dealers is contemplated, it must be kept in mind that there must be a great difference between wholesale and retail prices, because, as was mentioned previously, the dealer not only needs to pay his fixed expenses but is entitled to a fair profit besides. In general, specimens of good quality should be offered at from 40% to 60% of current retail prices, while those which are so plentiful that they promise to become a drug on the market should be offered at not more than 30% of retail value. Unusually fine examples may be bargained for separately, possibly from 75% to 80% of retail value. Very large or valuable specimens frequently have to be offered on consignment, that is, with the understanding that the owner will not receive payment until the dealer disposes of the specimen. It is extremely important that a wholesale price be agreed upon in writing, and if possible, a retail price. Vague verbal agreements cause no end of trouble, especially if considerable time has elapsed from the date of agreement to the date of settlement.

PACKING SPECIMENS FOR SHIPMENT

Packing mineral specimens for sending through the mails or via express is an art which is seldom mastered without a few bitter experiences to force one to do better. It is incredible how roughly parcels are handled during all stages of shipment, some arriving at their destinations looking as if they had been shot out of a cannon at least. Although we all have had parcels arrive in states of near-disintegration, and perhaps have addressed scathing remarks to postal and shipping authorities, complaints do not repair shattered specimens but the lessons learned help us wrap parcels so that they better survive future trips.

Perhaps the most commonly overlooked feature of minerals which calls for extraordinary efforts in packaging them properly is their great weight for small volume. Every time a package containing minerals is dropped or slammed against a hard surface, the minerals within tend to obey Newton's laws of inertia and to keep right on going even though the material containing them comes to an abrupt stop. This means that whatever packing material is used must be resilient in order to stand repeated crushings under the wight of the minerals and still retain its springiness.

Rough minerals such as bulk shipments of rock samples, agate, jasper and chalcedony masses or nodules, require practically no internal protection but must be packed tightly in very stout cardboard containers or wooden boxes. Boxes are best, and the rock masses should be surrounded by loose sawdust, excelsior, or shredded paper. In any event, if looseness develops, disaster is sure to follow, for few containers can stand the impact of heavy rock masses suddenly shifting position as containers are thrown about or rolled over. Many dealers who sell wholesale lots of rocklike material use double burlap potato sacks, cinched tightly at the throats with heavy cord or wire, and labeled with strong baggage tags. Single sacks are very apt to develop holes because of fiber crushing as sacks are dropped or dragged across hard surfaces.

Delicate minerals require the greatest care in shipment and, as a general rule, should be sent in individual containers despite the increased cost. Boxes for them may be corrugated cardboard but the solid cardboard used for shipping canned goods is far stronger and less likely to be crushed in transit. If much mailing or shipping is done it pays to buy boxes in bulk lots. When packing specimens, attempt to place them in the exact center, avoiding direct contact with any of the sides of the container. Line the bottom of the box with a single large pad of tightly crumpled newspaper, of a thickness that permits a pad of equal depth to be placed on top of the specimen. The wrapped specimen is now seated upon the pad and the spaces between sides and specimen are poked full of tightly crumpled newspapers. As a last step, place the cover pad over the specimen and *force* the lid or cover flaps over to the shut position. There must be so much paper in the container that sides, bottom and top bulge appreciably and require strong pressure to close. The box is now taped shut with thread-reinforced pressure-sensitive tape or corded with stout manila wrapping twine, mason's cord, or other string or line of considerable strength and abrasion resistance. Each crossover of cord is secured with loopings of cord knotted in place to prevent shifting. The test of a good wrapping and packaging job is whether or not *you* would be willing to throw the package down a flight of brick or concrete steps. If doubt is felt that the package could survive this treatment, it may be best to start all over again and do it up correctly.

Other padding and shock-absorbing materials which are superior to newspapers are excelsior, or shaved wood, which interlocks well but is messy to use and messy to unpack, and "balsam wool" blanket, commonly used as house insulation. The latter is exceptionally fine for packing minerals specimens on account of its wonderful resiliency and elasticity. This material is made from wood in continuous bats or strips which are sold by lumber yards in rolls; each bat consists of numerous crumpled, spongy brown, paper-like sheets loosely pressed together to a depth of about two inches. Sections may be easily torn off when desired or bats split to obtain thinner and more manageable wrappings. Packaging and box supply houses in large cities also stock similar battings of paper-like material in light colors which are perhaps more attractive than the house insulation just described but are more expensive and probably not much better for wrapping. However, they do give packages a professional look, which exerts some favorable influence upon their recipients. Another excellent packaging material, much used by the technical instrument industry, is rubber-impregnated Spanish moss and horsehair. Blocks of this material are cut to fit containers until they are filled to the tops, then spaces near the center sections are cut out to correspond exactly to the object being shipped. When finished, each package has the object located in the center, suspended in a mass of highly resilient material and nowhere touching the container walls. Plastic foam, polyurethane foam, sponge rubber, and other resilient materials may be used for shipping high-cost specimens but will prove to be too expensive for ordinary minerals.

Numerous small specimens of miniature or thumbnail sizes may be shipped in almost foolproof fashion in soft papier-mache egg cartons. These may be obtained in dozen-egg boxes which have identical top and bottom halves and are designed to fit snugly over eggs, shielding them from shock and preventing them from contacting each other. Large shipments may be made by inserting specimens in the square liners designed for use in wooden egg crates. Each specimen can be lightly wrapped in cosmetic tissue, so that it just fills the space meant to be occupied by an egg, or left unwrapped if it already fits rather snugly. Dozen-egg cartons must be further protected by placing them inside cardboard boxes lined with crumpled newspaper or insulation batting. Shifting of specimens within the cartons can be further prevented by stapling sides together or tacking with quick-drying cement.

Wrapping individual specimens is almost as much of an art as packaging, especially when long slender crystals perched on matrix are involved. Perhaps the simplest and safest scheme is to employ toilet tissue to wrap around crystals which protrude from the matrix, forcing some into crevices and spaces between other crystals. When properly done, the entire specimen will resemble a sphere or football. To prevent the paper from unwinding, strips of gummed tape or Scotch tape are used, or the parcel is held together with string or rubber bands. Further wrappings of tissue paper or newspaper are then applied to add bulk.

Another scheme uses wet tissue paper or any kind of clean soft paper (but not newspaper), which is poked into all openings and around all projections until the entire specimen is encased. This is then permitted to dry, at which time the specimen will be imbedded in a form-fitting papier-mache case highly resistant to shock.

A number of extremely delicate minerals are almost impossible to ship by any ordinary method and may indeed be so fragile that the only way they can arrive safely at their destination is by hand-carrying in an upright position. Some dealers have exercised a great deal of ingenuity in shipping fragile specimens; among the schemes which may be mentioned are fastening a matrix specimen with thick, water-soluble cabinet maker's glue to a piece of plywood which is then suspended in a much larger box by rubber shock cords, or covering a matrix with thin plastic film such as that used these days for protecting clothing sent from dry-cleaners and then imbedding it in papier-mache mix or in sawdust. Specimens with many small cavities or crevices should never be sent unprotected in sawdust, for the sawdust will prove to be almost impossible to remove completely. Another useful technique in packaging extremely fragile specimens is to dip them in paraffin or encase them in solid blocks of paraffin. Although this affords very good protection and adds little weight to each specimen, the drawbacks must be considered carefully before settling upon this method of packaging. Since paraffin requires heat for melting, some materials may not be able to stand the temperature, and if many small pores or crevices are present, it may be very difficult to remove all paraffin when specimens are dipped in hot water or solvent to clean them.

APPENDIX I

TABLE OF MINERAL SOLUBILITIES

About 250 of the most sought-after minerals are listed in the following table along with a number of common agents which dissolve them or affect them chemically. Species are listed in the left-hand column while columns to the right show the effect that agents may be expected to have upon them. Various agents, including ordinary water, are shown at the column headings. As many references as possible were examined for this information but a large number of blank spaces remain for which no reliable data could be found.

In using the table it is wise to remember that the ease with which any mineral dissolves or is attacked depends upon how finely divided or how porous it is. For example, compact goethite is only very slowly attacked by acids but is very quickly dissolved when it occurs as a powdery coating upon other minerals. Even the easily destructible calcite shows tremendous variations in solubility depending upon its solidity, uncracked crystals dissolving much more slowly than porous types such as calcareous sinter or calcite onyx. Comments on the effect of agents as well as the effects of other chemicals appear in the extreme right-hand column.

LEGEND

HCl—hydrochloric (muriatic) acid; HNO_3—nitric acid; H_2SO_4—sulfuric acid (oil of vitriol); HF—hydrofluoric acid; A.R.—aqua regia (a mixture of hydrochloric and nitric acids).

xxx—easily dissolved and damaged; xx—moderately dissolved and damaged; x—difficultly dissolved and slightly damaged; o—not affected.

Mineral	Water	HCl	HNO_3	H_2SO_4	HF	A.R.	Remarks
Acmite	o	x			x		Very slightly attacked by HCl
Actinolite	o				x		
Adamite	o	xxx	xxx	xxx	xxx	xxx	Easily soluble in dilute acids
Aegerite	o				x		
Albite	o				xxx		Rapidly dissolved in conc. HF

Mineral	Water	HCl	HNO₃	H₂SO₄	HF	A.R.	Remarks
Allanite	o	x			x	x	Partly decomposed in HCl.
Almandite	o				x		Very slowly attacked
Amblygonite	o	x	x	x	xx	x	Very slightly attacked by all except HF
Amphibole	o	o	o	o	x		
Analcime	o	xx			xxx	xx	
Andalusite	o	o	o	o	x	o	
Andesine	o	o	o	o	xxx	o	
Andradite	o	x			xx	x	
Anglesite	o		x				Slightly soluble in conc. acid; also soluble in ammonium citrate or acetate solution
Anhydrite	o	xx	xx	xx		xx	Soluble in hot acids; soluble in glycerine
Ankerite	o	xx	xx	xx	xxx	xx	Rapidly dissolved in warm acids only
Anorthite	o	x			xxx	x	
Antimony	o	o	x	x	o	x	Dissolves in hot conc. sulfuric acid; alters in conc. nitric acid
Apatite	o	xx	xx	x	xx	xx	
Apophyllite	o	xx			xxx	xx	
Aragonite	o	xxx	xxx	xxx	xxx	xxx	Easily soluble in dilute acids
Argentite	o	x	x	x	xxx	x	
Arsenic	o	o	x	x	o	x	
Arsenopyrite	o	o	xx	o			Decomposed
Augite	o				x		
Aurichalcite	o	xx	xx	xx	xxx	xx	Also soluble in ammonia solution
Autunite	o	xx	xx	xx		xx	
Axinite	o				xx		
Azurite	o	xx	xx	xx	xxx	xx	Partly decomposed in hot water; soluble in ammonia solution
Barite	o	o	o	x			Slightly soluble
Benitoite	o	x			xx		Slightly soluble
Beryl	o	o	o	o	x	o	Slightly attacked

Mineral	Water	HCl	HNO₃	H₂SO₄	HF	A.R.	Remarks
Biotite	o			x			Partly decomposed
Bismuth	o	x	xxx	xxx	x	xx	Soluble in hot acids
Bismuthinite	o	o	xxx	o			Insoluble in dilute acids
Bornite	o		xx				
Bournonite	o		x				Decomposed
Braunite	o	xx				xx	
Breithauptite	o		xx			xx	
Brochantite	o	xx	xx	xx		xx	
Brookite	o	o	o	x			
Brucite	o	xxx	xxx	xxx		xxx	
Bytownite	o	o	o	o	xxx		Rapidly attacked
Calaverite	o			x		xx	Decomposed in hot sulfuric acid
Calcite	o	xxx	xxx	xxx	xxx	xxx	Very rapidly attacked in dilute acids
Caledonite	o		xx				
Calomel	o	x	x	o		xx	Slightly soluble in hot acids; insoluble in alcohol
Cancrinite	o	xx			xx	xx	Bubbles in warm dilute acid
Carnallite	xxx	xxx	xxx	xxx		xxx	
Carnotite	o	xxx	xxx	xxx		xxx	
Cassiterite	o	x	x	o		x	Very slightly attacked
Celestite	o	x	x	x		x	Slowly soluble in hot conc. acids
Cerargyrite	o	o	o	o		x	Soluble in cyanide solutions
Cerussite	o	x	xx	x	xxx	x	Decomposed by hot water; soluble in warm dilute acids
Cervantite	o	xx	o	o		xx	
Chabazite	o	xx				xx	
Chalcanthite	xxx	xxx	xxx	xxx		xxx	Insoluble in ethyl alcohol
Chalcedony	o	o	o	o	xxx	o	Rapidly attacked
Chalcocite	o		xx				
Chalcopyrite	o		xx				
Chondrodite	o	x				x	
Chlorite	o			x			Slowly decomposed

Mineral	Water	HCl	HNO$_3$	H$_2$SO$_4$	HF	A.R.	Remarks
Chromite	o	o	o	o		c	
Chrysoberyl	o	o	o	o	o	o	
Chrysocolla	o	x	x	x	xxx	x	Decomposed in acids; dissolved in HF
Cinnabar	o	o	o	o		xx	
Clinochlore	o			x			Decomposed
Cobaltite	o		xx				Decomposed
Colemanite	x	xx				xx	Soluble in hot acids; very slightly soluble in water
Columbite	o	o	o	x	x	o	Partly decomposed by hot conc. acids
Copper	o	x	xxx	xx	o	xxx	
Corundum	o	o	o	o	o	o	
Covellite	o	x	xx	x		x	Soluble in hot conc. acids; soluble in cyanide solutions
Crocoite	o	x	x	x		x	Insoluble in acetic acid
Cryolite	x	o	o	x			Very slightly soluble in water; sulfuric acid releases HF
Cuprite	o	xx	x	x		xx	Soluble in concentrated acids; readily soluble in dilute HCl
Cyanotrichite	o	xx	xx	xx		xx	
Danburite	o	o	o	o	x	o	
Datolite	o	x			xx	x	
Descloizite	o	xxx	xxx	xxx		xxx	
Diamond	o	o	o	o	o	o	Crystals cleaned by dipping in HF
Diaspore	o	o	o	o	x	o	Very slightly attacked
Diopside	o				xx		
Dioptase	o	xx			xxx	xx	Very slowly attacked by dilute acetic acid
Dumortierite	o						
Dolomite	o	xxx			xxx	xxx	Rapidly dissolves in warm acids
Enargite	o		x			xx	
Enstatite	o	o	o	o	xx	o	
Epidote	o	x	o	o	xx	o	Partly decomposed in HCl

Mineral	Water	HCl	HNO$_3$	H$_2$SO$_4$	HF	A.R.	Remarks
Ferberite	o	x		x		xx	Slightly attacked by hot conc. acids
Fergusonite	o	x	o	x		xx	Decomposed
Fluorite	o	x		xx			Hot conc. sulfuric acid releases HF
Franklinite	o	xx					
Gahnite	o	o	o	x			Slightly attacked
Galena	o	x	x			x	Decomposed
Goethite	o	x			x	x	Soluble in conc. HCl; soluble in oxalic acid, citric acid, ammonium citrate
Gold	o	o	o	o	o	xx	Also soluble in potassium cyanide sol.
Gmelinite	o	xx				xx	
Graphite	o	o	o	o	o	o	
Greenockite	x	xx				xx	Destroyed by hot water; soluble in conc. HCl
Grossular	o	o	o	o	xx	o	
Gypsum	o	xx				xx	Soluble in hot dilute acid; soluble in glycerine
Halite	xxx						Soluble in glycerine; slightly soluble in alcohol
Halotrichite	xxx	xxx	xxx	xxx		xxx	
Hanksite	xxx	xxx	xxx	xxx		xxx	
Harmotome	o	xx			xxx	xx	Decomposed
Hedenbergite	o	o	o	o	xx	o	
Hematite	o	x				x	Soluble in hot conc. acid
Hemimorphite	o	x			xx	x	
Heulandite	o	xx			xx	xx	Decomposed
Hornblende	o	o	o	o	x	o	
Howlite	o	xxx	xxx	xxx	xxx	xxx	
Huebnerite	o	x		x		xx	Slightly attacked by hot conc. acids; decomposed by aqua regia
Hypersthene	o	o	o	o	xx	o	Very slightly attacked by HCl
Idocrase	o	x			x	x	Partly decomposed by HCl and A.R.

Mineral	Water	HCl	HNO$_3$	H$_2$SO$_4$	HF	A.R.	Remarks
Ilmenite	o	x					Slowly soluble in hot conc. acid
Ilvaite	o	x					
Inderite	o	xxx				xxx	Soluble in warm dilute acid
Inyoite	xx	xxx	xxx	xxx	xxx	xxx	
Iolite	o	x			xx		Slightly attacked by HCl
Iron	o	xxx	xxx	xx	x	xxx	Slowly soluble in acetic acid; insoluble in concentrated sulfuric acid
Jadeite	o				xx		
Jarosite	o	xx				xx	
Kernite	x	xxx	xxx	xxx		xxx	Slowly soluble in cold water; rapidly soluble in hot water
Kurnakovite	o	xx	xx	xx		xx	Soluble in warm acids
Kyanite	o	o	o	o	o	o	
Labradorite	o	o	o	o	xxx	o	
Laumontite	o	xx				x	Readily decomposes in HCl; loses water
Lazulite	o	x	x	x		x	Attacked by hot acids
Lazurite	o	xx				x	Decomposed in HCl
Lepidolite	o	x			xx		
Leucite	o	x			xx		
Linarite			xx				
Lithiophilite	o	xx	xx	xx		xx	
Loellingite	o	o	o	o		o	
Ludlamite	o	xx	xx	xx		xx	
Magnesite	o	xxx	xxx	xxx	xxx	xxx	Only slightly affected by cold acids but rapidly dissolved in hot acids; insoluble in acetic acid
Magnetite	o	x					Attacked by hot conc. acid
Malachite	o	xxx	xxx	xxx	xxx	xxx	Decomposed slowly in hot water
Manganite	o	x		xx			Attacked by hot conc. acid
Marcasite	o	o	x	o			Dissolves when powdered
Margarite	o	x				x	Partly decomposed

Mineral	Water	HCl	HNO$_3$	H$_2$SO$_4$	HF	A.R.	Remarks
Melanterite	xxx	xxx	xxx	xxx		xxx	Insoluble in alcohol
Metacinnabar	o	o	o	o		xx	
Metatorbernite	o	xx	xx	xx		xx	
Metazeunerite	o	xxx	xxx	xxx		xxx	
Meyerhofferite		xxx	xxx	xxx	xxx	xxx	
Microcline	o	o	o	o	xxx	o	
Millerite	o	o	xx	o		xx	Decomposed in hot water; slightly soluble in other acids
Mimetite	o	x	xx	x	xx	x	
Molybdenite	o		xx	xx		xx	Soluble in hot dilute acids; insoluble in conc. sulfuric acid and cold dilute acids
Monazite	o	x	x	x		x	Slightly attacked
Mottramite	o	xxx	xxx	xxx			
Muscovite	o			xx			
Nahcolite	xxx	xxx	xxx	xxx	xxx	xxx	Soluble in glycerine; slightly soluble in alcohol
Natrolite	o	xx				xx	
Natron	xxx	xxx	xxx	xxx	xxx	xxx	
Nepheline	o	xxx				xx	Decomposed
Neptunite	o	o	o	o	x	o	
Niccolite	o	o	o	o		xx	
Nickel-iron	o	x	xx	xx	x	xx	Slowly soluble in dilute acids; only slightly attacked by acetic acid
Niter	xxx	xxx	xxx	xxx	xxx	xxx	Insoluble in ether or alcohol
Oligoclase	o	o	o	o	xxx	o	
Olivenite	o	xx	xx	xx		xx	Soluble in ammonia
Olivine	o	xxx					Dissolves easily in hot conc. acid
Opal	o	o	o	o	xxx	o	Very rapidly attacked
Orpiment	x		x			xx	Slowly soluble in hot water; soluble in alcohol
Orthoclase	o	o	o	o	xxx	o	
Pectolite	o	x				xx	Decomposed by warm dilute HCl

Mineral	Water	HCl	HNO$_3$	H$_2$SO$_4$	HF	A.R.	Remarks
Penninite	o	x			xx		Partly decomposed by HCl
Pentlandite	o		x				
Perovskite	o	o	o	x	x		Decomposed by hot conc. sulfuric acid and by cold HF
Petzite	o		x				Decomposed
Phenakite	o	o	o	o	xx	o	
Phillipsite	o	xx			xxx	xx	
Phlogopite	o			x	xx		Partly decomposed by sulf. acid
Phosgenite	o		xx				
Platinum	o	o	o	o	o	x?	Slowly dissolved in hot aqua regia
Polybasite			x				Decomposed
Polyhalite	x	xx					Decomposed
Prehnite	o	x			xx		Slowly attacked by HCl
Priceite	o	xxx	xxx	xxx	xxx	xxx	
Proustite	o		x				Decomposed
Psilomelane		xx					
Purpurite	o	xxx					
Pyrargyrite	o		x				Decomposed
Pyrite	o	o	x	o			Insoluble except as powder in conc. acid
Pyrolusite	o	xx	o				Insoluble in nitric acid
Pyromorphite	o	x	xx	x	xx		
Pyrope	o	o	o	o	x	o	Slightly attacked
Pyrophyllite	o			x			Slowly decomposed
Pyrrhotite	o					x	Decomposed
Quartz	o	o	o	o	xx	o	
Realgar	o		x			xxx	
Rhodochrosite	o	xx	xx	xx	xx	xx	Dissolved in warm acids
Rhodonite	o	x			xx		Slightly attacked by HCl
Riebeckite	o	o	o	o	xx	o	
Rosasite	o	xx	xx	xx	xx	xx	
Rutile	o	o	o	x			Very slightly attacked
Samarskite	o	x	x	x			Very slowly dissolves when powdered
Sanidine	o	o	o	o	xxx	o	

Mineral	Water	HCl	HNO$_3$	H$_2$SO$_4$	HF	A.R.	Remarks
Scapolite	o	o	o	o	xx	o	
Scheelite	o	x	x				Decomposed in boiling acids
Scolecite	o	xx			xxx		
Scorodite	o	xx	xx	xx		xx	
Scorzalite	o	x	x	x			Slowly soluble in hot acids
Serpentine	o	x			xx		Decomposed
Siderite	o	xx	xx	xx	xxx	xx	Rapidly dissolves in hot acids
Sillimanite	o	o	o	o		o	
Silver	o	o	xx	x	x	xx	Soluble in cyanide solutions
Smaltite	o		xx				
Smithsonite	o	xxx	xxx	xxx	xxx	xxx	
Sodalite	o	xx		x			Decomposed in dilute HCl
Spessartine	o	o	o	o	x	o	Very slowly attacked
Sphalerite	o	xx	x				
Sphene	o				x	x	
Spinel	o	o	o	x			Slightly attacked when powdered
Spodumene	o	o	o	o	x	o	
Stibnite	o	xx	x				Decomposed in nitric acid; insoluble in acetic acid
Stilbite	o	xx			xxx		Decomposed in HCl
Staurolite	o						
Strontianite	o	xxx	xx	xx	xxx	xx	
Sulfur	o	o	o	o	o	x	Easily dissolved in carbon disulfide, toluene; slightly soluble in alcohol, benzene, ether
Sylvanite	o		x				Decomposed
Sylvite	xxx	xxx	xxx	xxx	xxx	xxx	Slightly soluble in alcohol; soluble in ether, glycerine
Talc	o	o	o	o	xx	o	
Tantalite	o	o	o	x			Partly decomposed by hot conc. sulfuric acid
Tennantite	o		x				Decomposed

Mineral	Water	HCl	HNO$_3$	H$_2$SO$_4$	HF	A.R.	Remarks
Tenorite	o	xxx	xxx			xxx	Dissolves in cyanide solutions
Tetrahedrite	o		x				Decomposed
Thenardite	xx	xx	xx	xx	xx	xx	Soluble in glycerine; insol. alcohol
Thomsonite	o	xx			xxx		
Topaz	o	o	o	x	x	o	Very slowly attacked by HF; decomposed by hot conc. sulfuric acid
Torbernite	o	xx	xx	xx		xx	
Tourmaline	o	o	o	o	x	o	Very slowly attacked
Tremolite	o	o	o	o	x	o	
Triphylite	o	xx	xx	xx			
Triplite	o	xx	xx	xx			
Trona	xxx	xxx	xxx	xxx	xxx	xxx	
Turquois	o	x			xx		
Tyuyamunite		xx	xx	xx			Insoluble in dilute acetic acid
Ulexite	x						Very slightly soluble in water
Uraninite	o	x	xx	xx	xx	xx	Very slowly attacked by HCl; solubility varies greatly
Vanadinite	o	xx	xxx				
Variscite	o	x					Incompletely soluble
Vivianite	o	xxx	xxx	xxx		xxx	Insoluble in acetic acid
Wardite	o	x	x	x			
Wavellite	o	xxx	xxx	xxx		xxx	
Willemite	o	xx		x	x		
Witherite	o	xxx	xx	xx	xxx	xxx	Insoluble in alcohol
Wollastonite	o	x					Decomposed
Wulfenite	o	x	x	x			Decomposed by HCl and nitric acid; sol. in conc. sulfuric acid; insoluble in alcohol
Wurtzite	o	xx	xx				Insoluble in acetic acid
Xenotime	o	o	o	x	o		Very slightly soluble
Zeunerite	o	xxx	xxx	xxx			
Zincite	o	xx	xx	xx		xx	
Zircon	o	o	o	o	o	o	
Zoisite	o						

APPENDIX II
Table of minerals requiring protection from atmospheric influences

LOSE WATER IN EXCESSIVELY DRY AIR

The following minerals are likely to be encountered by the average collector and require preservation in sealed containers to prevent crumbling due to loss of water. In addition, some chalcedonies and agates lose water, becoming paler in color and less translucent, while chrysoprase frequently changes to very pale shades as water is lost. Opals also lose water and may crack as a result but no practical way has been found to prevent this.

Autunite	Melanterite
Borax	Natron
Chalcanthite	Thenardite
Halotrichite	Torbernite
Kernite	Trona
Laumontite	Zeunerite

GAIN WATER IN MOIST AIR

The following minerals absorb so much water from the atmosphere that they may become moist, wet, or even dissolve in a puddle.

Carnallite	Melanterite
Halite	Sylvite
Hanksite	Ulexite (develops powdery
Kernite	coating)
Kurnakovite (develops powdery coating)	

TARNISH OR OXIDIZE

Surface tarnishes are seldom completely avoidable but intensification is prevented by keeping specimens in a dry atmosphere free of sulfur and acid fumes.

Argentite	Crocoite	Pyrrhotite
Arsenic	Cuprite	Realgar
Bismuth	Enargite	Silver
Bismuthinite	Iron	Smaltite
Bornite	Malachite	Sphalerite
Chalcocite	Marcasite	Stibnite
Chalcopyrite	Niccolite	Sylvanite
Cinnabar	Proustite	Vivianite
Cobaltite	Pyrargyrite	Zincite
Copper	Pyrite	

DAMAGED BY EXPOSURE TO LIGHT

Many specimens of the following minerals are affected by ordinary light and especially by direct sunlight:

Apatite (pink type loses color)
Argentite (alters)
Beryl (brown or orange types lose color, usually changing to pale pink)
Cerargyrite (alters and changes color)
Cinnabar (alters and changes color)
Fluorite (purple and green types change color)
Orpiment (decomposes)
Proustite (alters and becomes gray)
Pyrargyrite (alters and becomes gray)
Quartz (amethyst, smoky quartz, and rose quartz sometimes become paler in color)
Realgar (alters into orpiment)
Spodumene (kunzite becomes pale in color or loses all color)
Topaz (brown topaz loses color)
Tyuyamunite (alters)
Vivianite (quickly changes to dull dark blue-violet color)

DAMAGED BY FREEZING

Crystals containing water-filled cavities such as quartz, halite, gypsum, etc.

DAMAGED BY RAPID TEMPERATURE CHANGE IN CABINET OR STORAGE

Sulfur crystals.

APPENDIX III

Useful Addresses

The following offices and organizations of government supply geological information and materials. Additional directories and sources may be found in the bibliography in Appendix V.

CANADA

ALBERTA. Geological Survey of Canada, Institute of Petroleum and Sedimentary Geology, 3303 33rd Street, NW, Calgary.

BRITISH COLUMBIA. Geological Survey of Canada, Branch Office, 326 Howe Street, Vancouver 1.

British Columbia Department of Lands, Geographic Division, Parliament Buildings, Victoria (maps).

MANITOBA. Manitoba Department of Mines and Natural Resources, Winnipeg; includes a Lands Branch, Surveys Branch, and Mines Branch.

NEW BRUNSWICK. New Brunswick Department of Lands and Mines, Fredericton.

NEWFOUNDLAND. Newfoundland Department of Mines and Resources, St. John's; the Mines Branch includes: The Geological Survey of Newfoundland, Crown Lands and Surveys Division, and the Mining Division.

NORTHWEST TERRITORIES. Geological Survey of Canada, Branch Office, Yellowknife.

NOVA SCOTIA. Nova Scotia Department of Mines, Provincial Building, Halifax.

ONTARIO. Geological Survey of Canada, 601 Booth Street, Ottawa.

Geological Survey of Canada, Surveys and Mapping Branch, 615 Booth Street, Ottawa.

Geological Survey of Canada, Mines Branch, 555 Booth Street, Ottawa.

Department of Indian Affairs and Northern Development, Resource and Economic Development Group, 238 Sparks Street, Ottawa.

Ontario Department of Mines, Publications Office, Parliament Buildings, Queen's Park, Toronto 5.

PRINCE EDWARD ISLAND. Deputy Provincial Secretary, Provincial Government Offices, Charlottetown.

QUEBEC. Quebec Department of Mines, Quebec.

SASKATCHEWAN. Saskatchewan Department of Mineral Resources, Administration Building, Regina; includes the Saskatchewan Geological Survey in the Natural Resources Building, Regina.

YUKON TERRITORY. Geological Survey of Canada, Branch Office, Whitehorse.

UNITED STATES

U. S. Atomic Energy Commission, Washington, D. C. 20545 (publications on radioactive minerals, prospecting, sales of ores, etc., sold by Supt. of Documents, Government Printing Office, Washington, D. C. 20402).

362

U. S. Bureau of Land Management, U. S. Dept. of the Interior, Washington, D. C. 20240 (publications on land surveys, mining claims on public lands, etc., sold by GPO).

U. S. Bureau of Mines, U. S. Dept. of the Interior, Washington, D. C. 20240 (issues many publications sold by the GPO).

U. S. Forest Service, U. S. Dept. of Agriculture, Washington, D. C. 20250 (publishes maps of national forests; maps available in regional offices as given in state lists below).

U. S. Geological Survey, U. S. Dept. of the Interior, Washington, D. C. 20242 (issues general catalog of its publications, listed in Appendix V; maps may be purchased over the counter or by mail from the Map Distribution Office at Headquarters, or from numerous field activities and authorized agents; book publications are sold by the GPO and some field activities as listed under states).

U. S. Government Printing Office, Washington, D. C. 20402 (practically all publications concerning geology and related subjects issued by agencies of the U. S. Government are sold by this office; lists on a large variety of subjects are furnished free on request).

ALASKA. U. S. Geological Survey, Distribution Unit (publications), 310 First Avenue, Fairbanks, 99701.

U. S. G. S., Public Inquiries Office, Anchorage, Rm. 108, Skyline Building, 508 2nd Avenue, Anchorage, 99501.

U. S. Bureau of Mines, Mineral Resource Office, P. O. Box 2688, Juneau, 99801 (mineral identifications).

U. S. Forest Service, Alaskan Region Headquarters, P. O. Box 1628, Juneau, 99801 (maps of national forests).

State Division of Mines and Minerals, Pouch M, Juneau, 99801.

ALABAMA. U. S. Bureau of Mines, Mineral Resource Field Office, Univ. of Alabama, Box L, Tuscaloosa, 35486 (mineral identifications).

Geological Survey of Alabama, Post Office Drawer O, University, Alabama 35486.

ARIZONA. Arizona Bureau of Mines, University of Arizona, Tucson, 85721.

U. S. Bureau of Mines, Mineral Resource Field Office, University Station, P. O. Box 3928, Tucson 85717 (mineral identifications).

ARKANSAS. Arkansas Geological Commission, 446 State Capitol, Little Rock 72201.

CALIFORNIA. U. S. Geological Survey, Public Inquiries Office, Rm. 7638, Federal Building, 300 N. Los Angeles St., Los Angeles 90012.

U. S. G. S., Public Inquiries Office, Rm. 504, Customs House, 555 Battery St., San Francisco 94111.

U. S. Forest Service, California Region Headquarters, 630 Sansome St., San Francisco (maps of national forests).

California Division of Mines and Geology, Ferry Building, San Francisco, 94111 (publishes many books, maps, etc., on all phases of California mining and geology; issue informative monthly pamphlet *Mineral Information Service*, subscription $1.00 per year).

364

COLORADO. U. S. Geological Survey, Public Inquiries Office, Rm. 15426, Federal Building, Denver, 80202.
U. S. Geological Survey, Distribution Section (publications), Building 41, Denver Federal Center, Denver, 80225.
U. S. Bureau of Mines, Mineral Resource Field Office, Building 20, Denver Federal Center, Denver, 80225 (mineral identifications).
Mining Industrial Development Board, 204 State Office Building, Denver, 80202 (deals with state geology and mining).
CONNECTICUT. Connecticut Geological and Natural History Survey, Box 128, Wesleyan Station, Middletown, 06457.
DELAWARE. Delaware Geological Survey, University of Delaware, Newark 19711.
FLORIDA. Division of Geology, Florida Board of Conservation, P. O. Box 631 Tallahassee, 32302.
GEORGIA. U. S. Forest Service, Southern Region Headquarters, 50 Seventh Street, N.E., Atlanta 30323 (maps of national forests).
Department of Mines, Mining and Geology, 19 Hunter Street, S.W., Atlanta, 30334.
HAWAII. Division of Water and Land Development, Department of Land and Natural Resources, P. O. Box 373, Honolulu, 96809.
IDAHO. Idaho Bureau of Mines and Geology, Moscow, 83843.
ILLINOIS. Illinois State Geological Survey, 121 Natural Resources Building, Urbana, 61801.
INDIANA. Department of Natural Resources, Geological Survey, 611 N. Walnut Grove, Bloomington, 47401.
IOWA. Iowa Geological Survey, Geological Survey Building, 16 W. Jefferson Street, Iowa City, 52240.
KANSAS. State Geological Survey of Kansas, The University of Kansas, Lawrence, 66044.
KENTUCKY. Kentucky Geological Survey, University of Kentucky, 307 Mineral Industries Building, Lexington, 40506.
LOUISIANA. Louisiana Geological Survey, Box G, University Station, Baton Rouge, 70803.
MAINE. Maine Geological Survey, State Office Building, Rm. 211, Augusta, 04330.
MARYLAND. Maryland Geological Survey, 214 Latrobe Hall, Johns Hopkins University, Baltimore, 21218.
U. S. Bureau of Mines, Mineral Resource Field Office, College Park, 20740.
MASSACHUSETTS. Geological Museum, Harvard University, Oxford Street, Cambridge, 02138.
MICHIGAN. Michigan Department of Conservation, Geological Survey Division, Stevens T. Mason Building, Lansing, 48926.
MINNESOTA. U. S. Bureau of Mines, Mineral Resource Office, East 58th Street at Mississippi River, Minneapolis, 55417 (mineral identifications).
Minnesota Geological Survey, University of Minnesota, Minneapolis, 55455.
MISSISSIPPI. Mississippi Geological, Economic and Topographical Survey, P. O. Box 4915, Jackson, 39216.

MISSOURI. U. S. Bureau of Mines, Research Director, Rolla Metallurgy Research Center, P.O. Box 136, Rolla, 65401 (mineral identifications).
Division of Geological Survey and Water Resources, P. O. Box 250, Rolla, 65401.
MONTANA. U. S. Forest Service, Northern Region Headquarters, Federal Building, Missoula, 59801 (maps of national forests).
Montana Bureau of Mines and Geology, Montana College of Mineral Science and Technology, Butte, 59701.
NEBRASKA. Conservation and Survey Division, University of Nebraska, 113 Nebraska Hall, Lincoln, 68508.
NEVADA. Nevada Bureau of Mines, University of Nevada, Reno, 89507.
U. S. Bureau of Mines, Rare & Precious Metals Experiment Station, 1605 Evans Avenue, Reno, 89502 (mineral identifications).
NEW HAMPSHIRE. Department of Resources and Economic Development, Geologic Branch, Department of Geology, Conant Hall, University of New Hampshire, Durham, 03102.
NEW JERSEY. N. J. Bureau of Geology and Topography, John Fitch Plaza, Rm. 709, P. O. Box 1889, Trenton, 08625.
NEW MEXICO. U. S. Forest Service, Southwestern Region Headquarters, 517 Gold Ave. S. W., Albuquerque, 87101 (maps of national forests).
New Mexico Bureau of Mines and Mineral Resources, Campus Station, Socorro 87801.
NEW YORK. New York State Museum and Science Service, Geological Survey, N. Y. State Education Building, Rm. 973, Albany, 12224.
NORTH CAROLINA. Division of Mineral Resources, Department of Conservation and Development, P. O. Box 2719, Raleigh, 27602.
NORTH DAKOTA. North Dakota Geological Survey, University Station, Grand Forks, 58202.
OHIO. Ohio Division of Geological Survey, 1207 Grandview Avenue, Columbus, 43212.
OKLAHOMA. Oklahoma Geological Survey, The University of Oklahoma, Norman, 73069.
OREGON. U. S. Forest Service, Pacific Northwest Region Headquarters, P. O. Box 3623, Portland, 97208 (maps of national forests).
State Department of Geology and Mineral Industries, 1069 State Office Building, 1400 S.W. Fifth Avenue, Portland, 97201.
U. S. Bureau of Mines, Mineral Resource Office, P. O. Box 70, Albany, 97321.
PENNSYLVANIA. U. S. Forest Service, Eastern Region Headquarters, 6816 Market Street, Upper Darby, 19082 (maps of national forests).
Bureau of Topographic and Geologic Survey, Department of Internal Affairs, Harrisburg, 17120.
RHODE ISLAND. Brown University, Providence, 02912.
SOUTH CAROLINA. Division of Geology, P. O. Box 927, Columbia, 29202.
SOUTH DAKOTA. South Dakota State Geological Survey, Science Center, University of South Dakota, Vermillion, 57069.
U. S. Bureau of Mines, Rapid City Experiment Station, School of Mines Campus, Rapid City, 57701 (mineral identifications).

TENNESSEE. Department of Conservation, Division of Geology, G-5 State Office Building, Nashville, 37219.

TEXAS. Bureau of Economic Geology, The University of Texas, University Station, Box X, Austin, 78712.

U. S. Geological Survey, Public Inquiries Office, 602 Thomas Building, 1314 Wood Street, Dallas, 75202.

UTAH. U. S. Geological Survey, Public Inquiries Office, 8102 Federal Office Building, 125 South State Street, Salt Lake City, 84111.

U. S. Bureau of Mines, Mineral Resource Field Office, 1600 East First South Street, Salt Lake City, 84112 (mineral identifications).

U. S. Forest Service, Intermountain Region Headquarters, Federal Office Building, 324-25th St., Ogden, 84401 (maps of national forests).

Utah Geological and Mineralogical Survey, 103 Utah Geological Survey Building, University of Utah, Salt Lake City, 84112.

VERMONT. Vermont Geological Survey, University of Vermont, Burlington, 05401.

VIRGINIA. U. S. Geological Survey, Distribution Section, 1200 S. Eads Street, Arlington, 22202.

Virginia Division of Mineral Resources, P. O. Box 3667, Charlottesville, 22903.

WASHINGTON. U. S. Geological Survey, Public Inquiries Office, South 157 Howard Street, Spokane, 99204.

Washington Division of Mines and Geology, 335 General Administration Building, Olympia, 98501.

WEST VIRGINIA. West Virginia Geological and Economic Survey, P. O. Box 879, Morgantown, 26505.

WISCONSIN. U. S. Forest Service, North Central Region Headquarters, 633 W. Wisconsin Ave., Milwaukee, 53203 (maps of national forests).

Wisconsin Geological and Natural History Survey, University of Wisconsin, 1815 University Avenue, Madison, 53706.

WYOMING. Geological Survey of Wyoming, P. O. Box 3008, University Station, University of Wyoming, Laramie, 82070.

MEXICO AND CENTRAL AMERICA

MEXICO. Instituto de Geologia, Universidad Nacional Autonoma de Mexico, Ciudad Universitaria, Mexico 20, D.F.

BRITISH HONDURAS. Survey Department, Belize.

COSTA RICA. Geological Survey of Costa Rica, Geologic Department, University of Costa Rica, San Pedro de Montes de Oca, San Jose.

CUBA. Instituto Nacional de Investigaciones Científicas, Cerro 827, Havana.

DOMINICAN REPUBLIC. Servicio de Mineria, Ministerio de Industrio y Comercio, Santo Domingo.

EL SALVADOR. Centro de Estudios e Investigaciones Geotecnicas, Ministry of Public Works, 1-A Calle Poniente No. 925, San Salvador.

GUATEMALA. Sección de Geologia, Direccion General de Mineria e Hidrocarburos, 10a. Calle 11-46, Zona 1, Guatemala City.

HAITI. Geological Survey, Department of Agriculture, Damiens près Port-au-Prince.

JAMAICA. Geological Survey Department, Hope Gardens, Kingston 6.

NICARAGUA. Servicio Geológico Nacional, Ministerio de Economia, Apartado Postal No. 1347, Managua, D.N.

PANAMA. Departamento de Recursos Minerales, Panama City.

PUERTO RICO. Economic Development Administration, Industrial Research, Mineralogy and Geology Section, Box 38, Roosevelt Station, Hato Rey.

WINDWARD ISLANDS. Government Geologist, Castries, St. Lucia, T.W.I.

GREENLAND

GREENLAND. Grønlands Geologiske Undersøgelse, Østervoldgade 7, København K, Denmark.

APPENDIX IV

Reference Libraries

The following libraries maintain stocks of geological literature which may be consulted by residents of the states, provinces, or territories concerned.

ALABAMA.
Auburn : Alabama Polytechnic Institute.
Birmingham : Birmingham Southern College; Howard College; Public Library.
Mobile (Spring Hill) : Thomas Byrne Memorial Library.
Montgomery : Department of Archives and State History, State Capitol.
Tuskegee Institute : Hollis Burke Frissell Library.
University : University of Alabama; Alabama Geological Survey.
ALASKA.
College : University of Alaska.
ALBERTA.
Edmonton : Department of Lands & Forests Library; University of Alberta.
ARIZONA.
Phoenix : Department of Library & Archives; Department of Mineral Resources; Public Library.
Tempe : Matthews Library, Arizona State College.
Tucson : University of Arizona.
ARKANSAS.
Clarksville : College of the Ozarks.
Fayetteville : University of Arkansas.
Jonesboro : Arkansas State College.
Little Rock : Arkansas Geological Survey.
Magnolia : Southern State College.
Russellville : Arkansas Polytechnic College.
BRITISH COLUMBIA.
Kamloops : Kamloops Historical & Museum Association Library.
Trail : Consolidated Mining & Smelting Co. of Canada, Ltd., Central Technical Library.
Vancouver : Art, Historical & Scientific Association Library; Public Library.
Victoria : Department of Lands & Forests Library; Provincial Museum of Natural History Library.
CALIFORNIA.
Arcata : Humboldt State College.
Bakersfield : Kern County Free Library.
Berkeley : University of California.
Claremont : Pomona College.
Davis : University of California.
Eureka : Eureka Free Library.
Fresno : Fresno County Free Library; State College Library.
La Jolla : Scripps Institution of Oceanography.
Long Beach : Public Library.

Los Angeles: Department of Water & Power; Los Angeles Public Library; Los Angeles County Museum; Los Angeles State College; Occidental College; University of California at Los Angeles; University of Southern Calif.

Northridge: San Fernando Valley State College.

Oakland: Oakland Free Library.

Pasadena: California Institute of Technology.

Redding: Shasta County Free Library.

Redlands: University of Redlands.

Riverside: Public Library; University of California.

Sacramento: California State Library; City Free Library.

San Diego: University of California, La Jolla.

San Francisco: California Academy of Sciences; California Division of Mines; Mechanics Mercantile Library; San Francisco Public Library; San Francisco State College; Sierra Club; State Mineralogist.

San Jose: San Jose State College.

Santa Barbara: Santa Barbara Public Library.

Stanford University. Branner Geological Library; University Library.

Stockton: Free Public Library; College of the Pacific; Stockton College.

COLORADO.

Boulder: University of Colorado.

Colorado Springs: Colorado College.

Denver: Colorado Geological Survey; Colorado State Library; The Mining Record; Museum of Natural History; Public Library; Regis College; State Bureau of Mines; University of Denver; U. S. Geological Survey Offices at Denver Federal Center and 468 New Custom House.

Fort Collins: Colorado State University.

Golden: State School of Mines.

Grand Junction: Public Library.

Gunnison: Western State College.

Idaho Springs: Western College of Mining.

CONNECTICUT.

Bridgeport: Public Library.

Hartford: Connecticut State Library; Geological & Natural History Survey; Public Library; Trinity College.

Middletown: Wesleyan University.

New Haven: American Journal of Science; Yale University.

New London: Connecticut College.

Storrs: University of Connecticut.

DELAWARE.

Newark: University of Delaware; Delaware Geological Survey.

Wilmington: Wilmington Free Institute.

DISTRICT OF COLUMBIA.

Washington: George Washington University; U. S. Geological Survey Library; Library of Congress; U. S. National Museum; Department of Interior; Howard University.

FLORIDA.
  Coral Gables: University of Miami.
  Deland: John B. Stetson University.
  Gainesville: Florida State Museum; University of Florida.
  Jacksonville: Public Library.
  Lakeland: Public Library.
  Miami: Miami Public Library.
  Tallahassee: Florida Geological Survey; Florida State Library; Florida State
    University.
  Tampa: University of Tampa.
  Winter Park: Rollins College.
GEORGIA.
  Athens: University of Georgia.
  Atlanta: Division of Mines, Mining & Geology Library; Public Library.
  Emory University: Asa Griggs Candler Library.
HAWAII.
  Honolulu: Bishop Museum; College of Hawaii; University of Hawaii; Geologi-
    cal Survey, 225 Federal Building.
IDAHO.
  Boise: Public Library.
  Caldwell: Strahorn Memorial Library.
  Moscow: University of Idaho; Idaho Bureau of Mines & Geology.
  Pocatello: Idaho State College.
  Rexburg: Rich College.
ILLINOIS.
  Carbondale: Southern Illinois State Normal University.
  Chicago: John Crerar Library; Museum of Science & History; Field Museum;
    Public Library; University of Chicago; University of Illinois; Western
    Society of Engineers.
  Elsah: The Principia Library.
  Evanston: Northwestern University.
  Joliet: Public Library.
  Monmouth: Monmouth College.
  Normal: Illinois State Normal University.
  Peoria: Public Library.
  Rock Island: Augustana College; Rock Island Public Library.
  Rockford: Public Library.
  Springfield: Illinois State Library.
  Urbana: Illinois Geological Survey; University of Illinois.
INDIANA.
  Bloomington: Indiana Department of Conservation; Indiana University.
  Crawfordsville: Wabash College.
  Evansville: Public Library.
  Fort Wayne: Public Library.
  Greencastle: De Pauw University.
  Hanover: Hanover College.

Huntington: City Free Library.

Indianapolis: Indiana State Library; Public Library; Department of Conservation.

Lafayette: Agricultural Experiment Station; Purdue University.

Muncie: Public Library.

North Manchester: Manchester College.

Notre Dame: Notre Dame University.

Terre Haute: Indiana State Teachers College.

Valparaiso: Valparaiso University.

IOWA.

Ames: Iowa State College.

Cedar Falls: Iowa State Teachers College.

Council Bluffs: Free Public Library.

Davenport: Public Museum.

Des Moines: Drake University; Iowa State Mine Inspector; Iowa State Traveling Library; Public Library.

Dubuque: Carnegie Stout Free Public Library.

Grinnell: Grinnell College.

Indianola: Simpson College.

Iowa City: Iowa Geological Survey; State University of Iowa.

Lamoin: Graceland College.

Mount Vernon: Cornell College.

KANSAS.

Baldwin City: Baker University.

Emporia: Kellogg Library; Kansas State Teachers College.

Hays: Fort Hays Kansas State College.

Lawrence: Kansas State Geological Survey; University of Kansas.

Manhattan: Kansas State Agricultural College.

Pittsburg: Kansas State Teachers College.

Salina: Kansas Wesleyan University.

Topeka: Kansas State Library; Kansas State Historical Society; State Board of Agriculture.

Wichita: University of Wichita; Porter Library.

KENTUCKY.

Ashland: Public Library.

Bowling Green: Western Kentucky State Teachers College.

Lexington: Kentucky Geological Survey; University of Kentucky.

Louisville: Free Public Library; University of Louisville.

LOUISIANA.

Baton Rouge: Louisiana State University; Louisiana Geological Survey.

Lafayette: Southwestern Louisiana Institute.

Lake Charles: McNeese State College.

Natchitoches: Northwestern State College.

New Orleans: Law Library of Louisiana; Loyola University; Public Library; Tulane University.

Ruston: Louisiana Polytechnic Institute.

Shreveport: Shreve Memorial Library; Centenary College.

MAINE.
Augusta: Maine Public Library.
Bangor: Bangor Public Library.
Brunswick: Bowdoin College.
Lewiston: Bates College.
Orono: Maine Geological Survey; University of Maine.
Portland: Portland Society of Natural History; Public Library.
Waterville: Colby College.

MANITOBA.
Winnipeg: University of Manitoba.

MARYLAND.
Annapolis: Maryland State Library.
Baltimore: Enoch Pratt Free Library; Johns Hopkins University; Peabody Institute.
College Park: University of Maryland.
Westminster: Western Maryland College.

MASSACHUSETTS.
Amherst: Amherst College; University of Massachusetts.
Boston: Boston Museum of Science; Boston University; Public Library; State Library of Massachusetts.
Cambridge: Harvard University; Harvard University Museum; Massachusetts Institute of Technology.
Medford: Tufts College.
Northampton: Smith College.
Springfield: City Library.
Wellesley: Wellesley College.
Williamstown: Williams College.
Worcester: Free Public Library; Clark University.

MICHIGAN.
Ann Arbor: University of Michigan.
Bloomfield Hills: Cranbrook Institute of Science.
Detroit: University of Detroit; Public Library; Wayne University.
East Lansing: Michigan State College of Agriculture and Applied Science.
Grand Rapids: Public Library.
Houghton: Michigan College of Mining and Technology.
Ishpeming: Lake Superior Mining Institute.
Lansing: Michigan State Library.
Muskegon: Hackley Public Library.
Saginaw: Hoyt Public Library.

MINNESOTA.
Collegeville: St. Johns University.
Duluth: Public Library.
Minneapolis: E. J. Longyear Company; Minnesota Geological Survey; Public Library; University of Minnesota.
Northfield: Carleton College; St. Olaf College.

St. Paul: James Jerome Hill Reference Library; Minnesota Historical Society; Minnesota State Library; Public Library; Science Museum.

St. Peter: Gustavus Adolphus College.

MISSISSIPPI.

Columbus: J. C. Fant Memorial Library.

Hattiesburg: Mississippi Southern College.

Jackson: Mississippi State Library.

State College: Mississippi State College.

University: University of Mississippi; Mississippi Geological Survey.

Vicksburg: Mississippi River Commission.

MISSOURI.

Cape Girardeau: Southeast Missouri State College.

Columbia: University of Missouri.

Fulton: Westminster College.

Jefferson City: Lincoln University.

Kansas City: Linda Hall Library; Public Library; Rockhurst College; University of Kansas City.

Rolla: School of Mines; State Geologist.

MONTANA.

Bozeman: Montana State College.

Butte: Montana School of Mines.

Helena: Historical Society of Montana; Public Library.

Missoula: State University.

NEBRASKA.

Fremont: Midland College.

Lincoln: Nebraska Conservation and Survey Division; Nebraska State Library; University of Nebraska.

Omaha: Public Library.

NEVADA.

Carson City: Nevada State Library.

Las Vegas: University of Nevada; Southern Regional Division Library.

Reno: University of Nevada; Nevada Bureau of Mines.

NEW BRUNSWICK.

St. John: New Brunswick Museum Library.

NEW HAMPSHIRE.

Concord: New Hampshire State Library.

Durham: Hamilton Smith Library; New Hampshire Planning and Development Commission; University of New Hampshire.

Hanover: Dartmouth College.

NEW JERSEY.

Atlantic City: Free Public Library.

Bayonne: Free Public Library.

Camden: Camden Free Public Library.

Convent Station: College of St. Elizabeth.

Elizabeth: Public Library.

Jersey City: Free Public Library.

Madison: Drew University.

New Brunswick: Free Public Library; Rutgers University.

Newark: Public Library.

Princeton: Princeton University.

Trenton: Department of Conservation and Development; Free Public Library; New Jersey State Library.

NEW MEXICO.

Albuquerque: University of New Mexico.

Santa Fe: State Library.

Socorro: School of Mines.

State College: New Mexico College of Agriculture and Mechanical Arts.

NEW YORK.

Albany: New York State Library; New York State Museum.

Alfred: Alfred University.

Brooklyn: Brooklyn College; Pratt Institute Free College; Public Library.

Buffalo: Buffalo Museum of Science; Grosvenor Library; Public Library.

Canton: St. Lawrence University.

Clinton: Hamilton College.

Farmingdale: State Institute of Applied Agriculture.

Flushing: Queens College.

Glens Falls: Crandall Free Library.

Hamilton: Colgate University.

Ithaca: Cornell University.

Jamaica: St. Johns University.

New York City: American Geographical Society; American Museum of Natural History; College of the City of New York; Columbia University; Cooper Union; Engineering & Mining Journal; Engineering Societies; Fordham University; Hunter College; H. W. Wilson Company; New York Academy of Sciences; New York Botanical Garden; New York University; Public Library (Astor Branch); Public Library (Lenox Branch); Public Library (Queens Branch); Scientific American; The Chemists Club; Torrey Botanical Club.

Potsdam: Clarkson College of Technology.

Poughkeepsie: Vassar College.

Rochester: Rochester Academy of Science; Rochester Public Library; Rochester University.

St. Bonaventure: St. Bonaventure College.

Schenectady: Union College.

Staten Island: Wagner College; Staten Island Institute of Arts & Sciences.

Syracuse: Syracuse University.

Troy: Public Library; Rensselaer Polytechnical Institute.

Utica: Public Library.

NORTH CAROLINA.

Chapel Hill: University of North Carolina.

Davidson: Davidson College.

Durham: Duke University.

Greensboro: Agricultural and Technical College.

Greenville: East Carolina College.

Raleigh: North Carolina State Library; North Carolina State College, D. H. Hill Library; State Geologist, Division of Mineral Resources, Department of Conservation and Development.

Wake Forest: Wake Forest College.

Winston-Salem: Public Library.

NORTH DAKOTA.

Bismarck: State Historical Society.

Fargo: North Dakota Agricultural Society.

Grand Forks: North Dakota Geological Survey; University of North Dakota.

Minot: State Teachers College.

University: North Dakota State University.

NOVA SCOTIA.

Halifax: Dalhousie University; Nova Scotia Museum of Science Library; Nova Scotia Research Foundation Library; Nova Scotia Technical College Library.

OHIO.

Akron: Municipal University of Akron; Public Library.

Alliance: Mount Union College.

Athens: Ohio University.

Bowling Green: State University.

Cincinnati: Cincinnati Society of Natural History; Public Library; University of Cincinnati.

Cleveland: Adelbert College, Western Reserve University; Case Institute of Technology, Main Library; Public Library.

Columbus: American Ceramic Society; Geological Survey of Ohio; Ohio State Library; Public Library; State Board of Agriculture; State University.

Dayton: Public Library.

Delaware: Ohio Wesleyan University.

Granville: Denison University.

Hiram: Hiram College.

Marietta: Marietta College.

Oberlin: Oberlin College.

Oxford: Miami University.

Toledo: Public Library.

Yellow Springs: Antioch College.

Youngstown: Public Library.

OKLAHOMA.

Ada: East Central State College.

Alva: Northwestern State College.

Durant: Southeastern College.

Edmond: Central State College.

Enid: Carnegie Library.

Langston: University Library.

Norman: University of Oklahoma; Oklahoma Geological Survey.

Oklahoma City: Oklahoma State Library; Oklahoma City Library.

Shawnee: Oklahoma Baptist University.

Stillwater: Oklahoma State University.

Tahlequah: Northeastern State College.

Tulsa: University of Tulsa.

ONTARIO.

Chalk River: Atomic Energy of Canada, Ltd., Library.

Hamilton: Hamilton Public Library.

Kingston: Queens University, Douglas Library.

London: London Public Library & Art Museum.

Ottawa: Department of Mines & Technical Surveys Libraries.

Toronto: Department of Mines Library; Northern Miner Library; Royal Ontario Museum Library; University of Toronto Libraries.

OREGON.

Ashland: Southern Oregon College of Education.

Corvallis: Oregon State College.

Eugene: University of Oregon.

Forest Grove: Pacific University.

Portland: District Engineer, U. S. Geological Survey; Library Association of Portland; Mazamas Library; Reed College; State Department of Geology and Mineral Industries.

Salem: Oregon State Library.

PENNSYLVANIA.

Allentown: Muhlenberg College.

Bethlehem: Lehigh University.

Bradford: Carnegie Public Library.

Bryn Mawr: Bryn Mawr College.

Carlisle: Dickinson College.

Erie: Public Library.

Harrisburg: Pennsylvania State Library; Topographic and Geologic Survey.

Haverford: Haverford College.

Huntington: Juniata College.

Lancaster: Franklin and Marshall College.

Meadville: Allegheny College.

Media: Delaware County Institute of Science.

Philadelphia: Academy of Natural Sciences; American Philosophical Society; Franklin Institute; Free Library of Philadelphia; Philadelphia Commercial Museum; Temple University; University of Pennyslvania; Wagner Free Institute of Science.

Pittsburgh: Carnegie Library; Carnegie Free Library of Allegheny; Engineer's Society of Western Pennsylvania; University of Pittsburgh.

Reading: Public Library.

Scranton: Public Library.

State College: Pennsylvania State University.

Swarthmore: Swarthmore College.

University Park: Mineral Industries Library; Pennsylvania State University.

Warren: Warren Library Association.

Washington: Washington and Jefferson College.

Wilkes-Barre: Wyoming Historical & Geological Society; Kings College.

Williamsport: James V. Brown Library.

PUERTO RICO.

Hato Rey: Mineralogy and Geology Section, Industrial Laboratory.

Mayaguez: University of Puerto Rico, College of Agriculture and Mechanical Arts.

Rio Piedras: University of Puerto Rico.

QUEBEC.

Hull: Public Printing & Stationery, Publication Branch, Documents Library.

Montreal: Arctic Institute of North America Library; Canadian Institute of Mining & Metallurgy Library; Ecole Polytechnique Library; McGill University.

Quebec: Bibliotheque du Ministere des Mines.

RHODE ISLAND.

Kingston: University of Rhode Island.

Providence: Brown University; Public Library; Rhode Island State Library.

Westerly: Public Library.

SOUTH CAROLINA.

Clemson: Clemson College.

Columbia: South Carolina Geological Survey; University of South Carolina.

Orangeburg: State Agricultural and Mechanical College.

Rock Hill: Winthrop College.

SOUTH DAKOTA.

Brookings: Lincoln Memorial Library.

Mitchell: Dakota Wesleyan University.

Pierre: South Dakota State.

Rapid City: State School of Mines.

Sioux Falls: Carnegie Free Public Library.

Spearfish: Black Hills Teachers College.

Vermillion: South Dakota Geological Survey; University of South Dakota.

Yankton: Yankton College.

TENNESSEE.

Chattanooga: Public Library.

Johnson City: East Tennessee State College.

Knoxville: University of Tennessee.

Memphis: Cossitt Library.

Nashville: Nashville Public Library; State Geological Survey; Tennessee State Library; Vanderbilt University; Joint University Libraries. Sewanee: University of the South.

TEXAS.

Abilene: Hardin-Simmons University.

Alpine: Sul Ross State College.

Austin: Texas State Library; State Bureau of Economic Geology; University of Texas.

Brownwood: Walker Memorial Library.
Canyon: West Texas State Teachers College.
College Station: Agricultural and Mechanical College of Texas.
Commerce: East Texas State Teachers College.
Dallas: Public Library; Southern Methodist University.
Denton: North Texas State College.
El Paso: Texas Western College; Public Library.
Fort Worth: Public Library; Texas Christian University.
Galveston: Rosenburg Library.
Houston: Public Library; Rice Institute.
Huntsville: Sam Houston State Teachers College.
Kingsville: Texas College of Arts and Industries.
Lubbock: Texas Technological College.
San Antonio: Texas Natural Resources Foundation.
Waco: Baylor University.
UTAH.
Logan: Utah State College.
Provo: Brigham Young University.
Salt Lake City: University of Utah; Free Public Library; Utah Geological and
    Mineralogical Survey; Utah Academy of Sciences; U. S. Geological Survey,
    504 Federal Building.
VIRGINIA.
Blacksburg: Virginia Polytechnic Institute.
Charlottesville: University of Virginia; Virginia Geological Survey.
Emory: Emory and Henry College.
Fort Belvoir: U. S. Engineer School.
Lexington: Virginia Military Institute; Washington and Lee University.
Richmond: Virginia State Library.
VERMONT.
Burlington: State Geologist; University of Vermont.
Middlebury: Middlebury College.
Montpelier: Vermont State Library.
Northfield: Norwich University.
WASHINGTON.
Olympia: Division of Mines and Geology, Washington State.
Pullman: Washington State University.
Seattle: Public Library; University of Washington.
Spokane: Public Library; U. S. Geological Survey.
Tacoma: College of Puget Sound; Public Library.
Walla Walla: Whitman College.
WEST VIRGINIA.
Athens: Concord College Library.
Charleston: State Library; Department of Archives and History, State Library.
Huntington: Marshall College.
Morgantown: State Geologist, Geological and Economic Survey; West Virginia
    University.
Salem: Salem College.

WISCONSIN.
  Appleton: Lawrence College.
  Beloit: Beloit College.
  Madison: State Geological and Natural History Survey; State Historical Society; University of Wisconsin; Wisconsin State Library.
  Milwaukee: Public Museum; Public Library.
  Platteville: Wisconsin Institute of Technology.
  Racine: Public Library.
  Stevens Point: Wisconsin State College.
  Superior: Public Library; Superior State Teachers College.
WYOMING.
  Casper: Natrona County Public Library.
  Cheyenne: Wyoming State Library.
  Laramie: University of Wyoming.

APPENDIX V
Suggested Reference and Reading Material

Note: many of the publications listed below are out of print but are included nevertheless because of the value of their information. (Numbers inside parentheses are Zip Codes)

PROSPECTING AND COLLECTING

ANDERSON, D. L. *Prospecting for Placer Gold in South Dakota.* South Dakota Geological Survey, Report of Investigations 15, Vermillion, 1933.

———. *Prospecting in Washington.* Washington State Division of Mines and Geology, Information Circular 31, Olympia, 1959.

ATOMIC ENERGY COMMISSION & U.S. GEOLOGICAL SURVEY. *Prospecting for Uranium*, Revised Edition. Washington, D. C.: Government Printing Office, 1951. A very useful booklet. (20402)

AVERILL, C. V. *Placer Mining for Gold in California.* California Division of Mines and Geology, Bulletin 135, San Francisco, 1946.

BOERICKE, W. F. *Prospecting and Operating Small Gold Placers*, 2nd Edition. New York: John Wiley & Sons, 1936.

CANADIAN INDUSTRIES LIMITED. *The Blasters' Handbook.* Procured from any C. I. L. Depot; comparable to blasters' handbooks published in U. S.

COOK, E. F. *Prospecting for Uranium, Thorium, and Tungsten in Idaho.* Idaho Bureau of Mines & Geology, Pamphlet 102, Moscow.

COX, H. S. *Prospecting for Minerals*, 8th Edition. Philadelphia: J. B. Lippincott Co., 1921.

CRAWFORD, J. E. and PAONE, J. *Facts Concerning Uranium Exploration and Production.* Washington, D. C.: U. S. Bureau of Mines, 1956. Handbook with much information on all aspects of prospecting, mining, and marketing of radioactive ores.

DAKE, H. C. *Popular Prospecting: A Field Guide for the Part-Time Prospector.* Mentone, California: Gembooks, 1955.

E. I. DU PONT DE NEMOURS. *Blasters' Handbook*, 14th Edition. Wilmington, Delaware: E. I. Du Pont De Nemours & Co., Inc., 1958. Describes explosives, detonators, etc. and best methods to use them. (19898)

GARDNER, E. D. *Guide to Prospecting for Lode Gold.* U. S. Bureau of Mines, Information Circular 7535, Washington, D. C., 1950. Excellent summary of outcrop features of gold-bearing veins; also many practical hints to prospectors. (20240)

GARDNER, E. D. and JOHNSON, C. H. *Placer Mining in the Western United States, Part I.* U. S. Bureau of Mines, Information Circular 6786, Washington, D. C., 1934. Practical information for the prospector with sections on mining laws, equipment, camping tips, etc.; also a brief but useful summary of placer deposit geology. (20240)

GEOLOGICAL SURVEY OF CANADA. *Prospecting for Uranium in Canada.* Canada Geological Survey, 1952. Ottowa.

HUNTTING, M. T. *Gold in Washington.* Washington State Division of Mines & Geology, Bulletin 42, Olympia, 1955.

LANG, A. H. *Prospecting in Canada*, 3rd Edition. Canada Geological Survey, Economic Geology Series 7, 1956. Although directed toward Canadian prospectors, this book is extremely valuable to prospectors and collectors anywhere. (Ottawa)

PEARL, R. M. *Mineral Collector's Handbook.* Colorado Springs; Mineral Book Co., 1947. Contains much useful information on assembling and caring for collections.

U. S. DEPARTMENT OF THE ARMY. *Map Reading.* Field Manual FM21–26. Washington, D. C.: Government Printing Office, 1956.

VON BERNEWITZ, M. W. *Handbook for Prospectors and Operators of Small Mines,* 4th Edition Revised. New York: McGraw-Hill Book Co., Inc., 1943. Much useful information not readily available elsewhere.

WALKER, J. F. *Elementary Geology Applied to Prospecting*, Revised Edition. Victoria: British Columbia Department of Mines.

CLAIM INFORMATION

BUREAU OF LAND MANAGEMENT. *Information in Regard to Mining Claims in the Public Domain.* U. S. Department of the Interior, Bureau of Land Management Circular 1278, Washington, D. C.

————. *Lode and Placer Mining Regulations; As Amended to and including November* 1, 1955. U. S. Department of the Interior, Bureau of Land Management Circular 1951, Washington, D. C.

CALIFORNIA DIVISION OF MINES AND GEOLOGY. *Legal Guide for California Prospectors and Miners.* San Francisco: California Division of Mines and Geology, 1952. An excellent guide which also contains pertinent Federal laws.

CLAWSON, M. *Locating Mining Claims on the Public Domain.* U. S. Bureau of Mines, Information Circular 7535, Washington, D. C., 1950.

SOURCES OF GEOLOGICAL INFORMATION

FLOE, C. F. and MASSON, D.L. *Sources of Information for the Prospector,* 2nd Edition. Washington State College, College of Mines Information Circular 1-R, Pullman, 1946.

HOWELL, J. V. *Glossary of Geology and Related Sciences.* Washington, D. C.: American Geological Institute, 1957.

HOWELL, J. V. and LEVORSEN, A. I. *Directory of Geological Material in North America,* 2nd Edition Revised. Washington, D. C.: American Geological Institute, 1957. *Supplement,* 1961. Very useful compilation of sources of literature, equipment, maps, photographs, and other material of interest to geologists.

LANG, A. H. *A List of Publications on Prospecting in Canada and Related Subjects.* Canada Department of Energy, Mines and Mineral Resources, Paper 54–1, Ottawa, 1954.

LAPIDARY JOURNAL. *The Rockhound Buyer's Guide,* April issue annually. San Diego, (92112) Large special issue devoted to lists of clubs, selling organizations, equipment and material guides, and other valuable information.

LEAFLOOR, L. B. *Publications of the Geological Survey of Canada* (1917–1952). Ottawa: Canada Department of Energy, Mines and Mineral Resources, 1952.

MASON, B. *The Literature of Geology.* New York: The American Museum of Natural History, 1953. A guide to geological bibliographies, glossaries, dictionaries, and other sources and directories.

PANGBORN, M. W. *Earth for the Layman.* Washington, D. C.: American Geological Institute, 1957. (20005) A list of nearly 1400 good books and pamphlets of popular interest on geology, mining, mapping, and kindred subjects.

PEARL, R. M. *Guide to Geologic Literature.* New York: McGraw-Hill Book Co., Inc., 1951.

RICE, C. M. *Dictionary of Geological Terms.* Published by the author; Princeton, N. J.

U. S. GEOLOGICAL SURVEY. *Publications of the Geological Survey.* Washington, D. C.: U. S. Geological Survey, 1961 (latest edition), with *Supplements* provided thereafter.

REFERENCES AND TEXTBOOKS

BATEMEN, A. M. *Economic Mineral Deposits,* 2nd Edition. New York: John Wiley & Sons, Inc., 1950. Thorough treatment of mineral deposits of all types and how they came into being.

———. *The Formation of Mineral Deposits.* New York: John Wiley & Sons, Inc., 1951. A condensation of the previous work and better for the beginner.

BERRY, L. G. and MASON, B. *Mineralogy: Concepts, Descriptions, Determinations.* San Francisco: W. H. Freeman and Company, 1959. Excellent college-level text.

CAMERON, E. N. et al. *Internal Structure of Granitic Pegmatites.* Monograph 2. Urbana, Illinois: Economic Geology Publishing Co., 1949. Discusses in detail the features of pegmatites which are of interest to miners and prospectors but on a technical level.

CRONEIS, C. G. and KRUMBEIN, W. C. *Down to Earth; An Introduction to Geology.* Chicago: University of Chicago Press, 1936. Excellent beginning text.

DANA, E. S. and FORD, W. E. *A Textbook of Mineralogy,* 4th Edition Revised. New York: John Wiley & Sons, Inc., 1932. Despite its age, this textbook is still a most useful reference.

DANA, E. S. and HURLBUT, C. S. *Dana's Manual of Mineralogy,* 17th Edition. New York: John Wiley & Sons, 1959. Standard college text.

———. *Minerals and How to Study Them,* Revised Edition. New York: John Wiley & Sons, 1949. Excellent beginning text.

DIETRICH, R. V. *Mineral Tables.* Blacksburg, Virginia: Virginia Polytechnic Institute, 1966. (24060) Very complete tables of mineral properties designed to aid in their identification.

ENGLISH, G. L. and JENSEN, D. E. *Getting Acquainted with Minerals.* New York: McGraw-Hill Book Co., 1959. Beautifully illustrated beginning text.

FENTON, C. L. and M. A. *The Rock Book.* New York: Doubleday & Co., 1940. Beginning text written in easy style and handsomely illustrated; highly recommended.

FRONDEL, C. *Systematic Mineralogy of Uranium and Thorium.* U. S. Geological Survey, Bulletin 1064, Washington, D. C., 1958. Detailed compilation of all the data on the radioactive minerals.

GLEASON, S. *Ultraviolet Guide to Minerals.* New York: Van Nostrand Reinhold, 1960. Easily the most complete on the subject and written for amateur use.

NININGER, R. D. *Minerals for Atomic Energy*, 2nd Edition. New York: Van Nostrand Reinhold, 1956. An excellent reference book for the prospector of radioactive minerals.

PALACHE, C. et al. *Dana's System of Mineralogy*, Vols. I, II, III. New York: John Wiley & Sons, Inc., 1944, 1951, 1962. The standard reference works on mineralogy in the English language containing all the significant details known.

PIRSSON, L. V. *Rocks and Rock Minerals*, 3rd Edition revised by Adolph Knopf. New York: John Wiley & Sons, Inc., 1947. A standard textbook of considerable value.

SINKANKAS, J. *Mineralogy for Amateurs.* New York: Van Nostrand Reinhold, 1964. Specially written to bring to amateurs modern concepts in mineralogy in an easily understandable manner; numerous illustrations.

―――. *Mineralogy. A First Course.* New York: Van Nostrand Reinhold, 1966. Adaptation of the above as a beginning college-level text.

―――. *Standard Catalog of Gems.* New York: Van Nostrand Reinhold, 1968.

SMITH, O. C. *Identification and Qualitative Chemical Analysis of Minerals*, 2nd Edition. Princeton, New Jersey: D. Van Nostrand Company, Inc., 1953. The most complete compilation of testing and identification procedures available.

LOCALITY INFORMATION

BIRCH, R. W. *Wyoming's Mineral Resources.* Laramie: Wyoming Natural Resources Board, 1955.

BUDGE, C. E. *The Mineral Resources of North Dakota.* North Dakota Research Foundation, Bulletin 8, Bismarck, 1954.

CONLEY, J. F. *Mineral Localities of North Carolina.* North Carolina Division of Mineral Resources, Information Circular 16, Raleigh, 1958. Explicit instructions on how to reach deposits and what to find.

DAKE, H. C. *Northwest Gem Trails.* Mentone, California: Gembooks, 1950.

―――. *California Gem Trails.* Mentone, California: Gembooks, 1952.

DAVIES, J. F. et al. *Geology and Mineral Resources of Manitoba.* Winnipeg: Manitoba Department of Mines and Natural Resources, 1962. Detailed and thorough with much locality information.

DEL RIO, S. M. *Mineral Resources of Colorado, First Sequel.* Denver: Colorado Mineral Resources Board, 1960. A supplement to *Mineral Resources of Colorado* by Vanderwilt et al. (see below).

DIETRICH, R. V. *Virginia Mineral Localities.* Blacksburg, Virginia: Virginia Polytechnic Institute, 1960 with *Supplements* in 1961 (I), 1963 (II), 1965 (III), and 1967 (IV). Excellent presentations.

―――. *Virginia Minerals and Rocks*, 4th Edition. Blacksburg, Virginia: Virginia Polytechnic Institute, 1964.

DUKE, A. *Arizona Gem Fields*, 2nd Edition. Yuma, Arizona: Alton Duke, 1959.

ECKEL, E. B. *Minerals of Colorado: A 100-Year Record*. U.S. Geological Survey, Bulletin 1114, Washington, D. C., 1961. Thorough compilation of locality information.

EKBLAW, G. E. and CARROLL, D. L. *Typical Rocks and Minerals in Illinois*. Illinois Geological Survey, Educational Series 3, Urbana, 1931.

ELLSWORTH, H. V. *Rare Element Minerals in Canada*. Canada Geological Survey, Economic Geology Series 11, 1932.

EMMONS, W. H. and GROUT, F. F. *Mineral Resources of Minnesota*. Minnesota Geological Survey, Bulletin 30, Minneapolis, 1943.

FLAGG, A. L. *Mineralogical Journeys in Arizona*. Scottsdale, Arizona: F. H. Bitner Co., 1958. Informal and interesting.

GALBRAITH, F. W. and BRENNAN, D. J. *Minerals of Arizona*, 3rd Edition Revised. Tucson: University of Arizona Press, 1959.

GIANELLA, V. P. *Nevada's Common Minerals*. University of Nevada Bulletin, Vol. 35, No. 6 (1941). Geology and Mining Series 36.

GORDON, S. G. *Mineralogy of Pennsylvania*. Academy of Natural Sciences of Philadelphia, Special Publication 1, Philadelphia, 1922.

GREENSBURG, S. S. et al. *Guide to Some Minerals and Rocks in Indiana*. Indiana Department of Conservation, Geological Survey Circular 4, Bloomington, 1958.

HENRY, D. J. *Gem Trail Journal*, 2nd Edition. Long Beach, California: L. R. Gordon, 1952.

———. *The Rock Collector's Nevada and Idaho*. Long Beach, California: L. R. Gordon, 1953.

HEWITT, D. F. *Rocks and Minerals of Ontario*. Ontario Department of Mines, Geological Circular No. 13, Toronto, 1964. An excellent, detailed guide to many localities.

JANUZZI, R. E. *The Mineralogy of Connecticut and Southeastern New York State*. Danbury, Connecticut: Mineralogical Press, 1961. Directions to over 60 localities.

JOHNSON, P. W. *Field Guide to the Gems and Minerals of Mexico (Exclusive of Baja California)*. Mentone, California: Gembooks, 1965. Detailed travel and collecting guide to many localities.

JOHNSTON, R. A. A. *A List of Canadian Mineral Occurrences*. Canada Geological Survey Memoir 74, 1915. Old but still useful.

JONES, R. W., JR. *Nature's Hidden Rainbows*. San Gabriel, California: Ultra-Violet Products, Inc., 1964. Much detail on the fluorescent minerals of Franklin, N. J.

———. *Luminescent Minerals of Connecticut: A Guide to Their Properties and Locations*. Branford, Connecticut: Fluorescent House, 1960.

KELLER, W. D. *The Common Rocks and Minerals of Missouri*. University of Missouri Bulletin, Vol. 62, No. 27 (1961). Missouri Handbook 1.

LAPHAM, D. M. and GEYER, A. R. *Mineral Collecting in Pennsylvania*. General Geology Report G-33, Pennsylvania Geological Survey, Harrisburg, 3rd edit. 1969. Excellent details and directions.

LEADBEATER, J. E. M. *Maine Minerals and Gems.* Privately published, 1963.

LEIPER, H. *The Agates of North America*, Revised Edition. San Diego: Lapidary Journal, 1963. Compilation of articles from the *Lapidary Journal*, with much locality information.

LUEDKE, E. M. et al. *Mineral Occurrences of New York State with Selected References to Each Locality.* U.S. Geological Survey Bulletin 1072 (F), 1959.

MAINE GEOLOGICAL SURVEY. *Maine Pegmatite Mines and Prospects and Associated Minerals.* Department of Development of Industry and Commerce, Mineral Resources Index 1, Augusta, 1957.

————. *Maine Mineral Collecting.* Department of Economic Development, Augusta, 1960. Fine pamphlet with 11 maps showing 15 good mineral localities.

MANCHESTER, J. G. *Minerals of New York and Its Environs.* New York: New York Mineralogical Club, 1931. Still the most detailed listing of mineral occurrences within a 50-mile radius of New York City.

MARTENS, J. H. C. *Minerals of West Virginia.* West Virginia Geological and Economic Survey, Morgantown, 1964. A well written pamphlet with some good localities.

MEYERS, T. R. and STEWART, G. W. *The Geology of New Hampshire*, Part 3: *Minerals and Mines.* Concord: New Hampshire State Planning and Development Commission, 1956.

MONTGOMERY, A. *The Mineralogy of Pennsylvania.* Philadelphia: Academy of Natural Sciences of Phila. Special Publ. 9, 1969. Supplements and updates Gordon's work above.

MORRILL, P. *New Hampshire Mines and Mineral Localities.* Hanover: Dartmouth College Museum, 1960.

MULLIGAN, R. *Beryllium Occurrences in Canada.* Gelogical Survey of Canada, Paper 60–21, 1960. Numerous localities for beryl in pegmatites.

MURDOCH, J. and WEBB, R. W. *Minerals of California.* California Division of Mines and Geology Bulletin 189, San Francisco, 1956; with *Supplement* for 1965-1968 (see PEMBERTON, H.E.).

NORTHRUP, S. A. *Minerals of New Mexico*, Revised Edition. Albuquerque: University of New Mexico Press, 1960. Contains much historical information in addition to detail on localities and deposits.

OLES, F. and H. *Eastern Gem Trails.* Mentone, California: Gembooks, 1967. Popular account of some localities from New Jersey to North Carolina.

OSTERWALD, F. W. *Wyoming Mineral Resources.* Wyoming Geological Survey Bulletin 45, Laramie, 1952.

OSTRANDER, C. W. and PRICE, W. E. *Minerals of Maryland.* Baltimore: Natural History Society of Maryland, 1940.

PALLISTER, H. D. *Index to the Minerals and Rocks of Alabama.* Geological Survey of Alabama Bulletin 65, 1955.

PEARL, R. M. *Colorado Rocks, Minerals, Fossils.* Denver: Sage Books, 1964.

————. *Colorado Gem Trails*, 2nd Edition. Denver: Sage Books, 1965.

PEGAU, A. A. *Mineral Collecting in Virginia.* Virginia Geological Survey, Virginia Minerals, Vol. 3, No. 2 (1957).

PEMBERTON, H.E. *Supplement to Bulletin 189, California Div. Mines and Geology, Minerals of California for 1965 through 1968.* Montebello: Mineral Research Soc. Calif. Bull. vol. 3, No. 2, 1969.

POINDEXTER, O. F. et al. *Rocks and Minerals of Michigan.* Michigan Geological Survey Bulletin 2, Lansing, 1965.

RANSOM, J. E. *Arizona Gem Trails and the Colorado Desert of California.* Mentone, California: Gembooks, 1955.

————. *Petrified Forest Trails.* Mentone, California: Gembooks, 1955.

RICHARDSON, C. H. *The Mineralogy of Kentucky.* Kentucky Geological Survey, Geologic Reports, Vol. 33, Frankfort, 1925.

ROBERTS, W. L. and RAPP, G., Jr. *Mineralogy of the Black Hills.* South Dakota School of Mines and Technology, Bulletin No. 18, Rapid City, 1965. Much detailed information on the localities is also provided.

SABINA, A. P. *Rocks and Minerals for the Collector: Sudbury to Winnipeg.* Canada Geological Survey, Paper 63–18, Ottawa, 1963.

————. *Rocks and Minerals for the Collector: Bay of Fundy Area.* Canada Geological Survey, Paper 64-10, Ottawa, 1964.

————. *Rock and Mineral Collecting in Canada*, Vol. I, *Yukon, Northwest Territories, British Columbia, Alberta, Saskatchewan, Manitoba*; Vol. II, *Ontario and Quebec*; Vol. III, *New Brunswick, Nova Scotia, Prince Edward Island, Newfoundland.* Canada Geological Survey, Miscellaneous Report 8, Ottawa, 1964. All of these reports are in detail with precise instructions for reaching deposits and occurrences.

SHANNON, E. V. *The Minerals of Idaho.* U. S. National Museum, Bulletin 131, Washington, D. C., 1931. Old but still the best information on many localities in this state.

SIMPSON, B. W. *Gem Trails of Texas*, Revised Edition. Granbury, Texas: Gem Trails Publishing Co., 1962.

SINKANKAS, J. *Gemstones of North America.* New York: Van Nostrand Reinhold, 1959. Over 2000 localities and the most comprehensive work available on the subject.

SOHON, J. A. *Connecticut Minerals.* Connecticut Geological and Natural History Survey, Bulletin 77, Storrs, 1951.

STRONG, M. F. *Desert Gem Trails.* Mentone, California: Gembooks, 1966. Covers some localities in the Mohave and Colorado deserts and adjacent areas in Nevada and California.

STUCKEY, J. L. *Geology and Mineral Resources of North Carolina.* North Carolina State Division of Mineral Resources, Educational Series 3, Raleigh, 1953.

TOLSTED, L. L. and SWINEFORD, A. *Kansas Rocks and Minerals.* Kansas State Geological Survey, Lawrence, 1957.

TROXEL, B. W. and MORTON, P. K. *Mines and Mineral Resources of Kern County, California.* California Division of Mines and Geology, County Report 1, San Francisco, 1962. Much detail on deposits and occurrences.

VANDERWILT, J. W. et al. *Mineral Resources of Colorado.* Denver: Colorado Mineral Resources Board, 1947. Much detailed data on deposits of all types with mineralogy and localities.

WEBER, F. H. *Geology and Mineral Resources of San Diego County, California.* California Division of Mines and Geology, County Report 3, San Francisco, 1963. Very thorough coverage of the famous gem mines of this county.

WHITLOCK, H. P. *List of New York Mineral Localities.* New York State Museum, Bulletin 70, Albany, 1903.

WILKERSON, A. S. *Minerals of New Jersey.* Geological Society of New Jersey, Report 1, State Museum, Trenton, 1959.

WILLIAM, L. D. *Gem and Mineral Localities of Southeastern United States.* Jacksonville, Alabama: Jacksonville State College (privately published). Numerous localities in Alabama and Georgia.

ZEITNER, J. C. *Midwest Gem Trails*, 3rd Edition Revised. Mentone, California: Gembooks, 1964.

MAGAZINES AND JOURNALS

AMERICAN MINERALOGIST—The Journal of the Mineralogical Society of America. Editor: William T. Holser, Chevron Oil Field Research Company, Box 466 La Habra, California 90631. Articles by professional mineralogists and usually too advanced for beginners.

CANADIAN MINERALOGIST—Mineralogical Association of Canada. Editor: L. G. Berry, Miller Hall, Queen's University, Kingston, Ontario. Similar in scope and professionalism to the above.

CANADIAN ROCKHOUND—Lapidary, Rock and Mineral Society of British Columbia, P. O. Box 194, Station "A", Vancouver 1, B. C. Editor: Donald J. Wells. Popular coverage of all aspects of the earth sciences in Canada.

EARTH SCIENCE—Official publication of the Midwest Federation of Mineralogical Societies. Editor: Richard M. Pearl. Earth Science Publishing Co., Inc., Mount Morris, Illinois 61054. Popular mineralogy, geology, and gemology, with stress on paleontology.

GEMS AND MINERALS—Official magazine of the California Federation of Mineralogical Societies. Editor: Don MacLachlan, P. O. Box 687, Mentone, California 92359. Popular presentations of mineral collecting, gemology, paleontology, and gem cutting.

GEOTIMES—American Geological Institute, 1444 N Street, N.W., Washington, D. C. 20005. Editor: Linn Hoover.

LAPIDARY JOURNAL—Lapidary Journal, Inc., P. O. Box 2369, San Diego, California 92112. Editor: Pansy D. Kraus. Popular coverage of all aspects of gemology, lapidary work, and gem mineralogy. The specially enlarged April issue is called *The Rockhound Buyer's Guide* and is replete with lists of clubs, selling organizations, products for lapidaries, localities, etc.

ROCKS AND MINERALS—Official magazine of the Eastern Federation of Mineralogical and Lapidary Societies. Rocks and Minerals, Box 29, Peekskill, New York 10566. Editor: James N. Bourne. Popular coverage of mineralogy, geology, and gem cutting with emphasis on Eastern localities.

ROCKS AND MINERALS IN CANADA—William W. Reid, Editor and Publisher, Box 550, Campbellford, Ontario. Popular earth science magazine stressing Canadian localities and interests, especially in eastern Canada.

Index

About the author . . .

John Sinkankas, known the world over for his writings on mineralogy and gem cutting, dated his interest in minerals to the age of seven when he collected minerals in his native Paterson, New Jersey. Since retiring from a twenty-five-year career as a naval aviator, he has pursued a second successful career in mineralogy.

He is the author of four other books. In addition, he contributed hundreds of articles to amateur and professional journals, and was a member of many gem and mineral societies. His expertise in lapidary work is evident in the many very large gems which he cut for the Smithsonian Institution and which are on display there.

John Sinkankas was a fellow of the Mineralogical Society of America and the Mineralogical Society of Canada; an honorary member Rochester Academy of Sciences, the San Diego Mineral and Gem Society, and the Cosmos Club of Washington, D.C.; and a honorary Fellow of the Gemmological Association All-Japan. In 1982 he was awarded the "Distinguished Associate Award" from the Gemological Institute of America, and was presented with a degree of Doctor of Human Letters by the Board of Trustees of William Paterson College. He was presented the Carnegie Mineralogical Award in 1989.

Another John Sinkankas title from Echo Point Books You May Enjoy

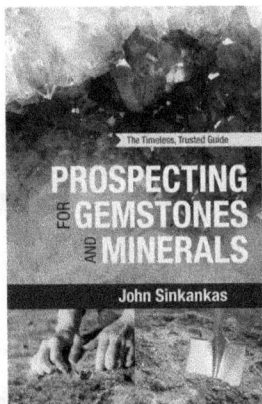

Prospecting for Gemstones and Minerals

Loaded with information about how, where and why mineral deposits form, *Prospecting for Gemstones and Minerals* is the perfect primer for the amateur collector. Featuring advice on where to find deposits, what they contain and how to remove crystals from the ground, this guide also covers maps and tools, and provides an introduction to geology.

PAPERBACK ISBN 978-1-63561-063-5

Our books may be ordered from any bookstore or online purveyor of books, or directly through our Web site, www. echopointbooks.com. Or visit our retail store, located in Brattleboro, Vermont.

www.ingramcontent.com/pod-product-compliance
Lightning Source LLC
Chambersburg PA
CBHW060132280326
41932CB00012B/1494